"AMERICA FOR THE AMERICANS" THE NATIVIST MOVEMENT IN THE UNITED STATES

SOCIAL MOVEMENTS PAST AND PRESENT

Robert D. Benford, Editor

Abolitionism: A Revolutionary Movement
by Herbert Aptheker

The American Communist Movement: Storming Heaven Itself
by Harvey Klehr and John Earl Haynes

The American Peace Movement: Ideals and Activism
by Charles Chatfield

American Temperance Movements: Cycles of Reform
by Jack S. Blocker Jr.

*The Animal Rights Movement in America:
From Compassion to Respect*
by Lawrence Finsen and Susan Finsen

*The Anti-Abortion Movement and the Rise of the Religious Right:
From Polite to Fiery Protest*
by Dallas A. Blanchard

The Antinuclear Movement, Updated Edition
by Jerome Price

The Charismatic Movement: Is There a New Pentecost?
by Margaret Poloma

The Children's Rights Movement: A History of Advocacy and Protection
by Joseph M. Hawes

Civil Rights: The 1960s Freedom Struggle
by Rhoda Lois Blumberg

The Conservative Movement, Revised Edition
by Paul Gottfried

The Consumer Movement: Guardians of the Marketplace
by Robert N. Mayer

Controversy and Coalition: The New Feminist Movement
by Myra Marx Ferree and Beth B. Hess

The Creationist Movement in Modern America
by Raymond A. Eve and Francis B. Harrold

Family Planning and Population Control:
The Challenges of a Successful Movement
by Kurt W. Back

Farmers' and Farm Workers' Movements:
Social Protest in American Agriculture
by Patrick H. Mooney and Theo J. Majka

The Health Movement: Promoting Fitness in America
by Michael S. Goldstein

The Hospice Movement: Easing Death's Pains
by Cathy Siebold

Let the People Decide, Updated Edition:
Neighborhood Organizing in America
by Robert Fisher

Populism: The Humane Preference in America, 1890–1900
by Gene Clanton

The Prison Reform Movement: Forlorn Hope
by Larry E. Sullivan

The Rise of a Gay and Lesbian Movement
by Barry D. Adam

Self-Help in America: A Social Movement Perspective
by Alfred H. Katz

The Senior Rights Movement
by Lawrence Alfred Powell, Kenneth J. Branco,
and John B. Williamson

Social Movements of the 1960s: Searching for Democracy
by Stewart Burns

"AMERICA FOR THE AMERICANS"

The Nativist Movement in the United States

Dale T. Knobel

Twayne Publishers
An Imprint of Simon & Schuster Macmillan
New York

Prentice Hall International
London Mexico City New Delhi Singapore Sydney Toronto

"America for the Americans": The Nativist Movement in the United States
Dale T. Knobel

Twayne Publishers
An Imprint of Simon & Schuster Macmillan
1633 Broadway
New York, NY 10019

Library of Congress Cataloging-in-Publication Data
Knobel, Dale T., 1949–
    America for the Americans : the nativist movement in the United
States / Dale T. Knobel.
        p.   cm. — (Social movements past and present)
    Includes bibliographical references and index.
    ISBN 0-8057-7846-2 hardcover
    1. Nativism—History. 2. Social movements—United States—
History. 3. Xenophobia—United States—History. 4. United States—
Ethnic relations. 5. United States—Race relations. I. Title.
II. Series.
E183.K645   1996
320.5'3—dc20   96-42171
                                                                      CIP

The paper used in this publication meets the minimum requirements of American National Standard for Information Sciences—Permanence of Paper for Printed Library Materials. ANSI Z3948-1984. ∞

10 9 8 7 6 5 4 3 2 1 (hc)

Printed in the United States of America

Contents

To the memory of my son,
Matthew Winsper Knobel, 1979-1992

Preface

"Aliens," "immigrants," "undocumented workers." These terms are the currency of the contemporary news media, appearing even more frequently since the winter of 1994-1995—when voters in California approved Proposition 187, withholding social services from so-called "illegal aliens." *Time* magazine, as it headed toward its year-end wrap-up in 1994, ran a cover story, "Down on the Downtrodden," in an effort to place the California issue in a historical context. The "yearly number of immigrants, legal and illegal," Richard Lacayo reported rather breathlessly, "tops one million," adding that "the last time the United States faced a comparable flood" was during the first decade of the century. He observed that the response of the nation to mass immigration then had been "jingoistic"—a rather curious term, borrowed from the history of foreign relations and more appropriate for describing something like the muscle flexed by President Theodore Roosevelt's world-circling "great white fleet" than for the complexity of Americans' response to our nation's ethnic and cultural diversity.[1]

Only a month earlier, Jeff Jacoby of the *Boston Globe* circulated a column, "Immigrant Bashing Is an American Tradition," through the Knight-Ridder News Service to daily papers nationwide. "The scapegoating of immigrants is one of the enduring prejudices in American history," Jacoby concluded—again, a curious choice of words, confounding behavior ("scapegoating") with attitude ("prejudice"). At about the same time, *USA Today,* discussing disagreements within the Republican party over the California law, reported the former secretary of Housing and Urban Development, Jack Kemp, as saying, "There are those who want the party to be the equivalent of the Know-Nothing party that was anti-immigrant, anti-Catholic, anti-black"—a third strange reference, confusing historical intercultural hostility with interracial hostility. Addressing not the California situation but a controversy in Texas involving a disputed symbol—San Antonio's Alamo—a column by James C. Harrington for the *Houston Chronicle* attributed Texas' postrevolutionary (the Texas revolution, that is) "spiral of racism" to "the dramatic increase in Anglo population, the Know-Nothing movement and the rise of the Ku Klux Klan." Harrington, too, revealed a little confusion about timing and sequence in American history and more than a little confusion about the objectives of the Know Nothings and perhaps of the Klan as well.[2]

In fact, there is a good deal of mystification over concepts like "prejudice," "discrimination," "racism," and "nativism," and probably a good deal more about historical mass movements, especially movements with racist or nativist goals. It is easy to have sympathy with that. It is confusing when, in contrast to the overwhelmingly European immigration of the nineteenth and early twentieth centuries, over 80 percent of today's immigrants come from Asia, Latin America, or the Caribbean, representing a host of nationalities, cultures, and "colors." How do the news media describe friction between those already here and newcomers? Is it "xenophobia"? Is it "racism"? Or is it something else? It is confusing, too, when there has not been just one Ku Klux Klan in American history but at least three Klans: of the 1860s and 1870s, of the 1910s and 1920s, and of the 1950s and 1960s. There may even be a fourth Klan today, in the 1990s—or more, because there are so many factions calling themselves "the Klan." And what about the "Know Nothings"? This is such an amusing, expressive term that it is hard to resist using. But just who were they, anyway?

Still, sympathy should not displace the discomfort that we ought to feel when such important words and representations of the past are tossed about carelessly, particularly because public policy makers are constantly being called on to "learn" from the past. *Time*'s "Down on the Downtrodden," for example, would have us believe that the "lesson" of the early twentieth century was that anti-immigrant "jingoism" (that odd expression) weakened when "Washington tightened [immigration] quotas in the 1920s and gave the nation time to absorb the influx"—a misleadingly simplistic representation of what was really a very complex phenomenon.

No one book can untangle all of these half-notions or restore appreciation for the historical complexities of American ethnic and race relations. But this volume tries to make a start by closely addressing one of the issues. In the United States, the "nativist" movement was an organized effort—lasting up to 150 years—to define American "nationality" restrictively by identifying who among those residing in the United States was authentically "American" and who was "alien." It proposed reserving the fullest privileges of citizenship for "Americans." The movement is most often associated with hostility to mass immigration from Europe, but it actually defined "alien" both more narrowly and more broadly than just as "foreign-born." Sometimes, nativists found the native-born "foreign" and immigrants suitably American. The nativist movement was rarely "xenophobic," that is, reflexively or unexceptionally antiforeign. It was certainly "ethnocentric," setting up as a standard for judging all comers to the United States its own understanding of American culture. But this does not really tell us very much. Most Americans of the late eighteenth, the nineteenth, and the early twentieth centuries—the approximate duration of the nativist movement—were ethnocentric. What we really want to know is why some people (and not others) were attracted to a particular version of American culture and were disposed to join organizations that discriminated between citizens and "aliens" on the basis of it. We do know—or at least I hope to show—that, for the most part, nativist activists were not much attracted to what we usually think of as "racism." Nativists typically shared the racial prejudices of their times but were reluctant to make blanket attributions of culture (and, consequently, of American nationality) to race. This was partly ideological and partly practical. What nativists believed was important in culture they also believed was acquired rather than innate. As for their organizational purpose, they intended to sort out "Americans" and "aliens" themselves; they did not want distinctions of "race" to do that for them.

Nativists' lack of enthusiasm for "racial" definitions of nationality and their promotion of themselves as the best judges of who was and was not "American" should tell us something about the participants in the nativist movement. They were not simply selfless (if misguided) patriots with disinterested concerns about preserving a particular American "national character" but people who derived private satisfaction from organized nativist activism. Their satisfaction, too, was both ideological and practical. Nativist activists joined national identity and personal identity—and, for that matter, they joined organizational identity and personal identity. In doing so, they received not only a sense of belonging and an affirmation of personal worth but also social benefits and sometimes material advantages.

This reminds us that the nativist movement was a movement of organizations. Since these organizations had origins and ends, we can also place the nativist movement in time and follow its development. Hints of a nativist movement were apparent by the end of the eighteenth century, but the movement itself flourished from the 1820s through the 1920s, with only a few shadows remaining afterward. The "nativist movement" alternately fed on and encouraged "nativistic" attitudes shared by a wider American public, but it was separate from them.

What, in fact, may set this book apart from others is its focus on the nativist *movement* in particular rather than on the broader phenomenon of public nativism, or what the eminent historian John Higham calls a popular "state of mind." My focus is on the movement's core ideas, constituent organizations, incentives for participants, public successes, failures, and ultimate decline. Much of my attention turns to internal organizational dynamics and to the mechanisms of organizational descent. The development of the book is essentially chronological. I have combined original research, particularly institutional evidence of nineteenth-century nativist organizations, with much synthesis of modern scholarship. I hope that the reader will come to know something about the "Know Nothings" and a good deal more about nativist organizations and their membership.

"Prejudiced," "bigoted," "discriminatory": participants in the nativist movement were all of these—in particular ways at particular times. This is important to recognize. For these are big, broad concepts, and if we are ever to understand them—let alone address them and expunge them from contemporary society—we must grasp all of the complexity they mask. When we are troubled today by the public reaction to "aliens," it is not very useful to attribute that reaction to historical "Know Nothingism" or "nativism"—or to historical "racism." But perhaps by studying the complexities of the past we will be more likely to uncover the complexities of the present which set people against one another and mock the inherent tolerance of our national creed.

This volume had its start over a decade ago, as I was bringing to conclusion another book, *Paddy and the Republic: Ethnicity and Nationality in Antebellum America* (Wesleyan University Press, 1986). That work gave me an opportunity to study closely public "conversation" about immigrants to the United States in the mass media of the mid-nineteenth century, and it particularly allowed me to make contrasts between everyday speaking and writing about immigrants and ethnic minorities in pre-Civil War verbal culture and the calculated rhetoric of the organizations in the nativist movement. In the course of that study, I concluded that it was worth examining the nativist "movement" apart from a popular nativistic "state of mind."

I am grateful for the patience of the editorial staff of Twayne Publishers and of the originator of the "Social Movements" series, Professor Irwin Sanders, as I inched my way through the preparation of this book. Its completion survived difficult family passages—the sudden death of a beloved adolescent son and an equally cherished daughter's completion of childhood and departure from home for college—as well as my own occupational passage from a relatively contemplative professorship to crisis-driven, overscheduled university academic administration. I would not have been able to see this book through without the care of my wife, Tina, the encouragement of my colleagues in the Texas A&M University Department of History, and the support of my friends and compatriots in the administration of undergraduate and honors programs: Sallie Sheppard, Susanna Finnell, Julie Cowley, and Fran Lamb. I am pleased that I have been gently prodded along by my own former doctoral student, Professor D. Gregg Cantrell, a successful young historian recompensing me by allowing me to learn from him.

Introduction:
American Nativism—
A Movement Lost and Found

"What constitutes an American citizen?" asked a delegate holding the floor at a political rally in Philadelphia's Independence Hall on a warm September day in 1830. Other participants at the meeting knew what was coming next. "Is it that he lives within the limits of the United States—that he was born within certain boundaries, or has since submitted to certain ceremonies of naturalization?"[1] Even today, 165 years later, we can recognize this as a rhetorical question—a question with an obvious answer, asked for effect. We would answer "yes." Not so the delegate, Dexter of Michigan. The answer he expected from his audience was a loud "no."

For about a century and a half, from the 1780s—the earliest years of the American republic—through the 1920s, Dexter's question (and his answer) was a permanent fixture of American public life. It was asked over and again at political rallies and conventions. It was printed in newspapers, books, and magazines. People who were certain that the answer was "no," and who tried to establish this "no" in law and social custom, came in time to be called "nativists." They were men and women who believed that they knew best who was *really* "American." There was much arrogance in that, but the true believers thought of themselves as patriots. To their mind, the freedoms of the American republic were imperiled because the nation was falling into the hands of "aliens." Actually, "nativist" was something of a misnomer for them, although they generally assumed that anyone native-born in the United States had a head start in meeting their criteria of Americanism. For they were perfectly content to read certain classes of "natives" out of the ranks of *real* Americans—and were sometimes willing to count certain classes of the foreign-born in.

Nativists' zeal could easily turn ugly. At their most civil, nativists pursued legal and political goals which included changes in naturalization law and in voting regulations. But even in these instances, while their methods might be conventional, their solutions could be extreme. Some nativists would have required immigrants to the United States to wait 21 years before applying for citizenship; some would have barred even native-born Americans of the wrong religious background from holding elective office or even voting. At their least civil, nativist rowdies were not above forcibly preventing "un-American" voters from casting ballots and not above committing violence against "aliens" they believed were not living up to "American" cultural standards. Obviously, even the most refined nativists provide no excuse for nativism. For nativists to propose that they alone knew who was authentically American, and to allege that with or without the law on their side those who were not real Americans did not deserve the rights and protections of full citizens, was to give legitimacy to private grievances and public prejudices alike.

Nonetheless, it is far too simplistic to write all nativists off as cranks and thugs. To be sure, nativists had many personal interests at stake in their efforts to make or remake American nationality, yet nativism was more than a collection of personal grudges and anxieties. It was decidedly an "ism," a body of interconnected ideas about American government and society, about the past and future of the United States. It had an ideology which was more or less systematic and which nativist leaders tried to keep consistent. This ideology was relied on to justify not only the individual but the collective conduct of nativists. For "nativism" has assuredly been a collective phenomenon in American history. It has, in fact, taken the form of a social movement, an orchestrated effort to bring about change in political and social structure. It has involved thousands, and occasionally hundreds of thousands, of activists. As a movement, it has been replete with organizations and publications, editors and ideologists, politicians, and of course a rank and file. Its lineage includes some of the best remembered (though not always the best understood) institutional names in American history—the "Know Nothings," the Ku Klux Klan, the American Protective Association.

Rediscovering the Nativist Movement

The nativist movement may fairly stake a claim to being the lost "ism" of United States history. Routinely included on lists of American social "reform" movements, it is customarily footnoted as an exceptional case and then ignored. Yet it was among the most sustained social movements in the first 150 years of the United States. In absolute numbers of active participants, it faced little competition from more famous rivals for public attention, such as abolitionism and women's suffrage. Its ability to mobilize a significant portion of the American electorate for political action and to actually achieve many of its goals far outstripped the record of the agrarian reformers of the Populist movement. Before the organized nativist movement folded its tents in the late 1920s, deflated—but not really satisfied—by the dramatic restraints imposed on immigration to the United States by federal legislation, it was unmatched for longevity and visibility by such organized movements as those that pursued universal free public education, international peace, or prison reform. Only the temperance movement, perhaps, was its peer.

What most people remember about American nativism is also what accounts for their not knowing much about it. They remember it as an "anti" movement, a crusade that was apparently against much and for little.[2] It was, to be sure, a movement hostile to unregulated immigration (which from the 1770s to the 1920s was, for the most part, European immigration), to the routine enfranchisement of foreign-born citizens by uniform naturalization procedures, and to allegedly excessive "foreign influence" in American life. "America for the Americans" is its most memorable rallying cry. Yet for many people this is what makes nativism just historical trivia. It seems too negative and defensive to deserve much attention as "real" reform. It seems too ill defined and emotional to warrant treatment as a coordinated, ideology-driven movement of any kind. It is easier to see it as raw xenophobia—simple revulsion to anything "foreign."

Paradoxically, advances in scholarship that have increased our understanding of another crucial American "ism" have also had the effect of decreasing our understanding of the nativist movement. These advances have been in the analysis of American racism. Almost half a century ago, Gunnar Myrdal helped redirect that study by making a persuasive case that the racism victimizing black Americans was neither a narrow interest-group problem (despite the notoriety of the Ku Klux Klan) nor a regional problem (despite the reputation of the old south) but an *American* problem—an "American dilemma," built into the very structure of American society.[3] After Myrdal, it seemed to make little sense to study the history of American racism in terms of movements, though there have been organizations and even movements pursuing racist objectives. It has seemed more important to study American culture, American social structure, and the American psyche to find out how racism grew and how it has been sustained.

It is all too easy to take nativism as nothing more or less than a cousin of racism. If many Anglo-Americans have been hostile to blacks, Native Americans, and Asians, then why not assume that some have despised Irish Celts and Balkan Slavs and that a few even have been uneasy about Germans and Swedes? Nativism, in this view, sits somewhere in the middle of a yardstick of bigotry with color prejudice at one end and indiscriminate xenophobia at the other. This outlook is what makes it so convenient to turn a few sentences by Abraham Lincoln about the nativistic American or "Know Nothing" party of the 1850s into a sort of blanket dismissal of nativism: "As a nation, we began by declaring that *'all men are created equal.'* We now practically read it 'all men are created equal, except *negroes.'* When the Know-Nothings get control, it will read 'all men are created equal, except negroes, and foreigners, and catholics.' "[4] This, of course, makes it important to study nativism as a kind of recurring popular emotion but eliminates the need to spend much time on its organizational or ideological aspects—that is, on nativism as a movement.

Viewed as a sort of racism stretched to the breaking point, American nativism can easily be dismissed as ridiculous. How could Americans of the first post-Revolutionary generation, already of well-mixed European heritage—much less those of the fifth or the sixth generation—have regarded themselves as so distinctively and purely "American" that they could express horror at the arrival of the Irish? How deep did they think national differences ran? And how did they propose to distinguish between the Anglo-Americans, Germans, and Irish anyway? The impression most people have today of the organizations created to achieve nativist objectives does nothing to dispel their apparent laughability or to encourage more thorough study. Almost any list of nativist societies will amuse modern ears: Loyal Men of American Liberty, Order of the Little Red Schoolhouse, Order of the Mystic Brotherhood, American Knights. These are names that conjure up images of silly rituals, nonsensical passwords, and comic-opera lodge costumes. And, undeniably, most of the nativist organizations had all that. "The ceremonies of our Order on the late anniversary of the birth of Washington were imposing in the extreme," reported the March 1852 number of the *Republic,* the monthly magazine of the nativistic Order of United Americans (OUA):

At the head of the procession was a cavalcade of about fifty horsemen, wearing the Continental hat and regalia of the Order, each carrying a baton; these were followed by the Grand Marshal and his special Aids, all mounted; next came the Chancery of New York, preceded by Willis's magnificent band; and following the Chancery, the several Chapters of the Order, in five divisions, each escorted by a military corps, with bands of music. Washington Chapter made a magnificent display, having a car drawn by eight white horses, elegantly caparisoned, on the car was a massive temple, occupied by three young ladies representing, in costume, Liberty, Justice, and Plenty, guarded by thirteen youths in naval uniforms, representing, with banners, each of the original States.[5]

It is not hard to make fun of that, and it is easy enough to write off OUA and similar organizations as havens for cranks, misfits, and lovers of gaudy uniforms.

But what if we check for fire behind the smoke? In 1907, when Albert C. Stevens prepared the second edition of his compendious reference book *The Cyclopedia of Fraternities,* he counted nearly 70 organizations like the Order of United Americans strewn across the preceding 125 years. He found 38 of them still active—some, in fact, newly formed. They represented one-tenth of all of the "friendly societies" (ranging from the Masons to the Sons of Hermann to the Grange) that Stevens was able to identify in the United States. He called them "Patriotic and Political Orders."[6] Despite some variation in particular aims and structure, most shared this basic outlook: that the American "national character" was menaced by internal "aliens," both foreign and native-born, and that persons and things "native" deserved precedence over persons and things "foreign." They constituted, in fact, the organizational fabric of an American nativist movement.

Before we smirk at these organizations, it is wise to consider that at the very time that Albert Stevens was compiling his institutional catalogue, pressure was mounting in the United States for the abolition of parochial schools as dangerously foreign and there was debate in the state legislatures and city councils across the land over whether a campaign to permit professional baseball on Sundays was an alien plot to undermine "traditional" American Protestant cultural values. Was it only coincidental that the most serious political challenge to routinely naturalizing immigrants and making them voting citizens had accompanied the rise of the Order of United Americans and its sister societies 50 years earlier? And what have important recent historical studies of the mid-nineteenth-century craft union movement taught us if not that the rituals, the formulaic rhetoric, and even the regalia of reform groups are not to be taken lightly but need to be understood as evidence of elaborate "movement cultures" which educated, emboldened, and sustained the enthusiasm of participants?[7]

"The inevitable takes a lot of hard work." This observation—very likely apocryphal, but often attributed to Lenin—appeals to historians and social scientists.[8] To them, not much happens in society or politics that simply can be shrugged off as the "spirit of an age" or as sudden mass hysteria. Yet scholars forget this from time to time, and write a history of actions without actors or of change without agents. Such may fairly be said to be the case with some of the modern study of American nativism. Nativism is often treated as a matter of mass social psychology or discounted as a preoccupation of cranks.

Think, for a moment, of nativism not as it may be defined but by what it produced in American history. Recall, for example, the "literacy test" for naturalization. Decade after decade in the late nineteenth and early twentieth centuries, bills mandating such tests were introduced in Washington, clearly aimed at favoring certain classes of prospective citizens over others. We must also include the periodic tinkering by state legislatures with residency requirements for exercising the vote—climaxing in the 1850s. We also need to remember local enactments related to the religious content of public education (as well as the secular content of parochial education) and the property rights of church authorities, which peaked in frequency during the quarter-century preceding the Civil War, in the quarter-century that followed it, and once again in the early twentieth century. This is only the merest beginning of a list, but it may be enough to show we can get some idea about what nativism is from what nativism does—or has done, anyway. And what it has done can fairly be attributed—at least as concerns instigation and, often, a high degree of public mobilization—to doers. To the extent that the doers have been organized in some fashion, we can talk about a nativist movement.

Early in this century, "Progressive" historians were inclined to see organized group interests (and, consequently, movements) at work behind most major social and political developments. Among these they included a nativist movement. The native-born with jobs to keep and taxes to pay resented immigrants who took away employment by working for less and who raised taxes by falling into poverty, crime, and disease. A little later, scholars' sensitivity to the extremist racial and religious prejudices of European fascism made it difficult to see American nativist hostility toward "aliens" and "foreigners" as anything other than the work of highly organized, dedicated fanatics.[9] But since the end of the Second World War, scholars have been tempted to see nativism less as an orchestrated social movement than as a widespread public temper, a recurrent mass paranoia about "outsiders." This is a point John Higham made explicitly in his pathbreaking postwar study *Strangers in the Land: Patterns of American Nativism, 1865-1925.* Higham informed his readers that this was "not . . . a book about crackpots . . . ; it deals with the American people." Nativism was not a movement but a "set of attitudes, a state of mind"; consequently, it revealed key themes in American culture.[10]

Historians' interest in nativism primarily for what it might reveal about broader patterns in the national psyche has largely been maintained up to the present, as is evident in such relatively recent works as David Bennett's *Party of Fear: From Nativist Movements to the New Right in American History.*[11] The only sustained departure from this trend has been the interest of a generation of political historians in the role played by nativist politics in the collapse of the so-called "second party system" and the rise of the Republican party on the eve of the Civil War. Most of these scholars, however, have been far more interested in examining where voters came from and where they ended up than in the nativist parties, orders, and societies they passed through. And, with a few notable exceptions, they have usually treated nativist organizations as empty vessels, hollow forms through which great waves of voters passed, fragmented, ideologically inconsistent, and weighed down by insincere, opportunistic leaders.[12]

Undoubtedly we have learned a good deal from postwar scholarship on American nativism. We now take it as well established that anti-"alien" prejudice has often been widespread in American society; it is not only the possession of zealots. We are especially indebted to John Higham for demonstrating that nativism is a "certain kind of nationalism" which elements of the "native" American public found attractive in

times of collective stress. And we have come to recognize that antiforeign attitudes could be manipulated for political gain by people who
had no ideological investment in nativism. Yet in reaching these conclusions, modern scholarship has neglected what earlier historians
took for granted: that for a century and a half of American history there
was, after all, a distinctive "nativist movement." From the late eighteenth century into the early twentieth, there was a succession of organizations sharing broadly similar outlooks and goals, pursuing a
nativist public policy agenda, subscribing to an elaborate nativist ideology, and serving as a catalyst for nativist aggression against immigrants and "aliens" in both politics and society.

There is good reason to think that it will be profitable to reexamine
American nativism as a movement. By neglecting the nativist movement in the study of nativism, we have forfeited the opportunity to put
modern scholarship to work to determine who nativist activists were
and what set them apart from other citizens less energized by nativistic
enthusiasm. And we have impoverished even the study of "popular"
nativism by overlooking the way in which a movement kept nativistic
concerns and proposed public policies alive between spikes of public
interest. It would be naive to think that the activists' ready-made
rhetoric and programs did not help shape mass attitudes when
interethnic rivalry or defensive nationalism—or dislocations in the
political party system—produced a broadened constituency for nativistic initiatives. In fact, the tendency of much contemporary scholarship
to treat nativism as a societal impulse overstates its episodic character.
Popular manifestations of nativist prejudices—and nativistic activity—
did indeed rise and fall. But the nativist *movement* was much more sustained. While it is certainly an exaggeration to treat the nativist movement as a great, seamless, uninterrupted web of organizations involved
in a vast conspiracy, there is little doubt that there were patterns of
organizational relationship and descent; that there were shared, or at
least communicating, leaders; and that there were some common outlooks which help explain why—under the right social conditions—
nativistic enthusiasm could become channeled and focused with such
speed. Moreover, to examine nativism in cultural terms rather than as
a movement is to obscure the ideological consistencies—and inconsis-
tencies—which help explain both the public appeal of the nativist
movement and its inability to hold public attention for long.

Consider what we would like to ask about nativism as a social movement. Who were the participants? Why was their enthusiasm for

nativism more intense and sustained than that of most of their contemporaries? What led them to organize, and what kept them together? What sort of institutional culture did they develop? What personal satisfaction did they derive from nativist activism? How did they go about appealing to their contemporaries? How did they react to success? How did they respond to failure? These questions are far different from those it would be appropriate to ask about a cultural style or a national psyche.

Accepting the relationship between nativism and nationalism that modern scholarship has identified helps us place some natural boundaries around our subject. It confines us, obviously, to the national period of American history; there really could be no *American* nationalism or American nativism in the British colonial period. Moreover, it requires us to exclude certain specific types of interethnic hostility, i.e., hostility directed at "alien" minorities who were not regarded as a threat to the "national character" or national existence, if you will, of the American people. Anti-Semitism is a good example: it remained a peculiarly transnational prejudice. Another example—for most of American history, anyway—is hostility to minorities from Asia or Latin America, who have been objects of racism but (partly on dismissive, racist grounds) have rarely been considered a "national" threat.[13] Such hostilities are no less interesting or important but do not fall within the purview of a study of the nativist movement.

To turn from the generic history of cultural nativism to the study of the nativist movement in America is to take up what Ronald Walters, a leading student of the American abolitionist movement, calls an "inner history," an examination of the "interplay between personality, culture, and environment" which defines an organized interest.[14] Environment, of course, is a combination of social, political, and intellectual conditions characterizing a time and place in which an organized nativist movement manifested itself. But culture, in this context, is what scholars sometimes call "movement culture," the perception of world, of self, and of symbols separating participants from outsiders. To study personality in a movement is to get at the incentives and rewards connected with participation, to penetrate the motivation of activists. What were the symbols that drew nativist activists together? What was the language of group communication that helped distinguish insiders from outsiders? What benefits did participation in nativist organizations provide to activists?

Part of studying the "inner history" of a movement is examining its central ideas and its efforts to maintain ideological consistency. Ideology—as a system of belief—is partly what sets a movement apart from a popular emotion or a cultural style; it is a cord that runs from organization to organization and participant to participant. Ideologies are sometimes called "highly constrained systems of thought." To seem convincing to prospective recruits and to hold even true believers in the long run, all of the elements of an ideology must somehow work together with reasonable internal consistency. To follow the ups and downs of the nativist movement is to follow its struggle to maintain ideological consistency and to transmit its institutional culture from one organizational vehicle to the next.[15]

Connecting Ideology and Organization

Throughout its long history, nativism was, in the words of the historian Jean Baker, a phenomenon of "the dedicated few and the casual many."[16] The casual many, of course, were a resource that the dedicated few sought to mobilize, and they were often able to do so because nativistic prejudices were widespread among Americans from the late eighteenth through the early twentieth centuries. Historians have documented the sources of antagonism between the native and the foreign-born and have found them quite diverse. They, ranged from objective conflict between interest groups—over jobs, neighborhoods, or political power—to cultural prejudices against neighborhood reference groups to ill-defined anxieties about strangers and change. But intergroup friction did not necessarily make a nativist. It could sometimes win a recruit for a mob to break immigrants' skulls, or provoke individual acts of discrimination, or motivate a vote, but by itself it rarely inspired anyone to seek public policies that would systematically exclude the "alien" from the full measure of American life. In fact, this would have been difficult because of countervailing pressures in the official culture of the American republic—to value uninterrupted population growth, to treat men (at least white men) as civil and political equals, to accord individuals an opportunity to participate as free competitors in the race of life.

To overcome the elements of official culture demanding opportunities open to the native and foreign-born alike and to turn ill-defined prejudices and visceral antagonisms into real nativism required sustained effort on the part of the dedicated few. To be brought into the nativist movement, casual sympathizers had to be attracted to an organization, persuaded that their anxieties about "aliens" were justified by the threat aliens posed to the republic, convinced that this danger demanded corrective public action, and—in most cases—encouraged to see that they had a personal stake in the consequences. What dedicated nativists sought was to enlist the casual many into a nativist mass movement.[17] Ronald Walters has observed that in the mid-nineteenth century abolitionist activists were on the whole not so different in their fundamental moral, social, and political outlook from the majority of their contemporaries in the northern and western states; where they differed, he argues, was in how they "connected all the points together, in how they formed them into a shell of feeling."[18] American nativism was like that, too, and the key to its successes and failures was its variable ability to attach the vaguely like-minded to a network of organizations that dignified prejudices as patriotism and converted individual indignation and anxiety into coordinated action.

Although occasionally nativists turned to the independent political party as their organizational vehicle, the backbone of organized nativism was the voluntary association, particularly the benevolent "fraternal" association. In the time that has passed since sustained scholarly attention was last devoted to American nativism as a movement, a good deal has been learned about the nature of voluntary associations. One thing we have discovered is that no matter how urgent the cause and how excited the activists, no organized movement will survive for long without creating incentives for sustained participation. Some students of voluntary associations talk about three kinds of incentives for participation: utilitarian, normative, and affective. Most studies of American nativism have focused on only one of these: normative incentives. Normative incentives are fairly obvious. They include the public recognition and political validation, or legitimacy, that come with success in shaping public policy. By linking cherished societal values with organizational objectives, such incentives attract members by appealing to social obligation. Clearly, American nativists did identify their objectives with good citizenship; and apparently one of their long-term problems in retaining members was their failure to secure some of their key goals. But affective and utilitarian incentives, though much less emphasized in the historical literature, were also at work in the nativist movement. Affective incentives included the personal relationships that developed within nativist organizations and the ways in which group membership contributed to personal identity. When touched on by historians, this dimension of American nativism is usually dismissed as little more than a juvenile love of grandiloquent titles, mock secrecy, and amusing costumes. Utilitarian incentives constitute the practical "goods and services" that an organization provides to its members—a subject completely neglected in most studies of American nativism, yet one that is essential for understanding the ability of the movement to hold its supporters, although it was often under fire from the very native-born citizens it purported to represent.[19]

Conclusion: Roots of a Nativist Movement

Nativism survived in American public life for so long—and recurrently flourished—because it meant many different things to many different people. It could assuage many different anxieties, justify many hatreds, and rationalize many personal and group objectives. But it also survived because it could persuade many people to "connect the points" in their lives and the world about them in the same way, and it did so by binding them to organizations that purveyed ideology by both argument and example. What allowed nativist ideology to provide apparently simple explanations for mystifying events in a complex world was, as we shall see, the particular intellectual inheritance of the early American nation and the anxieties associated with building a nation. And what allowed nativist ideology to become bound to organizations was a sense—shared by numbers of citizens during the first half-century of the United States—that personal identity as Americans required participation in voluntary associations. Between 1780 and 1820, the first hints of a nativist movement appeared.

Chapter One

Citizens and Brethren:
The Ideological and Organizational
Roots of American Nativism

In January 1851, the "grand sachem" of the Order of United Americans (OUA) spelled out the central objective of his nativist fraternity. The brethren, he declared, "will not slumber until the American people are . . . renationalized."[1] Two years later, a similar society, the Order of United American Mechanics, began its constitution with a close paraphrase of OUA's commitment to the creation of an American "nationality" but added a longer second article: "The objects of this Order shall be: First—To assist each other in obtaining employment. Second—To encourage each other in business in preference to all others. Third—To assist a sick and funeral fund. Fourth—To aid members who through Providence, may become incapacitated from following their usual avocations, in obtaining situations suitable to their afflictions." Such homely goals did not die out with the nativist activists of the 1850s. Almost half a century later, in 1889, the Patriotic Order, Sons of America arranged its bylaws with a "Declaration of Principles" second and the following objectives first: "home benevolence, the care of its sick, the burial of its dead, the protection of and assistance to all connected with it."[2]

During the 150-year history of the nativist movement in the United States, not every nativist ideologue copied the grand sachem's language and not every nativist organization constituted itself as a benevolent brother or sisterhood—but a remarkably large number did. The relationship between the ideology and structure of the nativist movement in the United States throughout its long career is one of its most significant features and offers insights into who was attracted to nativist activism and why. The most meaningful words in nativist rhetoric were "nationality," "independence," and "organization." Nationality was collective and political; independence was personal; and organization (depending on whether it was the tool of friends or of alleged foes) was understood to be something that could aid or block the achievement of either nationality or independence. What made nativists nativists was the way they saw "nationality" as an issue of individual independence and organized to pursue it.

Nation Building and "National Character"

The nativist movement began with an idea as old as the American republic itself. While nativist ideology gave this idea a special twist, it is fair to say that the movement might never have originated unless the idea was so widely shared at the inception of the United States that it became part of the political culture. American historians properly identify nativism with nationalism. Yet one of the weakest points in much of the scholarship of American nativism is that it applies a modern definition of "nationality" to the past. The difficulty is not just that today's ordinary understanding of "nationality" does not fit into the vocabulary of the nativist movement but that it does not represent what *most* Americans took to be nationality much before the end of the nineteenth century. During the whole first century of American history—and for a while thereafter—nationality meant "national character." And "national character" meant not at all what we take it to mean today, that is, something like stereotyped habits and collective personality, but just what the words said: "having the character of a nation." Thus it was entirely possible in eighteenth- and nineteenth-century terms for a people organized into a political state to have no "national character" at all. Such a population did not act as or like a nation and consequently could not be treated by others as a nation; in fact, it was probably bound not to survive as a nation.[3]

Noah Webster, who was an American nationalist theorist before he was a compiler of dictionaries, talked as early as the 1780s about the need for a people to have the "sense of a nation" before they could actually be regarded as a nation. But there was a circularity in early American thought about the meaning of nationality, captured in Gouverneur Morris's observation that "a national spirit is the natural result of national existence."[4] In either case, it was not the practice of the first citizens of the United States—even those legitimately ranked among the "founding fathers"—to regard American nationality as a fact established by the Declaration of Independence, by the Constitution, or even by the experience of putting into motion a new government. No amount of declaring, enacting, or administering could create an American nation. Nationality was more than a legalism. You could not set down—or even artfully construct—the legal and institutional bones of a nation and expect nationhood just to grow on them. As the early-nineteenth-century Whig politician Rufus Choate put it, a nation was "more than an encampment of tents on the great prairie, pitched at sundown, and struck to the sharp crack of the rifle the next morning." "Our national consciousness," Choate continued, "is, to an extraordinary degree, not a growth but a production."[5] If Americans were to be a nation, they would have to work at it.

To fail to become a nation spelled almost certain disaster. Americans would neither receive the respect of the world's actual nations nor, in the long run, be able to rule themselves. From their earliest existence as a political state, Americans who were familiar with notions of "natural rights" associated with philosopher John Locke gave them a twist derived from Scottish "faculty psychology": that rights had no meaning except when exercised within and defended by an organized human community. Thus pressure for the United States to become a real and enduring nation took on personal urgency. Moreover, a nation in the making needed to reach a sense of its nationality quickly, for only nationality could take the place of a history to help provide some reasonable prediction of what the future held for it. Americans saw the problem of nation *building* as especially acute because they believed it to be virtually untried, a task forced on them by the Revolution.[6]

For the first two or three generations after the American Revolution, there were apparently two ways to create a sense of a nation. These were bound up in the two meanings of the word "nation" itself. One definition was institutional and geographical: a nation consisted of political and administrative forms—of structured transactions among citizens operating over a territory with established boundaries. This might be thought of as a "compact" theory of nationality, the people agreeing to act like a nation or, as in the case of most contemporary European nations, having a compact imposed on them by a monarch or evolved from feudal traditions of obligation. The second definition treated nationhood as synonymous with "peoplehood" and regarded it as cultural or even ethnic. A people acted like a nation because they were bound to each other by common traditions, common values, shared culture, or common "blood."[7]

There was some basis for expecting the second mechanism of nation building to be workable in the American case. While there was already much ethnic diversity within the 13 colonies at the time of the Revolution, English cultural and political institutions were well established. But Americans of the Revolutionary generation hastily rejected a nationalism based on British descent and culture, however much some of them hoped to retain what they took to be the best features of British life. It would never do for a revolutionary people to say that they acted as a nation because of their common education under discredited British masters. Ironically, though, one of the most obvious things that had given diverse American colonists anything like a unified character was loyalty to Great Britain and integration into the British economic and political system. As John Murrin has pointed out, "to repudiate Britain meant jeopardizing what the settlers had in common while stressing what made them different from one another."[8] Consequently, it made the quest for an alternative source of American nationality more urgent.

The preferred solution for early American nationalist thinkers was to stress shared commitment to a set of political values ("life, liberty, and the pursuit of happiness") and loyalty to the Constitution. This gave a uniquely affirmative nature to nationality, making it a matter of individual choice. An American was one who subscribed to the principles of the Declaration of Independence and who committed himself (note the male pronoun; this was an age that made women politically invisible) to uphold the Constitution of the United States. The American nation was a compact of all those accepting this obligation. From this grew one definition of the "outsider": in the words of a nineteenth-century patriotic orator, "He who is not in sympathy with the American idea that breathes in our political institutions, is an alien."[9] Foreign observers frequently commented—sometimes with a sneer—that this was the only way Americans could claim nationhood. In the 1840s, the Englishman Alexander McKay, writing with some sympathy about the predicament of American nationality, observed that American personal and national identity was bound up more with laws and procedures than with culture or geography: "The American exhibits little or none of the local attachments which distinguishes the European. His feelings are more centered upon his institutions than his mere country. . . . His affections have more to do with the social and political system with which he is connected than with the soil he inhabits."[10]

Yet outside observers were also aware that there was some fuzziness in the distinction Americans liked to make between the old world and new world forms of nationality. The legal values and constitutional principles that Americans placed at the heart of nationality were, in fact, something less than universal and owed much to Americans' particular historical experience. "In doing homage to law," a contributor to the *North American Review* reminded early-nineteenth-century readers, "they [Americans] do homage to themselves, the creators and preservers of law."[11] Likewise, even Americans of the Revolutionary generation—perhaps especially Americans of the Revolutionary generation—clung to the view that no one *could* live up to constitutional expectations without displaying certain standards of moral and intellectual enlightenment. This was likely to be a problem in a society which, after all, did possess a core culture that was undeniably Anglo-American and which implicitly defined intelligence and morality in cultural terms.[12]

Obviously, from the first, the two potential mechanisms for creating a "sense of a nation" in the United States were not entirely separate from one another, and this was recognized early on. In the middle of the Revolution, John Adams speculated that the *kind* of government Americans installed was bound to go far toward creating a national culture and thus a distinctive people—a "decisive Colour" which would define the essence of being American is how Adams phrased it. Three-quarters of a century later, Congressman Alexander Stephens voiced the same sentiment: "The institutions of a people . . . are the matrix in which the germ of their organic structure quickens into life, takes root, and develops."[13] It was presumed, in short, that there was a cause-and-effect relationship between political institutions and distinctive "peoplehood." Conversely, it seemed beyond argument to the architects of American republican institutions that the character and culture of a people largely dictated the nature of the government they created for themselves. Many Americans noted with smug satisfaction the political difficulties of the early-nineteenth-century Latin American republics, observing that political models appropriate to North Americans did not suit the traditions or temperaments of the former Spanish colonies to the south.[14] Looking at the prospects for nationhood optimistically, the first generations of nationalist theorists in the United States implied that while Americans lacked the historical peoplehood of European nations and would have to rely on loyalty to common principles and institutions in order to take on a national character, they could still take heart. For life under common laws and values would progressively give them more of the character of a common people and, at the same time, demonstrate that there were core values already apparent which identified the essence of peoplehood.

The Intellectual Inheritance of a Nation in the Making

What provided an opportunity for a specific social movement directed at aggressively creating and shaping American "national character"— a nativist movement—to arise and sustain itself for more than a century was the extraordinary intensity of popular attitudes about the need for, prospects of, and impediments to developing a distinctive American peoplehood. This intensity was a legacy of the intermixed intellectual and cultural traditions of republicanism, rationalism, millenialism, and revolutionism.

For the first generation of American citizens, as well as for the second and the third, "republicanism" meant more than replacing a king with sovereign citizens. Instead, it was a whole way of understanding the relationship between government, citizen, and state. Partly, early American republicanism was borrowed from antimonarchist political theorists of the Commonwealth period of English history, the time between the beheading of Charles I in the 1640s and the restoration of Charles II over a decade later. Theirs was a language that had a special resonance in North America, because the Commonwealth coincided with the earliest colonies' development of local self-government and growing suspicion of distant authority. Its principal themes were reinforced by rhetoric that circulated through the British empire at the time of the Glorious Revolution of 1688, which led to a closer balance of power between the king and parliament—a rhetoric which harped on the dangers of excessive executive authority and the desirability of representation responsible to the political public. This emergent "republican" outlook was sustained in English (and, consequently, American) political discourse by the development of a political opposition in early-eighteenth-century England (variously styled "real Whig" or "Country party") to a "managed" Parliament led by the king's ministers, who rounded up votes by the distribution of titles, jobs, and contracts. Cultivated by members of the traditional landed gentry of the countryside and provincial towns, this opposition rhetoric reflected suspicion of London, which not only was geographically distant but had become home to new and suspect institutions of modern commerce, manufacturing, and moneymaking—banks, joint stock trading companies, and investment markets—that seemed to threaten property holders' prized independence.

Some scholars have called this evolving set of political outlooks "classical" republicanism because it glanced back at the only sustained European experience of representative and at least quasidemocratic political forms, the republics of ancient Athens and Rome. In fact, it took its interpretation of the rise and fall of the "classical" republics from Renaissance political theorists like Niccolò Machiavelli. From the Renaissance in particular it borrowed skepticism about the longevity of "republican" forms of government that ruled without kings, or at least without tyrants. Popular governments consisting of a king restrained by a parliament, or no king at all, were held to be perpetually in danger of subversion by a powerful few who would create a tyrannical oligarchy, or by a lawless many who would bring about tyrannical anarchy. In either case, the fault lay with corrupted self-interest that caused individual citizens to fall under the sway of powerful patrons or persuasive demagogues. Ironically, the same conviction about the diversity of individual citizens' interests that representative government was meant to serve seemed to be a source of danger to representative government.[15]

If these notions seemed relevant in eighteenth-century England as an established nation struggled with questions of leadership, representation, and economic modernization, they had even greater immediacy in England's North American colonies, which found themselves with a distant imperial government, no hereditary aristocracy, strong traditions of elected local government, and relatively wide access to political participation. As the colonies stumbled through the eighteenth century toward revolution and the formation of an actual republic, "republicanism" seemed a way of explaining who Americans were and where they were headed. In fact, the political rhetoric that we have labeled "republican" helped propel the colonies toward independent nationhood by conveying to many colonists the idea that Britain's parliamentary monarchy was degenerating into tyranny as the predictable forces of selfishness and greed took hold. Simultaneously, it persuaded numerous Americans that if any people were to have a fair chance of sustaining republican government, they—because of their simplicity, equality, and experience with local self-rule—were it. Yet the republican outlook also left the first "Americans" with a dread that their experiment was perilous, that the chief threats came from within, and that selfish interests and factions were poised to tumble the republic into tyranny or anarchy. Properly constructed laws and government institutions could at best balance and mediate competing interests, and the Constitution of 1789 was intended to do just this. But the prevailing understanding of the history of republics suggested that such a balancing act was difficult to sustain. Only some more enduring form of mutual obligation and self-restraint—a sense of shared peoplehood—was likely to help republican citizens avoid the degeneration of their state.

The origin of the state through revolution intensified the anxiety to establish common peoplehood. Not only did the Revolution discredit reliance on British ancestry or culture as a basis for common nationality but, as Thomas Archdeacon has noted, "participation in the Revolution legitimized the claim of non-English Europeans to a full share in the new nation," ensuring that from the first American nationality could not have a purely ethnic basis.[16] Moreover, by specifically rejecting aristocracy, the founding generation made it inevitable that the body of the people rather than a select group of leaders would be relied on to define moral and political character. With the artificial social distinctions and privileges of aristocracy gone, however, it was more likely that individuals would be free to pursue private interests, divide into factions, and (potentially) tear the republic apart.

Classical republicanism was not the only intellectual inheritance of the new American nation. The rationalistic, scientific outlook of the eighteenth-century intellectual enlightenment also invested the quest for peoplehood with both urgency and expectancy. "The men of the Revolutionary era," Neil Harris has noted, "were the conscious heirs of a tradition of European thought which perceived connections between the character of a people and the nature of its society." Such an outlook was a logical outgrowth of the assumption that this was "a world of mechanistic cause and effect in which what happens does so only because something happened before."[17] If a nation was to successfully implement republican government, its inhabitants would need to display the character appropriate for republicans. If this created an incentive to cultivate the germ of peoplehood, the rationalist outlook also made it seem reasonable to do so. For well into the nineteenth century, Americans, Gordon Wood reminds us, "could scarcely conceive of a moral order that was not based on intention."[18] Accordingly, it was assumed that citizens of the United States could, if properly motivated, *will* themselves into common peoplehood. During the "age of improvement" that characterized the late eighteenth and early nineteenth centuries, Americans applied to the development of something as intangible as nationality the same can-do practicality that they brought to the engineering of canals or the organization of volunteer fire brigades.[19] The expectation of success was reinforced by the evangelicalism spreading throughout American Protestantism during the first half of the nineteenth century. Evangelical Christianity posited that an individual "could be a force in history," and thus that for the republic to work, each of its citizens must be properly motivated. This perception was matched by a conviction that people *could* be motivated, could be changed, could adopt the shared characteristics that would mark them as a true national people (the political equivalent of voluntarily renouncing sin and embracing godliness). The evangelical notion that "moral deeds implied moral doers" had important implications for those who believed that the character of a people influenced the character of a nation's political institutions. The evangelical outlook assumed that a godly republic was a voluntary compact of people who cultivated the moral temperament that suited them for self- government.[20]

Paradoxically, the intellectual environment that suggested both the necessity and the possibility of creating common peoplehood also focused attention on the obstacles to such an achievement. The revolutionary origins of the United States heightened the sense of expectancy about its future. Casting itself adrift from the old world, America represented a whole new beginning—not only political but cultural and intellectual. A contemporary exulted, "The Revolution of America . . . seems to have broken off all those devious Tramels of Ignorance, prejudice and Superstition which have long depressed the Human Mind. Every door is now open to the Sons of genius and Science to enquire after truth. Hence we may expect the darkening clouds of error will vanish fast before the light of reason; and that the period is fast arriving when Truth will enlighten the whole world."[21] As self-flattering as such sentiments may have been, they also created an awful anxiety about failure. If America ceased to endure as a nation, much more was at stake than just the political independence of a few million souls—perhaps the future of the world.

Anxiety about living up to expectations fostered a sense of danger and a suspicion that nationhood was under threat. This reinforced the

doubt, implicit in classical republican thought, that republican nationhood could endure at all in the face of the forces ranged against it.
These included not only warring and divisive "interests" but
entrenched elites, corruptible leaders, and jealous foreign powers.
Moreover, republican thought—born, as David Brion Davis has indi-
cated, of "Protestant fears of the Counter-Reformation, by English
Whig interpretations of the Glorious Revolution"—proposed that these
forces were frequently in alliance with one another and that hidden
conspiracy was the chief threat to national survival. This created a tendency to connect apparently unrelated circumstances and to find in
them concealed danger. Well into the nineteenth century the kind of
"causative" reasoning process that Robert Wiebe has found characteristic of Jefferson's generation guided American nationalist thought.
Just as the Revolutionaries saw a threatening coherence in British
activities which were seemingly unconnected, Americans over the next
century manufactured threats to American nationality from incredibly
diverse circumstances and events.[22] Adoption of moral free agency as
an element of American Protestantism made it more difficult to see
adverse or even positive developments as simply accidents or coinci-
dences. Each republican failure was likely to be attributed to some sinister design, accentuating the sense of danger. If Americans failed in all
circumstances to act as a true "people," there was probably someone or
something intent on pulling them apart.[23]

   Although it is sometimes dismissed by historians as a kind of collective paranoia characteristic of a suspicious, premodern people, the fear
of conspiracies against American nationhood actually owed a great
deal to modern rationalism. On the one hand, it was appropriate to the
expansive new American nation spread out initially along 1,500 miles of
coastline, and eventually an even greater distance inland—appropriate
to the reality that unseen, distant events were politically consequential.
This reality took on yet another dimension in the nineteenth century as
a few American cities grew into complex metropolises and telegraph
and railroad gave distant and often puzzling events immediate impact.
In a growing and geographically mobile populace, strangers increasingly became a part of most people's lives, encouraging healthy suspicion and a rational need to be wary.[24] That this was an age which no
longer attributed social or political events to divine mystery only
heightened skepticism. If freely acting individuals were understood to
be the prime movers of human events, there was no dismissing political failure as blind fate. Consequently, there was every reason to exam-

ine the ways of men closely and to investigate their motives. "If bad effects continually resulted from the professedly benevolent intentions of an actor," Gordon Wood has observed of the early republican popular mind, "then something was wrong. Some sort of deceit or dissimulation was to be suspected."[25] Even the evangelical temper affirmed that the ways of Satan as well as the ways of God took form in the ways of men and women. In short, while there was every reason to think that the emergent nationhood of the American people could be realized, there were equally good reasons to believe that republican "national character" was constantly jeopardized by enemies seen and unseen.

Nationality and Individual Identity

The idea that in North America not just a state was being created but a "nation" that would guarantee permanence to the state, was a double-edged sword. It filled people with optimism: no matter that the traditional characteristics of European nationality were incomplete or altogether absent; a republican "nation" was a product of careful construction rather than an accident of nature or history. But it also filled them with dread: the republican state might never become a nation, in which case it would not survive. These were collective, social issues. And there were also personal issues involved—another double edge. In a created nation, an individual could be either inside or out. After all, it was not place of birth, not ethnic descent, and not present residence that made a person a part of the "nation in progress." This is what cut both ways. It created conditions whereby the "nationality" of all others—of neighbors, of strangers, of the native-born, of the foreign-born, of coreligionists and those of other faiths—was always open to question. But it meant that one's own national identity was subject to question too. Were you in or were you out? What did you think? What did others think? Worries about self and self-image could produce even more anxiety than fears about others.

If peoplehood—as an essential feature of nationality—was not natural but created, what, then, was the material out of which it was to be formed? From the time of the Revolution (and for a long time thereafter) the answer most widely subscribed to was fundamentally political. The material consisted of those who should be and could be active in (to use Jefferson's formulation in the Declaration of Independence) the "pursuit of happiness." It may seem strange to us that this would not include everyone, but, then, we have redefined "happiness" to suit our own generation. "Americans," wrote the columnist George Will for a piece that appeared in newspapers across the country a few years ago, "are happiest when pursuing happiness, happiness understood as material advancement."[26] Although they hardly lacked material ambitions, Americans in the Revolutionary and early republican era would scarcely have understood such an interpretation of Jefferson's phrase. The happiness Jefferson had written about was the satisfaction of the individual who has the opportunity to take an active role in the government of society and thus in shaping the conditions under which all private ambitions might be pursued. This happiness was civic—in the sense that it had to do with taking responsibility for the welfare of others—but also intensely personal, because only if one had a hand in public decision-making could one really be free.[27] That the "pursuit of happiness" might mean the freedom to take the time and effort (and even the risk) to participate in the political process may seem strange to our generation, with its exceptionally low rates of voter registration and its frighteningly lower rates of actual voting. But in the eighteenth century it was quite real to former Europeans and their offspring, who recognized that in America this was an opportunity that might be seized by a larger proportion of the populace than in any other place (although by modern standards, it remained narrowly constricted by race, class, and gender).

It is easy to get carried away here and see the generation of the founders as an unusually noble breed. But the truth is that they saw participation in government as being at the root of their personal interest. This was true both at the high end of society and in the middling orders. George Washington talked about taking up civic responsibility as a matter of "honor" but acknowledged frankly that the honor in which a man was held directly affected how he fared in dealings with his neighbors. John Adams preferred "reputation" or "distinction" to "honor" (as suited his background as an ambitious small-town lawyer, in contrast to Washington the established great planter), but he too believed that active participation in public affairs was a way to promote all kinds of private interests.[28] The colonial legislatures were made up of many such men, eager for "honor" and "reputation," and one incentive for the American Revolution itself was their perception that a progressive tightening of British imperial administration over the North American colonies was limiting their ability to increase their personal roles in public affairs.[29]

Participation in public life was not just an interest of the rich and upwardly mobile. The historian Charles Sydnor reminds us that in Virginia, as in many other colonies and, subsequently, states, the proudest ("happiest") day of the year for many ordinary freemen was election day, when polls were taken by voice vote: "As each voter came before the sheriff to proclaim his preference among the candidates, he held for one brief moment the center of the political stage. Then at least he felt that he counted for something in government."[30] In some places, political participation even had theological overtones. Though traditional New England Puritanism had been watered down by the time of the Revolution, there was still a surviving sense that political participation was an act which symbolically bound an individual to the community and maintained social order. By participating, one was also agreeing to abide by community decisions. In areas swept by the evangelical revival of the mid-eighteenth century (the so-called "great awakening"), participation in public life was another way of showing that individuals were responsible to God without intermediaries.[31]

Ironically, two Europeans—one a sometime resident and the other strictly a visitor—publicized for Americans what this matter of participation meant: it meant that political responsibility was the hallmark of citizenship and, in turn, that citizenship was the criterion of nationality, or peoplehood. Writing from France in the early 1780s after some 20 years of living in the English North American colonies, now becoming the United States, Hector St. John de Crèvecoeur reminded his former neighbors in his *Letters from an American Farmer* that what made them Americans was not that the state governed them but that they governed the state and that they could be assured of this because they appeared "in the civil lists of their country"—were participating citizens. "His country" gave the American "land, bread, protection" but, most important of all, "consequence." This is what made the citizen loyal. Without the right of participation, without the consequence, the land, bread, and protection were all insecure. Fifty years later, the French visitor Alexis de Tocqueville put his observations of the Americans this way: "I maintain that the most powerful and perhaps the only means . . . of interesting men in the welfare of their country is to make them partakers in the government. . . . Civic zeal seems to me to be inseparable from the exercise of political rights." Europeans might experience nationality in that "instinctive, disinterested, and undefinable feeling which connects the affections of man with his birthplace"; but in America, where men came from all over and often did not stay in one place very long, "it grows by the exercise of civil rights; and in the end, it is confounded with the personal interests of the citizen."[32]

If the most authentic definition of "American" was "participating citizen," who should participate? The somewhat circular answer was "everyone with a stake in activities of government." In fact, the theory was that one would have the freedom to pursue one's private stakes—whatever they might be—only if one was enough of a participant in public affairs to ensure that government did not frustrate those stakes. But what, then, of the individual who chose to live among Americans but not to participate in public affairs? Newcomers arrived on American shores all the time, for any number of reasons, some eager to participate as citizens and some not. Should the latter be accounted "Americans"? The question of *should,* however, was overshadowed by the question of *could.* Who could participate in republican self-governance? Republican political theory gave citizenship a qualitative dimension. Who could safely be expected to honestly represent his own interests, uncoerced, when exercising citizenship rights? For it was commonly believed that republican government could work only when "natural" majorities of shared interests produced public policy. If one citizen could manipulate another to produce an "artificial" majority, not only would bad public policy result but degeneration would begin: a democratic republic—ruled by the many—would devolve inexorably into an oligarchy, government by a few.

The only reliable—hence the only authentic—American citizen was one who was unmanipulable and uncoerced. Republican thought offered up a rather long catalogue of conditions that might make a person vulnerable to manipulation. These included economic conditions like debt, employment, tenancy, and even business patronage. But they also included "moral" or intellectual conditions. Pliability of character, unscrupulousness, intemperateness, ill education, superstition, and plain lack of intelligence were among these. And they even incorporated coercion. The power that other individuals or organizations had over a person because he chose to bind himself or was bound against his will could also prevent him from acting as a proper citizen. Various interpretations of these conditions were believed to justify the exclusion of adult women and white men of little or no property from participation in the franchise in most places in early republican America. Did it keep them from being part of the "nation"? Probably not in the case of women, who were considered—rather like children—as the legal extensions of male relatives. But the situation of the poor was open to debate and would not come close to being resolved until the last state eliminated property requirements for the vote, after the United States was over half a century old. When Africans or the descendants of Africans were not disqualified by the dependence implicit in slavery itself, a majority of white citizens went out of their way to embrace increasingly elaborate theories of the perpetual mental and moral dependence of the black race. They were written out of citizenship and American peoplehood for a very long time.

The catalogue of disqualifications from effective citizenship was so long and varied that it encouraged people to scrutinize one another. One historian of the early national period points out that for a good while, everyday politics seemed to be built around pointing out why one's foes were inadequate or unsuitable republicans.[33] But if scrutiny was easily directed at people who lived nearby and whose character was relatively well known, what about the continuing flow of newcomers from the British Isles and western Europe who would trickle in for a while before, in the mid-nineteenth century, turning into a flood (to say nothing of the much more diverse flow of immigrants later)? *Would* they be full and enthusiastic participants in public life, or would their loyalties stretch back across the ocean? *Could* they be participants? Did they display the independence requisite of the citizen—independence of such an extensive catalogue of dependencies? And if they spoke a foreign language or differed much in culture from Anglo-American norms, how much more difficult to evaluate their independence and how much greater the opportunities for skepticism.

But the length and variety of the catalogue of disabilities could also produce self-doubt, doubt that oneself was really fulfilling the role of republican citizen. Particularly during the United States' first century, when nation building coincided with fantastic geographical expansion and economic modernization, there was plenty of uncertainty in many people's lives. When personal fortunes were adversely affected, individuals and families suffered materially. But popular civic ideology also gave their suffering political meaning. Did adversity lead to dependency? When was dependency so great that others might call into question one's reliability as a citizen? Moreover, in a time of rapid change, an individual could become ineffective as a citizen not by change of fortune but by the changing circumstances or activities of others. What if others gained power over you? What if others conspired in unrepublican ways to make your participation in public affairs meaningless? In some sense were you de-Americanized, denationalized?

It was only because these were widely shared notions that a nativist movement could arise in the early United States. Though they were articulated with varying degrees of sophistication among different strata of American society, it is fair to say that these ideas were part of the popular culture. Probably it is because the United States was both a new nation and one formed on an untried principle that such a high level of political consciousness existed. People became part of a nativist movement when their anxieties about nationality and peoplehood propelled them to organize and attempt to take public action. But in most cases they were anxious about themselves, too. Nativist activists came from all ranks and walks of life, but *in their minds personal identity and national identity became joined.* More to the point, *they took threats to "national" identity as threats to personal identity.*

Although it was George Washington's warning about the dangers of foreign influence to republican institutions that nativists professedly admired most, the founding fathers who provided them with the most quotable advice on national character were Jefferson and Hamilton. Jefferson had written that effective civil government "must be conducted by common consent" growing out of popular subscription to common "principles." Hamilton not only handily observed that "the safety of a republic depends essentially on the habits of a common national sentiment; on a uniformity of principles and habits," but also, more to the point, recommended that "to render the people of this country as homogeneous as possible, must lead as much as any other circumstance to the permanency of their union and prosperity."[34] The nativist movement that had emerged by the end of the United States' first half-century consisted of men—and women—who selectively picked out sentiments like these and attempted to turn them into prescriptions for separating "Americans" from "aliens," taking personal satisfaction that by their very organizational activity they were proving themselves to be among the Americans. In their self-serving selectivity, they plainly ignored the injunctions of another founding father, James Madison, about the safety of diverse interests and sentiments in a republic. Nativist nationalism demanded uniformity. Since in a republic sovereignty was invested in the citizens, and government in the citizens' elected representatives, both had to be rendered as uniformly "American" as possible. The need to police the national character rationalized the very existence of nativist fraternities and societies, which not only labored to establish homogeneity as a principle but also offered themselves as reliable judges of American nationality. The "American" organizations would separate the sheep from the goats, or at least call to account the public officials whose responsibility this might be.

The host of nativistic voluntary associations—most, as we shall see, organized on the fraternal model—that emerged between the 1780s and the 1920s looked both inward and outward. Collectively constituting a mass movement, they offered participants a sense of identity seemingly related to the national identity they proposed to secure. And they provided tangible benefits for the brethren that mimicked the mutual obligation that nativist ideologues promised would result from the development of harmonious American "peoplehood." No wonder they enlisted so many supporters. And by institutional example as well as by exhortation they sought to provide citizens outside the movement with new ways of connecting contemporary events, "new ways of looking at the world which would give meaning to a whole succession of previously unintelligible developments."[35] That nativist aspirations and anxieties were not wildly at odds with the popular prejudices of a large proportion of the American people made this a recurrently achievable object.

Rethinking the Origins of the Nativist Movement

Between 1780 and 1820 a variety of organizations appeared in the United States which appropriated to themselves some measure of responsibility for identifying who or what contributed to the national character and who or what was alien. A few of them evolved into wholesale nativist societies; some spawned nativist successors; and a larger number left behind organizational models and precedents which more overtly nativistic bodies would subsequently exploit.

These predecessors and paradigms for the nativist organizations of the mid-nineteenth century did *not* emerge in response to an upsurge of European immigration to the United States; in fact, the arrival of newcomers was suppressed during most of this period, first by the social and economic dislocations of the American Revolution and subsequently by the European wars of the French Revolution and Napoleon and their stepchild, the War of 1812. In fact, their very existence should remind us that a nativist movement was something more than a reaction to mass immigration, which did not really get under way until the 1820s.[36] Nor was it, for that matter, primarily a response to the dangerous international waters the young American republic found itself navigating during its first half-century, which might be expected to have produced a defensive xenophobia: fear of *all* things foreign. Rather, the roots of an American nativist movement can be traced to perceived opportunities within and supposed *internal* threats to republican government. They are to be found connected with the formation of mechanics' societies and Democratic-Republican clubs, with the Federalist Washington Benevolent Societies, with the Democratic Tammany, and even with the fraternal benefit and reform societies that flourished in the early American republic.

Ironically, the origins of an American nativist movement cannot be found in the circumstances surrounding the enactment of the Alien and Sedition Acts in 1798, the most visible evidence of anxiety about "foreigners" in the early republican period. The Alien Acts were, in fact, three measures. The Alien Enemies Act, providing for the restraint or expulsion of unnaturalized foreigners in the eventuality of war (presumably with France), never operated. The Naturalization Act did temporarily extend the probationary period for aliens seeking citizenship to 14 years, including five continuous years of residence in the state of naturalization. The so-called Alien Friends Act gave the president much leverage, even in peacetime, over noncitizens the administration found troublesome, but it too was more of a threat than an actuality.

But the Alien Acts were not about nationality, not about the definition of American peoplehood. In large measure they were a reflection of what Robert Wiebe has called early republican "neocolonialism," an assumption that North America would continue to be what it had been for the preceding 150 years, a focal point for competition between the great powers of Europe. Although this competition might take the form of commercial manipulation or conflict over control of the western half of the continent, few American politicians doubted that it really threatened American independence itself. Likewise, few seem to have doubted that the United States would be pushed and pulled between the great powers and that efforts would be made to sway American citizens to favor this European nation or that. Such sentiments reflected a pitiful lack of confidence in the republic's powers of survival and in Americans' ability to resist the enticements of either the French or the British. This anxiety was also reflected in the debates over the ratification of the Constitution: was centralization or decentralization of political authority was more likely to stand in the way of foreign manipulation? Although President John Adams's three commissioners stood firm against the bribe offered by the French foreign minister, Talleyrand, for a commercial treaty with the United States, the so-called "XYZ affair" of 1797 nonetheless left many people with the impression that Americans *might* be bought. And even the president had earlier speculated that in any serious domestic dispute, Americans might be tempted to turn to foreign allies.[37] In the aftermath of the XYZ affair, citizens of Vergennes, Vermont, reminded Congress that it had become more important than ever for Americans to advertise to the Europeans that they were "not that degraded nationless people who will tamely lay our well-won glory and natural Happiness in the scale with the barbarian demands of the Spoliators."[38]

Doubting themselves, republican leaders were disposed to try to minimize temptation. Such temptation included persons recently arrived from Europe and residing in the republic, transients or at least "pre-citizens." It was these who might attempt corruption on behalf of their homelands or, if nothing else, infect their neighbors with their own loyalties. Aliens seemed threatening not because they were unsuitable potential citizens but because they were likely to remain alien. To Federalists, they represented an "army of spies and incendiaries" dispatched by the French to undermine trade relations with Britain. To Democratic-Republicans, they were potential agents of the British—out to lock the United States into economic dependence on the former imperial master. What made the Alien Acts controversial was not the assumptions behind them but the fact that they could be used by the party in power—the Federalists—to selectively neutralize aliens supposedly connected with France. To Federalists, the enthusiasm that their political rivals had shown for the French Revolution and the loose emulation of the Jacobin clubs by American Democratic-Republican societies proved the power of alien influence.[39]

Fundamentally, the Alien Acts were not about aliens—or even about the threat of foreign influence. They were about the relationship between government and governed in America, and they reflected a greater anxiety among their authors about the conduct of those who were inside the American polity than about who was outside it. James Morton Smith's generation-old interpretation of the Alien and Sedition episode has held up rather well: "The years between 1798 and 1801 afforded the first instance under the Constitution in which American political leaders faced the problem of defining the role of public criticism in a representative government. . . . Both the Naturalization and the Alien Friends Law represented a growing distrust not only of aliens but also of the people in general; both acts were designed to restrict the growth of the opposition party."[40] In fact, in the late 1790s the whole question of the legitimacy of political opposition itself was at issue. The emergence of organized dissent behind Jefferson and Madison struck the ruling Federalists as not merely novel but actually conspiratorial. Once elected, after all, government was supposed to govern. The Democratic-Republicans proposed that popular sovereignty did not stop at the ballot box and that popular approval for a government and its policies could be withdrawn at any time. To many Federalists—and not just extremists—such a notion smacked of revolution or at least of subversion. Under these circumstances, the Alien and Sedition Acts were intended by the Adams administration to prevent the "overthrow" of the government.[41]

In reference to a later crisis in American political life, Michael Holt has observed that when citizens question the legitimacy of political opposition, they are likely to view opposition in nonpolitical terms and, consequently, seek nonpolitical ways to remove it. In the 1790s, given the neocolonial outlook of many of those in government, it was often easy to assume that the source of opposition to the administration was foreign. Miffed by the strength of American trade with Britain, France was conspiring to bring a more pliant administration into power in the United States. To do so, it was able to take advantage not only of a smattering of French emigrants to the United States but also of other European radicals and, most especially, of the Irish in America, who could be counted on to do anything to weaken Anglo-American ties. Robert Wiebe appropriately points out that this was scarcely a general xenophobia but rather a focused critique of particular elements among the foreign-born in the United States who were supposed to be in league with the Democratic-Republican opposition.[42]

In fact, Federalists clearly distinguished between good aliens (pro-administration) and bad aliens (anti-administration). Both before and after the Alien and Sedition Acts, Federalists went out of their way to woo immigrants. Jedediah Morse, famous for his diatribes about alien subversion in the late 1790s, had been instrumental earlier in the decade in building up the Massachusetts Society for the Information and Advice of Immigrants, and only a few years into the new century Philadelphia Federalists created a committee to assist aliens through the naturalization process.[43] Probably because, in the end, the Federalists' selective anxieties about immigrants were partisan rather than nationalistic, they were never able to make a convincing case that the American character was threatened by immigration. This is not to say that Federalists did not try to make such a case in 1798 and repeatedly for more than a decade. Sometimes they tried out a primitive contract theory of the American republic, arguing that post-Revolutionary immigrants were not party to the original union and could never feel a real loyalty to it.[44] But this was sure to ring hollow, given the apparent enthusiasm of many Federalists for English immigration. Nor was it appealing to an American people already famous for moving from place to place and claiming ownership in any number of preexisting state and community compacts.

The Alien and Sedition Acts, then, left little enough of a nativist legacy. Federalists' elitist assumptions about the illegitimacy of political opposition weakened in the aftermath of Thomas Jefferson's election as president in 1800, and Federalism *became* the opposition. The need to place greater trust in the people and to credit their powers of resistance to foreign manipulation weakened Federalists' resolve to find alien agents behind domestic politics. And ultimately, the national self-confidence that grew out of the War of 1812 dispelled much of the residual neocolonialism that had assumed that the United States was destined to remain a pawn of the great powers. Perhaps more important, the Federalists never convinced a broad constituency that their anxieties about immigrants went beyond party interest, that the accumulation of aliens actually threatened the ability of Americans to function as a nation.

Yet the Alien and Sedition episode does highlight one of the key conditions that led to the emergence of a pre-nativist movement in the early republican period. Sponsors and critics of this legislation alike subscribed to the classical republican theory of history, which saw the fate of nations resting on the circumference of a great wheel. At the top of the wheel stood a successful, self-governing republic; a quarter-turn to one side was anarchy, a quarter-turn to the other tyranny. Keeping the wheel upright and without rotation downward in either direction was the chief object of a republican people. This was no simple task, for the slightest motion either way could set the wheel turning. Once the wheel was rolling, momentum made it unlikely that it could be stopped or that circumstances could be reversed: the rotation would continue until something other than a republic took its place. This outlook had numerous consequences for the political life of the young American republic. "Every republic had its Rubicon," Robert Wiebe writes, "and after it was crossed, no one could turn back the march. The republic simply perished. Hence . . . leaders set their lines of defense far in front of its banks and scanned the horizon. . . . To a man they decried the terrible 'tendencies' toward another form of government because anything more substantial meant irremediable disaster."[45] Obviously, this built a kind of conservativism into republican thought, a sensitivity to change and a suspicion that change was likely to be for the worse. Moreover, it encouraged the stereotyping of political opponents as enemies of republicanism itself. Those who were not at the top of the wheel with you must be working to roll it one way or the other—and either way was down.

No doubt Federalist fear of Revolutionary France was encouraged by this aspect of republican thought. Better to nip political opposition and unconventional definitions of popular sovereignty in the bud than to discover too late that they were actually the first shoots of foreign intrusion on American independence. Likewise, better to keep people of doubtful loyalty out of the political process than to discover too late that they were carriers of foreign radicalism.

The classical republican outlook unquestionably played an important role in the germination of a nativist movement in the early republic. Over the years, historians have found it tempting to attribute early nativist sentiment to that part of the republican tradition which stressed the necessity of "civic virtue"—high moral character represented by willingness to sacrifice for the corporate good. This explains the confusion of the Alien and Sedition Acts with authentic nativism, for Federalist rhetoric was loaded with denunciation of "radicals," "rabble," and "aliens" who were ungrateful for the leadership of a virtuous administration. But there was another side to classical republican thought, a side which stressed the importance of individual independence, participation in government, and civic equality.[46] It was to this side that organized nativist activism actually traced its roots.

Republican Notions of Reliable Citizenship

Sometimes called the "popular" side of classical republican thought, concern with citizens' independence and political participation was actually another dimension of "virtue," which was more than the exclusive concern of "elite" republicanism. Citizens' participation in republican government confirmed a sense of ownership in government and was central to Americans' "pursuit of happiness." As

Hannah Arendt once pointed out, "Americans knew that public freedom consisted in having a share in public business, and that the activities connected with this business by no means constituted a burden but gave those who discharged them in public a feeling of happiness they could acquire nowhere else."[47] Republican anxiety about patronage and dependence was in part rooted in a conviction that such conditions interfered with political participation. No citizen ought to feel compelled to surrender his voice in public affairs to another because he fell under someone else's control. Dependence, in fact, could lead a man to be either a nonparticipant in the political community or an unreliable participant, following the dictates of patron and master rather than conscience and interest. These concerns were far more than intellectual abstractions. As Rowland Berthoff observed, they reflected the "peasant-smallholder or artisan-proprietor outlook" of the large majority of early republican citizens. Personal interest in economic autonomy and the happiness of public participation intersected with some of the principal themes of classical republican rhetoric.[48]

What conditions conferred personal independence and, hence, reliable republican citizenship? Education was one. According to one early-nineteenth-century editor, it was lack of education that made a man "liable to be imposed upon, misled, betrayed, and ruined": in short, reduced to dependency.[49] Likewise, freedom of conscience was advanced as critical to proper republicanism. A popular stereotype was that the Protestant Reformation was an essential precursor of American liberty, allegedly providing for "the emancipation of the mind from subjection to every restraint but that which common sense and truth imposes."[50] Yet independent citizenship required resistance to other, less obvious kinds of dependence. "Clubbing together," as one early republican put it, could, by magnifying the political power of the participants, effectively disfranchise others. To avoid contributing to such distortions of the political process, the good republican had to be sure to place individual conscience ahead of loyalty to neighborhood, family, or clan.[51]

In the late eighteenth and early nineteenth centuries, even the traditional definition of republican virtue began to change to reflect a heightened emphasis on independence and participation. The public good was increasingly perceived as being benefited more by independent economic achievement than by self-sacrificing commitment to the community. Having virtue meant preserving the capability to make independent choices of all kinds. Such values as autonomy, self-reliance, and thrift seemed keys to this sort of republican virtue, as did, for that matter, the acquisition of property. Geographical mobility, too, seemed another manifestation of personal independence and thus of political reliability.[52]

If independence and participation had always been chief characteristics of the good citizen in republican theory, circumstances in the history of the early republic placed more pressure on Americans to assure themselves that the nation's population was growing only by the addition of people meeting republican requirements. As the euphoria of the Revolution wore off, there was a natural tendency to look for signs of decline. Republican theory, of course, suggested that small signs were often weighty, potentially signifying the rotation of the wheel of history. Besides, disappointment was almost inevitable, given the inflated expectations of the nation-building period. Many shared the feeling that the Revolution was more than a political or even a social event but that it actually "would remove long-standing constraints to national development and thereby unleash vast reservoirs of untapped energy within American society and within individual personalities, . . . that postrevolutionary America would become the cultural as well as the political capital of the world."[53] Failure to achieve such lofty goals might easily be perceived as a failure of republicanism itself. Moreover, there was a sense that the achievements of the Revolution and the Constitutional period had been brought about precisely because crises had extracted an extraordinary republican commitment from the people, a commitment that might not last after these crises had passed. Finally, the millennial theme in American Protestant Christianity at once affirmed that Americans were very likely a chosen people and that a chosen people face awful justice should they fail to live up to human and divine expectations.[54]

As it happens, there were signs enough of disappointment and failure in the four decades between 1780 and 1820. An expanding commercial economy brought an increasing proportion of Americans into impersonal economic exchanges with one another. As informal constraints on economic behavior in face-to-face transactions receded, there seemed to be increasing evidence of fraud, sharp dealing, and personal gain at the expense of others. From the perspective of "elite" republicanism, this was a demonstration that too many citizens had lost their self-sacrificing civic virtue. But to many Americans, the greater affront to republicanism was in the economic power some citizens gained over others—as customers, suppliers, creditors, or employers—

creating dangerous patron-client relationships. Such relationships struck at the very heart of the independence and equality of participation in public affairs required of the republican citizen.[55]

Evidence of commercial greed was matched by signs of self-serving political ambition. Republican distrust of political power was another manifestation of anxiety about the preservation of individual independence and participation. Republican theorists of the eighteenth and early nineteenth centuries, according to Harry L. Watson, "believed that power had an insatiable appetite for liberty and that forceful exercise of state authority was subversive to America's most precious asset." In *The Washington Community* James Sterling Young has theorized about how hostility toward power actually caused early-nineteenth-century congressmen to doubt the legitimacy of their legislative activity and, accordingly, to suspect one another's virtue. Yet the governments of a growing nation and its constituent states inevitably found more reasons to govern, and, ludicrous as it seems by modern standards, the perceived rise of too much government persuaded more than a few contemporaries that politicians and voters alike were turning their backs on true republicanism.[56]

In short, Americans of the early national period had strongly affirmed and very specific notions about the kind of citizens that were required for a republic to function as a nation—to have a national character. And not only were they conditioned by republican theory to suspect that the most important attributes of a self-governing people were likely to come under assault; they also read recent national experience to mean that these characteristics were in real jeopardy. Yet citizens of the fledgling nation were not uniformly pessimists. There was a sustained theme in popular political thought which affirmed that men could be suited and, for that matter, re-suited for effective participation in a self-governing republic. In particular, confidence was expressed in some quarters that personal independence could be cultivated and equal participation in public affairs encouraged. What if dependence was a matter of being held down—by ill education, or superstition, or misinformation, or even intemperance or other personal vices? These were all remediable conditions. In the early republic, as Roland Berthoff points out, liberating the ignorant or the intemperate "seemed to promise the perfection of American liberty."[57] Such liberation required a plan of action. Men would not be educated in the ways of republicanism by experience only. Systematic preparation for republican citizenship should begin early in life. In the 1780s, Benjamin Rush was already publishing papers on the special forms of childhood education required to mold good Americans. It was at this time that "schooling emerged as the taproot of a uniform republican culture, and the felt need for civic institutions sparked an enduring national commitment to education, not for its . . . economic training within a modernizing economy, but as a political tool training Americans in the 18th century understanding of civic order."[58] The 1790s saw a proposal for a national university, an idea endorsed by Washington. That its principal object was to teach citizenship is clear from Rush's proposal that the Constitution be amended to qualify only the university's graduates as candidates for public office. George Washington himself was held up to youth as the foremost example of what was sought in the good republican: "unvarying habits of regularity, temperance, and industry . . . ability to act independently."[59]

Organizing for Participatory Citizenship: The Trade, Political, and "Patriotic" Societies

Between 1780 and 1820, elements in American society which found themselves vulnerable to losing the prerequisites for effective republican citizenship, or which regarded themselves as somehow especially representative of republican character, organized. The resulting organizations implicitly and sometimes explicitly defined what (or who) was acceptably republican—and, consequently, "American"—and what was not. These organizations included mechanics' and democratic societies, Tammany, the Federalist Washington Benevolent societies, and a variety of other clubs describing themselves as benevolent and fraternal. Although they were not specifically nativist, in this phenomenon lie the authentic roots of the American nativist movement.

The urban mechanics' societies of the 1780s and 1790s were descendants of the compacts of craftsmen and merchants made during the nonimportation-home manufactures phase of colonial protest against British imperial trade policy in the early 1770s. Historians continue to argue over the real objectives of the mechanics' societies. Sean Wilentz, for example, insists that they were more than self-interested trade groups—that they were created "to prevent what they feared was the imminent collapse of republican ideas and institutions." Lashing out at a newly arisen commercial elite, they reminded Americans of the republican value of honest labor, useful products, and regard for neighbor. By contrast, John Diggins wonders if what journeyman craftsmen were really interested in was taking collective action to get ahead economically, to improve their working conditions and influence wages and prices.[60] In fact, both are right. The mechanics' organizations *were* created in defense of republicanism, but with a particular emphasis on the opportunity for craftsmen to achieve republican independence and full participation in public affairs. This independence—which obviously had economic ramifications—was at the nub of the mechanics' interpretation of republican "virtue."[61]

Consider the experiences of two well-documented urban mechanics' societies of the 1780s and 1790s, those of New York and Baltimore. In New York City, the General Society of Mechanics and Tradesmen was founded in 1785 in the tradition of the Revolutionary-era Mechanics' Committee. Though initially combining master craftsmen, journeymen, and merchants, the society was gradually abandoned by most masters and merchant capitalists. By the early 1790s, in fact, merchants and tradesmen were backing opposing slates of political candidates representing the divergent interests of the two groups. A consistent objective of the Mechanics' Society was economic autonomy. The organization sought legislation helpful to tradesmen, opposed the chartering of private banks (which members regarded as institutionalizing privilege), and sustained a nationalist hostility to British commercial imperialism and to Americans deemed too friendly to England. Much the same was true in Baltimore, where the Mechanical Society of the early 1790s traced its roots to the Mechanical Volunteers militia company of 1773. A modern scholar of Baltimore tradesmen notes that the society functioned as a "school of democracy" which honed individual skills essential to effective participation in public affairs and kept craft workers informed about public issues.[62]

The centrality of public participation to republican citizenship also helps explain the popularity of New York's Tammany Society (or, originally, Columbian Order), founded in 1786. Not yet the party tool that it would eventually become, Tammany was instituted as an instrument of participation in public affairs for the middling classes of the city, providing through organization some of the political clout that the "aristocracy" possessed by virtue of wealth or connections. Like the mechanics' societies, with which its membership overlapped, Tammany stressed individual self-improvement as a means to autonomy, and its early headquarters included a reading room as well as a historical and scientific museum. In the 1790s, Tammany also took up the campaign for social, legal, and penal reforms that promoted personal independence, including the establishment of public schools and the abolition of imprisonment for debt. Its charitable functions, including small loans and death and survivor benefits for dues-paying members, also were aimed at warding off dependence. While Tammany did not run its own tickets of political candidates and was officially nonpartisan, its populist character led to the departure of most members with Federalist leanings by mid-1795. The American Indian symbolism of the society—its name, borrowed from a fabled Delaware chief; its description of its officers as sachems; its Indian-style regalia; and its headquarters "wigwam"—served to reinforce its rhetorical commitment to personal independence.[63] So appealing were both the message and the symbolic elements of Tammany that imitative organizations sprang up in widely dispersed locations. During the first decade of the nineteenth century, a Tammany society was formed in Cincinnati, to be followed by branches in a number of nearby Ohio towns.[64]

More openly political in identity and purpose were the Democratic-Republican societies that spread up and down the Atlantic seaboard during the mid-1790s. Perhaps as many as four dozen major clubs appeared between 1793 and 1800. The first was founded in Philadelphia, and the largest and most powerful remained the Democratic Society of Pennsylvania. The societies were overtly antiadministration during the Adams presidency and, of course, were a major source of the Federalists' suspicion of political opposition. While the immediate provocation that led to their creation was the alleged subservience of the administration to Great Britain and its hostility to revolutionary France, the underlying theme was that the people were being left out of affairs of state, that unresponsiveness to the popular will mocked authentic republicanism.[65]

The models for the democratic societies were the correspondence committees of the Revolutionary crisis, and, as Richard Buel has made clear, their principal objective was not electioneering but "mobilizing public opinion." They acted on the suspicion that an unresponsive government needed to be constantly watched lest it begin to fall away from republican reliability. It was precisely because these societies were committed to broadening participation in public affairs that the Federalists despised them. Criticism of the organizations as "self-created societies" highlighted the Federalists' distinction between a proper republican society, which left its elected governors to govern; and artificial and (to their minds) anarchistic arrangements, which allowed periodic public intrusion into the affairs of the administration.[66] In fact, in 1794 and 1795 the democratic societies did prove successful in stimulating increased public interest and participation in elections.[67]

Connection with the committees of correspondence of the 1770s was more than symbolic; the Democratic-Republican societies included a number of former participants in these institutions of participatory politics as well as alumni of the Sons of Liberty and Revolutionary committees of public safety. They explicitly identified the Revolution as a model of republican participation. For this reason, they not only made much of celebrating Revolution- hallowed holidays like the Fourth of July and Washington's birthday but also commemorated them in ways that maximized popular participation, with parades, public addresses, fireworks, and picnics. In these, they were joined by Tammany and the various mechanics' societies. Likewise, in the tradition of citizens' involvement in the Revolutionary crisis, the Democratic-Republican societies were quick to volunteer manpower for militia drills or building fortifications.[68] Although not particularly noted as social reformers, the Democratic-Republican societies also joined Tammany and the mechanics in pursuit of a free school system that would liberate the individual; and toward the end of the 1790s, some clubs began to dabble in fraternal benefits on the "mutual assessment principle," whereby all members chipped in equal amounts to bury a brother or help him in illness. The creation in New York City of a Juvenile Republican Society in 1795 also reflected the idea that good republican citizens could and should be nurtured. Although congressional endorsement of the Jay Treaty took much wind out of the Democratic-Republican societies' sails, suggesting their impotence in foreign policy and putting an end to their rapid growth, remnants of the organizations survived into the early 1800s. More important, their alumni lived on, remembering not only the organizations' emphasis on republican independence and participation but also their structure, regalia, and celebrations.[69]

In fact, the appeal of the themes and forms of such "republican" organizations knew no partisan bounds, and as the Federalists became more sensitive to the fact that any viable political party must attract a mass following, they turned to creating societies along similar lines. Beginning about 1800, Washington or Young Federalist Associations began to form in cities from Alexandria, Virginia, to Augusta, Maine. Perhaps the most famous was New York City's Washington Benevolent Society of 1808. These societies did represent a modest shift by a new generation of Federalists away from the extreme anglophilia identified with Alexander Hamilton; but they represented less a break with

traditional Federalist foreign policy than a tighter embrace of the classical republican themes of independence and participation that so far
had been appropriated by the Democratic-Republicans.[70]

Like Tammany, the mechanics' organizations, and the Democratic-
Republican societies, the new Federalist organizations had mutual benefit features and highly public and participatory patriotic celebrations,
and they appealed to Revolutionary veterans and the populist dimension of the Revolutionary experience. By 1812, there were more than
200 local Washington Benevolent Societies spread as far west as Ohio.
Massachusetts alone counted 52 clubs in 1815.[71] David Hackett Fischer
describes the fraternal benefits provided by many of the societies:
"Some of its members received weekly support. . . . Others were given
occasional cash assistance, help in obtaining employment, free legal
advice and medical care, firewood and warm clothing in winter, aid in
the recovery of debts or the satisfaction of creditors. . . . Other societies maintained free schools."[72] Although tradesmen and shopkeepers
were undoubtedly attracted to Federalist clubs as the foreign policy of
the Jefferson administration—especially the Embargo of 1807—began
to cause economic pain, perhaps the principal effect of the societies
was to confirm the importance of personal independence and participation to the popular definition of the good republican citizen. Federalist
hostility to the War of 1812 ultimately brought the Washington Benevolent Societies into disrepute and led to their demise, but both their
themes and their form would be remembered.[73]

Predecessors to a Nativist Movement

What was nativistic about all this? Immigrants or the foreign-born
were rarely explicit objects of concern in the rhetoric of any of these
organizations. The "foreigners" most likely to be criticized were
French ministers or English lords. Yet the roots of a nativist movement were here—in the selective emphasis given to the requisites of
good citizenship in classical republican thought. The only proper
American was independent of all patronage—economically and intellectually. The good American was ready and able—through education, information, and experience—to participate in public affairs. The
ability of the United States to function as a nation—that is, to have a
national character—hinged on its citizens' living up to these republican requirements. To put it another way, these were nationalist societies, and organizations which—because of the republican view of his-

tory—represented nationalism with a rather suspicious outlook. The implicit assumption was that people who lacked both independence and the prerequisites for reliable participation in the governance of the nation were posing as American republicans. As diverse as were the goals of mechanics' societies, Tammany organizations, Democratic-Republican clubs, and Federalist Washington Societies, all considered it their mission to nurture good republicanism *and* to make judgments about who was a suitable American republican.

Actually, to define who was a good American republican was also to define who was not—that is, who was alien. The early national patriotic and political societies focused their attention on anything that purportedly interfered with individual independence or blocked equal participation in public life. Of course, they had some tradition to work with. One legacy of the Anglo-American colonial past was a notion that among the most morally and intellectually dependent people of all were Roman Catholics. Although the historical question of Catholic loyalty to the English king and constitution was now academic, and despite the meritorious conduct of many American Catholics in the Revolutionary crisis, Catholics found no relief from charges that they were expected to surrender mind and conscience to the will of priest and prelate. Confounding the theological and the political, a Connecticut minister opined that, for Protestants, "the whole plan of Redemption is comprised in procuring, preaching, and bestowing liberty to the captives, and springing the prison to the bound."[74]

The selective emphasis of the republican societies on equal participation actually cast suspicions on any group regarded as clannish and under central direction. Of course, all those without appropriate education were also regarded as misled by ignorance and lacking the independence of the proper American citizen. Yet who was to decide what was appropriate education? The patriotic societies assumed that they knew, and they were likely to exclude education that was parochial, ethnic, or unconventional. To these issues were added concerns about the patronage exercised by family or clan and the likelihood of the poor to fall into economic dependence. The European-born, of course, were likely to run afoul of one or more of these suspicions. Yet immigration languished for most of the 40 years between 1780 and 1820, and the suspicions were more potential than actual. Nor did the patriotic societies' republican rhetoric set the stage for a general xenophobia; instead, it focused suspicion on particular elements among both the native- and the foreign-born. Still, the patriotic societies' selective

emphasis of republican themes and their experimentation with tech-
niques of mass mobilization paved the way for a more explosive situation once an invigorated European immigration commenced in the
1820s.

Key elements in the selective republicanism of the turn-of-the-century "patriotic" societies were perpetuated by a host of new benevolent
and fraternal organizations that sprang up in the years before 1820. In
fact, they were also implicit in many of the reform societies which
experienced luxuriant growth in the aftermath of the War of 1812. By
1820, Richard Brown has calculated, some 70 new fraternal and reform
organizations were being formed each year. Brown astutely notes that
the proliferation of such bodies was itself a reflection of the participatory theme in classical republicanism, representing "non-subservience
to public officials" and the combined power of average men where once
elites alone would have acted to produce reform. Putting it slightly differently, Lois Banner observes that voluntary associations were seen
by many of their members as "a way of involving citizens with their
government and thus insuring that democracy would actually function
within the republican framework."[75] In this way, the voluntary associations of the early nineteenth century carried on the republican themes
of their predecessors.

In fact, personal independence was the main objective of turn-of-the
century reform. Participants in reformist voluntarism saw as their chief
aim the nurturing of individual self-reliance and self-control, to set
Americans "free . . . from evil institutions and stifling environments":
these could include everything from the Roman Catholic Church to
debtors' prisons, from alcoholic drink to ill education.[76] As strictly voluntary associations, the reform bodies stressed their members' independence from identities prescribed by family, class, or community
and gave preference to initiative over obligation. "One's commitment to
voluntary community is determined more by carefully calculated personal goals . . . than by deep primordial bonds to kinship and place,"
Don H. Doyle observes. Voluntary reform associations offered liberation to insiders as well as clients.[77] Moreover, by rejecting either government action or the paternal benevolence of elites as an appropriate
method of republican social reform, the voluntarists made a powerful
statement about independence and participation. These themes were
reinforced by the reform associations' intentional efforts to cultivate
members' communication and managerial skills, powerful tools of personal independence in a modernizing society.[78] By tackling social prob-

lems of national or even international dimensions, the voluntary societies expanded their members' vision beyond local communities and gave them new avenues for participation in public affairs.[79]

A special kind of voluntary association—the fraternal mutual benefit society—went to extraordinary lengths to nurture republican independence and participation. Its practical economic benefits—primitive life, health, and unemployment insurance—gave individuals a certain freedom from reliance on family and community and encouraged geographical mobility away from place of birth. The "brotherhood" of the lodge cut across class and occupational identities and suggested that any man of good conduct could achieve respect. Even the commercial contacts made through brotherhood were a spur to independent economic achievement. The lodge was particularly attractive as a point of entry to public affairs for young men, and they seem to have embraced the form enthusiastically. Richard Brown notes not only the explosion of chapters of the Masonic order in the period from 1790 to 1810 but also the growing proportion of men under 30 in lodge leadership roles.[80] Obviously, for many, fraternal orders provided a perfect opportunity to harmonize personal ambition with republican principles.[81]

The voluntary associations—fraternal or reformist—of the early United States saw themselves as uniquely "American," connecting their structure and goals with hallowed republican principles. Of course, they assumed the right to admit or exclude from membership individuals whom they found lacking in republican character, and implicitly they extended those standards to inclusion in the national family. Operating outside the political system, they were not antiparty but antipolitical. They were not averse to organized effort, the hallmark of party; but they were hostile to patronage and compromise, the stock in trade of politics. Yet these organizations also obviously saw the attributes of effective republicanism as objects of nurture. They sought to function both as training grounds for effective citizenship for their members and as missionary agencies to nonmembers. Accordingly, they saw Americanism itself as a learned and earned status.

The nativist potential of such organizations is obvious. They posed as gatekeepers of republican citizenship and had the structural characteristics that could turn their efforts to include or exclude into a genuine mass movement. The creation of such organizations in the early national period had much more enduring consequences for the nativist movement than the contemporaneous evidence of sporadic, disorganized interethnic rivalry and violence. In major cities with ethnically and religiously diverse populations, like Boston and New York, St. Patrick's Day took the place of the colonial Pope's Day as an excuse for working-class hooliganism. In the late 1810s, competition between Anglo-American and Irish-American cartmen in New York led to an ordinance restricting the most lucrative kinds of hauling licenses to native or naturalized citizens, but it would be hard to say that this incident represented a larger pattern of institutionalized economic discrimination in the city.[82] Outside of the larger cities, anti-Catholic rhetoric proved useful to clergymen made anxious by new schisms in mainstream Protestantism. In New England the challenge of Methodism, Baptism, Unitarianism, and Universalism prompted Congregational traditionalists like Jedediah Morse to remind coreligionists of the importance of remaining united in the face of the Catholic "anti-Christ." In the south and west, the rise of the Cumberland Presbyterians and the Disciples of Christ prompted a similar strategy, among some clerical and lay leaders of more established denominations, to promote Protestant unity by vilifying Catholics.[83]

The organizational forms that a movement assumes are typically harmonious with its goals. Yet it is not always the objective that dictates the structure: organizational requirements may actually help shape ideology and outlook.[84] Both conditions operated to produce and sustain an American nativist movement. Consequently, the usual form assumed by nativist organizations in the United States from at least the 1820s (when true "nativist" organizations became evident) to the 1920s was that of the fraternal benevolent society. So prevalent was this institutional type that even nativist organizations initially founded on a different basis often adopted at least parts of the fraternal style. For a movement committed to establishing American peoplehood, the fraternal form associated with groups like the Masons, early craftsmen's societies, and "patriotic" orders offered a perfect reinforcement of its message. Each local society set itself up as a close-knit community, a society of "brothers" (and, since many of the nativist orders created women's affiliates, of "sisters"). These societies were to be microcosms of the national "people" nativists sought to cultivate. Like the American "nation," such societies were not inherent, organic, or blessed by a long history. They were systematically created—just as it was believed an American peoplehood could be created. As voluntary associations, they consisted of members who committed themselves to the ideals of the organizations by choice, just as American nationality was believed to require choice. Like the Masons, Odd Fellows, and other fraternal organizations, the nativist societies ritually stressed social harmony and committed brethren to maintain concord with one another in all of their interactions—never to let "interest" come in the way of shared goals.[85] Moreover, despite the secrecy of these organizations and their elaborate procedures for admission and withdrawal, they aggressively recruited new members.[86] The networks of local nativist fraternal organizations that stretched across states and even across the nation were calculated to remind members that they were part of a *national* people.

By acting out their ideology through participation in voluntary fraternal societies, men and women were staking a claim to individual identity.[87] We should not underestimate the attractiveness of such an assertion of identity in a society which, throughout the nineteenth century, was geographically expansive, socially fluid (with people moving up and moving down), and undergoing rapid economic development. Some historians have treated such associational activity as conservative, defensive, and premodern, but it actually showed every sign of being adaptive to a modern world. The identity that an individual took by participation in a nativist society was based not on assigned social status or inheritance but on a voluntary contract. As a result, taking an individual into a group was fully in harmony with the modern ethic of individualism. Likewise, as organizations with a public purpose, the nativist societies implicitly accepted the modern state and ascribed to it certain responsibilities that in a more traditional society might have been exercised by family, church, or clan. Community, in short, was understood in relatively modern terms.

Don Doyle has observed that the explosion of voluntary interest groups in the mid-nineteenth century represented acceptance of "a new definition of community, not as a network of self-regulating personal and family relationships but as a collection of individuals subject in some areas to the regulation of public institutions."[88] Highly participatory in structure (despite the grandiloquent titles of their leaders), nativist fraternities offered a kind of microcosmic experience with popular democracy for those who chose to share the culture of the group. Members were participatory "citizens." Accordingly, they mimicked the nation they wished to create.

Brotherhood involved more than lip service; the nativist fraternities *did* provide disability, burial, and survivors' insurance on the mutual-assessment principle, and ultimately (in the late nineteenth century) on an actuarial basis. In 1888, the Pennsylvania chapter of the Patriotic Order, United Sons of America reported over $300,000 in its relief

accounts; and the American Protestant Association, which was not organized nationally as a beneficial society, authorized local chapters to offer
"relief" related to distress, burial, and bereavement.[89] Membership in a
nativist fraternity thus had many of the same advantages as participation in any beneficial fraternal group; at a time when the modern insurance industry was still in its infancy, when geographical expansion and
a revolution in transportation were taking more and more people away
from the secure support of family, when the assumption was becoming
widespread that the risks of life could and should be managed, fraternal
benefits were extraordinarily attractive, especially to men and their families who were in middling economic circumstances. The emotional
trappings of "brotherhood," including a respectable crowd and a dignified service at one's funeral, added to the fraternities' appeal.

But the real "utilitarian" benefit of belonging to the Order of United
Americans in the early 1850s or to the Junior Order of United American Mechanics four decades later was less emergency relief in times of
disaster than assistance in seizing prosperity—and, consequently, in
republican political terms, a greater likelihood of "independence." For
a merchant, a professional, or a tradesman, membership in a nativist
fraternity—no less than in a social fraternity like the Odd Fellows—
gave access to a world of economic contacts. One met customers or
suppliers or prospective employers and came to call them "brother."
The nativist fraternities encouraged the brethren to trade with one
another and sometimes actually promoted their goods and services.
This was a time when credit reporting had yet to be perfected, but
advances in communications and transportation were constantly bringing newcomers into a community and taking commercial transactions
out; thus dealing with sworn brothers made good business sense. The
insistence of the nativist lodges that members deal equitably with one
another and the enforcement of ethical conduct made possible by the
threat of suspension from lodge membership added to the security participants could feel in conducting their affairs within a fraternal circle.
At the very least, brethren could be assumed to share a similar outlook
and similar values and to have undergone a certain scrutiny before
being admitted to membership.

Obviously, membership could be especially valuable to a man on
the move, who could take his identity as a brother with him into a new
community where he was otherwise unknown. All of the nativist organizations established on the fraternal model had elaborate procedures
for distributing transfer cards to members striking out to new loca-

tions. As Don Doyle has demonstrated of nineteenth-century fraternal organizations generally, participation in a nativist society encouraged the internalization of an entrepreneurial "moral discipline" that "enhanced opportunities for upward social mobility."[90] Finally, the nativist fraternities, no less than the Druids or the Red Men or the Sons of Temperance, provided a "sanctioned avenue away from the family," a weekly evening of male conviviality, boyish ritualism, and informal self-improvement that violated none of the emerging values of middle-class respectability.[91]

In general, American fraternalism—and particularly nativist fraternalism—has received short shrift from historians, who are inclined to treat the lodges as reactionary, refuges from the modern urban, industrial world that began to emerge in America in the early nineteenth century. In our own time, when fraternalism has gone out of fashion and seems hopelessly quaint, it is all too tempting to go along with Alexis de Tocqueville, who suggested as early as the 1830s that American voluntary associations of all types offered Americans relief from individualism and competitiveness. That they did foster an appealing sense of community is certain. But they also offered to abet opportunities that American society provided for individual achievement and mobility. In fact, in creating communities that were based on common values and goals rather than geography or inherent mutual obligation, they were decidedly modern and forward-looking.[92] That the nativist fraternities shared these characteristics should make us wary of unsophisticated stereotypes of nativist activists as backward-looking protesters against change of all sorts. In fact, the very similarity of the nativist fraternities to other fraternities may provide a key to understanding why they fell as well as why they rose. A fraternity with instrumental objectives—say, the Order of United Americans—would never provide as useful a transfer card as a purely expressive fraternity like the Masons. The circle of brothers would inevitably be more constricted, and the strength of the order would rise and fall as its instrumental objectives were or were not achieved. Many members of nativist societies were joiners who also belonged to other fraternities; they would drop the least useful memberships first. Whenever the nativist movement was instrumentally potent, flexing its political muscle, its constituent organizations grew—and growth nourished itself as more people saw advantages in belonging to an enlarged brotherhood. Conversely, whenever nativism went into political decline, it lost much of its expressive utility as well.[93]

The long and virtually uninterrupted life of the nativist movement is explained only by the adaptability and resiliency of both its ideology and its organization. In time, the nation-building phase in the history of the United States passed, and a majority of citizens—even nativists—accepted the fact that the republic was functioning "as a nation" and was able to survive the most severe challenges to nationhood. The Civil War, whatever else it did not resolve, seemed to prove that. And the old classical republican warnings about the dangers of degeneracy into oligarchy or anarchy became time-worn. But the elements of the civic culture inherited from the Revolutionary era which drew attention to the characteristics of good citizenship continued to offer support to a nativist movement that claimed for itself the exclusive right to determine who was suitably American and who was not. Moreover, the utopian character of American nationalism, which supposed that the United States had a mission to regenerate the world, was bound to take on weight once the nation had proved not only that it could survive but that it had the potential of being a world power. This offered an opportunity for nativists to argue that "national character" was now more important than ever—"national character" not in the sense of ability to function as a nation but in the sense of collective values. The fraternal form of nativist organizations, with their membership oaths and tests, was well suited to their definition of themselves in the late nineteenth and early twentieth centuries as judges of values. At the same time, they could claim that only organizations such as they could resist the challenges posed to authentically American values by well-organized "aliens." And they continued to provide opportunities for individuals with doubts about their personal identity to prove that they were among the "real" Americans.

Conclusion: Toward National Character by Exclusion

The fact that for a full half-century after the Declaration of Independence Americans were still seeking to establish that they *had* a national character is demonstrated by national reaction to the War of 1812. The response of the American people as a whole to the crisis, President Madison told Congress, represented "proofs of the national character." How was that demonstrated? At two levels, collective and individual. Having fended off Great Britain again, the United States showed that it might survive as a nation. But this was made possible by citizens who exhibited "self-control," "resiliency," and "public spirit," that is, individual independence and participation in public affairs.[94] That these could be powerful tools of exclusion as well as inclusion in the national family—especially when wielded by efficient voluntary associations—would be fully demonstrated during the succeeding 30 years, during which a nativist movement flourished.

Chapter Two

The Nativist Network in the Mid-Nineteenth Century

The Common Council of New York City, rumor had it, was about to purge the last of a handful of aged Revolutionary War veterans from their municipal jobs. As the rumor made the rounds of neighborhoods of craftsmen and shopkeepers in late 1835 and early 1836, it turned into a tale of conspiracy. Democratic party politicians, it was alleged, wanted to get these 75- and 80-year-old heroes out of the way to appoint in their places immigrants from Ireland—a payback for Irish Catholic voters' support in recent elections. Outraged, native-born Protestant Democrats jumped from their party's ranks to join a New York Native Democratic Association that had been formed earlier, in 1835, primarily by discontented Whigs who believed their political leaders, too, had sold them out in pursuit of "foreign" votes. Was politicians' willingness to ignore the interests of the "American" voter and their eagerness to manipulate gullible aliens a fateful sign that the republic was unraveling as other republics had unraveled? Equally frightening, was it evidence that native-born workingmen, clerks, and small proprietors—already nervous about mystifying economic changes—were losing their public voice? If their economic autonomy was threatened and their vote became meaningless, could they really be republican citizens, really be "Americans"?

"In the antebellum period," the historian Amy Bridges has observed, "there were always nativists about."[1] True enough. Yet the mere accumulation of Americans with anxieties about accelerating

European immigration and white ethnic diversity did not make for a nativist movement. The distinction between interethnic prejudice and organized activity directed at confirming American "nationality" is critical. One of the dominant characteristics of the period between 1820 and 1850 was the ebb and flow of organized nativist activism as members of the native-born Anglo-American ethnic majority lost or found connections between their interethnic perceptions, their fears about their own identity as effective citizens, and their concern that the United States "act as a nation."

Social Change and Individual Anxiety in Antebellum America

The 30 years leading to midcentury were characterized by both widespread optimism and anxiety—often traceable to the same sources. For many Americans, it was a period of unusual geographical mobility, prompted not only by the expansion of the nation's borders but by the absorption and development of vast territories previously annexed. This was the time when the land between the Appalachians and the Mississippi was transformed from rude wilderness into the nation's breadbasket and the source of its most lucrative agricultural exports. But population was not migrating only from east to west. Economic development altered opportunities and horizons and produced large population movements within regions and between communities. Of course, there were major consequences for social organization among a mobile people. Movement sheared families from neighbors and individuals from families. Familiar sources of practical and psychological support evaporated. Neighbors were strangers. Of necessity, many antebellum Americans placed a new premium on shorthand sources of knowledge about one another, particularly ethnic, religious, and regional stereotypes.

Expansion across large spaces was matched by movement to a special kind of place: the city. In 1820, only 7 percent of Americans lived in places that could even remotely be called "urban"; during the 1850s, some 20 percent of a much larger population was nonrural. Urbanization peaked in the 1840s, town and city populations nearly doubling during that decade. The most startling change was represented by the growth of large cities. Between 1825 and 1850, New York City experienced a growth rate of 750 percent, outdistancing the Liverpool and Manchester of Dickens's England by two- or threefold. By midcentury, the population density of Manhattan's Fourth and Fifth Wards reached 45,000 per square mile.[2] But New York, Philadelphia, Boston, and Baltimore (and even second-tier eastern cities like Hartford, Lawrence, and Lowell) were not the whole story of antebellum urbanization. Chicago was transformed from a frontier fort in 1830 to a bustling city of more than 100,000 in the 1850s. A dozen inland towns along the Great Lakes, the Ohio, and the Mississippi became substantial urban centers.[3] The city—previously represented by only a few precincts in the east—was a different social proposition, throwing people of diverse social classes, religious denominations, interests, and origins into continuous interaction. To most Americans, this was a new kind of living.

Compounding the unfamiliarity of new people and new places were changes in the world of work. While the rhythms of agricultural life remained fairly constant, the spread of commercial agriculture continually expanded the number of propertyless agricultural laborers, as well as the number of workers constructing and operating the canals, steamboats, and railways spawned by expanded trade. The early stages of American industrialization—sometimes called "proto-industrialization"—had the greatest impact on work life in cities and towns. Although the emergence of a modern industrial workforce was not completed in this period, some traditional manufacturing institutions like craft apprenticeship fell into disuse; and as a result of expanded manufacturing contracting in key trades, craft shops staffed by skilled journeymen were replaced by a production process that passed a merchant capitalist's goods from hand to hand among workers who did not possess the materials, tools, or skills to improve their economic condition. The fact that these changes appeared selectively in particular trades probably compounded the sense of bewilderment and helplessness among downwardly mobile craftsmen in the affected industries. Employers, too, sometimes found themselves grappling with a new relationship to labor that gave them much less responsibility for or control over workers' lives outside the workplace than had been the case in the traditional patriarchal craft shop.[4] Obviously, the fundamental impersonality of urban market relationships affected the lives of buyers and sellers as well. A spreading market economy and the beginnings of an industrial economy created remarkable opportunities for some, just as geographical mobility and city life created unprecedented lifestyle opportunities. Yet winners as well as losers often found the new circumstances, relationships, and statuses unfamiliar, and the sources of change mysterious.

It is not enough to note that the changing economy of antebellum America brought opportunity to some and sorrow to others. Actually, dramatic boom and bust cycles could abruptly turn winners into losers and losers into winners. Waves of economic growth surged in the early 1830s and after 1844, but there were devastating lows at the very beginning of the 1820s and from 1837 through 1843. These instabilities had particularly keen effects on people who found themselves isolated from supportive families and communities or who were experiencing changes in their work life. In a society characterized by movement and growing impersonality, economic unpredictability sowed suspicion about strangers and their motives.

One of the chief effects of geographical expansiveness, urbanization, personal mobility, and economic development was increased diversification of interest and outlook among Americans. While neither the nation as a whole nor individual communities had ever been as homogeneous as contemporary popular lore supposed, these developments could easily be taken as signs of social fragmentation, challenging national unity. This perception was compounded by the consequences of the sustained evangelical revival, the "Second Great Awakening," which lasted from the 1790s into the 1830s (with echoes up to the Civil War), creating great churches from small sects and producing dramatic schisms which made American Protestantism remarkably diverse. The sense of religious disunity was especially acute in those regions which had left the Revolutionary era with an "established" church intact in law if not in fact. Likewise, the eruption of sectional conflict—epitomized by the debate over admitting Missouri to statehood in 1819-1821, by South Carolina's defiant "nullification" of congressional tariff legislation in the early 1830s, and by the struggle over the status of slavery in territory taken from Mexico by conquest in the 1840s—seemed evidence of a loss of common national outlook and purpose.

It was probably not coincidental that growing diversity was accompanied by some fundamental changes in the structure and conduct of American politics. Gradually, from the 1820s into the 1840s, a democratization of the American electorate took place. This assumed the form not only of a broadened franchise—to the point that it essentially took in all adult white males—but also of an expanded number of political offices filled by the voters' direct election. For example, in New York

City, the electorate grew by 30 percent as a result of franchise reforms in the early 1820s. Shortly thereafter, this expanded electorate acquired new power through statewide legislation which provided for direct election of sheriffs and justices of the peace and, a few years later, of mayors. Geographical mobility and urbanization greatly increased turnover in the electorate as well. Kenneth Winkle's careful study of population movement and the vote in antebellum Ohio suggests that even in rural areas, citizens were likely to cast ballots in only two or three elections before moving on. To prevent mass disfranchisement, communities and states gradually replaced "consensual" legal residence—in which the community determined its legitimate inhabitants and political participants—with "volitional" residence, in which individuals (at least white, male individuals) "themselves could choose legal residence . . . through their own free will, through their continuing presence alone."[5] Under these circumstances, it did not require a distrustful upper-class conservative like the diarist Philip Hone in New York City to complain that "the men who decide the elections are unknown."[6]

The United States entered the 1820s almost without competing national political parties. The Federalists had disappeared as an organized entity in most places. Nominally, almost every state or federal officeholder was a Democratic-Republican. The sectionally divisive Missouri crisis at the start of the decade illustrated how dangerous it could be for the nation to have no competing political coalitions that could cut across regional boundaries. The "second party system" that emerged between 1828 and 1832 was characterized by the first national parties that were more than alliances of elites and their personal followings. These new mass parties encouraged loyalty to platforms as well as to personalities and sought to hold voters' interest by connecting local circumstances with national events. By selecting candidates for public office by convention rather than by insider caucuses, they prolonged campaigning between elections and made politics a very public spectacle.[7]

Collectively, these political developments—the expanded franchise, direct election of officeholders, volitional legal residency, and mass political parties—raised new questions about the responsibilities of the voting public. While some conservatives harbored fears that there were few checks on an unpredictable and uneducated electorate, a more widely held concern was that one's vote should mean something: that participation, the mark of the republican citizen, should be effective and authentic. If politicians would now rule with a public mandate, how could the ordinary citizen ensure that his vote had the same weight as everyone else's? This created an inherent suspicion of voting blocs and political deals which, when captured in traditional republican rhetoric, took on apocalyptic significance.

The growing complexity of the American social fabric was bound to raise questions about national unity—about the ability of the American people to have the "character of a nation," which was still understood to be something different from and more enduring than a constitutional state. Traditional republican theory underscored this point by insisting on the need for a citizenry with enough mutual sympathy to make virtuous self-sacrifice for the community good natural and unforced. In its modified Madisonian version, at least, republicanism presupposed that competing interests among the electorate would be so equal in strength that fair compromises would ensure national harmony. But under the circumstances of antebellum America, the growing variety of interests seemed matched by great differences in access to power. Change was not new to antebellum America; the republic had been anything but stagnant since the ratification of the Constitution. But the survival of many of the hallowed founders up to the 1820s had lent legitimacy to change and had given a sense that the republic remained on course. Then, in quick succession, Monroe's retirement from the presidency, the deaths of John Adams and Thomas Jefferson, and the aging Lafayette's nostalgic visit to the United States made it apparent to all that the age of Washington had passed into history. In increasingly complex times, would the successors be able to ensure that the United States nurtured and protected its "national character"?

Into the antebellum cauldron of change came a greatly accelerated immigration from Europe, and consequently a bolder pattern of white ethnic diversity. Revolution in America and decades of war in Europe had combined to dampen the transatlantic migration which had fueled colonial expansion. But as the 1820s wore along, a trickle of immigrants grew into a stream, and by the mid-1830s an invigorated immigration was under way, most heavily from Great Britain, Ireland, and Germany. During the mid-1840s, European immigration was well along toward its pre-Civil War peak: more than 425,000 arrivals in 1854. The crest of immigration at midcentury was largely attributable to the European potato famine, which devastated Ireland as well as parts of the European continent. A combination of economic and political incentives produced a trailing wave of German immigrants in the late 1840s and early 1850s. By the mid-1850s, the proportions had been reversed, with Germans outnumbering even the sustained mass migration of the Irish.[8]

It is important to bear in mind that the effects and perceptions of antebellum immigration were uneven across the United States. The popular press, of course, reported its broad ebbs and flows. Peaks excited notice, especially in port cities, which had the most immediate experience with the newcomers. Between 1830 and 1860, for example, fully 3.5 million immigrants landed in New York City. From the early 1840s through the mid-1850s, New York was the point of disembarkation for 68 percent of all immigrants arriving in the United States.[9] By 1860, nearly 20 percent of all the nation's foreign-born lived in just six port cities; close to 40 percent were found in some 43 municipalities—mostly in the northeast—that constituted the primary, secondary, and tertiary centers of the nation's manufacturing and commerce. While many of the immigrants from Ireland and Germany who made up most of the flow spread out across the country, a substantial proportion were clustered in only a few areas, often at the ports of arrival. On the eve of the Civil War, half of the United States' Irish-born lived in New York, New Jersey, and Pennsylvania (with half of that number settled in New York state alone). Half of the nation's German-born lived in the states of the "old" northwest and neighboring Missouri. In some young states, comparatively small numbers of immigrants had a large demographic impact. At the end of the 1850s, California's population was nearly 40 percent foreign-born, and immigrants constituted 35 percent of the populations of Wisconsin and Minnesota. On the other hand—and this points up the concentration of immigrants in the north—among the southern states only Louisiana and Texas had proportions of the foreign-born as large as 10 percent. Elsewhere in the south, 1 or 2 percent was typical.[10]

It is possible to get an idea of the impact of antebellum immigration on public perceptions in places where it was most concentrated by considering the experience of New York City. In 1845, of a population of 371,000, fully 135,000 were foreign-born—overwhelmingly Irish and German (the ratio of Irish to Germans was 4 to 1). But just 10 years later, the city's immigrants numbered 300,000, making about 52 percent of its population foreign-born. By 1855, the most "foreign" wards of the city were up to 70 percent immigrant, and even the wards most heavily populated by the native-born were 35 percent foreign.[11] In one month—April 1851—almost 28,000 newcomers landed at New York harbor, including 15,000 from Ireland and 6,000 from the German states.[12]

The foreign-born in Philadelphia increased from 2 percent of the total population in 1830 to 20 percent at midcentury. Nationwide, the United States grew more from immigration than from native births (by a small margin) during the high tide of immigrant arrivals between 1845 and 1854; at the key points of entry, natives were likely to perceive themselves as being overwhelmed.[13]

Yet it was not numbers alone that made immigration so visible during the decades preceding the Civil War. The Irish and German arrivals overwhelmingly came from the working and middle classes. They had not necessarily been poor when they left their homes; but many had their resources depleted by the process of migration itself, and of course a substantial proportion of the famine-era Irish were desperately poor. Compounding relative poverty was ill health, aggravated if not initiated by the transatlantic passage. Historians have long since exploded the stereotype of immigrants as rootless isolates, shorn of kin and culture. We are now much better acquainted with the self-selection that took place in the decision to emigrate, which tended to pull out not the weakest or the poorest but the most intentional and those committed to preserving what status and property they had. And we have come to understand much better the ways in which kinship and communal networks structured the immigrants' choice of residence and work, creating channels of opportunity. Nonetheless, the attention of native-born Americans focused readily on the haggard, disoriented appearance of newly arrived immigrants, especially those who landed sick. The oldest, weakest, and poorest inevitably stood out from the rest and provided the raw material for stereotypes that magnified differences between the native and the foreign-born.

Immigrants also drew attention disproportionate to their numbers by their overrepresentation in particular jobs and industries. The famine-era Irish arriving in the late 1840s wound up heavily concentrated in day labor, carting, and domestic service, jobs requiring little training or investment.[14] By midcentury, "Irish" and "servant" had become near-synonyms in American parlance. In manufacturing, immigrants clustered in trades that were among the first to make the transition from traditional craftsmanship to contracting and putting-out, where cheap, unskilled labor was in demand.[15]

Along with their more obvious cultural characteristics, including religion (Catholic for most of the Irish and a substantial proportion of the Germans) and language (for all of the Germans and some of the west country Irish), immigrants bore some cultural baggage that was a product more of timing than anything else. Just when proto-industrialization and urbanization were becoming characteristic features of American life, most of the immigrant Irish and not a few of the Germans were rural, agricultural people who came with rural, agricultural outlooks and expectations. Immigrants out of the Irish peasantry, apparently locked into political impotence at home, sometimes brought with them a physical, confrontational style that had been the only resource of self-defense for those in no position to bargain.[16] Among the German arrivals of the late 1840s and early 1850s was a notable class of educated intellectuals, political refugees from the liberal "revolutions" of 1848, who had no intention of giving up their political activism. These characteristics, too, were bound to make immigrants visible out of proportion even to their growing numbers.

Accelerating immigration, the geographical concentration of the foreign-born, and the disproportionate visibility of immigrants—set against the background of change and sensitivity to change in antebellum America—created obvious potential for ethnic friction. The real surprise, perhaps, is that the potential exceeded the actual—a testament to the geographical and economic space the growing United States provided. But in particular times and places the mixture became volatile. Especially in burgeoning cities and in towns rapidly growing into cities, there was naked competition between the native and the foreign-born for residential and public spaces as well as for entertainment facilities. In these places, where assimilation of even native-born strangers was a struggle, any substantial immigration was bound to complicate unsettled circumstances. Immigrants who were ill or poor were likely to place unusual burdens on the relatively new institutions—poorhouses, prisons, or juvenile halls—that the nineteenth century used as caretakers for dependents. At a time when journeymen found their skills degraded and apprentices found their traditional status evaporating, immigrants could only too easily be cast as dupes or allies of merchant capitalists in the debasement of labor. As economic transactions spread out over an expanding nation and brought unseen buyers and sellers together in increasingly impersonal transactions, the introduction of people of diverse cultures made the person on the other end of the deal seem even more inscrutable and unpredictable. Likewise, a mobile population that was suspicious of new neighbors, even if the newcomers spoke in the same accents and professed similar versions of Protestant Christianity, would be much perplexed by newcomers as different as the Famine Irish or the German forty-eighters. At a time when change of all sorts seemed to be sapping national unity, immigrants not only interjected ethnic and religious diversity but accentuated class distinctions and set off areas where they were heavily represented from areas where they remained scarce.

The political developments of the antebellum period were also likely to provoke uncertain feelings about immigration. "Who elects our governors?" the New Yorker Philip Hone had wondered as he eyed the expanded *native* electorate. Imagine his discomfort with the accumulation of new voters who shared with him even less culture and education. This was not merely a complaint of conservative members of the elite like Hone. In fact, it was likely to be raised most loudly by the newly enfranchised, who would be the most sensitive about the value of their votes and their ability to make themselves heard in the political arena. Would immigrant voters dilute native voters' ballots by sheer numbers or, worse, vote in such regimented blocs as to wreck any authentic poll of citizens' interests? By the early 1850s, the foreign-born constituted one-third of the voters of the states of Rhode Island, Massachusetts, and New York; roughly half the voters in the cities of New Orleans, Detroit, New York, Boston, and Cincinnati; and a majority in Chicago, Milwaukee, and St. Louis.[17]

"Native Americanism" in the 1830s

Accelerating immigration, proliferating ethnic stereotypes, and suspicions about cultural diversity provoked by an environment of change did not lead directly to organized nativist activism in antebellum America. But these conditions did constitute an array of points which some people might connect into a pattern suggesting that the American people were failing at nationality—failing to act as a nation—and heading toward a boundary which, once crossed, meant the irreversible decline of republicanism. For those who thought they discerned such a pattern, the key element was the growing foreign-born population of the United States. The people who saw that pattern were prospective nativists. And they thrived for a time by taking advantage of some of the classical republican premises and rhetoric that still permeated popular culture. In particular, nativists argued that the consequences of immigration threatened the personal independence of the republican citizen, his ability to participate in republican government (to "pursue happiness" in a political sense), and his opportunities to join with his neighbors to forge an enduring peoplehood that would offer permanence to the American experiment of creating nationality by revolution. Nativists not only identified the sources of republican discontent but also salved popular anxieties by offering a program of redress and organizations which would model "proper" republican government while promising to help participants navigate in a world of change and uncertainty.

The nativist movement during the three or four decades preceding the Civil War is not to be confused with a "party," although it sometimes spawned political organizations. Nor was it anything like a nationwide monolith, although contemporaries referred to it with a singular noun like "native," "American," or later, "Know Nothing." Actually, it was a loose network of voluntary associations, operating at the local level, that occasionally combined to pursue larger objects. The popularity of these local clubs or temporary common fronts varied with a host of social, economic, and political conditions—often very local—most of which were not tied directly to the ebb and flow of immigration. In fact, participants in organized nativist activism were distinguished from their contemporaries not so much by the problems they identified in antebellum life as by the remedies they prescribed and the gloominess of their predictions for the nation's future if the dose was ` not taken. Moreover, nativism thrived on defeat—or at least on circumstances which nativist activists could portray as defeats. They treated each adverse circumstance in antebellum life as a product of some failure of native-born Americans to be good republicans. Although immigrants and Catholics were their villains, nativists rarely identified "foreign" or "papist" victories. They spoke instead of the failure of the native-born to live up to the high demands of republican citizenship. This conformed well with classical republican theory, which posited that republics were more likely to fall from their own self-centeredness and inattention to public needs than from external assault.

Nativists recurrently struck a responsive chord among their contemporaries by illustrating how accumulating threats to personal independence and to equal participation in public life undermined the security of republicanism. These themes had greatest appeal among the middle and working classes. Antebellum nativism was once portrayed by historians as primarily a movement of conservative elites for whom immigrants represented the forces of both modernization and democratization, but it is much better understood as something that appealed to middling folk who wanted to get ahead and feared falling behind. To these, the foreign-born could easily represent the perils of dependence and the muting of one's own public voice.

By the 1820s, the understanding of what a republican citizen needed in order to be really independent had broadened considerably from its original formulation in eighteenth-century political rhetoric. What now seemed to be required was not freedom from coercion but also a chance to realize one's personal potential and to cultivate one's higher faculties. The relatively impoverished, underemployed, at least nominally Roman Catholic Irish immigrants who were so prevalent in the Atlantic migration in the 1830s and 1840s were represented as embodying every dimension of dependence. They lacked not only economic resources but also, apparently, opportunity. Supposedly led and ordered about by priests, they were assumed to be held in thrall, with limited mental exercise. A good American public school education might hold out to them the cure for economic and intellectual dependence, but this seemed to be undercut by the growth of parochial schools in cities where immigrants congregated and the reluctance of Catholic parents to use the presumed repository of truth—the King James Bible—when their children remained in the public schools. Of course, republican theory held that people dependent in mind or purse were unreliable citizens whose hands must be kept off the levers of public power; moreover, their dependence gave inordinate and corrupting power to anyone capable of exploiting their want or their credulity. Much nativist animus, accordingly, was aimed at the *native* employer of immigrant labor or at the *native* politician who would speedily enfranchise the foreign-born to take advantage of their votes. In making these charges, nativists were revealing their own anxieties about economic change, which could unpredictably turn independence into dependence, and about the possibility of being effectively disenfranchised by the weight of other people's votes.

The gradual acceleration of European—especially Irish—immigration in the 1820s and 1830s provided the context but not the cause of a nativist movement. Likewise, incidents of friction between "Anglo-Americans" and the Irish did not lead directly to nativist organizing. For example, when New York Irish cart drivers and native competitors from Connecticut clashed in the spring of 1825 over the "just" size of loads, or when—a year earlier—Irish Catholics and Protestants rioted over the Protestants' celebration of the Battle of the Boyne, no one took it as a commentary on the ability of the republic to achieve effective nationality or on the future of republican citizenship.[18] Even the anti-Catholicism in American Protestant churches, heightened by Catholic Emancipation in Britain in 1829, did not directly promote nativist organizing. In quick succession between 1830 and 1832, ministers in New York City created a New York Protestant Association; the Reverend George Bourne initiated an anti-Catholic newspaper, the *Protestant;* and Samuel F. B. Morse published a series of hysterical letters about the diabolical designs of the Catholic Leopoldine missionary society of the Austro-Hungarian empire—all without creating much sense that the republic was in peril. Perhaps this was because Americans had lost the neocolonial outlook of the turn of the century, which had led them to suspect that continuing threats to nationhood came from overseas.

What was more likely to promote authentic nativism was "evidence" of domestic failure, of departure from the requirements of republican citizenship and from the capacity of the United States to function as a nation. Such a circumstance arose in New York City in the spring of 1835. A lecture at the New York Protestant Association on the evils of "popery" was broken up by a mob in which immigrant Irish Catholics were prominent. What captured public attention was not so much the brawl itself as its aftermath. The participants escaped arrest and indictment, and this prompted charges that the Democratic administration of the city was subordinating the law to the quest for Irish-American votes in the forthcoming elections. Ironically, the opposition Whigs drew this conclusion because they too had been lobbying for Irish ballots. When the Democrats won in April, it seemed to confirm that the politicians had placed partisan expediency ahead of justice. Subsequently, the assent given by local authorities to the creation of an all-Irish militia company, the O'Connell Guards, reinforced the impression that competition for the votes of the foreign-born had passed legitimate bounds.[19] The charge here was less that immigrants were corrupting the political system than that native-born Americans were shaming themselves. The right of native-born citizens to participate meaningfully in republican governance was diluted by politicians' aggressive solicitousness for the interests of the foreign-born.

Even before the New York City election returns were in, Samuel F. B. Morse broke from the Democratic party over the issue of immigrant voters, taking with him other dissident Democrats who may have been as distressed by what they took to be heavy-handed party leadership as by appeals to immigrant voters. Morse organized the New York Native

American Democratic Association (NADA) in March 1835. It would be a mistake to understand NADA as a citywide third party with the same degree of organizational cohesiveness as the Democrats or the Whigs. Rather, it was a coalition of ward associations and had something less than citywide coverage. Recent studies of its officers reveal that leadership was disproportionately drawn from shopkeepers, petty professionals, master craftsmen, and journeymen. Moreover, the journeymen were chiefly attracted from trades in which "putting out" (a process like the assembly line) had made the least headway and in which relations between master and employee remained the most traditional.[20] These were exactly the sort of people whose pride in personal independence was likely to make them unusually sensitive to allegations that their political voice was being weakened by the parties' eagerness to capture immigrants' votes. Additionally, NADA provided an opportunity for men who had been closed out of political leadership—either because of their class or for ideological reasons—to climb a new ladder of political mobility.[21] NADA ward associations were especially attractive to young Democratic activists who were on the outs with the "Tammany" faction that controlled city hall. Their political platform—publicized in a new newspaper, *Spirit of '76*—called for lengthening the probationary period for naturalization to 21 years and for making the foreign-born ineligible for elective office. NADA rallies, replete with artisan craft symbols, made clear the connection between economic independence and republican citizenship, implying that both were related to honest labor.

Rooted in a sense that Americans were failing to show a "national character," NADA was nurtured on evidence of "defeat." An ugly riot in June 1835 involving both native and foreign gangs in the crumbling "Five Points" slum seemed another failure of justice and order, and President Jackson's nomination of a Catholic—Roger Taney of Maryland—as Chief Justice of the United States Supreme Court in July was taken as calculated sellout to foreign-born voters. In republican parlance, these were the first turns of the wheel that would take the state to ruin if not immediately arrested. It was this rhetoric which proved successful for NADA candidates in November 1835: they captured places in city delegations to the state and national legislatures, pulling the votes of both traditional Democrats and Whigs.[22]

Across the East River in Brooklyn, another group, the Native American Democrats, also organized at the ward level for the fall elections in 1835, charging that immigrant voters were dominated by Catholic clergymen who told them that Americans were "too free" and dared to think for themselves.[23] Another apparent "defeat," the rumored purge of Revolutionary War veterans from public posts by Democratic city politicians and their replacement by Irish Catholics, propelled Samuel F. B. Morse into a campaign for mayor in the spring of 1836. In this case, however, the bipartisan support the Native American Democrats had received in the past failed to hold up. In a presidential year (with Morse openly supporting the Democratic candidate Van Buren), Whig nativists turned out in much lower numbers for the third-party candidate: Morse received only 6 percent of the vote.[24]

Early nativist organizing followed a roughly similar pattern in a number of other cities during the 1830s, although few communities were home to so many of the foreign-born as New York. In fact, the common elements were traditions of fraternal organizing, perceived "defeats" for republican principles, anxiety over independence, and self-criticism—not just immigrants. Several well-publicized incidents of ethnic or religious friction that turned violent took place in metropolitan Boston: these included the destruction of a Catholic girls' academy in Charlestown by a mob in 1834 and a wild affray between an Irish funeral procession and a volunteer fire company on Broad Street in 1837, but none of them led directly to nativist organizing.[25] More consequential was Whig Governor Edward Everett's chartering of a Boston militia unit composed of Irish immigrants and the sons of immigrants—the Montgomery Guards—at the beginning of 1837. This was denounced as a shameless bid for Irish-Catholic political support; the Montgomery Guards were publicly snubbed by the other militia companies at the city muster of September 1837; and the continuing outcry led the governor to disband the unit in the spring of 1838. Significantly, the chief complaint about the Montgomery Guards was not that it was dangerous to arm "foreigners" or that a military force had been created which supposedly owed its primary allegiance to a "foreign potentate" (the pope), though such wildly exaggerated rhetoric could be found in pamphlets and the press. Rather, it was the governor and his party who came in for most of the abuse, for putatively placing political interest ahead of public interest.[26] This was the kind of "defeat" that nativism thrived on. In Boston (unlike New York), it did not lead immediately to nativist ward associations, but it did produce an enlivened nativistic sentiment within existing militia and fire companies, which had many of the elements of fraternal organizations.

Reinforcing the lesson taught by Massachusetts—that nativist organizing did not directly accompany dramatic changes in the pattern of immigration itself—the District of Columbia's first experience with a Native American Association in 1837 featured anti-*British* rhetoric and charges that the republic was sacrificing sturdy native culture to imitate English manners.[27] Charges of a political sellout for advantage among immigrant voters punctuated the debate over the position taken by Democratic delegates to the Pennsylvania Constitutional Convention of 1837 that native-born African-Americans should be excluded from citizenship while naturalization should be made easy for the European-born. In Germantown, outside Philadelphia, a public mass meeting agitated the issue of naturalization fraud by politicians eager to turn immigrants into voters and called for the revision of naturalization legislation.[28] Although Philadelphia had a large immigrant population, it would require an economic downturn in 1837-1838 to raise widespread "republican" anxiety about personal independence and political effectiveness and to energize a nativist movement there. Still, the issue of naturalization in Pennsylvania was just the sort of thing to provoke suspicions that an irreversible descent into political tyranny had begun.

Although both European immigration and nativist organizing rose to peaks in the mid-1840s, it would be simplistic to draw too close a connection between the two, interpreting them mechanistically as cause and effect. In fact, the two pivotal developments in the acceleration of organized nativist activism were the prolonged economic downturn of 1837-1843 and the spread of fraternal, patriotic, self-improvement societies. These phenomena were related. In stages between 1837 and 1839, the land and currency boom of the mid-1830s collapsed. British restriction of gold outflows combined with a new federal requirement that the purchase of public land take place in hard cash combined to burst the bubble of inflated land and commodity prices. In American cities, prices of manufactured goods slumped—and with them jobs and wages. Wage rates in New York City dropped by one-third from 1836 to 1842.[29] Among the consequences was an invigorated search for personal survival strategies among the urban middle and working classes, including temperate habits; the education of the young; Protestant evangelicalism, which connected self-discipline with earthly as well as eternal salvation; and the abandonment of newly formed workers' organizations (which might have muted interethnic conflict by contributing to a common working-class identity). At the same time, the depression bid up the value of fraternal mutual benefit societies which offered their members practical aid and useful economic contacts. Especially, the conditions of the times raised anew old republican questions about personal independence and the capacity of individuals to participate in public decision making.

There is no question that the depression put a new face on some old issues and gave them nativistic potential. For both the middle and the working classes, tax-supported public education became a pressing concern. Access to education seemed critically important as traditional ways of making a living began to disappear and upward mobility appeared to hinge increasingly on individual ability. The kind of education that seemed most appropriate for youth would at once teach them to navigate a world full of changes by reference to moral absolutes and (paradoxically) encourage creativity and flexibility of action.[30] Control of the public schools, moreover, had important symbolic value for groups who feared that their economic marginalization represented a loss of political effectiveness. In major cities with populations both ethnically and religiously diverse, this created new tensions that far exceeded any historical rivalry between Protestants and Catholics.

In both Philadelphia and New York, Catholic parents—often (though not always) foreign-born—had periodically complained during the 1830s about the overtly Protestant tenor of the public schools, particularly about the use of the King James Bible as a standard text and, in some cases, the use of outright anti-Catholic literature in the classroom. Actually, sins of omission were equally common; as one Catholic clergyman pointed out, it was quite possible for Catholic children to come away from the schools without a clue that even one of their coreligionists had played any constructive role in the history of the republic. In 1834, the bishop of New York objected to the way New York City managed public education by vesting responsibility for the schools in a private Public School Society with strong connections to institutional Protestantism. This produced a Protestant outcry but no immediate impetus for nativistic organizing. But when Catholic criticism was renewed at the beginning of the 1840s, different circumstances led to an aggressive response, particularly from the self-described "producing classes" of artisans, neighborhood merchants, aspirant entrepreneurs, and petty professionals.[31] Ostensibly, these people rose to defend the moral content of public education, which seemed essential for arming young people with the independence of thought and strength of character that would allow them to survive in an unpredictable environment. But the real issue was a growing fear of political marginalization which accompanied a suspicion that economic marginalization had already taken place. To risk losing political effectiveness as well as economic self-determination was to risk losing republican citizenship—and hence nationality itself. Elected officials' position on issues concerning the content and administration of public education emerged in the early 1840s as a bellwether of political responsiveness to the popular will and therefore as a measure of the "producing" classes' continuing effectiveness as citizens. If politicians bent to the will of others, this was evidence that office-mongering had replaced public service; and of course republican theory gave to such a circumstance apocalyptic significance, as a road to tyranny.

That a nativist reaction to the school issue in New York and Philadelphia assumed the form of an organized social movement was largely because the same economic conditions that provoked anxiety in the urban middle and working classes also promoted the proliferation of fraternal clubs and societies. These included temperance societies, trade organizations, benevolent brotherhoods, and patriotic orders. Promoting individual economic independence and effective participation in public affairs, this network of small groups lay at the core of organized nativist activism.

The Schools Controversies and "American Republicanism" in the 1840s

Although the particulars of the school controversies of the 1840s in New York City and Philadelphia were different, the themes were the same. Nativism flourished whenever events could be interpreted as evidence of a loss of independence by republican citizens, and it assumed the character of a movement whenever it could take advantage of fraternal models of organization. In New York, dissidents broke with both the Whigs and the Democrats over the issue of school control and curriculum, perceiving political expediency in the actions of party leaders. In 1840, the Whig governor, William Seward, announced that he favored a statewide system of local school control which would allow students to be instructed by teachers of their own religion; and the secretary of state, John Spencer, subsequently proposed to extend to metropolitan New York the upstate model of district schools supervised by locally elected boards. Both Seward and Spencer were denounced within the party as selling out to attract

immigrant Catholic votes.[32] In 1841, New York City Democrats frac-
tured when Archbishop Hughes called for Catholic voters to support
only that part of the Democratic ticket that seemed sympathetic to a
school districting plan. When the state legislature passed the Maclay
Act of 1842, placing control of New York City schools in the hands of
elected district boards, the concerted action of voters in both parties
initially ensured that the schools remained under the direction of
native-born Protestants, frequently members of the former Public
School Society. That the nativistic potential of the issue was primarily
in the alleged affronts of politicians to republican citizens, rather than
the school curriculum, is demonstrated by the muted reaction to the
gradual passing of the local boards out of the hands of Public School
Society loyalists in 1843 and 1844, and by the quiet elimination of the
King James Bible as a school text in heavily Catholic districts.[33] Additionally, while the school issue led to substantial public agitation, it did
not leave nativism with much of an organizational legacy. Samuel F. B.
Morse's attempt to reassemble the Native American Democrats of the
mid-1830s as a "Democratic American Association" for the spring elections of 1841 proved lame; and an American Protestant Union led by
ministers captured media attention but had little appeal to the middling folks who could make up a nativist rank and file, suggesting the
limited appeal of a movement resting purely on anti-Catholicism.[34]

In Philadelphia, similar circumstances led to a more sustained
nativist response, perhaps because of the Temperance leaders in emergent nativism brought with them practical models for ward-level organization. As in New York, a key issue was power, or, more to the point,
the political effectiveness of economically threatened elements of the
native-born Protestant middle and working classes. This was abun-
dantly evident in the events which immediately preceded the cresting
of the school issue in Philadelphia in the mid-1840s. During 1839,
Protestant Democratic voters had flexed their political muscle and
demonstrated their independence of party leadership by abandoning
an Irish-Catholic candidate for alderman, leading to his defeat by the
Whigs.[35] Two years later, they did the same with the Democratic candidate for county treasurer. The Whig leadership, thinking to benefit
from their rivals' disorganization, sought a deal with the rump of the
regular Democratic party to split victories by running candidates for
alternate offices, but this only provoked suspicion among their own
rank and file that the Whigs would sell out on issues of concern to
native-born Protestants in order to win the votes of an alliance of old

Democratic party loyalists and immigrant Irish Catholics.[36] Already fearing that their adequacy as republican citizens was threatened by economic precariousness, suspicious middle-class Whig and Democratic voters jumped to the conclusion that they were being marginalized by the party leadership. To lose one's voice in public affairs, of course, meant losing one's claim to the essence of American nationality. To compound their fury, the established political community appeared willing to turn for votes to immigrant populations which seemed even less capable of republican independence.

The collection of dissidents from the two major parties into "nativist" organizations began at the ward level right at the beginning of the 1840s. In many places, nativist organizations were grafted onto the neighborhood craft-related benevolence and temperance societies that flourished during the depression, products of workers' efforts to retain their economic independence and their self-respect.[37] Early in the decade, they were given an ideal issue. Regular Whig and Democratic politicians alike came under criticism as unprincipled office-mongers during the Philadelphia campaign of the Irish Repeal Association in 1841-1843. Aimed at rescinding the Act of Union which joined Great Britain and Ireland, Daniel O'Connell's Irish civil rights movement initially appealed to many Americans' latent hostility toward England; but after O'Connell broadened his libertarian message by lashing out at American racial slavery, the Repeal movement in America ran into charges that it was trying to involve the United States in foreigners' business and foreigners in American business. Philadelphia politicians who had initially endorsed the Repealers' fund-raising suddenly confronted vicious accusations that they were placing their attractiveness to Irish-American voters ahead of the national interest. Accordingly, it was alleged, they weakened the opportunities of native-born citizens to participate in public decision making by diluting their votes in an expanded electorate and thereby ignoring their will.[38]

Participants in an emergent nativist movement were on the lookout for political "deals" which seemed to court the foreign-born voter and ignore the native-born. It was precisely in this context that the public schools of metropolitan Philadelphia became an issue. In the spring of 1842, public school directors in the working-class suburb of Southwark dismissed a Catholic teacher who refused to open the school day with the prescribed reading from the King James Bible. When Catholic parents and Archbishop Kenrick protested—they wanted children to have the option of the reading the Catholic Douay Bible—Protestant denominational agencies and newspapers raised the alarm and called for the election of school officials who would make no compromise.[39] Archbishop Kenrick's formal request to the Board of School Controllers in November for the Douay Bible as an option touched off a concerted response from Philadelphia's Protestant clergy. Several dozen—and eventually well over a third—of the city's ministers put their signatures to a charter for an "American Protestant Association," which committed itself to publicizing the threat of Catholic pressure on what they took to be an appropriately republican school curriculum, protecting the sanctity of the sabbath, and distributing Bibles and religious tracts.[40] School officials' proposed compromise—to continue readings from the King James Bible but to allow children whose parents objected to excuse themselves from the classroom during a reading—provoked rather than satisfied Protestant activists. It smacked of the secularization of the schools at a time when it was deemed increasingly important to teach republican and Protestant values and seemed a defeat to majority rule.[41]

Mounting suspicion that the leadership of both major political parties had sold out native-born Protestant middle-class citizens was taken as confirmed when an Irish Catholic school director, Hugh Clark, suspended classroom Bible reading entirely in a Kensington district school in February 1844, on the ground that the voluntary withdrawal of Catholic students had become disruptive. Leaders of an embryonic nativist movement attacked this new development both as a weakening of the school curriculum (and thus of an avenue of social mobility and economic independence) and as evidence of disregard for the political voice of the native-born Protestant majority. Although it was the clergy-dominated American Protestant Association that attracted the most attention by staging mass "save the Bible" rallies, it was the ward associations of dissident Whigs and Democrats—which had begun calling themselves "American Republican"—that channeled native working-class and middle-class outrage into a sustained movement. Taking a stand for direct election of city and county school officials (which purportedly would reduce the influence of professional politicians), the American Republicans were surprisingly successful in the local elections in April.[42]

While these initial electoral victories provided an impetus for American Republican organizing in wards across the metropolitan area over the next several months, "defeat" continued to energize the institutionalization of a nativist movement. At the beginning of May, an

American Republican public meeting in heavily immigrant Kensington turned into a scuffle between nativists and Irish-American residents. To a native working class which had already found its access to upward social mobility—its "equality"—jeopardized and its political position eroded, this event was interpreted as an attack on its very ability to organize to maintain its political voice. When a larger American Republican mass meeting in Kensington was also broken up by residents of the Irish Catholic neighborhood and a young participant was killed, three days of rioting ensued: it was quelled only by martial law and the appearance of 3,000 troops. Subsequently, 6,000 people turned out at a protest rally in, significantly, Independence Square, where nativist speakers compared the actions of the foreign-born and pliable politicians to British affronts to American liberty on the eve of the Revolution.[43]

Overt manipulation of republican symbols and mobilization of ward and fraternal organizations characterized increasing nativist militancy in Philadelphia during the late spring and summer of 1844. Taking advantage of the Fourth of July, some 50 American Republican ward associations and dozens of trade societies paraded to remind the public—and especially the politicians—of tradesmen's right to economic and political centrality and the republican requirement that an authentic citizen be both economically competent and politically independent.[44] Such a show of force, highlighted by the paramilitary aspect of some of the parading units, provoked a defensive response among elements of the metropolitan Irish Catholic community. In the suburb of Southwark, residents placed muskets in St. Philip's Church to discourage a renewal of May's mob violence. When this was reported to hotheaded native Protestants, it set off a flurry of counterarming. And when, allegedly, Sheriff Morton McMichael refused to take the initiative and seize the arms in the church, a nativist mob took matters into its own hands, citing the hallowed Revolutionary tradition of civil self-defense and popular recourse. Once again, the charge was made that the civil authorities were scorning the bone and sinew of society in exchange for short-run political gains among those less suited to be effective republican citizens.[45] The ensuing riots were ultimately suppressed by an even larger militia than had been called out in May, and the use of the state's uniformed forces reinforced the nativists' conclusion that the producing classes had been abandoned by the political system. Philadelphia elites were appalled by both the riots and the appropriation by the rioters of republican language and symbols associated with mechanics' associations and tradesmen's societies, confirming that the heart of the emerging nativist movement lay in the middling classes.[46]

Unquestionably, the Southwark riots of 1844 contributed to the alienation of many native-born Philadelphians, who already saw their ability to function as effective citizens by traditional republican standards threatened by economic circumstances. Although the worst of the depression was past, it was becoming increasingly apparent that permanent structural changes in the manufacturing economy were changing the status and prospects of the worker. Nativist organizing was a way of reclaiming political clout and asserting the continued "independence" of local tradesmen and shopkeepers from domination by "manufacturers" or "middlemen." In the midst of the Southwark disturbances, the American Republican ward organizations began agitating for the election of "reform" mayors throughout the metropolitan area who would restore the authority of real republican citizens.[47] On July 6, 1844, delegates from many of the nativist ward associations opened two weeks of discussions aimed a producing a unified American Republican party for Philadelphia.[48] Although the party rules hammered out were similar in most respects to those of the Democrats and the Whigs, new safeguards were devised to ensure that control of the party would not fall into the hands of an unresponsive professional elite. The key element was a sort of direct primary system whereby all party nominations for public office would have to begin in the ward associations. Although two-thirds of the ward organizations quickly ratified the rules, the initial convention of ward delegates in August divided over how much authority to give to a central executive committee. So anxious were many nativist activists about retaining control by the rank and file that an arrangement had to be negotiated whereby the ward units would have to ratify any decisions of the executive committee. Within a few weeks, a parallel American Republican party structure was assembled for the county outside of Philadelphia.[49]

The American Republican political initiative depended on effective organization of the party at the ward level. This was made possible by the existence of ward associations that had many of the characteristics of fraternal societies. In fact, many of them had their origins in trade-based mutual-assessment insurance societies, fire company auxiliaries, or fraternal benefit societies like the Improved Order of Red Men. Leonard Tabachnik has pointed out how the new convention system itself seems to have been borrowed from an earlier proposal for the political organization of the temperance fraternities developed by the American Republican activist Lewis Levin.[50]

In accordance with its republican rhetoric and demonology, the American Republican party of greater Philadelphia established both a Committee of Superintendence and a Board of Correspondence. The former was charged with providing poll watchers for elections to see that only legally qualified voters cast ballots. The latter, in the Revolutionary tradition, was to share information with similar nativist organizations around the country, arranging for nativist speakers, demonstrating the strength of the movement, and unearthing evidence of apparent "conspiracies" to take government out of the hands of the majority of republican citizens.[51]

The American Republicans were able to combine the "evidence" of an effort to politically marginalize solid republican citizens that could be extracted from the schools controversy and the 1844 riots with an appealing plan for the reform of the electoral process; and they were remarkably successful in the political campaign in the fall. Two of four available congressional seats went to American Republican organizers Lewis Levin and John H. Campbell, both of whom attracted strong followings in the previously Democratic industrial suburbs. In addition, a county commissioner, the auditor, and a state senator were nativists. In the suburbs, four mayors and six representatives to the state legislature were elected from the American Republican ticket; four suburban boards of commissioners had American Republican majorities. Throughout the metropolitan area, American Republicans attracted about 20,000 votes.[52]

Recent studies of American Republican activists are quite uniform in their conclusions. The first rank of leadership was held by the petit bourgeoisie: lawyers, merchants, tavern keepers, and insurance agents. In the second rank were skilled tradesmen who either represented the last of their breed in crafts being disrupted by merchant capitalism or worked in areas of manufacturing which still retained a traditional organization. This was not some stereotyped conservative elite, holding out for Puritan values and social rigidity, or, for that matter, a new elite of manipulative employers seeking to control an increasingly immigrant workforce. Michael Feldberg's examination of 464 American Republican activists identified many tavern keepers but found no significant industrialists. David Montgomery noticed that neither the metropolitan nor the ward-level leadership was well connected to institutional Protestantism in the Philadelphia area. What both observed was that American Republican leaders were by and large new to politics.[53] Economically, they were as likely to be on the way up as on the way down; but they were in a position to feel that their opportunities were being squeezed, and they were intensely concerned about being recognized as economically competent and politically effective.

Fraternalism and Nativism

At least one historian has noted that the local cells of the Philadelphia American Republicans bore an "eerie resemblance to the Sons of Liberty."[54] In fact, it is possible to make a good case for loose descent, not just resemblance. For the nativist cells of Philadelphia—and other cities, including New York—often had roots in fraternal, Masonic, Democratic-Republican, and mechanics' organizations which had originated in the Revolutionary and early national period. The character of these organizations took on new relevance for members of the working and middle classes in the uncertain economic circumstances of the late 1830s and early 1840s. All emphasized economic self-help, security in the form of fraternal aid or mutual assessment insurance, opportunities for public participation, and a secular or deistic morality. Although the anti-Masonic movement of the late 1820s had seriously weakened the most powerful of these societies, by the mid-1830s new orders were being founded. Some of these emphasized fraternal ritual and mutual support: the Ancient Order of Foresters (1834), the United Ancient Order of Druids (1834), and the Independent Order of Odd Fellows (initially imported from Great Britain in 1819 but independently American by 1843). In fact, by the beginning of the 1840s, Freemasonry itself was again growing nationwide.[55]

Not only were some older models of fraternal organization revived by the economic hazards faced by many Americans—especially in the cities—during the middle antebellum period, but some new forms took shape. With fledgling tradesmen's unions broken by the depression, journeymen joined with vulnerable masters in new fraternities. Perhaps the largest, the Mechanics' Mutual Protection, was founded in Buffalo in 1841 but soon spread to New York City and into Ohio, Pennsylvania, Michigan, and even Wisconsin. With strength particularly in the building trades, the Mechanics' Mutual Protection offered the emotional satisfactions of a secret brotherhood in a trying time and, more important, the practical advantages of sickness benefits on the mutual-assessment principle (where each "brother" chipped in support as needed) and a labor exchange for members out of a job.[56]

The early 1840s also witnessed the rise of a new kind of temperance organization with strong appeal to tradesmen and workers. Like some of the new mechanics' organizations, these temperance organizations took the form of fraternal benevolent societies. The Order of the Sons of Temperance, founded in New York City in 1842, patterned its rites and regalia on the Odd Fellows. By 1844, the Sons of Temperance had established "grand divisions" throughout the mid-Atlantic and New England states and west to Ohio.[57] Jed Dannenbaum's study of the Sons in Cincinnati reveals a membership similar to that of the mechanics', benevolent, and nativist societies. A minority of neighborhood lawyers, physicians, and petty professionals offered much of the leadership; middling proprietors or craft-shop masters occupied a second tier; and skilled workers—especially in the construction trades—made up most of the rank and file. The Sons emphasized self-control and self-help, political effectiveness through combination, opportunities for personal growth in leadership, business and employment contacts, and mutual assistance. Some offshoots of the Sons of Temperance, like the Templars of Honor, developed elaborate systems of sickness and death benefits through mutual-assessment insurance. Their secret rituals, Masonic-related roots, and working-class ribaldry kept the Sons and other temperance fraternities like it out of favor with institutional Protestantism and genteel society.[58]

Organizations such as these were like the American Republican ward associations of Philadelphia and similar nativist organizations elsewhere, and they attracted members for much the same reasons. They offered to arrest the descent of self-described "producers" into economic and political ineffectuality. To some extent, this was symbolic. Whether temperance, trade, or benevolent, all of the fraternities offered a sense of supportive brotherhood, of strength in numbers, and of individual self-worth. They made a member *feel* that he was important and a contributor to a larger whole. The rhetoric of fraternal organizations was calculated to build that feeling, emphasizing that brethren were equal and membership was earned. But much more than symbolism was operating. The concentration of numbers in a fraternity *did* magnify the public effectiveness—whether in political or benevolent activity—of each individual member. Each organization offered practical aids to personal economic achievement, albeit to varying degrees. At the least, they all provided informal employment and trade contacts. Many fraternities institutionalized this by encouraging brethren to patronize and deal equitably with one another and even by carrying advertisements for members' businesses and trades in their publications. For members on the move within a metropolitan area, around a region, or across states, the transferable memberships that came with the larger organizations gave instant economic connections at a new address.[59]

By implicitly—and often explicitly—reaffirming that freedom from economic manipulation and the ability to have one's voice and vote matter in public decision making were essential to effective American citizenship, antebellum fraternal organizations reinforced traditional republican norms and provided a basis for distinguishing between insiders and outsiders, Americans and aliens. It is not very surprising that some fraternities elaborated on this theme or that they could trace their roots back to the more nakedly political fraternal societies of the Revolutionary and early national periods. This, for example, was the case with the Improved Order of Red Men (IORM), the fraternity that Arthur M. Schlesinger Sr. once described as the United States' "first adult secret society" to distinguish it from friendly societies that had their roots in the Masonic or Odd Fellows rituals imported from England.[60]

IORM traced its origins to the St. Tamina organizations of Philadelphia and Annapolis and through them to the Sons of Liberty and the nonimportation leagues of the Revolutionary period. St. Tamina societies (named for a legendary Delaware chieftain) were founded in reaction to two loyalist societies: St. George's and St. Andrew's. After independence, the St. Tamina societies remained hostile to the pro-British slant of the emerging Federalist party and to the aristocratic pretensions of the military officers who founded the Society of Cincinnati; and they came into connection with the Democratic-Republican societies. Although the St. Tamina organizations gradually faded away, some former members on militia duty during the War of 1812 reorganized into a patriotic club called the Society of Red Men, carrying forward the American Indian motif of St. Tamina and the Sons of Liberty. By the 1820s, tribes of Red Men had spread from Baltimore as far north as Albany, New York. Chapters were highly independent secret social and political fraternities with relatively little central organization. During the anti-Masonic hysteria of the late 1820s and early 1830s, their numbers declined precipitously, and as temperance enthusiasm increased they were denounced for the excessively "convivial" character of their meetings—taverns being their most popular gathering places.[61]

In Baltimore in 1834, several former Red Men sought to reorganize the fraternity on a new principle: it would avoid direct affiliation with any political party, becoming primarily social and fraternal and offering disability and funeral insurance, and it would also become more temperate. Adding "Improved" to its name, the Society created a Great Council of Maryland in 1835 and a District of Columbia Council a decade later. By 1847, the Improved Order of Red Men counted 19 tribes from Pennsylvania to Maryland and authorized a Great Council of the United States, with its headquarters in Baltimore. Rapid growth brought IORM to 45 tribes in an increasing number of states by the end of the decade.[62]

As the American Indian symbolism in its ceremony, regalia, and rhetoric suggested, IORM placed a premium on individual independence, nationalism, and patriotism. IORM also used all kinds of traditional republican iconography in its rituals. When Logan Tribe 1 was established in Baltimore in 1834, its constitution provided for the sacred Revolutionary number, 13: there would be 13 officers; 13 consecutive meetings without payment of dues would be cause for suspension; and the fine for absence from a meeting would be 13 cents. Washington's Birthday was a high holy day for IORM.[63]

IORM also staked out an attractive middle position on alcohol that appealed to industrious workmen and small-business men. It prohibited meetings in barrooms and consumption of alcohol at ceremonies, but it left decisions about responsible drinking up to "independent" brethren. Providing "mutual assistance in time of need, care for the sick, [and] relief of the widow and orphan," IORM was meant to help brothers maintain a decent economic independence, too. This was reinforced by encouraging members to trade within the circle of brothers.[64]

The Improved Order of Red Men and similar fraternities nurtured organized nativist activism. They catered to middle-class and upper-working-class hypersensitivity about independence—economic and political—and were connected in both ritual and rhetoric to authentic "Americanism." Not surprisingly, it did not take long for such organizations to begin attaching the label "alien" to those they identified as deficient in either kind of independence. And they often harbored a sense of grievance that aliens—by their definition—were taking on an oversized role in American affairs, marginalizing authentic Americans and threatening republican stability. Fraternities like IORM seldom became involved with concrete solutions to perceived dangers to the "national character," much less with actual political organizing in pursuit of nativist objectives. Yet they helped create an environment in which organized nativist activism might flourish and lent many of their members to other societies whose chief objective was to restore the putatively defiled national character. Also, they provided an appealing form, rhetoric, and iconography for nativist activists. By the mid-1840s, specifically nativist fraternities had been founded in both New York and Philadelphia which showed the influence of the Red Men. These organizations often borrowed not only the trivial (like the pseudo-American Indian nomenclature of New York's Order of United Americans) and the practical (like the mutual-benefit system of Philadelphia's Order of United American Mechanics) but also the working-class liberalism represented by the Red Men's moderate temperance proclivities and mild semi-Christian deism.[65] Eventually, the influence of the Red Men on the nativist fraternities of the 1840s turned around, and IORM became infected with the spirit of "American" exclusivism. Toward the end of the decade, this resulted in the expulsion from membership of a substantial minority of German-Americans.

Traditional republican themes associated with skilled tradesmen and small merchants were evident in the Order of United American Mechanics (OUAM), a nativist fraternity founded by a few skilled workers and masters at Philadelphia's Jefferson Temperance Hall in 1845. OUAM's motto, "Honesty, Industry, and Sobriety," stressed personal independence gained by self-control. Members were to renounce insobriety, "libertinism," cursing, and sabbath-breaking, keeping watch on one another for assurance. Repeated violations of these standards could bring suspension of mutual-insurance benefits or expulsion from the order altogether. OUAM sought to enhance workers' dignity symbolically by celebrating "producers" on public holidays and practically by offering instruction on such topics as "How to Accumulate Property."[66] The first two OUAM lodges, or "councils," were named "Enterprise" and "Perseverance."[67]

But OUAM did not put the whole burden of personal independence on the individual craftsman. A "fair day's wage for a fair day's work," another OUAM slogan, was aimed at employers. What was fair? That pay which would allow workingmen to "support themselves and their families in comfort and respectability."[68] Undermining this principle, the order alleged, was the willingness of employers to engage foreign-born workers at subscale rates, simultaneously perpetuating the dependent character of the immigrant and depriving native workers of jobs. Accordingly, OUAM propaganda called on employers to use native-born workers and on consumers to patronize native-owned shops. The organization appealed to many trade leaders who had been frustrated by the effects of the depression, and it attracted to its own leadership men like George F. Turner of the Journeyman House Carpenters and most of the officers of the Franklin Typographical Society. By the end of the decade, OUAM counted 100 lodges along the mid-Atlantic coast, fanning out from Philadelphia.[69]

Offshoots of OUAM were even more closely connected to labor radicalism. The Patriotic Daughters of America, a female auxiliary, was founded in 1845 by Harriet Probasco, who had been publishing an aggressively nativist newspaper, *American Woman,* since September 1844.[70] Appealing to self-supporting workingwomen, the Daughters denounced prevailing wages and working conditions in industries which used mainly female labor—especially the garment industry—and what were perceived as shrinking employment opportunities for native-born women. They charged that both "cheap" foreign-born workers and the capitalists willing to employ them were contributing to women's distress. As a remedy, the Daughters championed a head tax on new immigrants—a "workingman's tariff"—which would either restrict immigration or at least drive up the cost of employing the foreign-born. Although the Daughters observed cultural norms in encouraging mothers to educate themselves for the moral nurturance of republican youth, they also challenged conventional assumptions by calling for a revision of property laws which would allow married women the right to sell personal property and to retain their own earnings. Recognizing the value of engaging the whole family in nativist organizing, OUAM not only encouraged the Daughters but also made a point of inviting women to attend nativist mass meetings.[71]

Members of the nativist ward clubs and societies in cities like Philadelphia during the 1840s stood at a crossroads of older socioeconomic goals and exciting new opportunities. On the one hand, they were anxious about social and economic changes that threatened traditional sources of economic independence and public responsibility, characteristics that they believed essential to republican citizenship and, consequently, to the well-being of the republic itself. The nativist club salved this anxiety, bringing men together in an egalitarian face-to-face community of "brothers," frequently from a familiar neighborhood or workplace. This was more than nostalgia; in a society where personal contacts still had substantial economic value, membership was as much a way of preserving access to individual opportunity as assuaging its loss. In this context, the secrecy practiced by many nativist organizations also had more than a symbolic character: it served to protect the brethren from falling into dangerous commercial relationships with "impostors and designers."[72] But the nativist brotherhoods were also avenues to wider opportunities in a new world of transportation, mobility, and impersonal interchange. These were *voluntary* associations that, as Mary Ryan has pointed out, helped participants escape the "confining trilogy of household, town, and church." Members joined a "community of limited liability" which did not consume all of their loyalty and as such was a tool which could be used to achieve personal objects.[73]

Modernization had not yet displaced partnership as the predominant form of business organization, and the personal contacts made and sustained through lodge membership were a key to entrepreneurship. Such memberships were especially useful, as David Brion Davis has observed, to "ambitious men . . . who were excluded from the most prestigious centers of local power"—especially young men or men on the move and new to a community. In this respect, the antebellum lodges, including the nativist fraternities, were forces of modernization, breaking the economic and political stranglehold of traditional elites and creating new opportunities for individuals. And even if the ranks and rituals of the lodges seemed ridiculous to outsiders, they nonetheless made the point that office and status were based on earned qualifications rather than inheritance or connections.[74]

Careful examination of antebellum fraternal organizations—particularly proto-nativist or nativist societies like the Improved Order of Red Men, the United American Mechanics, or New York's Order of United Americans—may go far toward resolving a conflict among some modern scholars of nineteenth-century popular republicanism. Scholars like Sean Wilentz see working-class goals of the time as a "fusion of independent liberty with social and corporate responsibilities"; their critics, like John Diggins, argue that "values of ambition, enterprise, and opportunity"—in short, individualism—were the hallmark of the antebellum "producing" classes.[75] In fact, antebellum Americans of the middle orders of society wanted and felt confident that they could have both—and their enthusiastic participation in fraternal orders is evidence of this. They sought independence and participation in public affairs that was intensely personal, but they could not imagine that these opportunities were available except in a society which offered rich community contacts. It is not at all surprising, consequently, that the nativist fraternities provided an attractive basis for political organizations that would contest the Democrats and the Whigs. With their roots in local clubs and ward societies, they offered both a progressive opportunity to be personally effective in public affairs and a nostalgic sense of community at a time when the two major parties were becoming increasingly impersonal and bureaucratized.

The nativist character of fraternal orders like the United American Mechanics lay in their suspicion that the foreign-born threatened American republicanism, both by contributing to the economic and political marginalization of the bone and sinew of the native-born population and by failing to display the economic and political independence that would make them reliable republican citizens themselves. In the rhetoric of popular republicanism, they threatened the "national character" by preventing the American people from succeeding at popular self-government. This was much more complicated than either knee-jerk economic defensiveness to newly arrived competitors or some culturally inbred Anglo-American anti-Catholicism. Yet it easily took on an hysterical character because of the republican language of endangerment, which suggested that any sign of declension from republican orthodoxy was the beginning of the end of republicanism itself.

There were many small signs that nativists exaggerated into large, dark forebodings. It is significant, for example, that the flurry of nativist organizing during the 1840s and 1850s fell into a fallow period for American fraternalism generally but paralleled the rise of fraternal organizing among the foreign-born. In 1836 Irish-Americans founded the American Order of Hibernians; in 1840 and 1847, respectively, German-Americans founded the Sons of Hermann and the Order of Harugari. By the end of the 1840s, German-Americans who had left IORM had formed the *Independent* Order of Red Men. (By contrast, there was little organizing of general membership fraternities without ethnic affiliation after the founding of the United Ancient Order of Druids in 1839 and the domestication of England's Odd Fellows in 1843.) The growth of these fraternities, consisting largely of immigrants, doubtless exacerbated the fears of some of the native-born that at the same time they were being economically and politically marginalized, the foreign-born (who were, in the thinking of many natives, ill suited to effective citizenship because of their economic, intellectual, or political dependence) were organizing for greater public influence. By 1848, even a remote frontier community like Milwaukee had no fewer than seven lodges of the Sons of Hermann. One can only imagine the *perceptual* impact, for the most sensitive native psyches, of an announcement in the *Cleveland Daily True Democrat* on November 16, 1848, that the Cleveland Hibernian Guards, a paramilitary fraternal order of Irish-Americans, was holding its annual ball at the *American* House Hotel.[76]

Members of proto-nativist organizations like the Improved Order of Red Men or actual nativist organizations like the Order of United American Mechanics almost always portrayed themselves as *counterorganizing* to preserve the influence of independent republican citizens on public affairs. David Brion Davis has it about right, I think, in suggesting that membership in antebellum fraternal organizations (he refers to the Masons, specifically, but his point can be generalized) was a "substitute for ethnicity." At a time when European newcomers—because they shared a religion, a distinctive tongue, or a neighborhood—seemed to have a cohesiveness that the native-born lacked, lodge membership created what Davis calls an "in-group" and also provided the "charity, solidarity, and social services" usually associated with specifically ethnic clubs and societies.[77] Nativist fraternities were particularly suitable for this purpose because of their nationalist ideology and rhetoric. "Anglo-Americanism" (let alone "Anglo-Saxonism") faced real barriers to becoming an effective native reaction to immigrant ethnicities, not only because the native population was actually of such mixed stock but also because of the widespread reluctance to Anglicize American culture. (After all, Americans celebrated their independence *from* England). A nativist fraternity provided an effective alternative. It offered to set men (and, through auxiliary societies, women) apart from the foreign-born not by inherited culture or "blood" but by self-proclaimed commitment to republican ideals and virtues. Accordingly, the nativist fraternities were surprisingly open to immigrants and their children who subscribed to the organizations' values, and these fraternities were remarkably free of the Anglo-Saxon or Anglo-American racialist rhetoric that was often tried out in public discourse during the 1840s and 1850s.[78]

Nativist Politics and Urban "Reform" before 1850

In the 1840s, New York City joined Philadelphia as a capital of organized nativist activism, and (as in Pennsylvania) fraternal orders were among its chief vehicles. Likewise, the school controversy which initiated the period proved to fit within a larger context of working- and middle-class anxiety over independence and public effectiveness, exacerbated by lingering economic recession. In New York City, in fact, hypersensitivity about the corruption of republican institutions flared and went out more quickly in the debate over the public school curriculum, and control of the schools, than it did in the prolonged excitement over the structure of municipal government.

American nativism cast itself in positive terms, as standing *for* American "national character," and it saw the ability of Americans to act like a nation as based on individuals' retaining the prerequisites of republican citizenship. Thus it erupted in the face of circumstances that seemed to threaten an independent citizenry or its control of public processes. Such circumstances were not always initiated by immigrants, nor were immigrants always the villains, although nativists were on the lookout for involvement of immigrants. Nativists were more than willing to treat as "alien" anyone, native-born or foreign-born, who did not meet their standards of good republicanism. This became obvious in the controversy over municipal reform in New York City, which vaulted nativism to political prominence. The reform campaign of the mid-1840s also demonstrated how the traditional republican rhetoric of organized nativist activism continued to resonate with a wider public and enabled nativists to expand their ranks when they could make a case that the "national character" was threatened. At the same time, it shows how the rhetoric of republicanism trapped nativists into simplistic notions of reform and good government which rendered their political successes fragile.

New York City entered the 1840s with a municipal charter which called for executive departments to carry out the work of the city but a tradition which turned over departmental functions to standing committees of the city council. This effectively politicized the day-to-day activities of city government; but since both major political parties benefited from the arrangement, there was little impetus for reform. Although the Democrats made significant political gains in the spring elections of 1843 by running on a reform platform, they reneged on their pledges once in office.[79] Then, in the summer months, meat market vendors vehemently protested what they took to be favoritism by the council's market committee, charging that it distributed the best market stalls to political allies. At a time when the marketmen were still complaining about slow trade, and perhaps fretting over what the

threats to respectable self-employment implied about their qualifications as independent republican citizens, they found it particularly troublesome that among these allies were a number of immigrant vendors.
The marketmen were, accordingly, among the earliest participants in
reenergized nativist ward associations which often counted among
their organizers alumni of the Native American Democratic Association (NADA) of the 1830s. The NADA, of course, had a ready-made
rhetoric which traced public ills to the manageability of foreign-born
voters and the greed of native-born politicians. As early as June 1843,
these ward-based organizations were agitating for reform of the city
charter through mass meetings and a newspaper, the *American Citizen*. Because civil service reform that would place municipal responsibilities in the hands of salaried executive managers had an appeal that
went beyond the anxieties of the native-born working classes or their
suspicion of immigrants, its advocates were able to sign on men who
were connected with national social and moral reform movements and
who brought with them political respectability.[80]

Municipal reform was clearly an issue which could be addressed in
the language of traditional republicanism, feeding on the anxieties of
people already economically pressured who found that their public
voice was weakened as well. Losing independence as both a producer
and a voter predicted the disappearance of the qualifications of American citizenship. At the same time, city politicians' alleged solicitousness for the foreign-born suggested that conditions were being established in which despots might rule by manipulating a dependent
proletariat. Cast in these terms, municipal corruption in New York City
could be taken as a threat to the "national character."

The nativist response to evidence of municipal corruption was both
to lash out at immigrants, who were held to be the politicians' dupes,
and to demand restoration of the native-born "producing classes" to
economic and political centrality. In July 1843, delegates from nativist
clubs and ward associations across the city formed a loosely organized American Republican party. The new party made a token
demand for the repeal of the controversial 1842 school law, but its
principal aims were a 21-year probationary period for naturalization,
exclusion of the foreign-born from public office, and municipal charter
reform which would finally replace the council committees with executive departments. It appealed to a broad public which included not
only the marketmen and other frustrated workers but dissident
Democratic party activists who had unsuccessfully challenged the

Van Buren establishment in 1842, as well as upper-middle-class "clean government" reformers.

Although the Democratic masters of city hall were its political targets, it would be quite wrong to view the American Republican party as just a stalking horse for the Whigs. It included many traditional Democratic voters and out-of-favor politicians, and to the extent that it did attract Whig voters, it actually sapped the Whigs' ability to contest the Democrats.[81] In fact, in New York (as in Philadelphia), the nativists found some of the strongest support among workers who had been drawn to labor activism over the preceding decade. Amy Bridges observes that several American Republican leaders had been key figures in the Mechanics' Mutual Protection or the General Trades Union, organizations which tried to preserve the economic centrality of the craft worker. Even those who came from the more genteel classes were rarely among the city's political or social establishment. Sean Wilentz's analysis of American Republican ward leaders in the 1840s identified about one-third as merchants and neighborhood professionals, nearly half as shopkeepers and master craftsmen, and the remaining 20 percent as journeymen and laborers. Leonard Tabachnik reached a similar conclusion, but by evaluating a smaller sample of activists in greater detail concluded that—in comparison with Whig and Democratic political leaders—these were mostly young, "new" men without the wealth or standing that was typical of the major parties' officers. Bridges suggests that part of the appeal of American Republicanism was its flattery of the craftsmen and shopkeepers, contrasting their historical independence with the allegedly dependent masses of "aliens," and the fact that it gave craft masters and journeymen (who were being repositioned by the forces of technological change as entrepreneurs and semiskilled workers) a revived sense of shared cultural and political objectives.[82] The organization of ward and citywide nativist associations along fraternal lines forged additional bonds between the diverse participants in nativist activism by creating a pseudoculture of lodge ritual.

Playing on the strength of both ward and fraternal associations, the American Republicans did well in the fall elections of 1843, stripping enough votes from the Democratic party to limit it to a slim victory over the Whigs. With the election past, the American Republican party sought to strengthen its reform credentials by driving from its leadership former Democratic officeholders and party officials.[83] Thus positioned to focus on municipal reform, the party nominated a political newcomer, James Harper (a master printer who had become an employer and an industrialist), for mayor, and in April 1844 elected him, along with two-thirds of the city council.

Harper had acquired a reputation as an anti-Catholic during the schools controversy and took advantage of the support of a newly formed American Protestant Society (which declared its goal to be the conversion of Catholics to "true" Christianity); but it would be a mistake to reduce his appeal exclusively to religious bigotry. Harper's candidacy succeeded because he was able to play effectively to working- and middle-class anxieties, which took on nationalist significance when couched in the terms of classical republicanism. Harper stressed a populist theme which promised restoration of public responsibility to an independent citizenry that would resist being manipulated. He supported the depoliticization of municipal services and a trimmed-down government bureaucracy. Presenting himself as a master craftsman, Harper deemphasized the emerging gulf between semiskilled workers and white-collar management, reminding craft workers that energy, initiative, and self-discipline would bring them independence and opportunity. It is not very surprising that this message was most effective among masters and journeymen in industries where the division of labor was not yet far advanced. If workers saw the Harper administration as offering them political recognition and preserving their effectiveness as republican citizens, many middle-class and even elite New Yorkers perceived it as a fresh breeze of municipal reform which would take power from the hands of self-serving demagogues.[84] In both cases, Harper's election seemed a step toward preserving the "national character"—at least in New York—by restoring public authority to "independent" citizens and depriving politicians of the ability to manipulate dependent and pliable voters. That growing numbers of "dependent" day laborers and semiskilled workers in sweated industries were foreign-born Catholics, and that they were more successfully courted by the selfsame Democrats who dominated city hall, added to Harper's allure. Despite the rough treatment given to Whig Governor William Seward by nativist activists during the school law controversy of the early 1840s, even Seward's publicist, Thurlow Weed—sensing the popularity of political reform—endorsed Harper in his Albany newspaper.[85] The Kensington riots in Philadelphia, immediately preceding the New York municipal elections, did not hurt Harper's candidacy either. Although some New Yorkers feared that electing American Republicans would lead to ethnic polarization of the city and thus increase the potential for the same sort of violence that had scarred Philadelphia, more voters seemed to think that the efforts of Irish-Americans in Pennsylvania to thwart nativist organizing was all the more reason to take a stand for the "right" of the native-born to hold onto the political initiative.[86]

Initially, the American Republican takeover of city hall added luster to organized nativism. A flurry of nativist political organizing took place in the Hudson Valley and upstate New York. In June, another American Republican, Simeon Baldwin, was elected to the New York City board of education. But voters had clearly felt that they were making more than a symbolic statement in bringing the Harper administration to office, and they expected delivery on the promised reforms. Both ideological and structural conditions, however, made it difficult for the American Republicans to fulfill public expectations. Ideologically, Harper and his associates proved that they were no cynics, that they really believed their rhetoric. Reform was primarily a matter of removing "dependent" foreigners from the political process, and this was to be accomplished simply by enforcing existing naturalization laws and by keeping noncitizens from the ballot box. Secondarily, reform was a matter of removing from positions of authority politicians who putatively thrived by manipulating pliable voters, and of ensuring the continued "independence" of republican citizens.

Thus American Republican reform was all-or-nothing reform. The issues were black-and-white and admitted little gray. Structurally, then—as a matter of practical politics—this was sure to cause problems and set Harper's nativist administration up for failure.[87] Almost at once, by indiscriminately replacing officeholders with American Republican loyalists, the administration lost the ability to form political coalitions that would broaden its base of support. This not only alienated the Democratic losers but precluded any advantageous alliance with Whigs by denying them a share of the victory. American Republicans rubbed salt into Democrats' wounds by loftily declaring their unwillingness to strike political deals, which they alleged would undo in secret what the voters had mandated in public. Yet Harper and his councilmen had difficulty keeping the voters in line. It was all well and good for Harper to describe sobriety and self-discipline as the means to economic self-sufficiency and political independence, but when he issued an executive proclamation shutting down street-corner drinking stands, he ignored the realities of life for many of his working-class supporters, leaving them wondering whether they had achieved any greater "independence" after all.[88] Harper was perceived by the lower socioeconomic orders as having taken reform too far, but he quickly drew middle-class and upper-class criticism for not taking it far enough. The credibility of the administration was particularly damaged by its failure to abolish the administration of the city through council committees. Admittedly, Harper was hamstrung by the weakness of the mayoralty under the city charter, but he was remembered for promising more than he could provide.

The political fragility of the American Republicans—their failure to reach accommodation with the Whigs, their inability to satisfy reformers, and the hazards of trying to graft bourgeois reform onto grizzled working-class and lower-middle-class stock—all showed up in the autumn elections of 1844. Without a national party to call home, the nativists of New York backed the Whig presidential nominee, Henry Clay; but the Democratic background of many American Republicans ensured that Clay would not pick up unanimous support from the nativist rank and file. Although American Republican candidates for Congress and the state legislature were well supported, the weaker showing of the Whigs demonstrated that there was little potential for a sustained, unified anti-Democratic coalition. Accordingly, over the next few months, the Whig leadership of New York City and the state backed away from any sort of formal cooperation with the American Republicans, taking with them many who had initially embraced the nativists as reformers. Removal of this leaven from nativist ranks left the American Republicans even more narrowly committed than before to cleansing the political system by eliminating "dependent" foreign-born voters. This made them more susceptible to charges that they would lead the city into a cultural polarization as dangerous as that in Philadelphia, and thus caused them to lose even more voters. Election-day riots in Brooklyn and Williamsburg involving nativist activists and Irish-American Democrats made this threat seem more than theoretical.[89]

Abandonment by the Whigs and failure to elect an opponent of the Democrats as president did little to dampen nativist enthusiasm in New York City. In fact, just enough evidence of Democratic ballot fraud turned up to confirm nativists' suspicions that republican political processes were being corrupted.[90] Nativism, after all, thrived on "defeat." Any sign that politicians were taking advantage of illicit votes to hold onto office simply confirmed apocalyptic republican imagery: that corruption, if not immediately reversed, would lead directly to utter despotism. Failure to succeed as a broad-based reform party also threw New York nativism back on its roots in neighborhood clubs and associations. In fact, it led to a new round of organizing. In December 1844, a small group of activists founded a nativist lodge first called the American Brotherhood but within days renamed the Order of United Americans (OUA).[91] With a pseudo-American Indian ritual, nomenclature, and regalia, OUA gave every evidence of having borrowed both ideas and brothers from the Red Men.[92] Though at its core were prominent and well-to-do nativist leaders, including James Harper and his brother, the membership of Alpha Chapter 1 was filled out with petty professionals, neighborhood retailers, and craft workers. It had far more than its share of insurance salesmen, who doubtless saw the lodge as a fertile ground for contacts, and its publications were full of advertisements for its storekeeper brethren.[93]

The dominant figure in the Order of United Americans from its early days until his death in the mid-1850s was Thomas Richard Whitney, its third grand sachem. Whitney's biography is instructive about the kind of person who might be attracted to nativist activism. Whitney was descended from a Connecticut family that could trace its lineage to the earliest days of New England; his grandfather had been a local hero in the Revolution. By Whitney's youth, the family had lost some of its earlier luster. His father was a not very successful jeweler and watchmaker in New York City, and his brothers were, respectively, a jeweler and a whip maker (who later became a grocer).[94] Thomas R. Whitney himself—perhaps more ambitious than his brothers—used his initial training as an engraver to move progressively into printing, editing, and publishing. At the time of the founding of the Order of United Americans, Whitney was still a young man on the make, just 37 years old, a craftsman with literary and political aspirations but an outsider with few connections and perhaps a bit of nostalgia about this family's more prosperous and more heroic past.[95]

For a man like Whitney, OUA offered just the right mix of ideology and opportunity. Celebrating a purer republican past now defiled by corrupt politicians and manipulable foreign-born voters, it offered balm for the anxiety of the present generation (of Whitneys?) that it might not be living up to the forefathers' standards of public responsibility. Equally important, it provided opportunities for a young man to show leadership and form the contacts necessary to make his mark in the world. Whitney used these opportunities to advantage. By 1846 he was grand sachem, following two much more prominent New Yorkers, John Harper (brother of Mayor James Harper) and Simeon Baldwin (president of the New York Exchange Company).[96] After working at the *New York Sunday Times* and the *Sunday Morning News,* he began, in 1851, to publish a stylish periodical intended for national circulation. Billed as a "monthly magazine of American literature, politics and art," The *Republic* was actually the official OUA organ and relied on the membership as subscribers.[97] Although the journal survived for only two years, it brought Whitney the exposure that led to a second term as grand sachem in 1853, election as a nativist candidate to the New York state senate in the same year, and election as a United States congressman in 1855. For Thomas R. Whitney, who died in 1858 at the age of 50 in his fine house on Broadway, the nativist brotherhood had rewarded youthful ambition with both economic autonomy and public effectiveness.

Like the Order of United American Mechanics, which had originated in Philadelphia, New York's Order of United Americans offered benevolent and fraternal features which neatly meshed with an ideology stressing equality and independence. OUA offered sickness and death benefits on the mutual-assessment principle and consequently made full membership available only to healthy men between ages 18 and 55. The mother chapter, Alpha 1, distributed about $1,000 per year in insurance benefits during each of its first half-dozen years, and other chapters reported similar expenditures.[98] Within a few years of its founding, the order arranged for the writing of a funeral service and prescribed that each chapter chaplain see that it be impressively performed and attended by a respectable representation of brothers.[99] The constitution of OUA made the usual fraternal references to aiding the sick and comforting the bereaved, but the real emphasis of its rhetoric was how the strong bonds of brotherhood rendered such aid more than just "the hand of cold charity to [the] needy." Rather, it stressed that fraternal aid was a sharing of resources among equals.[100] Likewise, the order had no compunction about "puffing" in the pages of its journal the goods and services offered by its membership of shopkeepers, craftsmen, lawyers, and insurance salesmen, encouraging prosperity among the brethren through mutual patronage. As editor of the *Republic,* Thomas R. Whitney called on each chapter to think of itself as a "school," teaching young men in commerce and the trades lessons in leadership as well as in "oratory and debate" which would make them more effective republican citizens.[101]

The full significance of the Order of United Americans and other fraternities like it became apparent in April 1845, when the voters' patience with the Harper administration ran out and a Democratic merchant, William Havemeyer, was elected mayor. Although the American Republicans ran a respectable second in these municipal elections, they lost not only the mayoralty but also their council seats. No longer taken by the majority of New York voters as effective reformers, the nativists were defeated by a "clean government" pledge much like the one that had worked for them a year earlier.[102] In fact, the American Republicans discovered that their efforts to create a grassroots nominating procedure through ward associations and nativist fraternities had worked to discredit them. By prolonging political campaigning and placing candidates more often in the public eye, they had the unintended effect of making nativist political aspirants look like single-minded office-seekers. That at least some American Republican candidates had previously held or sought office as Whigs or Democrats added fuel to their opponents' charges that nativists were not real reformers but opportunistic political hacks. Out of office and out of power, organized nativist activism in New York and its environs was kept alive in the lodge rooms of the Order of United Americans and newer fraternities like the Sons of the Sires of '76 (founded in 1848).

Actually, survival as a network of lodges and ward political clubs rather than as a political party allowed New York nativism to refurbish its image as a champion of independent republican workers and of honest government. Nativists found that it was much easier to stand for reform out of power than in. Likewise, a nativist ideology that thrived on perceived republican "defeats" fit a political opposition better than an administration. During the late 1840s, public anxiety again began to grow about the conduct of municipal government. City expenses had doubled during the decade, and the tax rate had increased by about the same amount from 1839 to 1846. As New Yorkers cast about for culprits, their attention frequently lit on the rapidly increasing numbers of the foreign-born. A New York City Reform Party, organized in 1847, reported that increases in expenditures for almshouses and prisons far exceeded population growth but matched the arrival rate of new— mainly Irish—immigrants. Even the Maclay Act, which had created district school boards, was again brought under scrutiny as a source of bureaucracy and expense. Arguably a concession to Catholic New Yorkers, it was charged to the foreign-born.[103]

While the costs of city business chiefly aroused middle- and upper-class taxpaying property holders, the issue easily became entangled with working-class apprehension over the continuing restructuring of manufacturing employment. If the City Reform Party saw immigrant "paupers" as an expense, craft workers who feared the expansion of merchant capitalism saw them as a cheap source of unskilled labor for greedy entrepreneurs. A mechanics' mass meeting in March 1847 took a position that conformed closely to the nativist predilection to find fault in native retreat from republican standards.[104] The Irish famine-era immigration was charged to capitalist rapacity, and the proposed solution was an immigrant head tax or a fine on "importers" of labor.[105] The meeting led both to a petition drive and to the establishment of a newspaper, the *Champion of American Labor,* which was edited by a member of an OUA lodge. In April, the enthusiasm crystallized into an organization which took the name American Laboring Confederacy. Consisting largely of mechanics and small employers, it held its meetings at the same American Hall that was a gathering point for nativist political and fraternal organizations.[106]

Evidence of public discomfort with immigration emboldened the Order of United Americans. The public dedication of a monument to George Washington in October 1847 afforded an opportunity for the order to display its strength by putting its members on the street. This was followed in February 1848 by an OUA memorial service for John Quincy Adams.[107] Whereas only 15 OUA chapters had been founded from 1845 through 1847, 22 new ones were chartered in 1848 and 1849 alone—mostly in New York City and its environs, but there were a few on Long Island, up the Hudson River Valley toward Poughkeepsie, and out along the Connecticut coast.[108] Resisting the temptation to reorganize as a political party, OUA preferred to use its lodge rooms as places to hear, debate, and endorse candidates running on other party tickets. Of course, the brethren themselves were encouraged to stand for public office and to count on fraternal support. In this way, two members of OUA running as Whigs were elected to municipal offices in April 1849. The semisecrecy of OUA made it difficult for outsiders to gauge its political strength. When a Democratic candidate for New York comptroller publicly ridiculed OUA in the campaign of autumn 1849, he played right into the nativists' hands. Democratic voters who were OUA members or who took OUA's counterattack seriously scratched his name from their ballots and he lost to his Whig opponent, running 1,000 votes behind others on the Democratic ticket.[109]

These developments were far more consequential in the history of organized nativist activism than the more celebrated agreement of the American Protestant Society and the Christian Alliance in June 1848 to cooperate on the proselytization of American Catholics, or the actual merger a year later of the American Protestant Society, the Christian Union, and the Foreign Evangelical Society into the American and Foreign Christian Union, which would promote Protestant ideals at home and abroad. While these events absorbed the energies of important clergy and lay churchmen and, perhaps, exhibited the cultural imperialism of native American Protestants, they contributed little to the debate over the "national character" and less to the organization of a popular mass movement. It is also somewhat misleading to pay too much attention to abortive efforts in the 1840s to create a national nativist third-party alternative to the Whigs and the Democrats. The assemblage of delegates from local nativist parties (especially New York and Philadelphia American Republicans) in 13 states (although 80 percent of them came from New York, Pennsylvania, and Massachusetts) at Philadelphia on July 4, 1845, to establish a Native American party attracted plenty of publicity. The Native Americans' selection of Henry Dearborn as party president tugged at republican heartstrings. Dearborn was the son of a Revolutionary hero and thus represented the glorious founding of the American state. Honored by being named to the Collectorship of the Port of Boston by John Quincy Adams, he had been unceremoniously removed by Jacksonian Democrats in an act of naked political retribution. Elected to Congress as a Whig in 1832, he had served one term and then had been defeated by a Democrat, in an election which was replete with charges of immigrant vote fraud. Yet the Native American party had neither deep roots at the community or ward level nor sufficient voter loyalty to challenge the major parties in national elections. Meeting in convention in Pittsburgh in May 1847, the Native Americans lamely endorsed Zachary Taylor for president (whom everyone expected would be nominated by the Whigs) and Dearborn for vice-president. It was the Native Americans' last formal act before evaporating.[110]

Conclusion: The Local Basis of Nativist Activism

The future of nativism lay in local organization, and particularly in quasipolitical fraternal organizations. This had been the lesson in New York City, and it also proved true in Philadelphia. The political ascendancy of the American Republicans in Philadelphia—though longer-lived than in New York—did not last. American Republicans' difficulties were caused not (as some historians have argued) by their failure as reformers, but by their very successes—at least in their own terms. Calling for economy in government and the reduction of opportunities for patronage and graft, the Philadelphia American Republicans opposed the construction of street railways just as public enthusiasm for this modern convenience was cresting. Remarkably successful in making their scheme of popular nominations for political office work, the American Republicans gave voters little incentive to call for a reforming state or national party. Voters, consequently, could happily cast their ballots for American Republicans in local elections and return to traditional loyalties in state and national races. Since the nativists did have objectives which required state and federal action— prohibition of foreign-born officeholders and a 21-year residence as a prerequisite for naturalization—the question inevitably arose whether the American Republicans would be best served by working with one of the major parties. But this immediately threatened to fracture their bipartisan constituency, which had traditional homes in the Democrats or the Whigs. When Lewis Levin and other American Republican leaders orchestrated a mass rally in 1846 to denounce the (low) Walker Tariff emerging from the United States Congress as calculated to cost manufacturing jobs, the fissure deepened. Tariff reduction was historically identified as a Democratic issue, and public agitation tended to drive voters back to their original party loyalties.[111]

Faced with fracture and losing their political grip on Philadelphia, nativist activists returned to traditional rhetorical themes and organizational strategies. Resuming the call for greater accountability of officeholders to republican voters, American Republicans (or Native Americans, the short-lived name of the national party, which was increasingly applied to the local organization) called for direct election of all public officials from the highest national positions to local deputy postmasters.[112] They also reiterated the demand for a head tax on immigrants, which had proved popular among the native-born working classes. Making the familiar connection between personal economic independence and American nationality, the nativist *Philadelphia Sun* began running a series of commentaries promoting workers' manufacturing cooperatives and profit-sharing programs identified with the French socialist Louis Blanc.[113] Finally, the American Republicans made the most of perceived republican "failures." President Polk's well-publicized meeting with Archbishop Hughes of New York to secure Catholic chaplains to accompany American troops during the Mexican War (not only to minister to Catholic soldiers but also to ease Mexicans' fears that the United States was conducting a Protestant crusade) gave nativists ample opportunity to denounce a presidential "sellout" to foreign-born voters.[114]

Philadelphia nativists also reverted to dependence on fraternal orders as the core of their organizational strength, although this was not without controversy. Determined to cling to as many of the political gains of 1844-1845 as possible, part of the American Republican-Native American leadership headed by Lewis Levin accepted a fusion deal with the Whigs in 1847-1848 which allowed the two parties to nominate candidates for alternate offices. Describing this as a debasement of the principle that the voters should have unrestricted opportunities to select public officials, an anti-Levin faction led by Reynell Coates, which had been gaining strength since 1845, called for the unification of all those with authentic concerns about the "national character" in a new nativist fraternity called the Patriotic Order, Sons of America (and its auxiliary, Patriotic Daughters of America).[115] Founded in December 1847 under the name of Junior Order, Sons of America, the organization offered conventional fraternal benefits and included among its officers many with experience in the Order of United American Mechanics. Coates insisted that, unlike the American Republican party, the Sons retain a secret membership and ritual and bind members by oath to organizational objectives. The Sons also installed an elaborate system of earned ranks leading to a "blue degree," which documented that a member was ideologically and morally fit to stand as a candidate for public office. The process was calculated to mirror what nativists took to be the "earned" nature of American citizenship itself.[116]

When the fusion of the American Republicans and the Whigs proved unsuccessful in 1847, leading to the loss of nativist officeholders throughout metropolitan Philadelphia, the Sons of America—or "true blues"—were emboldened. Although a fusion campaign in the spring elections of 1848 proved more satisfactory and the election of Zachary Taylor as president in the fall with the support of the Native American party (if not all nativist activists) gave the Philadelphia party a share of federal patronage, the "true blues" were encouraged to run their own candidates for office in 1849. Their suspicion of fusion was premonitory, for in 1850, when the Whigs divided internally, there was not enough combined support from Whig and nativist voters to keep even the popular American Republican congressman Lewis Levin in office. The American Republicans were for all intents and purposes gone, and the Native American party died aborning; but Philadelphia's

Order of United American Mechanics and Sons of America—like New York City's Order of United Americans—endured, keeping alive an appealing republican rhetoric which connected American nationality with personal economic independence and political effectiveness.[117] It was also in 1847 that the novelist of the Philadelphia working class, George Lippard, established a "Brotherhood of the Union" which grew to several thousand members before the end of the decade. Emphasizing self-improvement and mutual assistance along with advocacy of an immigrant head tax and "nonsectarian" public schools, it appealed especially to artisans. With its women's affiliate, the Home Communion, it regularly denounced "capitalists" for sapping workers' independence and thus their capacity for effective citizenship.[118]

Across the nation, during the 1830s and 1840s, the staying power of organized nativist activism varied directly with the creation of voluntary associations, usually benevolent and fraternal. Where these were established, nativist activism had a sustained life which took it past midcentury. Elsewhere, it was more episodic—particularly in the west, where the circumstances provoking nativist activism were a little different in character. North of Illinois or west of the Mississippi, town, city, territorial, and state populations were typically so thin that relatively small numbers of foreign-born residents had the potential to make relatively big political differences. Moreover, for cities writing charters and territories writing state constitutions, voters' qualifications had to be addressed not as a remedial issue but as a fundamental matter. Allegations that the German voters—and, to a lesser extent, the Irish voters—of St. Louis were capable of diverting Whig and Democratic officeholders from their responsibility to the majority of the electorate spawned a local Native American Association as early as 1840. Taking advantage of factional quarreling within the major parties, the Native Americans made major inroads into the city government in elections during 1845-1846. After the nativist mayor of St. Louis was defeated in 1847, however, nativism fell organizationally dormant until the 1850s, having failed to create institutions to sustain it.[119]

In Wisconsin territory, the issue of who should have the opportunity to vote for delegates to a state constitutional convention and who, in turn, should vote to ratify a constitution preparatory to statehood became a lively issue from the early 1840s. By January 1844, the question had been decided in a way that allowed all free white males in the territory to become voters on all issues after a three-month residence, whether they were United States citizens or not. Foreign-born voters' active and highly visible participation in Wisconsin and Milwaukee politics in succeeding months, particularly within the Democratic party, provided ample opportunity for elements of the native-born to worry about the diversion of officeholders' attention to immigrants' interests. Native backlash was evident in the Milwaukee area when the Democratic candidate for sheriff, a Catholic, ran well behind the rest of his ticket and was the only Democrat to lose. When the next Democratic slate pointedly excluded anyone who was known to have broken ranks in the sheriff's race, bolters declared the party under the thrall of foreign-born voters and placed their own ticket in contention. These Democratic nativists, backed by Whigs eager to take advantage of their rivals' fracture, were remarkably successful in the spring local elections of 1845.[120] Still, nativism in Milwaukee remained at the level of political protest and did not take an institutional form which could sustain it through the decade.

Things were a little different in another eastern city where voters also dabbled in third party politics: Baltimore. There, in November 1844, an "American Republican" party announced itself. It combined the goal of municipal reform with "purification" of the republican electorate through extension of the prenaturalization probation and restriction of officeholding to the native-born. An American Republican city ticket ran a weak third in the October 1845 elections, and plans for a statewide party faltered.[121] Yet in Baltimore, unlike St. Louis or Milwaukee, nativism maintained an organized presence through a variety of clubs and fraternal orders. Perhaps it owed something to the strength of nationalist fraternities like the Improved Order of Red Men, whose birthplace was Baltimore, or to the ability of the Order of United American Mechanics to spill over the state line from Pennsylvania. In fact, organized nativist activism would not only survive the 1840s but enter the 1850s best equipped to make a social and political impact in just those places where it had such an organizational basis.

Chapter Three

A Party of "Brothers":
The Rise of Know Nothingism

On July 25, 1856, Thomas R. Whitney, past grand sachem of the Order of United Americans (OUA) and chief ideologist for the nativist fraternity, wrote to Millard Fillmore at his home in Buffalo, New York, announcing the decision of OUA to endorse Fillmore in the coming presidential election. Although Whitney claimed that OUA was the "oldest of all the American organizations" (the "Old Guard," he called it), Fillmore was running not on an OUA ticket but as the candidate of the "American" party, which itself was rooted in a quasifraternal organization, the Order of the Star-Spangled Banner.[1] By 1856, however, the distinction between fraternal and political nativist organizations had become imprecise, participants and outsiders alike using the blanket term "Know Nothing." In fact, the field had become quite crowded with "American" organizations, the Order of United Americans and Order of the Star-Spangled Banner (which Whitney at one point had called an OUA "auxiliary") having been joined by the United Sons of America, United American Mechanics, and the United Daughters of America—to name just a few.

OUA and OSSB:
The Fraternal Basis of the Know Nothings

Whitney could rightly be sensitive about OUA's loss of visibility within the nativist universe, and he was correct in giving it first place in birth order among the politically active elements of the nativist movement. As early as 1846, scarcely a year after its founding, OUA staked out a public position on the proposed new constitution of New York state, denouncing clauses which provided for an elected judiciary, allowed the clergy to be candidates for public office, and permitted naturalized citizens to be candidates for the governorship. In 1849, OUA chapters in New York City rallied their members to help defeat a Democratic candidate for city comptroller who had expressed hostility to the fraternity. By 1850, OUA, with dozens of state chapters stretching from New York City up the Hudson River Valley (and, for that matter, into Massachusetts, Pennsylvania, New Jersey, Connecticut, and—more surprisingly—California), felt strong enough to take a more visible role in the campaign for a state school law turning control of the public schools over to local boards, which nativists surmised could be dominated by native-born Protestants. Anticipating that this was only a beginning of political action, the statewide executive council (or "chancery") of OUA adopted a new fraternal rule which required that the brothers vote for political candidates endorsed by the order or face expulsion. It is unclear how rigorously this rule was enforced, but OUA members belonging to both the Whig and the Democratic parties began to turn up as successful candidates for public office, including, in 1851, Grand Sachem Frederick A. Talmadge, who was elected New York City recorder, and Henry Storms, a Democrat who won the race for New York state prison inspector.[2]

Although OUA continued to represent itself as a "patriotic" benevolent and fraternal organization, Thomas R. Whitney—who, by 1852, was acquiring national visibility as editor of the *Republic*—began to lobby for a New York "Municipal party" of reformers to contest both the Democrats and the Whigs. Taking advantage of public revulsion to the corruption attributed to the "forty thieves" who made up the New York City Council of 1852, Whitney joined other local notables—some already associated with OUA, some not—to create a City Reform League. In fact, it was an internal fracture within this coalition which brought to public attention the fact that nativists in New York City were beginning to function like a political party for the first time since the mid-1840s.[3] The newspaperman Horace Greeley, a non-nativist member of the City Reform League, was so alarmed that he began to expose in print what he called a secret "Know Nothing" organization (he used this term because supposed members, when questioned, professed to know nothing about it). As OUA became increasingly open about its political activity, its chancellor, Joseph C. Morton, ran as an independent candidate for Congress from New York's Fifth District in the fall elections of 1852, and Thomas Whitney himself stood as a Whig candidate for the state assembly. Both lost, but Whitney was able to take some consolation in the fact that (by his own accounting, anyway) he outran all of the other Whigs on the ticket, apparently picking up bipartisan support. In 1853, when the City Reform League both prevailed on the state legislature to give New York a new municipal charter which strengthened the power of the executive and campaigned for the first officeholders to be elected under it, preexisting nativist ward associations that were already well organized were typically relied on to get out a bipartisan vote. As if to underscore the political clout of the nativists, Thomas Whitney was elected to the state senate as a Whig, despite the unhappiness of Whig regulars with his unorthodoxy.[4]

But at midcentury it was not only in New York City (or the state) that the nativist fraternities began to become politically more active. In Philadelphia, nativist "purists" entrenched within the United Sons of America denounced the traditional "American" leadership connected with Congressman Lewis Levin for crawling into bed with the Whigs and, particularly, for taking too conciliatory a view of "nonpolitical" Catholics. Surprisingly—even shockingly—an anti-Catholic street preacher named Joe Barker was elected mayor of Pittsburgh in 1850 as the "People's and Anti-Catholic Candidate," attracting to the polls in a municipal campaign nearly as many local voters as had cast ballots in the governor's race two years before.[5] In little more than a year after its birth in New York City, OUA had planted colonies in Massachusetts; and the former mayor of Springfield, the Reverend Alfred Brewster Ely, emerged as OUA's spokesman in Massachusetts. Nativist fraternities were poised to sound the alarm when a reform constitution was narrowly defeated in a statewide referendum in 1853. Providing greater legislative representation to the rural towns at the expense of Boston, the proposed constitution faced opposition from both urban immigrant Democrats and merchant Whigs, making plausible the charge that the two groups were in collaborating.[6]

Given this much success in local politics, it is no wonder that the nativist fraternities wasted little time before they began to speculate about the role they might play in national affairs. As early as June 1851, Thomas R. Whitney's *Republic* was beginning to promote prospective presidential candidates for 1852 and 1856 who might be acceptable to nativist tastes. Whitney was particularly enthusiastic about Millard Fillmore, who had become president on the death of Zachary Taylor, and OUA's Washington Chapter 2 turned out as an honor guard when Fillmore visited New York City to celebrate the completion of the Erie Railroad to the Great Lakes. Just a few months later, Whitney was calling for a convention comprising the "delegates from the several American orders throughout the country, for the purpose of forming a system of cooperative action." The creation of an effective "American National Union" could provide nativists with an alternative to the existing political parties. However, Whitney was scarcely rejecting the concept of "party" itself. In fact, he editorialized in the *Republic,* "party is essential to a safe execution of the affairs of government ... but ... that parties should exist in the same form forever, does not necessarily follow. ... The peculiar elements which call a party into existence, though they form a basis for action under certain emergencies, must in time become exhausted; and the party, having been deprived of its natural springs of action, falls into consequent decay, only to make room for a new one, based upon new and novel issues." The issues of the present, Whitney implied, called for a new party. Was the Order of United Americans itself a party? In reply to a reader of the *Republic* who asked just this question, Whitney claimed that it was and it was not, that it was "a political body, having a political object" but that it was also a bipartisan fraternity that stood outside of party. To hold together a "brotherhood" made up of voters with long-term ties to both the Whigs and the Democrats, the Executive Convention of the New York OUA found it wise to recommend both a Whig presidential candidate (Millard Fillmore) and a Democrat (Lewis Cass) in advance of the national party nominating conventions of 1852.[7]

In the summer of 1852, leading figures in the nativist fraternities moved to get beyond the limitations to forceful political action inherent in the fraternal model and specifically organize a party. Virtually simultaneously, and perhaps in concert, Whitney of OUA and representatives of what remained of Philadelphia's Native American party called for a national convention of delegates from "American" organizations. In July, 31 delegates from eight eastern seaboard states plus Ohio gathered in Trenton, New Jersey, and announced the formation of the American Union party. Rather presumptuously, the fledgling party immediately nominated Senator Daniel Webster for president of the United States and George Washington's grandnephew, George C. Washington, for vice-president. Both declined the honor, and Reynell Coates, one of the founders of the fraternal, nativist Patriotic Sons of

America, and Jacob Broom were nominated in their places. But squabbling broke out among the different organizations represented at Trenton over the question of naturalization reform, and the more militant orders, like Whitney's OUA, ignored the nominations in the general election. Whitney himself continued to promote a write-in campaign for Webster right up until Webster's untimely death, switching as a last resort to John Crittenden of Kentucky. The actual contest between the Whig Winfield Scott and the Democrat Franklin Pierce—which largely ignored the issues that nativists thought critical—only solidified nativists' conviction that the existing parties were unequal to the task of representing the public interest. In the November 1852 issue of the *Republic*, Whitney renewed his "proposition to form a new party, on the basis of pure Republican principles."[8]

Even while the American Union party was dying aborning, Whitney's OUA was exploring an alternative approach to effective political organization. Conscious of rivals, OUA leaders took time in the summer of 1852 to look into another New York City nativist society, the Order of the Star-Spangled Banner (OSSB), which had been founded two years earlier by a businessman, Charles B. Allen. Finding an attractive set of rituals and symbols in OSSB but scarcely any members, United Americans who wished to promote greater political activism seized on it as a useful vehicle. OSSB—unburdened of much of the fraternal and benevolent baggage of OUA—could be reworked as a tool for attracting mass voting support while OUA retained the luxury of selecting its membership and of keeping alive the notion that it was patriotically bipartisan. In only about a year, Allen was shoved out of the OSSB leadership by key members of OUA Washington Chapter 2, including James W. Barker, Jacob Bacon, and Daniel Ullman. By late 1853, New York City cells of OSSB, much enlarged by application of OUA's organizational expertise, began to stake out political positions. It was in November that Horace Greeley of the *New York Tribune* noticed it at work within the City Reform movement and referred to it as "Know Nothing." A month later, OSSB attacked the Whig mayor, Jacob Westervelt, for arresting an inflammatory anti-Catholic street preacher, Daniel Parsons. They were now ready for bigger game.[9]

In May 1854, James Barker presided over the formation of an OSSB—now beginning to style itself "American"—grand council of New York and, virtually simultaneously, a grand council of the United States. Almost at once, the order began to grow explosively, expanding in New York state alone from 91 local chapters at the beginning of sum-

mer to over 200 by the fall. The growing number of adherents, combined with a system of degrees and oaths which pledged members to
"vote in all political matters and for all political offices for second-
degree members of the Order, providing it shall be necessary for the
American interest," placed the Know Nothings (as even they were
beginning to call themselves) in a strong position to affect local and
state elections in the fall. Although a boomlet by OUA and OSSB members promoting Thomas R. Whitney within the Whig nominating caucuses fizzled and Barker's efforts to be elected mayor of New York as a
temperance candidate failed, the separate Know Nothing gubernatorial
candidacy of Daniel Ullman was remarkably successful. Though third
in a three-man race, Ullman was not far behind the Democrat, Seymour; and the presence of an independent ticket in the contest almost
certainly helped elect the Whig, Myron Clark. Moreover, candidates
endorsed by the Know Nothings took 19 of 33 congressional seats and
one-third of the positions in the state house and senate.[10] As David H.
Bennett aptly describes the public reaction, the "election of 1854 was a
stunning demonstration of the Know Nothings' magnetic appeal.
Within months, nativism became a new American rage: Know Nothing
candy, Know Nothing tea, and Know Nothing toothpicks were mar-
keted, omnibuses and stagecoaches received the charmed name, the
clipper ship *Know Nothing* was launched in New York." By February
1855, the New York state Know Nothings claimed almost 150,000
members in nearly 1,000 local chapters. Know Nothingism had not
pulled voters or legislators away from traditional party affiliations sufficiently to defeat the Whig senator, William Seward, for reelection in
early 1855; still, it was threatening enough to the established order to
wring from the Whig state administration support for an "Act for the
Suppression of Intemperance, Pauperism and Crime" largely aimed at
the supposed criminality of the foreign-born. In September, a state convention at Auburn formally reconstituted OSSB as the "American
party."[11]

The Know Nothing formula for third-party organization proved
effective outside New York state as well. The Whig politician Edward
Everett of Massachusetts called the nativists' success in the November
1854 elections in his state "the most astonishing result ever witnessed
in our politics." The Know Nothing gubernatorial candidate, Henry J.
Gardner, dominated the polling, winning every county but one. In addition to electing all of the statewide offices on the ballot, the Know Nothings won every state senate race, dominated the lower chamber, and

captured all 11 congressional seats. Careful analysis of the sources of Know Nothing voting strength by the historian Dale Baum indicates that Gardner did particularly well among traditional Democrats, ran almost as well among Whigs, and was particularly attractive to previous nonvoters. As in New York, the Know Nothings were most successful where there was a history of nativist fraternalism and seemed to be particularly popular in manufacturing towns where more or less traditional crafts like shoemaking (and the ideology of workers' independence) survived.[12]

In 1854, across the north in state after state, the particulars of the Know Nothings' political achievement were different but the results fundamentally similar. Philadelphia Americans swept the municipal elections under their own banner. At the other end of the state, candidates endorsed by the Know Nothings won all five state assembly races in Pittsburgh's Allegheny County. William Gienapp points out that, as in Massachusetts, the third-party initiative in Pennsylvania was about as successful in attracting former Democrats and previous nonvoters as Whigs.[13] The United Sons of America—a nativist fraternity with its origins in Philadelphia—established itself in Iowa by late 1852, to be followed within a couple of years by the Junior Sons of America. Thirty-six OSSB chapters were reported in Iowa by late 1854, and five newspapers were backing nativist candidates. Local Know Nothing tickets were successful in several key towns in the next spring's municipal elections, and elsewhere Democratic slates ran with Know Nothing endorsement. Fraternities like the United Sons of America spread in Michigan, too, where nativists variously ran their own tickets or endorsed sympathetic Whigs and Democrats. A "fusion" campaign conducted in many communities across Michigan, joining Whigs and nativists, elected a governor in the fall of 1854; but, as elsewhere, nativistic candidates also seemed remarkably successful at wooing Democratic voters.[14]

In Ohio, the *Cleveland True Democrat* estimated that Know Nothing lodges had 80,000 members by September 1854. Noting that the movement seemed to appeal to voters of different political persuasions, the paper offered as evidence the fact that the Cuyahoga County Democratic convention "refused to entertain resolutions repudiating the Know-Nothings." A year later, the candidate of the "People's Know Nothing" party defeated a former governor to win the mayoral election in Cleveland.[15] Even in faraway California, Know Nothingism quickly made its mark. At least some of the membership of a San Francisco "Vigilance

Committee" that was organized in 1851 to avenge crimes putatively committed by immigrants found it convenient to affiliate with the various nativist fraternities. OUA's Whitney heartily endorsed "vigilance" activities and noted that by May 1852 there were enough chapters of his own order to form a California state chancery. In 1854, Know Nothing candidates and candidates endorsed by the Know Nothings won a dominant position on the San Francisco city council, and all of the county's seats in both houses of the legislature. The evidence is that the nativists attracted voters away from both the Whigs and the Democrats.[16]

The Native American political movement of the mid-1840s—outside of the border states—had largely bypassed the south, but the Know Nothing enthusiasm of the mid-1850s did not bypass it. This would scarcely be surprising in New Orleans (which received one-eighth of all immigrant arrivals in the United States in 1851) or Baltimore (with a pre-Civil War population almost one-quarter foreign-born) or even smaller mercantile cities like Mobile, Alabama, or Natchez, Mississippi, which attracted diverse inhabitants. But the Know Nothing boom in the south was much more widespread. As in the northeast and midwest, it built on the proliferation of nativist fraternal orders in the early 1850s and took advantage of the willingness of both Whig and Democratic voters to break ranks. In the spring of 1853, Baltimore locals of the Order of United American Mechanics participated in an ironworkers' strike which—because of the association of the Democratic party with Maryland's elite of manufacturers, merchants, and planters—took on political overtones. On August 18, 1853, Maryland chapters of the United Sons of America staged a mass rally in Baltimore's Monument Square to impress candidates for the new state legislature with the extent of opposition to the Kerney Bill, legislation which had been introduced in the General Assembly the year before allowing private (including parochial) schools to participate in the public school fund. A Temperance ticket evenly divided between former Whigs and Democrats subsequently rode to office on a platform opposing the Kerney Bill. Candidates endorsed by the Know Nothings were successful in local elections in Cumberland and Hagerstown in early 1854, and later that year Frederick and Baltimore elected mayors running on nativistic tickets. In 1855, third-party nativist candidates won a majority of contested legislative seats and several statewide offices.[17] Independent-minded nativistic Whigs like Garrett Davis and Stephen F. J. Trabue had little enough impact on the political life of another border state,

Kentucky, until the wholesale organization of OSSB chapters in mid-1854 began to dislodge Democrats and Whigs alike from their traditional affiliations. Functioning as nominating conventions, these organizations put forward successful candidates for municipal offices in Louisville, Lexington, and Covington; won seats for nativist candidates in Congress and the state legislature; and paved the way for the creation of a state Know Nothing council in early 1855.[18]

Throughout the deep south, the sequence of nativist political development was much the same. OSSB chapters appeared in New Orleans in late 1853 and, taking advantage of widespread public belief that naturalization fraud had affected the outcome of the fall elections, rapidly coalesced as an "Independent" party. The Independents elected enough of their candidates for alderman in the spring of 1854 to take control of the legislative branch of the municipal government. Bolstered by this success in the metropolis, Know Nothings elected judges in both former Whig and former Democratic areas of Louisiana and, in the spring of 1855, elected the chief justice of the state supreme court from among their ranks.[19] From North Carolina, Tennessee, and Missouri to Alabama, Arkansas, and Mississippi, nativist fraternities quickly gave way to nativist political organizing between mid-1854 and mid-1855.[20]

The rapid emergence of local and even statewide third parties from a core of nativist fraternities naturally created pressure for a national political union and began to influence the fraternal orders themselves. A national Know Nothing convention in Cincinnati in November 1854 found itself unable to bask long in the glory of political success but had to confront what it meant to be an emerging political party. If there were exciting prospects in unified action on a national scale, there were also great dangers, since individual state American parties were more or less dominated by Whigs or Democrats, depending on the local conditions that gave rise to them, and potential sectional frictions threatened to produce ruptures when the subject of extending slavery—provoked by the introduction of the Kansas-Nebraska Bill in Congress—came up. Trying to anticipate the latter, one delegate, Kenneth Rayner of North Carolina, oversaw the addition of a third degree to the OSSB ritual. Whereas the first and second degrees required the brethren to favor "American" interests as voters and elected officeholders, the third was styled the "Union" degree and called on members to reject those "whom you know or believe to be in favor of dissolution of the Union of these states."[21] Potentially, this could deter agitation on issues likely to split Know Nothing ranks along sectional lines. But who was to determine what constituted a divisive issue and what was essential core ideology that defined Know Nothingism itself? Even at the height of the Know Nothings' success, these questions loomed large and unanswered.

Such extravagant political achievements coming so rapidly caught the traditional nativist secret societies somewhat by surprise. Used to operating behind the scenes and recommending to the brethren "sound" candidates nominated by the existing political parties, they suddenly found themselves part of a new political coalition promoting its own tickets. They scrambled to catch up. Finding the exclusivity which had characterized their membership practices and the secrecy of their proceedings politically disadvantageous, they began to make new arrangements. In the spring of 1855, the Order of United Americans overlaid on top of its fraternal chapters "executive associations" of nativist political leaders and an "Executive Convention" that could provide political coordination with the American party. About the same time, the Order of the American Star reorganized itself similarly, placing individual "temples" under the political direction of a "grand temple." By midsummer, formal talks were taking place between OUA, the Templars of OAS, and OSSB about how to work more closely politically.[22]

On the national level, the OSSB-American party also discovered that political success made it necessary to back away from most of the trappings of a fraternal brotherhood. Suddenly possessed of majorities in city councils and state legislatures, it found itself needing to prepare legislative agendas and campaign platforms as well as distribute party patronage. The National Council of OSSB met in early June 1855 and substituted for the fraternal oaths and degrees a new "pledge of honor" for party members that committed them to support the party platform and candidates. At the American party convention in Philadelphia that immediately followed, irregular state fraternities like Mississippi's Order of the Stars and Stripes were brought into line, and the party sought to give itself the kind of national programmatic definition that would allow it to get ready to compete in the next year's presidential contest.[23] The charged intersectional issues of the mid-1850s made this exceptionally challenging. Section 12 of the national platform adopted at Philadelphia was intended to keep the issue of extending slavery out of congressional debate by ruling it beyond the competence of Congress, but this merely transferred the debate to the party itself. Some heretofore Know Nothing voters and political leaders fled the party while others agitated for a reconsideration of the issue.

Less spectacular but still troublesome was the issue of what to do about naturalized and Catholic voters, who in some locations (like Louisiana) had been pushed by complex political circumstances into the Know Nothing camp. All of the traditions of nativist fraternalism implied their exclusion, while the practicalities of political campaigning suggested the wisdom of some kind of accommodation. Secrecy was abandoned by some OSSB chapters at the local level and by some state grand councils. Not everyone was comfortable with the way party activity began to overshadow pure nativist fraternalism. New York Know Nothings wrangled as early as the fall of 1854 over whether their cause was best served by running an independent ticket or by endorsing candidates of other parties on a case-by-case basis. Section 12 of the 1855 platform was so resented by some antislavery Know Nothings in the north that it began to provoke defections, rival tickets, and endorsement of unauthorized candidates almost as soon as it was announced.[24] Still, the political record of the nativist movement during the first half of the 1850s was nothing short of remarkable.

Accounting for the Know Nothings' Appeal

The puzzling thing about the nativist political boom of the 1850s was its brevity, and historians' need to account for its expiration has often colored their explanations of its explosive beginning. There is no question that as a major political party, Americanism was short-lived and that its life and death were caught up in a wholesale reorganization of the American political party system. Whigs and Democrats went into the 1850s, and Democrats and Republicans came out; and along the way, both leaders and voters reshuffled so much that even the continuity of the Democratic rank and file was lost. There has been a long debate over whether political nativism was the cause or just the temporary beneficiary of the breakdown of the second party system. But, either way, political historians tend to treat the rise and the fall of the Know Nothing-American party as symmetrical: what brought the party up must also be what brought it down.

The temptation is to look backward from what happened after 1855 to provide an explanation of what happened before. In the course of the collapse of the Whig party, did former Whigs vote Know Nothing before winding up as Democrats, and did Democrats pass through the

Know Nothings before becoming Republicans? If so, it is easy to conclude that from the beginning the Know Nothings must have been a haven for "political fugitives and opportunists." After 1856, was the American party forced to abandon a single national platform and accept local autonomy? Why not decide, then, that from the first the Know Nothing party had been a "conglomeration of interests attracted by a catchall program"? Did political nativism in the 1850s rise and fall so fast as to seem just a flash in the pan? Explain this, then, by arguing that "die-hard nativists . . . because of their single-minded commitment were a minority in the Know Nothing movement [even] during its ascendancy."[25] Of course, there were political opportunists in the American party, and most nativist leaders and followers eventually found new political homes. But this is a far cry from concluding that political opportunism brought about the Know Nothings' success or that voters left their traditional political allegiances *planning* to use the American party as only a temporary stopping point. Likewise, among the hundreds of thousands of Know Nothing voters there were undoubtedly men harboring competing interests. Yet this is quite different from saying that nativism had no ideological core. In fact, the Know Nothings attracted opportunists precisely because they were able to attract so many voters. And the party was able to embrace so much diversity because its central message had such a strong appeal. As Jean Baker has pointed out, the Know Nothings' political opponents liked to charge that the party "was little more than an ephemeral creation of intolerant bigots and greedy politicians," but just because they said this does not make it true.[26] To discover the real sources of the successful politicization of Know Nothingism in the 1850s (and its abrupt failure), it is necessary to look closely at the ideological themes that characterized the nativist movement over a much longer period but took on particular political appeal during the 1850s, and at the attractions of the nativist fraternalism that provided an institutional foundation for the political movement.

What broadened the appeal of nativism to the point where it became a potent political force during the 1850s was the way nativist ideology seemed to speak to the issue of individual autonomy—a sacred theme of American republicanism which took on new significance in an age of urbanization, industrialization, and geographical expansion. Whereas autonomy or "liberty" had once seemed to mean only freedom from control, in the more romantic culture of the 1850s, for many Americans (so long as they were white males, anyway), it had come to mean, as

Robert Berkhofer aptly puts it, "the opportunity to develop their natural talents to the fullest in order to realize their inner potential."[27] This broadened definition of liberty made Americans much more sensitive about threats to personal autonomy. In fact, J. Mills Thornton has argued that antebellum politics "turned almost wholly on the discovery and elimination of all sources of coercive dependence." To lose one's autonomy was to become a "slave," a particularly charged expression in the period before the Civil War. Under such conditions, the way to appeal to the voters was to promise to uncover and then remove obstacles to personal autonomy. This had a tendency to increase the paranoia of the electorate and encourage conspiracy theories, for it was much easier to think of coercion as coming from persons and groups than from impersonal social or economic forces.[28]

But sensitivity about personal autonomy was encouraged not only by the republican political tradition and newfound optimism about individual potential but also by actual developments in economic and social structure which seemed to be sapping the independence of many Americans. A modernizing economy in which large-scale manufacturing and the specialization of labor were taking a bigger role really did seem to be widening the gap between the richest and the poorest and making it increasingly unlikely that those near the bottom—whatever their talents—could ever rise near the top. While economic modernization did lead to a proliferation of white-collar jobs at the level of clerk, foreman, copyist, and petty manager, the occupants of these positions had no doubt about their dependence on "bosses" and large organizations. Nor was dependence strictly a northeastern, urban phenomenon. The spread of commercial agriculture west of the Appalachians produced increasing numbers of landless, often transient farmworkers and their counterparts in urban food-packing and processing industries.[29]

Structural economic change, which had the effect of making dependency at the very least more visible and more consciously experienced by many, was exacerbated in some places by the boom and bust cycle in the commodity and financial markets and the unpredictability of nature. Inflation, which began to affect the cost of living as early as 1851-1852, struck hard at foodstuffs between 1852 and 1854. Poor crop yields at home and abroad and international demand for grain encouraged by the Crimean War generated increases in the price of food that were largely responsible for driving the cost of living in nonagricultural areas up as much as 40 percent over four years in the middle of the decade. In the northeast, a terrible winter hit particularly hard in 1854-1855, overwhelming the ability of urban charities to feed and house displaced elements of the working classes. For many, humiliation was added to dependency. Even more comfortable members of the middle and upper classes were aware that their autonomy was being limited by the impact of inflation and—in cities like New York—a social services crisis and rapid increases in local taxation. The New York City almshouse budget more than tripled between 1853 and 1856, following hard on the heels of 33 percent increase in property taxes between 1851 and 1853. Under these circumstances, no fortune seemed secure.[30]

Unquestionably, growing sensitivity about dependence and independence gave further encouragement to the benevolent fraternalism which had flourished in the 1840s. The business contacts provided by the Masons or the Odd Fellows or the Improved Order of Red Men (or, for that matter, the Order of United Americans) seemed to provide a form of economic insurance in an uncertain environment, and the "benevolent" services represented by burial, sickness, and survivors' benefits offered a final safety net between at least nominal independence and abject "slavery" to the almshouse or private charity. Perhaps it is for these reasons that so many Americans became such aggressive joiners at midcentury. Over and again, we find men like Andrew J. Baker of Philadelphia, who made the rounds from night to night among his Odd Fellows lodge, his Red Men's wigwam, his Masonic chapter, and his two volunteer fire companies (really another sort of fraternal organization). The young Cincinnatian Rutherford B. Hayes (later president) dutifully committed to his diary an exhaustive weekly calendar of fraternal activities.[31]

In Hayes's case, one fraternal obligation was to his temperance lodge. He was scarcely alone in this. In the 1850s, temperance rhetoric typically linked drink to "slavery," to loss of self-control (or at least control of the higher faculties), and thus to loss of autonomy. "By taking away rationality," notes Jed Dannenbaum, a historian of temperance ideology in Ohio, "alcohol deprived its users of free will, of freedom."[32] Not surprisingly, one of the key temperance orders of the early 1850s, the Sons of Temperance, attracted a youthful membership made up of economically vulnerable men. Besides promising freedom from bondage to the bottle, temperate habits also seemed well calculated to keep an employee in the good graces of his boss at a time when long-term economic change and short-term volatility seemed to make many jobs precarious. The banner of a local temperance society of the period combined potent symbols—a broken bottle, an upended whiskey barrel, bound sheaves of grain, the national eagle, and the stars and stripes—representing independence from drink and its benefits for economic prosperity and participatory citizenship.[33]

The achievement of the nativists was to identify a single plausible cause for the descent into dependence (real, imagined, or feared) of so many mid-nineteenth-century Americans. They attributed it, of course, to what they took to be the growing influence of the foreign-born in American life, but also to what they called a loss of "national character." This involved much more than the simple charge that, by competing with natives for employment, immigrants took jobs and drove down wages, although this was an appealing idea in cities where the foreign-born congregated during the half-decade after 1848, when European immigration was at its pre-Civil War peak. The public was only too willing to believe that immigration was actually responsible for some of the structural changes that seemed to be coming to American manufacturing. They were receptive to charges that the decline of the traditional apprentice-journeyman-master hierarchy in some industries was due to the availability of large numbers of adult male immigrants who could accomplish through sheer numbers on a piecework basis what a smaller force of painstakingly trained skilled craftsmen had traditionally achieved.[34]

But these were really old arguments that had been around since at least the 1820s. Even though they struck a more sensitive public nerve around midcentury, they cannot account for the enhanced appeal of nativism that led to its rather abrupt political success. What no one did better than nativist ideologists was to tie these developments to what they portrayed as a larger assault on individual autonomy, victimizing both natives and immigrants. The Philadelphia nativist John Hancock Lee, for example, shrilled that the "free labouring men of America" seemed doomed to fall "to a level with serfs, [peons], and slaves" if wages continued to drop, skilled labor was devalued, and the traditional route to economic independence which led from apprentice to master craftsman was destroyed.[35] Even if there was enough work for all, the life that would result for workers would be one of abject dependence. Moreover, by driving down the cost of labor, immigration was lining the pockets of the rich, who consequently found themselves in an even stronger position to control the poor. As Thomas R. Whitney of the Order of United Americans put it, "the unnatural excess of the producing element caused by immigration is . . . well-calculated to create an aristocracy of wealth, fatal to the moral and social interests of the producing classes."[36] At a time when even white-collar jobs were coming to seem more tenuous and dependent, this was a warning that resonated among the middle classes. Symbolism, too, was all-important. As Robert H. Wiebe has pointed out, in many lines of work, direct competition between skilled native workers and unskilled immigrants was slight, yet at a time when a host of forces seemed to be working against individual independence, struggling immigrants "represented above all the horrors of the bottomless, propertyless pit."[37] A state in which more and more of the populace lacked independence of action could not—in a republican sense—be a nation (have a "national character") at all, for what created republican nationhood was shared, uncoerced participation in public affairs.

Even more effectively than they had in the 1840s, the nativist fraternal lodges after midcentury played on the fears of men—and women— that they were living on the brink of dependence. In organizations like the Order of United Americans, the cash benefits dispersed in a primitive form of insurance and unemployment assistance were more than window dressing. Not only did the ordinary activities of chapters include regular benefit fund-raisers, but full beneficiary membership remained open only to healthy men no older than 55.[38] Such financial assistance could mean the difference between dignified independence and dependence on private handouts or the public almshouse, but equally important were the symbolic ways in which the nativist fraternities bolstered individual self-respect. OUA, for example, lavished attention on the development of a stately funeral ritual, ensured that the death of a brother was advertised in his neighborhood, required members to attend funerals in full regalia, and saw to it that even in the absence of family a body was respectfully interred. OUA went so far as to make plans for the purchase of New York City property in 1852 to serve as a fraternal burying ground (laden with the heavy symbolism of a 350-foot-high monument to George Washington above a funeral chapel, both "to be built only by American hands, with American materials"). Over and again, nativist rhetoric stressed the difference between dependence on strangers and the independence preserved through the mutual assistance of benevolent fraternalism. As opposed to the "hand of cold charity," "with us there is something that impels each member to a more hearty recognition of a brother under all circumstances; and when we do meet—no matter where—we are no longer strangers, though we may never have met before . . . and on the spot where we knew no face, and could claim no other sympathy, the bond of the *American Brotherhood* is thrown around us, and we find ourselves suddenly in the midst of *friends,* earnest and hearty in their welcome."[39] Such reminders of fraternal egalitarianism were sure to have broad public appeal at a time when many people were becoming concerned about hardening social-class distinctions and new challenges to personal independence.

The value of nativist fraternalism was actually enhanced as the American orders began to acquire greater political visibility. OUA's *Republic* was consistently full of business notices for "Brother Kellogg's" hats, "Brother Haight's" family groceries, and "Brothers Walnut and Radford's" oyster and dining saloon. And the growth of the fraternities themselves created a large and well-advertised industry involving the manufacture and sale of fraternal regalia, membership certificates, and printed business cards. In fact, by the mid-1850s, the very success of Know Nothingism created for imaginative brethren a captive market which, for example, a New York City marketer of "Ray's Superior Zephyr Merino Undergarments" sought to tap by advertising that the lucky wearer would "Know Nothing of the morning chills, Nothing of the mid-day heats, Nothing of the evening dews." Some nativist publications specifically endorsed products sold by cooperatives of old-fashioned craft shops, like New York's "Hat Finishers' Union," reinforcing the equation of nativist fraternalism with individual autonomy.[40] With the spread of political nativism, the "withdrawal cards" provided by OUA or the Order of United American Mechanics or the Sons of America for members in good standing who were moving to a new location had enhanced economic value, not only admitting a member to a new chapter and a new band of "brothers" but providing a sort of business reference at a time when modern credit reporting was still in its infancy. There is some evidence that "seafaring men" who called at many ports found membership in nativist fraternities particularly useful for this reason.[41]

What the nativist orders were able to accomplish by the early 1850s was a reworking of the fraternal model, which in the hands of the Masons in 1820s and 1830s had come under popular attack as elitist and antirepublican, by infusing it with an ideology which made it appear the soul of republicanism itself. There is no doubt that the essential organizational principles of the nativist orders were borrowed. An early grand sachem of OUA attributed the beneficiary features of the Order to the example provided by the Odd Fellows, and contemporaries frequently noted the similarity between the nativist Brotherhood of the Union and the Masonic order. A nativist author, C. Edwards Lester, gave the oration at the dedication of New York City's new Odd Fellows Hall (which was used as a meeting place by the New York Know Nothing grand council) in 1854; and elsewhere, as in Cleveland, after nativist fraternalism slipped into decline, the OSSB lodge rooms were taken up by other fraternal organizations.[42] E. Z. C. Judson, one of the founders of Philadelphia's Patriotic Order, United Sons of America, borrowed liberally from the Masonic ritual that he had become acquainted with through his father, and across the country well-known members of the American party (like Kenneth Rayner of North Carolina or Sam Houston of Texas) used their Masonic connections for political advantage. Jean Baker has pointed out that nativist politicians in Maryland were much more likely than their counterparts in the traditional parties to be Masons, and Ronald R. Matthias has made the same observation about frontier Iowa.[43]

Its proven structure and ritual, its emphasis on mutual support and independence, and its identification of unrestricted immigration and naturalization with threats to personal autonomy gave midcentury nativistic fraternalism strong appeal, leading to a proliferation of organizations. In addition to OUA, the quasifraternal Order of the Star-Spangled Banner, the Order of United American Mechanics, the American Brotherhood, and the Patriotic Order, Sons of America, numerous lesser fraternities appeared, some local, some aspiring to be national: examples include the American Knights, Native Sons of America, and Sons of the Soil. Not only was there considerable communication among the leadership of these organizations, but many "joiners" belonged to two or more. In 1851, the *Cincinnati Daily Enquirer* reported that Judson of the United Sons of America had appeared on one of the city's lecture stages dressed "in the full regalia of five American Orders." Given the ideological and practical appeal of the nativist societies, evaluations like that of the historian John Mulkern are far too simplistic: "delicious nonsense, with its allure of mystery and promise of adventure, brought out the boyish exuberance concealed in the hearts of many men and drew countless numbers of middle-aged Tom Sawyers into Know Nothingism."[44]

If the appeal of the nativist fraternities had been limited to the utility of brotherhood combined with an egalitarian ideology which invoked traditional republican ideals, they would never have become more than the "patriotic societies" that Albert Stevens, compiler of the *Cyclopedia of Fraternities,* would later call them. But they became launching pads for a potent political movement because their ideologues charged that many of the contemporary challenges to individual autonomy were political in nature and had political solutions. Nativists warned that the equality represented by the franchise and its capacity to serve as a way for individuals to assert their will (their independence) were under threat. Refugees from famine in Ireland and political unrest in the German principalities added approximately 3 million newcomers to the United States between 1846 and 1854. This represented more than one-seventh of the whole population of the country at the time that the upsurge began. With a federal naturalization period of five years, many of the arrivals were in a position to vote by the early 1850s. At the state level—particularly in the new states of the west—the franchise was frequently offered before citizenship. In areas with high concentrations of immigrants, the foreign-born could make up a large proportion of the electorate. By 1855, nearly half of New York City's voters were foreign-born, and immigrant voters outnumbered native in at least nine wards. As early as 1850, half of the population of St. Louis consisted of immigrants, many looking forward to voting early in the new decade. Nor was this phenomenon confined to major urban centers. During the late 1850s, more than one-third of the population of Wisconsin and Minnesota and almost 20 percent of the population of Illinois and Iowa were foreign-born. The thinly populated western states, particularly, awarded the vote to immigrants who met a residency requirement of as little as four months (though in most it required a year after a declaration of intent to become a citizen).

The argument advanced by nativists was that this explosive growth of the enfranchised was "unnatural," having the effect of diluting the ballot of the individual native voter, who had waited 21 years to earn it. It increased the likelihood, they alleged, that one's vote did not matter and hence that one's fundamental mark of republican equality—the vote—was depreciated. Of course, this fit nicely with charges that immigration was also a source of growing economic dependency, suggesting a sort of conspiracy that anxious minds were only too eager to believe in. Nativist remedies ran a gamut: from (1) completely excluding the foreign-born from the franchise except when it was specifically conferred by Congress on an individual in recognition of exceptional public service (the official position of the Order of United Americans); to (2) requiring a waiting period of 21 years before naturalization (the rationale being that this was the period of republican seasoning for an American-born youth); to (3) harmonizing state franchise require- ments with the federal naturalization probation period of five years. In any event, nativists argued that these were political questions that the traditional parties seemed unwilling to address, providing added justifi- cation for the first efforts of the nativist fraternities to dabble directly in politics.

An Alternative Party

Ironically, the rationale for the very existence of political parties, worked out over the first half of the nineteenth century, was that they served as the mechanism for individuals to regulate the power of the state. In a sense, they served as an extension of the individual, another preserver of personal autonomy. But at the same time as nativists charged that immigrant voters were diluting the ballots of natives through sheer numbers, they attacked the political parties for bending over backward to earn the immigrant vote. Nativists denounced Presi- dent Franklin Pierce's appointment of James Campbell, a Roman Catholic from Pennsylvania, to the cabinet—in the patronage-rich position of postmaster general—as soon as it took place, early in 1853. According to the nativists, Campbell had been pointedly rejected by the voters when he ran for the Pennsylvania supreme court in 1851, the only Democratic candidate for the court to lose; and he had subse- quently been named state attorney general as a bow to the Irish Catholic electorate. His appointment to the president's cabinet, nativists alleged, demonstrated how the parties had been converted into mere machines for getting votes and distributing patronage and how little the individual native-born voter mattered.[45]

It was not just the Democrats who came under fire for their conduct before and after the election of 1852, but also the Whigs. In real danger of losing their southern wing entirely to the Democrats (who seemed the more uncompromising defenders of racial slavery), the national Whig hierarchy made a conscious effort to woo immigrant voters from the Democrats, particularly in populous northeastern states like Penn- sylvania and New York. The Whig presidential candidate General Win- field Scott backtracked on some earlier public statements he had made on the need for naturalization reform and particularly praised the ser- vice of Irish-Americans in the recent war with Mexico. At the same time, a rather far-fetched story was concocted charging Franklin

Pierce and the New Hampshire Democrats with anti-Catholicism because the state's electorate had not eliminated a religious test for public office from its revised constitution of 1850. All of this drove nativists wild and seemed to give them plenty of grist for charges that ordinary voters had lost their influence.

Throughout the early 1850s, the nativist press was full of alleged examples of state and local offices being quietly promised to different ethnic blocs as a way of sewing up elections; and newspapers like the *Inland* of Lancaster, Pennsylvania, published figures suggesting that foreign-born voters had come to control elections. (The *Inland* counted the immigrant vote of Pennsylvania at 43,300 and the Democratic majority for Franklin Pierce at 19,400.)[46] If this was too subtle, nativist publicists made it plainer (and linked native-born Americans' alleged loss of freedom of political action to other supposed threats to their autonomy), charging that immigrants were "crowding our cities, lining our railroads and canals, occupying our kitchens, driving our carriages, and *electing our rulers.*" Moreover, the parties were guilty accomplices in this affront to republican voters. Even the general press was supposedly part of this corruption. The Order of United Americans' *Republic,* for example, was incensed when the New York papers seemed to pay more attention to Irish-American units participating in the funeral procession for the city's last Revolutionary War veteran than they did to the (self-reported) 1,000 OUA members marching in full regalia.[47]

That a large proportion of the recent arrivals from Ireland and Germany were Roman Catholics only encouraged the nativists' argument. The relatively centralized, hierarchical nature of the Catholic Church gave superficial plausibility to nativist accusations that the foreign-born were able to exercise disproportionate political influence because they were organized to do so by a cadre of priests and bishops. Know Nothing newspapers functioned like Revolutionary-era "committees of correspondence," spreading the alarm when new Catholic clergy entered a neighborhood, suspecting that furtive political organizing was going on. Even the courtly planter Kenneth Rayner, a North Carolina Know Nothing, could descend to demagoguery on this subject, charging that the nation was faced with "a great spectacle calculated to humiliate every patriotic heart, of both the great parties bowing down before this foreign horde, truckling to them for votes—and of a Protestant people huckstering for votes with the Romish priesthood." For a public anxious to prevent a seeming loss of economic independence from being confirmed by a loss of personal political effectiveness, this seemed a reasonable explanation for the political parties' appeals to foreign-born voters. Few nativists thought they were exaggerating, then, when they denounced Roman Catholicism as "slavery" which stripped the liberty of the independent vote from Catholics and non-Catholics alike.[48]

The notion that the political parties to which the electorate had become accustomed had grown unresponsive to the individual voter and his concerns, and that these parties wanted to perpetuate their hold on office by manipulating blocs of voters, was encouraged by the "insider" methods that were used to nominate candidates for office. A letter to the editor of a nativist magazine described the party caucus system in a major northeastern city this way:

It is never generally known where the polls are to be held, nor who are chosen to serve as delegates in support of the different candidates to be presented in convention. . . . But, sir, these parties, being naturally quiet, do not seek the confusion and clamor of public meetings, where work is not done but drawn out, it having been previously cut and dried by the "wire-pullers" and private caucuses. And, sir, if the good citizens did go to the meetings, what could they do there? . . . Committees arrange the time and place for holding the polls, and make these known to the elect and their forces, that they may be on hand, drilled, primed, and (spiritually) loaded. But, sir, the time, and place for hold-ing the primary contest are designedly withheld from the public until within a few hours of action, and then only is communicated the time and duration of the polls, without the naming of delegates chosen to support the different can-didates and or even the localities in which the polls are to beheld.[49]

Historians routinely confirm that by 1850 the nominating conven-tion system was in disarray and was drawing the attention of political reformers of all stripes. What made reform of party nominating machinery such a potent issue in the hands of nativists in the early 1850s was the way they connected it with other evidence of party unre-sponsiveness, particularly the alleged attractiveness of immigrants and Catholics to politicians seeking "drilled," organized voters. Equally important, Know Nothingism, with its roots in the nativist fraternities, was able to offer what seemed to be a populist alternative to closed, managed caucuses. The nativist club, lodge, or ward organization itself would serve as the setting for an open primary convention among members. To enhance the democratic appearance of such a procedure, members were enjoined before voting to consult their friends and neighbors about the candidates. Obviously, this system was something less than public, but to those who participated in it (and during the peak of nativist organizing in the mid-1850s, there were many) it seemed not only less manipulated but more empowering, restoring political responsibility to ordinary voters. Nativists capitalized on this reformist theme by often styling themselves at the local level as the "People's party," and once they did come into positions of real power in state legislatures in the mid-1850s, they promoted a variety of structural political reforms, including primary reform, voter registration, and legislative reapportionment.[50] During his single term in Congress, OUA's Whitney went down swinging in the prolonged controversy over an election of a House Speaker, repeatedly calling for a secret ballot and a simple majority to break the reflexive loyalty to party which had created a months-long impasse.[51]

Once again, the focus of nativist rhetoric was on *individual* autonomy and participation—the traditional mark of the republican citizen. "I am one of the millions who have too long allowed a few men to do their political thinking for them," wrote a nativist publicist. "I have determined to think for myself, read for myself, and, as far as I can, to understand for myself." This could easily be interpreted as a rejection of political parties altogether. But as the effort to substitute lodge meeting for caucus shows, most nativists were opposed not to *party* itself but to the existing Democratic and Whig organizations. In fact, one typical nativist plaint was that the parties were insufficiently organized— "agglomerated only at times of election" for the purpose of winning votes, but without long-term vision or objectives. "Yet what is the remedy? Organization in a form likely to prompt and develop the mind . . . with that culture which may lead to the recognition of the principles evolved through our institutions, and which should base our general, political, and philanthropic action. . . . Such schools are now in operation. They are called Chapters."[52] The nativist fraternities putatively offered a new kind of party, calculated to restore morality to politics and amplify the voice of the individual voter. Moreover, they would provide fraternal benefits, conviviality, employment and business contacts, and a sense of status that conventional parties tried to but could not quite match. Not surprisingly, nativist rhetoricians were careful to flatter the voter at the same time that they denounced politicians: "The masses are sound but the old party leaders and political hacks . . . will ruin us."[53]

As the historian Michael Holt has effectively documented in *The Political Crisis of the 1850s,* a variety of circumstances around midcentury really did conspire to make the national Whig and Democratic organizations seemingly less responsive to voters' concerns. According to Holt, in a time when parties were regarded as bulwarks against abuse of power rather than wielders of power, what voters most wanted was a clear choice between parties. This could allow voters to decisively shift their favor at election time, the ultimate defense of "liberty" against party "tyranny." If their platforms were too much alike, the parties seemed to offer little alternative to one another and gave the appearance of being nothing but machines for winning office.

Between 1850 and 1853, many of the key issues which had traditionally distinguished the national parties from one another evaporated. An inflationary economy, bolstered by the California gold rush and European investment (particularly in American railroads), stimulated bank deposits and dissipated much of the interparty conflict over paper banknotes and bank charters which had divided Whigs from Democrats since the 1830s. Enthusiasm for the railroad boom weakened the northern Democrats' anticorporation temper. Rising prices and business profits plus the demand of an industrializing economy for capital goods like British steel rails weakened the Whigs' insistence on protective tariffs. A wave of state constitutional reform addressed many historically divisive issues, including standards for business incorporation and the capacity of states to fund debt. The issue of extending slavery, which might have distinguished the parties at least in the north, was temporarily undercut by the zeal with which the national party organizations—particularly the Whigs—promoted the Compromise of 1850. Zachary Taylor had campaigned in 1848 as something of a nonpartisan "people's" candidate, trading on his reputation as a war hero, and the subsequent Fillmore administration pulled out all the patronage stops to see that the party faithful accepted the Compromise, making difficult the local waffling on slavery that had allowed the Whig party to survive in many areas. In the midwest, where the Whig apparatus was opposed to extending slavery, the Democrats found it wise to soft-pedal their support for the Compromise. Having backed away from the traditional economic issues that had originally set them apart during Andrew Jackson's time—and, for that matter, having backed away from slavery as the core of partisan difference—the parties seemed reluctant to take up other matters that appealed to many voters: issues like franchise and naturalization reform that were central to the nativist movement.

This only heightened the parties' appearance of bland sameness and unresponsiveness. In the presidential election of 1852, the Whig vote fell off markedly and the Democrats fared little better. In many locales voters simply stayed home, doubting that it mattered whether they voted or not or which party's candidate won.[54] As Holt astutely concludes, "Much more was at stake in the waning of perceived party alternatives on issues by 1852. . . . The lack of choice between the parties was equated with an end of republicanism, a loss of popular control over government."[55] Generally speaking, in states where voters' old loyalties to parties survived longest, local issues continued to provide substantial grounds for distinction between the parties.

It is all too easy to jump to the conclusion that popular distrust of the major parties reached a point where any alternative would do and that the American party, simply being at the right place at the right time, was sucked into the vacuum. To this way of thinking, almost any alternative party might have served; and it is no surprise that scholars of the breakdown of the second American political party system in the mid-1850s who offer this interpretation tend to see political nativism as little more than an umbrella for diverse interests and political manipulators, without much ideological substance, relying on old stereotypes and bigotries as the lowest common denominator of unity. But it was not just because the nativist movement was available as an alternative that popular faith in the major parties waned. Nativism had both a message and a form of organization well calculated to respond to voters' fears and to make it a particularly suitable repository for their political loyalty.

Because nativists initially entered politics not as a party but as fraternal cells endorsing nominees of both major parties, the "Americans" gave the appearance of being above partisanship, seeking only the "best" men. And when they did begin to offer their own tickets, the relative openness of their local chapter meetings made them look very democratic. Their appealing organizational model also enabled them to grow swiftly as a political coalition by masking their activities until they had gained strength. Throughout the early 1850s, Whig and Democratic political leaders expressed frustration and alarm at being unable to distinguish the nativists in their midst who might pick and choose among the candidates of their party and those of their rivals. The New York state Democratic convention of 1853 was shocked when a quarter of the delegates abandoned the meeting. Most of the renegades turned out to be nativist organizers, editors, and candidates. Three years later, a resolution to force delegates to the Democratic state nominating convention to renounce membership in nativist organizations faced so much opposition that it was withdrawn. A historian who compared nativist lodge membership rolls and voter participation in Lancaster, Pennsylvania, in the years right after midcentury discovered that the number of "brothers" equaled a quarter of the total number of eligible voters, and up to 40 percent of the average number of citizens casting ballots in most elections. This suggests how nativism could so swiftly transform itself from a coalition of friendly societies into a successful political party.[56]

As we shall see, far from being "antiparty"—that is, opposed to sustained, organized political action—mid-nineteenth-century nativists were committed to an expansion of the party concept. A good part of their criticism of the existing parties actually focused on what they took to be the part-time nature of conventional party activity. They argued that party ought to permeate everyday life and serve as an instrument to restore dignity and autonomy to the individual citizen. According to nativist ideologues, one of the things to be feared most in the modern republic was that citizens would become strangers to one another. Strangers would feel less reciprocal commitment, share fewer common goals, and more often experience the powerlessness of social isolation. The nativists' cultural narrowness was part and parcel of this fear of a nation of "strangers." So was their attraction to fraternal and—in the case of the OSSB-American party—quasifraternal organization. For the fraternal chapter was specifically calculated to take advantage of what one scholar of friendly societies calls "neighborhood ties" and "job-associated friendships." It brought together people who were already neighbors and then bound them more formally with a new set of symbols and mutual obligations. In this, there was a strong conservative inclination which resisted not only the tendency of a growing, industrializing nation toward impersonal, commercialized relationships but also the privatization of social life promoted by the emerging middle-class family. The "order," unlike the conventional parties, was *not* expected simply to regroup during elections to nominate and support its candidates and in between monitor patronage appointments. Rather, it was to provide an ongoing educating, acculturating, and nurturing community. Nor was it to back away from its ideology and accept expedient political deals. It was, if anything, to politicize life, and many communities discovered that the days of nonpartisan local elections were gone once the Know Nothings had organized. Nativists insisted that there was nothing like nonpartisanship; one either embraced nativism or was part of the problem it sought to confront.[57]

Conclusion: The Appeal of "New Men" in Politics

Because ideology was everything to the nativist movement, it made few moves that were not in harmony with its pledge to restore the "autonomy" of American citizens, even when its actions, as a matter of political tactics, were unwise. It gloried, for example, in its ability to bring to political office new men with little or no previous experience in government. A new political movement was bound to attract outsiders and disappointed political aspirants anyway, but the Know Nothings went out of their way to promote just such men. Nominating candidates who seemed to have no political connections or debts, no previous commitments or baggage, suited perfectly a movement which stressed independence and protection of the citizenry from unresponsive, self-perpetuating oligarchies. Only four of the Know Nothing candidates elected in the first wave of nativist victories to the lower house of the Maryland legislature had previous legislative experience; and in Massachusetts, 90 percent of the Know Nothing members of the new general court of 1855 were newcomers to the statehouse.

From Florida to Michigan, the evidence is that nativist officeholders at all levels were, on average, decidedly younger than their Whig and Democratic counterparts—were, in fact, young men, often in their twenties or thirties. Perhaps in part because of their youth, they were also on the whole less affluent than their rivals. This did not mean they were poor, although the Know Nothings were much more likely than the traditional parties to nominate tradesmen and shopkeepers, but it did mean they were less likely to draw their incomes from landed wealth, investments, or the traditional professions of gentlemen. They were apt to be agents, factors, brokers, salesmen, and shipmasters as well as clerks, copyists, printers, storekeepers, master craftsmen, and restaurateurs, men who had not traditionally played a large role in political leadership. Thus Know Nothingism had less to do with class than with occupation and, possibly, ambition. The Know Nothings included many of the "wannabes" of the mid-nineteenth century, young men who aspired to both commercial and political achievement.[58] This suited the nativist message just fine. Nativist lodges took special pride in advertising themselves as training grounds for prospective state legislators and city councilmen. A grand sachem of the Order of United Americans lauded chapters which had adopted the practice of "giving a course of private lectures in their halls . . . affording, as it does to the young members, an opportunity for practice in the school of oratory."[59]

The conviction that the old parties no longer effectively represented citizens' interests, and that new men were likely to have a freedom from obligation that would make them more reliable stewards of popular will, provided nativists with potent ammunition when Whigs and Democrats counterattacked. They were the "old hack politicians, ever ready for preferment." In fact, nativist leaders were very nearly paranoid: they felt that everywhere opportunistic politicians had insincerely professed loyalty to nativism simply because, as an OUA representative put it, "ever eager to seize upon whatever may seem to command influence, [they] have noticed our rapid and solid increase in numbers." This could be effectively portrayed as another assault on voters' independence and worked into the nativists' overall theme: "What claim . . . have Whig politicians upon *American* votes?" Do Whig politicians imagine that the voters are "spaniels, to bend before your insults in humility and subjection?"[60]

Of course, reliance on this proposition could make nativists vulnerable to public rejection if they, too, began to act like the political parties they criticized. But what played a bigger role in the growing political appeal of mid-nineteenth-century American nativism was the consistency of its message about threats to personal autonomy and the effectiveness of its constituent organizations in providing avenues for members to prove to their own satisfaction they remained free and effective citizens. Ironically, nativism lost its political clout when other movements hijacked this message.

Chapter Four

The Politics of Autonomy: Know Nothingism in Ascendancy and Decline

Nativists were able to work their enthusiasm for autonomy into an effective political message because they broadly defined the contemporary threats to personal independence and the equality of citizens. It was not just the old political party system which led to dependence. Consider both the breadth and the single-mindedness of the political goals that a nativist editor laid out for the his movement in 1852:

1.   In no case should a State have the power of conferring the right of suffrage upon aliens.
2.   Our present law of wholesale naturalization should be abolished.
3.   More rigid practice of economy in the public expenditures must be enforced. . . . Nothing tends so much to foster corrupt ambition as luxurious example and lavish expenditures on the part of government.
4.   The public domain should be held as a sacred legacy to the people.
5.   Manufactures and the arts should be encouraged.
6.   A large army and navy are not needed . . . because a free people will stand always ready to protect alike their government and themselves . . . ;

besides, a large standing army, being, as it must, a creature of the government, is well calculated to excite the just jealousy of the citizens.

    7.   The emoluments of public office should be reduced.[1]

Many of these goals are not usually recognized as part of nativist agenda. But they all fit, and the apparent consistency of their message is part of what lent midcentury nativism popular appeal. All had to do with the preservation of personal autonomy, and all made some sense to people who thought their own independence was threatened.

Nativist Ideology: Dependence and Independence

Nativist goals were more than rhetorical; activists pursued them throughout the 1850s. They showed up, for example, in the criticism of General Winfield Scott's presidential candidacy in 1852. Bad enough that Scott and the Whigs seemed bent on wooing the immigrant vote; worse that "after having spent a life-time in *war,* he shall now, without an apprenticeship, put on the coronal of *peace,* and become a ruler in *civil,* as he has heretofore been in martial affairs." For nativist ideologues, the promotion of military men for civilian offices was the lowest common denominator of politics, seemed a further sign that the major parties stood for little of substance, and smacked of government disregard for the sovereignty of the people: "We are opposed to the growing habit of choosing our Presidents from the army . . . for no other purpose than to make 'available' candidates." Occasionally, they went further and used scare tactics, arguing that this practice could lead to "eventually, perhaps, a military dictatorship."[2] The parties, and the government that their loyalists staffed, the nativist argument ran, were out of touch with and unconcerned about the average citizen.

Far more likely than military dictatorship was the prospect that government was aiding and abetting forces driving the national economy into a configuration that accentuated personal dependence. Michael Holt has shown how concern about the effect of (publicly subsidized) railroads on commercial river traffic and the livelihoods it supported helped excite political nativism in Pittsburgh and western Pennsylvania. J. Mills Thornton suggests how, in Alabama, sympathy for nativist candidates was encouraged not only by anxieties wrought by the transportation revolution but by the expansion of government activity itself, by the growth of public expenditures, debt, and taxes. All of these

seemed to reinforce nativists' contention that the nation was moving in
a direction in which increasing constraints were placed on the individual. In power, nativist officeholders—at least on the national level—
sought to cultivate voters' sensitivities on this issue by calling persistently for economy in government.[3]

At a time when the nation was focused on geographical expansion
(and the associated debate over extending slavery), resourceful
nativist thinkers managed to connect the disposition of public lands in
the west with insensitive big government, political corruption, public
debt, and domineering big business—threats to individual autonomy.
"The Land Robbery Bill," a nativist headline shrieked, referring to congressional debate on homestead legislation. Rather than "squander all
the acres that are left of the public domain," a nativist congressman
argued in 1856, why not turn them to a "national" purpose by leasing or
selling them to eliminate all federal public debt and relieve the citizenry of wealth-sapping taxation? "We believe it to be a truism, that
republican simplicity abhors a public debt, in the same ratio that a free
people abhor direct taxation." Just as bad was a proposal to turn a
checkerboard of alternate sections of western land over to private
entrepreneurs in compensation for transportation improvements, to
"vote them away by millions of acres at a time to projectors of railroads,
canals, etc., whose philanthropy, however comprehensive it may seem
to be, has self-interest for its source and center."[4] These, too, were the
soulless corporations that were allegedly hemming in the individual
and making him something less than the independent, unmanipulable
republican citizen envisioned by the founding fathers.

Nativists had no problem, moreover, tying pressures for the distribution of the public lands to the influence of "aliens." The "land robbery
bill" was supposedly being pushed by "European advocates" and
"imported reformers" who promoted a socialistic equalization of property which struck at individual initiative and made private citizens
dependent on the state. Worse, nativists claimed to see a hidden purpose: "The ultimate object of the ostensibly philanthropic scheme, is
the peopling of the valley of the Mississippi with Europeans of the
poorer class; and, if passed into a law, it will be at a premium offered to
Papal and pauper immigration."[5] What particularly seemed to offend
nativists was that in the thinly populated newer and candidate states of
the west, the franchise was opened to men after only a short residence
in the community. While this made sense in communities where *everyone* was new and all had a stake in building the society, it reawakened

the fears that nativists harbored about the dilution and cheapening of the individual vote. This became an issue for nativists in the debate over the revised constitution of Indiana in the early 1850s and again in the discussion of the admission of Minnesota and Oregon as new states later in the decade. Nativists did not hesitate to try to connect the franchise issue with their objections to a liberal homestead policy, insisting that agitation for the homestead bill was part of a conspiracy led by the Roman Catholic Cardinal John Hughes "by which he promises to give to the Papacy the political control of these United States." "The enemies of civil and religious liberty," speculated OUA's *Republic,* "know very well that it will not do to allow their poor, ignorant followers to become Americanized before they can use their political influence. If they do, there is some chance of losing their sympathy and support."[6]

The political appeal of nativism was in its ability not only to play on many Americans' fear of dependency but also, apparently, to connect diverse developments in American life to "explain" to the satisfaction of uncomfortable natives why personal autonomy seemed under siege. Take, for example, the way midcentury nativist propagandists stressed a special kind of autonomy, intellectual autonomy. The 1856 nativist tract *A Defense of the American Policy* tied the inalienable right to liberty in the Declaration of Independence to freedom of *thought.* Nativists played out this theme in a variety of ways. For instance, one form was the nativist fraternities' endorsement of free public libraries which could support the informed citizen and encourage individual self-improvement. But it also spilled over into nativist dogma about the relationship of church and state. Although we usually associate mid-nineteenth-century nativism with militant Protestantism, serious nativist thinkers were not hesitant to attack the cozy relationship between leading Protestant denominations and the government. Thomas Whitney, for one, argued that whatever the denomination, "the first effect of a combination of the affairs of religion with the affairs of State policy, is to restrain the consciences of men." Theology was "speculative," he argued, and therefore involved a surrender of intellectual autonomy to emotion and faith. Politics, on the other hand, "has been a speculative science, but is so no longer. The experiment of the American republic . . . has abolished all doubt, and settled all speculation."[7] Hence, citizens, operating within the known parameters of American republicanism, could allow their intellect free rein. For that reason, Whitney repeatedly denounced Protestant intrusion into what he believed was the sphere of government. He called on ministers to cease speaking on "political" topics from the pulpit. He criticized the exemption of church property from taxation, using as his example New York City's famous Trinity Episcopal Church. And he editorialized against the efforts of Baptist and Dutch Reformed officials to garner public tax support for denominational schools.[8]

Nativists struck a particularly responsive chord when they related the intellectual autonomy of the individual to public schooling. We have already seen how the economic hard times of the late 1830s and early 1840s caused many working-class Americans to place exaggerated hope in the ability of public education to provide economic security and mobility to the next generation. If anything, homage to the public school increased as the nation grew and became more complex. As the *Williamsburg Daily Times* put it in an 1854 editorial, "Our public schools offer an escape from the evils of ignorance. . . . A thing of vast moment—they overcome the social differences which wealth and cultivation imposes upon the intercourse of men and gather each day into intimate relations the children of every rank in our society, and of different national origins, and of various and conflicting creeds. . . . We regard our public schools as beyond all price and praise."[9] Such sentiments set the stage for a paranoid watchfulness that was sure to interpret any proposed alternative to the public school as a direct assault on it. Renewed efforts on the part of Catholic parents to have public funds directed to denominational schools during 1852 and 1853 in states like Pennsylvania and Michigan were seized on by nativist activists not only as examples of religious imperialism but as challenges to "freedom of thought" itself.[10]

In fact, nativists could find no end to the connection between immigrants—particularly Roman Catholic immigrants—and threats to the intellectual autonomy of the individual and were able to make much political capital out of it. Respectable, educated middle-class Protestants might not feel much attraction to coarse anti-Catholic street preachers like Daniel Parsons or the "Angel" Gabriel or to the wild slanders of the former Italian priest Alessandro Gavazzi (whose speaking tour in America in 1853 was sponsored by the American and Foreign Christian Union, which had connections with nativist fraternities). But when such rabble-rousers succeeded in provoking outrage from offended Catholics, the Protestant bourgeoisie reacted quickly and affirmatively to nativist charges that the protesters were attacking independence of mind and freedom of expression.[11] In this environment, it was easy for nativist ideologues to interweave the defense of public schools and of free expression with a new outbreak of Protestant anxiety about free access to scripture. Use of the Bible in the curriculum of the public schools, which had been an issue in the 1830s and 1840s, continued to be a political hot potato after midcentury. As late as 1858, school officials in New York City were fighting over whether Bible reading could be left to the discretion of local district officials or had to be defended citywide. Significantly, the press described this as a contest over "free" education. But the issue also spread beyond the schools; nativists made much of the fact that the Roman Catholic church had banned the distribution of unauthorized Bibles in Europe and that, in the mid-1850s, the government of Tuscany took legal steps to suppress non-Catholic Bibles. Nativists supplied an interpretation which attributed all of this to Catholic and European resistance to individual freedom.[12]

The expression that the (Protestant) Michigan *Christian Herald* used to describe the conduct of a group of rebellious trustees seeking increased lay control of the affairs of St. Mary's Catholic Church in Detroit was "manly independency." And when the bishop of the diocese excommunicated the ringleaders, it was taken by suspicious minds among the Protestant public as an assault on "independency" itself. Slanders about Catholics that had been kicking around since the early part of the century (like Samuel F. B. Morse's charge that immigrant Catholics were "human priest-controlled machines") now took on new meaning as nativists grafted them to an alleged pattern of Catholic resistance to individual autonomy. This contributed to a suspicion that almost everything the American Catholic church did was part of a larger assault on personal freedom. In Michigan in 1852, this became an issue in a debate over taxation of church-owned property and in competition between public and private charity.[13] A few years earlier in Mississippi (where there were only nine priests in eleven parishes statewide as late as 1853—scarcely a threat to Protestant dominance), a tremendous row ensued when the Roman Catholic church sought to purchase and reopen the defunct Jefferson College. Protestant clergymen took to their pulpits to denounce the surrender of an institution named for the author of the Declaration of Independence to an allegedly authoritarian organization. The depth of this hostility can be gauged by a headline in the *Jackson Mississippian* about the conversion of a southern Episcopal clergyman to Roman Catholicism: "Bishop Ives a Pervert to Rome!"[14] Likewise, new anxieties about nuns and convents were expressed aboveground in a series of official inquiries by nativist state legislators in Massachusetts, Pennsylvania, and Michigan and underground by mob threats in South Carolina, Rhode Island, and Louisiana. These all played on the fear that Catholic sisterhood was depriving women of their individual liberty.

When the pope deputed Gaetano Bedini as nuncio to resolve conflicts between the American clergy and defiant lay trustees over control of local church property in the mid-1850s, it was taken by many as confirmation of nativist allegations that an international conspiracy was afoot to impose Roman authoritarianism on the United States. Nativist publicists could dredge up all sorts of alleged confirming evidence. Much was made of the fact, for instance, that by 1854 the United States had 40 Catholic bishops, archbishops, and cardinals whereas the larger Catholic population of Ireland was organized into only 28 dioceses.[15] People were apt to read what they wanted into information about church growth and decline, such as data from Massachusetts showing that the number of Roman Catholic churches increased from 1 to 88 in the five decades after 1810 while the once-dominant Congregational churches had declined from 64 percent to 32 percent of all Christian houses of worship. People anxious for many reasons about personal autonomy and already predisposed to lend credence to nativist accusations were not reassured by the efforts of the administration of Pius IX—widely reported in the American press—to restore greater papal authority within the church and over the Italian papal states.[16]

Nativist denunciation of Roman Catholicism as incompatible with freedom of belief and expression set the stage for distinctions between the "religious" church and the "political" church, between "native" Catholicism and "foreign" or "immigrant" Catholicism, between "American" Catholics and "Roman" Catholics. In each case the former, "mere professors of the Catholic religion," were held by nativists to be resistant to the "authority" and "supremacy" to which the latter were allegedly addicted. This allowed nativists to deny any religious prejudice, as Thomas Whitney did in a *Republic* editorial of 1851 on "Romanism": "if any reader should imagine that we are about to enter upon a crusade against the Catholic *religion,* as such, he will be greatly mistaken. We look at nothing in this issue but *political* tendencies." Accordingly, nativists could eat their cake and have it too, posing as defenders of individual conscience while badgering Catholics.[17]

National Autonomy and Personal Autonomy
in Nativist Thought

Popular anxieties about autonomy also gave new life and political potency to old nativist charges about the subversive designs of European states on the American republic. The nativist press renewed speculation, which had been common during the 1830s, that European monarchies were "dumping" the worst of their populations on American shores as an act of aggression, unloading people who not only lacked the independent character required of American citizens but also diluted the vote and the public voice of native citizens by their sheer numbers. "In five years from the day of their landing," one nativist editorial predicted, "each one of the emancipated felons will become . . . what no native American felon could become—a *citizen,* in good standing, invested with political rights and powers equal to those enjoyed by the most upright and intelligent, and qualified, not only to vote, but to stand behind the ballot-box, and be the arbiter and judge of the right of others to deposit a ballot." Not content to work at only one end of the social spectrum, nativist activists looked closely for any sign of intrusion in American affairs by European diplomatic officials or other notables. The British ambassador to the United States in the early 1850s, Henry Lytton Bulwer, came under especially heavy criticism in the nativist press for having "presumed to enter the arena of American politics" by endorsing a presidential contender.[18] This, too, could be portrayed as an assault on American independence, individual and national.

Historians have characteristically underemphasized the hypersensitivity of midcentury American nativists to international—especially European—developments and the ability of political nativism to milk popular anxieties about American national independence. It had been characteristic of nativist boilerplate for decades to incorporate into its rhetoric the wording of George Washington's farewell address about the danger of "entangling alliances" to American independence.[19] But since the end of the War of 1812 and the explosive expansion of the United States across the North American continent (abetted by a brief and exhilarating war with Mexico in the 1840s), there had been little to make the American public very mindful of these sentiments. During the late 1840s and early 1850s, however, European affairs attracted renewed American attention. Political unrest in Europe, culminating in the liberal "revolutions" of 1848, was taken by many Americans as a validation of American republicanism and a repudiation of European monarchism. There was particular enthusiasm for the Hungarian revolutionary Louis Kossuth and, in nativist circles, initial support for his visit to the United States in 1851-1852. Interestingly, nativists were especially encouraged by the widely shared impression that Kossuth was coming to stay—that the "distinguished exile" was seeking to become an American citizen.[20] This prospect not only flattered Americans' image of the republic as a haven for those who had fought tyrants but also conformed to nativists' argument that citizenship should be conferred on the foreign-born only individually, taking special merit into account. Kossuth seemed a worthy candidate.

But nativists soon soured on Kossuth, and their reaction was symptomatic of a growing nervousness that political turmoil in Europe— even when inspired by "republicans"—was likely to involve the United States in situations that would restrict its liberty of action. Henry Clay won nativist hearts when he publicly lectured Kossuth that the United States best served itself, Hungary, and the world by staying out of the "tangled web of European politics." And as it became increasingly apparent that the object of Kossuth's visit was not refuge but financial and diplomatic support for Magyar nationalism, the Order of United Americans' *Republic* offered the caution that "the asylum we offer to [this] person, is misconstrued—our sympathies are distorted into an alliance, and with an egotism unparalleled, he proceeds to dictate the foreign policy of the United States." Nativists craftily associated the loss of national freedom of action that might be produced by international adventurism with loss of personal independence, arguing that even private funds pledged to Kossuth might be better spent in "liberating" the needy at home: the poor, the widow, the orphan, the aged, the Mexican War veteran, and, especially, the "surviving relatives of that *Revolutionary* patriot who died in the service of his country, and whose helpless daughter dwells in yonder garret."[21] Nativist publicists expressed the same skepticism about the Italian nationalist Giuseppe Mazzini, though they actually had kind words for the Irish Catholic Thomas Francis Meagher, who escaped from a British prison but turned down the invitation of the New York Council to a triumphal reception.[22]

Nativists' anxiety about national obligations in the international arena also made them skeptical about the wilder American expansionist schemes that abounded in the 1850s. The *Republic*'s Whitney repeatedly ran editorials denouncing American filibusters who sought to seize Cuba from Spain, although he professed a desire to see the Cubans freed to pursue republicanism. But it was the nativist argument, anyway, that the only people who could manage republicanism were those who had shown their capacity for it by independence of temper, and, consequently, in the case of Cuba, "when she determines to adopt that course, she will doubtless find ready sympathy."[23] Nativists thought they saw a relevant example in France, which had just "elected" an emperor in Napoléon III. "The people of France possessed under the Republic of 1841, more liberty than they were capable of employing and enjoying rationally," wrote Whitney, and, unready for freedom, they "voted away their own liberty." This, he insisted, should make Americans cautious about claiming that the United States had an obligation to assist other nations take the road to freedom: "Just as the 'Yankee nation' was about to republicanize all Europe at a single puff, republican France took a fancy to throw a somerset and come up a despotism."[24] During his term as a Whig president, the future Know Nothing presidential candidate Millard Fillmore won nativist hearts by reminding Congress that it should "remember that Revolutions do not always establish freedom." Foreign policy, nativist activists argued, was best restricted to opening up trade to American merchants, manufacturers, and farmers. One of the chief things that commended Millard Fillmore to nativist political strategists in the mid-1850s was that during his administration he had aggressively pursued agreements with nations like Japan which were restricted to eliminating barriers to commerce.[25]

Nativist activists—who were always looking for revealing patterns in national and international affairs—were both horrified and gratified when European political exiles began to take advantage of the United States' ethnic diversity. They were horrified because this seemed to illustrate what they feared most about immigrants: that they would not become "Americans." On the other hand, they were gratified because it seemed not to be accidental: there were conspiracies afoot, just as nativists had been reporting. Louis Kossuth's appeals to German-Americans brought howls of protest from nativist quarters over what was taken to be his effort to have the United States intervene in Hungarian affairs and to have Germans in America "compel it to do so, through their influence at the ballot box." By late 1852, nativist publications had taken to calling Kossuth a "viper" who was intent on "coercing the government and the people." This was a code that was sure to be understood by people sensitive about influence and coercion in their own lives.[26] It was easy for nativists to tie these allegations of foreign intrusion to charges that the American ballot box was being corrupted by naturalized voters misled by outside attachments and ulterior motives. At least that is what they tried to do when German immigrant liberals in 1854 announced a "Louisville platform" which condemned European monarchism but also American "race and class privilege" and American racial slavery. A "Freie Verein" established in San Antonio, Texas, at about the same time came in for similar abuse for announcing political goals which included support for a homestead act and elimination of racial slavery.[27]

Know Nothing anxiety about the activities of refugees from the failed European revolutions of 1848 was rooted less in ideological disagreement than in hypersensitivity about national "dependency." Good evidence is the similar anxiety they displayed about the effects of illiberal "reactionary" forces on the European continent. In fact, nativist ideologues often linked the two, stressing the need to preserve the United States' "free and rational system of government from the radical influences of a lawless European democracy on the one hand and the retrograde influences of aristocracy and legitimacy (so called) on the other." In both cases, concern focused on whether European unrest could force American engagement in foreign affairs in a way that would limit the nation's freedom of action. Accordingly, Russian "aristocracy" made nativists squirm when the Russian ambassador to Brazil visited Haiti and Mexico, potentially stirring up trouble in two of the United States' close neighbors. Always seeking connections between events which seemed to have explanatory power, Know Nothings noted that the combination of Russia, Austria, and Prussia at the Frankfurt Diet was more than a response to liberal unrest in Europe; it was a gathering to find "the most effective means of extinguishing civil liberty all over the world." And they noted darkly that reactionary forces in Europe seemed to be in combination with a reinvigorated Roman Catholic church, pointing out examples of civil enforcement of church policy—state and church combined to hem in individual liberty.[28]

Commitment to individual autonomy placed organized nativism in a strong position to capitalize on popular anxieties about unrest in Europe, saber-rattling adventurism in the Caribbean, and foreign "intrusion" into American politics, but it could also—if strictly adhered to—divide the potential nativist political constituency. Such was the case with the nativist response to the "temperance" issue of the mid-1850s. Nativist rhetoric was full of denunciations of "the sounds of coarse revelry issuing from the 'Wein Halles' and 'Lager-bier shops'" of

German-American neighborhoods, to say nothing of the liquor-dispensing "groceries" associated with Irish-American communities; but it is not always clear whether alcohol itself or its cultural context was the chief object of nativist hostility.[29] Often, historians have been too quick to link midcentury temperance activism with nativist activism. To be sure, the American temperance crusade, which was moving in the direction of legislated prohibition, bore some superficial similarities to nativism, having a distinctly Protestant, anti-Catholic flavor (although there was a parallel Catholic temperance movement). Because of these similarities, some scholars of the late antebellum period have assumed that the movements were almost one and the same. Leo Hershkowitz has made the colorful assertion that in New York City, the temperance movement "brought together nativists, Whigs, do-gooders, anti-Catholics, anti-immigrants, Fundamentalists and assorted sour apples—generally the most conservative anti-urban, anti-democratic elements."[30] All of these types could probably be found in the ranks of temperance, but this is a far cry from making a case that the two movements marched hand in hand or that enthusiasm for temperance was one of the things that brought people into political nativism. Several historians, in fact, have noticed that the leading figures in temperance political parties (which sprang up in many locales) rarely emerged as nativist officeholders. Some—like Dale Baum—have even documented hostility between the crusty craftsmen and workers who made up the backbone of the nativist rank and file and the more genteel participants in the temperance movement. As Baum puts it, "prohibition . . . cut across the lines of nativism and frequently exposed the inner tensions" of Know Nothingism.[31]

Indeed, temperance was a potent political issue in the early 1850s. Beginning with Maine in 1851 (hence the term "Maine law"), state after state across the north passed prohibitory legislation affecting the sale of alcoholic beverages. Even in those states which did not install such a law—like Pennsylvania and Ohio—the battle was close and spun off other legislation which made the purchase of liquor more difficult. But in almost every case, temperance was an issue without a party home and, in fact, divided men who voted together on other issues. Both states with Whig legislatures and states with Democratic legislatures approved "Maine laws," and most political historians argue that the major parties tried to avoid taking a stand on the matter.[32] So did the American party, despite the popular association of immigrant cultures with alcoholic beverages. Partly, this was just good politics.[33] Vot-

ers' attitudes toward temperance were so personal that it was difficult
to determine whether embracing it was a net vote-getter or vote-loser.
But beyond that, legislated prohibition (or even regulation) was quite
at odds with nativist dogma, which stressed individual independence.
Recognizing that, nativist ideologists and political leaders often went
out of their way—sometimes dramatically—to show that nativism and
temperance were not the same thing. According to his political biographer, Gregg Cantrell, the North Carolina Know Nothing Kenneth
Rayner "would down a 'stiff toddy' from the speaker's stand to demonstrate the party's correctness on the liquor question." This was more
than a case of practical politics in the south, where temperance
activism was weak. The New Yorker Thomas R. Whitney, of the Order
of United Americans, calculatingly passed along to the readers of his
Republic that he had received a welcome "basket of champagne" from
one of OUA's brethren who ran an emporium offering such delec-
tables, sneering that "teetotalers will take warning from this notice, and
keep away from his premises." And although Henry Gardner, the
Know Nothing governor of Massachusetts, signed a prohibitory law
passed by the legislature, he also was a conspicuous public drinker and
had promoted wine production in Massachusetts.[34]

For many nativists, legislated temperance was simply another effort
to hem in the individual and take away autonomy—freedom to choose
to drink or not drink. For just the same reason, nativist leaders periodically denounced legislation against gambling, as when such a law was
proposed for New York in 1851. "Reforming the world," wrote a contributor to a nativist periodical, "will never be done by . . . committees.
It must be individual work, every man reforming himself. . . . The laws
have no influence upon the man who does right; he does so because he
feels it wrong and abhorrent to do otherwise." This was a characteristic
nativist stance and was repeatedly endorsed by ideologues like Whitney, who preferred encouraging citizens to attend an entertaining and
"moral" drama like the popular play *The Bottle,* because he believed it
was "exercising a more wholesome influence in the cause of temperance than all the Maine Laws that can be adopted."[35] Not surprisingly,
temperance activists often regarded political nativism with suspicion if
not outright hostility. Sometimes, they merely expressed dismay that
Know Nothings could not be counted on to stand in unbroken ranks
behind temperance. At other times, they attacked the backbone of
nativism—the fraternal orders—as "un-Christian." In any event, there
is plenty of evidence from states as far apart as New York and Iowa that

temperance voters did not necessarily become nativist voters or vice versa. In fact, they were frequently at odds.[36]

Nativist reluctance to embrace prohibitionism helps us understand the political appeal of Know Nothingism in the south, where the foreign-born—in most locales—were few. Here was an entire region of the United States which placed a special premium on both individual and sectional autonomy. It is not surprising that in states where the ultimate loss of autonomy was so glaringly visible in the form of racial slavery, (white) men should be anxious to advertise their own freedom to make choices for themselves. It is undoubtedly in part because of this that the south proved hostile to most antebellum reform movements—like temperance—which seemed to restrict autonomy. But "reform" also was taken to challenge regional autonomy. If behavior connected with drinking, for example, could be regulated by law, then why not behavior connected with the control of labor? If temperance or observance of the sabbath or the schooling of children was a legitimate object of legislation, then why not the preservation or extension of slavery? The more effectively nativism stressed "autonomy," the more appeal it would have in the south. It might even appear, as it did for a while in the mid-1850s, as a defender of "southern rights," and its leading spokesmen in the region attempted to position it just that way. In 1855, Gile Hillyer, a Know Nothing candidate for Congress from Mississippi, artfully wove resistance to the Fugitive Slave Law in Wisconsin and support for the emerging antislavery Republican party to that state's population of immigrant voters and their "foreign" ideas about what should be regulated by law.[37]

But personal autonomy was more than a preoccupation of the south and southerners, and it is useful to inquire about to whom it appealed in the north—where, after all, it became much stronger politically. Some close scrutiny of the Order of United Americans, the oldest of the major nativist fraternities, is useful. Although the first grand sachem of the OUA, John Harper, ran a major publishing house and the second, Simeon Baldwin, was a leading figure in insurance and investments, the third, Thomas Whitney—at the time of his election— was an engraver. Up to the end of the 1850s, he was followed in office by a rice broker, ship's grocer, auctioneer, tailor, truss-maker, clerk, upholsterer, and frame gilder. A directory of OUA's Alpha Chapter in 1848 reported the occupations of 70 percent of its membership of 220. There were 45 men employed in law and medicine, banking, insurance, real estate, and manufacturing (just two of the latter), but they were far outnumbered by clerks, craftsmen, retailers, restaurateurs, and men in maritime occupations. In fact, the two largest categories were storekeepers and skilled craftsmen. It is probably too easy to confuse OUA's small group of founders with its subsequent membership or with the citizens who later became the political base of Know Nothingism.[38] Studies of voters' support for the American party in states as diverse as Maryland and Iowa suggest that political nativism was especially attractive to small proprietors, clerks, and neighborhood professionals. These, of course, were exactly the sort to value individual autonomy—and perhaps to be most sensitive to perceived threats. They were neither captains of industry commanding others nor unskilled laborers who were resigned to being commanded. Here was the real secret of nativist political success in the 1850s: matching a message to a constituency.[39]

The nativist message, of course, had to do with "nationality," immigration, and naturalization, but it also had to do with other things touching on "autonomy," and in this was both power and vulnerability. As suited a movement that built on a fraternal base populated by craftsmen and shopkeepers, midcentury nativism went out of its way to defend opportunities in manufacturing and sales for petty capitalists. Nativist literature was consistent in criticizing the taste of "fashionable" Americans for European goods, and in 1855 the Know Nothing governor of Massachusetts announced a "buy American" publicity campaign. Know Nothingism also supported tariffs on imported manufactured goods; this is sometimes taken by historians as nothing more than a carryover from the Whig party, but it fit entirely with nativists' defense of economic opportunities for American laborers and merchants.[40] Some nativist spokesmen went much farther, criticizing what they took to be misguided public attention to "foreign productions" in art, literature, "eloquence," "mechanics," and drama. This was not merely a patriotic sentiment but reflected a conviction that these, too, were a basis for professions that offered income and hence "autonomy" to many Americans. OUA's Whitney continued to think of himself as an engraver, an artist, and a printer well after he had become, successively, a publisher and a congressman.[41] He repeatedly pointed out that one of his objectives in publishing the *Republic* was to show that "there is many a flower of literature in the prolific American field, 'blushing unseen,'" and he drew some attention in New York City by attacking the city Art Union for mismanaging funds intended to underwrite "subscription" exhibitions in support of local artists. Significantly, one of his last acts as a congressman was to criticize a new Coinage Act for putting the Treasury in the engraving business and taking work away from independent artists and engravers. This would, he argued, "prostitute the Government into a common workshop, in competition with the mechanics of our land." Whitney's OUA was particularly successful in attracting as members well-known figures in the New York arts community, like the engraver William Walcutt and the actor Edwin Forrest.[42]

There is little question that "old" political names showed up in the "new" Know Nothing political party of the mid-1850s. It took only the first glimmers of success for Know Nothingism to begin to attract from both of the major parties "establishment" politicians who saw the appeal of nativism to large chunks of the electorate. It is all too easy to conclude from this that the Know Nothings were primarily a "conservative" party committed strictly to the restoration of a supposedly better past. This is a fallacy that flies in the face of much evidence that the popularity of nativism with its voter base was closely related to its willingness to challenge a status quo in which dependence and limitation seemed to be the lot of more and more Americans. In fact, consistent with its championship of individual autonomy, there was a significant "populist" element to midcentury political nativism, particularly an economic populism that was likely to make conservatives and "better" people of all kinds uneasy. Defense of economic autonomy grew out of the nativist fraternal orders of the late 1840s and fit with the fraternities' emphasis on self-help and brotherly support. The constitution of a local chapter of Pennsylvania's Order of United American Mechanics (OUAM), a fraternity which appealed particularly to workingmen, spelled out the brotherly objectives that contributed to individual autonomy: "to assist each other in obtaining employment," "to encourage each other in business in preference to others," to provide a sickness and funeral fund, to make available resources to widows and orphans, and "to aid members who, through Providence, may become incapacitated from following their usual avocations, in obtaining situations suitable to their afflictions." OUAM's motto, "Honesty, Industry, and Sobriety," likewise capitalized on the notion that individuals should be responsible for their own opportunities. Significantly, after OUAM was founded in Philadelphia in 1845, its first council took the name "Enterprise" and its third "Perseverance." At the same time, as Bruce Laurie points out, OUAM "also vowed to employ 'every honorable means to obtain a fair day's wage for a fair day's work' so that workers could 'support themselves and their families in comfort and respectability.' These means included pressure on employers to hire only native-born Americans. They also included encouraging consumers to patronize American craftsmen and to boycott businesses owned by foreigners in the hope that employers would increase their business and then pay better wages."[43] To that end, OUAM supported a landing fee or head tax on immigrants, a so-called "working man's tariff."

Not surprisingly, a movement with these kinds of objectives attracted men who were also active in the tradesmen's movement; and in holiday parades workingmen's and nativists' floats and marchers were almost indistinguishable. No wonder nativist political candidates went out of their way to identify themselves as skilled craftsmen or independent small businessmen.[44] More extreme was the rhetoric of the Philadelphia-based Brotherhood of the Union, which described the workingman's pursuit of a living wage as a "war of labor." Founded by George Lippard, who attracted public attention in the 1840s as the author of what have sometimes been described as "Christian socialist" novels, this fraternal order stressed a combination of self-culture and hostility to trends within industrial capitalism increasing the ranks of dependent wage laborers.[45]

Although OUAM treated the skilled workers in its membership as independent entrepreneurs and seemed to go out of its way to discourage the notion that there was any fundamental difference between "big" businessmen and "small" businessmen, nativists could display a deep hostility to employers they perceived as furthering economic and technological processes that were shrinking workers' opportunities and compromising their independence. Interestingly enough, some of the earliest and most intense hostility came from affiliates of the nativist societies whose dependence was most acute—women. As early as 1845, chapters of United Daughters of America (UDA) were organized, some of which became affiliated with the Order of United Americans (based in New York) and others with OUAM (based in Philadelphia). These were more than the usual "female auxiliaries" that developed around other antebellum social movements. They could be counted on to offer the obligatory praise of hearth and home, treating members, for example, to lectures on the moral influence provided by George Washington's mother and reminding them that the character of the child was fixed by the actions of the parent. But they also criticized the low wages and deteriorating working conditions for women in the mechanized spinning and weaving industries and the sweated garment trades, called for expanded educational opportunities for girls and young women, campaigned against prostitution, and denounced the effects of male intemperance on family relationships.[46] While these were fairly advanced (and politically risky) positions for women's organizations, they seem to have been embraced by the mainstream male fraternities as in line with the nativist rhetoric of personal independence and self-development. Advertisements for nativist lectures and rallies often included special invitations to "ladies."[47]

It would be convenient if we could write off OUAM and the more strident chapters of UDA as radical antebellum nativists, out of step with the "conservatives." But we cannot. There is too much evidence that they not only shared the main themes of the other nativist orders but also were actively courted by them. Throughout 1851 and 1852, Thomas R. Whitney of the Order of United Americans—the nativist fraternity most closely associated with conservative Whigs—kept up a campaign in the pages of his *Republic* to bring about a merger of OUA and OUAM. He was a popular speaker at OUAM meetings and advocated joining OUA, OUAM, UDA, United Sons of America, and the Sons of Liberty into "one great American Order." Key leaders of OUAM offered compliments to OUA, and their own plan for union. One went so far as to propose converting OUAM councils into OUA chapters.[48]

Whitney himself charged that the independent American worker needed to be defended against an emerging "aristocracy of wealth" as well as against immigrant competitors. After all, he reasoned, what drove down wages was employers, usually native, who took advantage of a growing labor supply—not the supply itself. And at a time when middle-class New Yorkers were celebrating the opening of A. T. Stewart's fabulous new department store, Whitney brought the attention of the *Republic*'s readers to "the blood and flesh of . . . wives, widows, and children . . . coined into gold" in attic tailoring operations which kept Stewart's shelves full—and called for a boycott! Likewise, while Whitney had numerous friends "on change" (the stock and mercantile exchanges), he wondered about the fairness of a proposed antigambling law that would outlaw the recreation of the poor but leave untouched "Wall-street, the private saloons of the money aristocracy," and its kind of gambling for "money or property. Nativist populism also showed up in public support for the establishment of New York City's Central Park ("This is a good investment. The people who really pay the taxes, with the sweat of their foreheads; the men, women, and children who labor to swell the coffers of the millionaire, are entitled at least to God's gifts, fresh air and exercise"); and in Philadelphia nativist politicians pursued legislation to promote public health and safety through construction standards for housing, factories, and public transportation.[49]

"Nationality," Immigrants, Ethnicity, and Race

This concern for individual "autonomy" showed up in quite a different form in nativists' charges that Americans' health and safety—the fundamental prerequisites for any meaningful kind of individual freedom—were jeopardized by the growing ranks of the foreign-born. This was a kind of populism, too, but it was aimed at other "workers" rather than at capitalists. In the larger eastern cities, public order *was* threatened by economic change. The rise of wage labor and the collapse of traditional apprenticeship did undermine some of the traditional forms of social control—as did the very size of cities like New York, Philadelphia, and Baltimore. Young men and casual laborers attracted the most attention, and it was all too easy to associate these with immigrants. Immigrant populations like the Irish were disproportionately young and male and unlikely—at first—to be in long-term employment relationships.[50] Moreover, the visibility of first-generation immigrants made them targets for overstretched urban police forces eager to show by their arrest records (even if these arrests were for the most petty infractions) that they were doing their best to maintain order. Not surprisingly, in major immigrant centers like New York City, up to half of all the names on police blotters were Irish. According to nativists, these facts demonstrated that the foreign-born were ill-suited to handle freedom from traditional European social restraints. Nativists also argued that crime and violence infringed on the liberty of the law-abiding native-born. Particularly when immigrants demonstrated against nativist demagogues or anti-Catholic street preachers, Know Nothings treated it as an assault against individual freedom of speech itself.[51]

Nativists' response to alleged immigrant lawlessness was militant. Most of the nativist fraternities had at least paramilitary organization, and many actually established "military" units—sometimes affiliated with the local militia, though sometimes not. The humorist Ned Buntline created an armed "Guard of Liberty" in Maine in the mid-1850s, allegedly to defend Know Nothing speakers; and the Order of United Americans supported the American Rifles, a militia company "composed entirely of the 'sons of the soil,' native born Americans."[52] Sometimes these were not far removed from urban gangs (like New York's infamous Bowery Boys) that claimed to be "native" and sought out combat with their "foreign" counterparts. That nativist ideologues could turn even these into defenders of American "liberty" is evident in their praise for "Butcher Boy" Poole of the Bowery Boys, who was killed in 1855 in a brawl with the "Irish" gang of John Morrisey. It is little surprise, then, that nativists sought to make much of any evidence they could find of poverty or disease among immigrants, arguing that even these sapped the freedoms of the native-born by affecting the quality of life, driving up public charity expenses, and making citizens "slaves" to taxation.[53]

In the late 1840s and the 1850s, nativism wrapped its concerns about autonomy and its anxieties about the foreign-born and their offspring together in its promotion of "nationality." Mordecai Noah, a New York newspaperman with loose connections to leading figures in the Order of United Americans, captured nativist anxieties exactly when he opined on Washington's Birthday in 1851 that "the truth is, we want nationality." John Hancock Lee, an activist in Pennsylvania's United Sons of America, offered further clarification by calling for the development of "national characteristics" among the American people. Thomas R. Whitney asserted that there was just "one idea" to express what would give "to the people of the United States a distinct *nationality*," and that was "independence." Such "independence" was defined broadly. It could be independence from "any allegiance or obligation of any description to any foreign prince, potentate, or power," as the 1856 American party national platform put it. Or it could be independence from illiteracy and lack of education. Or it could be the freedom from economic or intellectual subservience that defined the "manly" republican citizen. Only individual autonomy, the argument ran, could ensure that a republic of equally influential, responsible, and unmanipulable citizens would survive and flourish.[54]

Nativists, of course, found the foreign-born (or others they identified as "foreign") lacking in one, some, or all of these forms of independence. What sharpened their hostility was a perception that "foreigners" did not crave republican independence and even resisted it. This, at least, is what seemed to lie behind the Know Nothing assault on "hyphenism"— long before the term entered colloquial American speech. "If you are

Americans, say so," insisted a nativist publicist, "but don't choose a mongrel name, as American-Celt, Irish-American, or American-Irish. Don't stand on the fence; pop down on one side the other. You have shown your country; stick to her, and every honest American will glory in your spunk."[55] To nativists, continued identification with another nation in name betrayed unwillingness to shed the shackles of monarchy, religion, or culture which allegedly held Europeans in thrall. Moreover, they treated the persistence of "foreign" clubs and societies as evidence not just of timidity about throwing off dependence but of cultivated resistance to independence. Thus nativist publications took particular offense at the formation of St. George's Societies for the English-born, Societies of St. Patrick for the Irish, St. David's associations for the Welsh, Scotch Thistle Clubs, and fraternities for German immigrants such as the Sons of Hermann and the Order of Harugari. OUA's *Republic* especially mocked New York's St. George's Society for the subservience displayed in styling members as "majesty's most dutiful and loyal subjects."[56]

When some of these ethnic organizations took the form of militia companies, nativist hostility was fanned to a white heat. Purportedly, here was an armed defense of dependence itself, even if the logic was tortuous. Consider the *Republic*'s conclusion about "Irish Military Companies": "So, then, an Irishman cannot serve against the Pope; hence, so long as the services of his followers anywhere are likely to aid his cause, he will let them fight; but when they are against it, he will forbid them. What kind of troops will they make then for Protestant America, whose most dangerous foe is the church Political?" It made quite a display to put this all together as the editors of the *Jersey City Daily Sentinel and Advertiser* did in 1854:

Foreign tongues are heard on every hand. Foreign newspapers flood the country. Districts of foreigners, townships of foreigners, counties of foreigners, with foreign hearts, and foreign manners, and foreign institutions, dot the whole country. Foreign quarters are found in our cities, and bands of armed foreigners parade our streets with foreign insignia. Foreign priests employ the thunders of a foreign politico-religious power to force from the hands of legal trustees the property of American citizens.

These, it was argued, were marks of studied dependence, a disinclination to throw off old roles and relationships which could prevent immigrants from becoming reliable citizens.[57]

The nature of its plaint about "foreigners" made nativism of necessity assimilationist. If foreigners were to be rid of old dependencies, then they must become more "American." This was no easy matter, nativists agreed:

Man is a creature of habit and custom, wherever, and under whatever auspices his lot is cast. Opinions, morals, usages, are all the fruits of training and education, and all these, by training and education, become, not impressions merely, but absolute convictions, or what is sometimes called second nature. To root out these convictions, to annul this second nature, to unleash the mind of what has been learned through years of precept, example and discipline, is not the work of a day or of a few years."[58]

In fact, nativists frequently charged that the main problem with mass immigration was that it worked "to prevent the assimilation . . . with the American people . . . [and] to preserve and perpetuate the habits, customs, peculiarities, and distinctive characteristics of the immigrants." The American party platform of 1855 claimed that "Americans only shall rule America" but acknowledged that proper Americans were to be made not only by "birth" but also by "education and training."[59]

Nativists actually had both ideological and practical reasons for this assimilationist stance. As a matter of ideology, it was illogical to hold that "independence" was not achievable for most persons in a nation which had among its core values the idea that no one (at least no white person) was totally bound by the conditions of birth. If anything, the American nation was to unlock individual potential and replace inherited suitability for citizenship with demonstrated accomplishment. Moreover, if the United States was to have an ennobling international purpose, to function as what Ernest Lee Tuveson has called a "redeemer nation" for the rest of the world, then it had to show both that outsiders could be reshaped into effective Americans and that other nations could emulate its republican form. Nativists also had a pressing practical reason for advocating assimilation, which touched on the reason for the existence of the nativist fraternities. They supposed that someone had to distinguish between the appropriately independent, reliable American citizen and the dependent, unreliable would-be citizen, and that separating the sheep from the goats was the responsibility of a "national American association" like the Order of

United Americans or the Patriotic Order, Sons of America or the Order of United American Mechanics. For both reasons, ideological and practical, the politicized nativism of the 1850s rarely promoted outright restriction of immigration and, in fact, repeatedly pointed out that the United States was—as the 1856 Know Nothing platform put it—a "land of liberty and the asylum of the oppressed."[60]

Nativists clung to assimilationism even when division of opinion over its terms threatened to fracture the movement. During its one presidential campaign in 1856, the Know Nothing party called for revising the naturalization laws to require a "continued residence of twenty-one years" as an "indispensable requisite for citizenship."[61] This had been a nativist position since the 1830s and was predicated on the notion that it would take 21 years for an immigrant to duplicate the acculturation and political maturation of an American-born youth. A Know Nothing congressman—carrying this analogy with adolescence one step further—called it an "extended period of republican schooling." But for some nativists, even 21 years was far too generous; they questioned the whole concept of naturalization, wondering whether an immigrant could ever become a reliable participant in republican politics. "The word *naturalization*," one wrote, "may be appropriately called a *misnomer*, because the process of naturalization is one of the most *unnatural* of all proceedings." This technical procedure could legally invest an individual with specific "rights and privileges," but not with the "home sentiment" or natural patriotism which came effortlessly to those who were "natural to the soil and reared on its institutions."[62] According to this theory, there was a legitimate distinction between "resident" and "citizen," and it was possible to enjoy civil rights without political rights. Among the most vocal proponents of this view was the Order of United Americans. Its position was that the United States Congress should enact a "uniform naturalization law," binding on the states, which would provide that "no foreigner hereafter arriving in this country ... shall, upon any consideration whatever, become a naturalized citizen ... but that he shall, however, as a resident, be subject to, and receive the protection of our laws, and enjoy all the rights of a citizen, excepting that of the elective franchise, or the holding of office of high trust." The only exceptions, OUA argued, should be conferred (rarely) by Congress itself "only as a reward of individual merit." Why confer full citizenship after 5, 10, or even 21 years? If no harm was done to immigrants by making them wait 21 years, what harm could be done by withholding the franchise in perpe-

The Politics of Autonomy 139

tuity? The 21-year requirement was actively disputed at an "American" national convention which brought together representatives of the major nativist fraternal organizations at Trenton in 1852, and it was finally dropped from the "principles" adopted by that assembly.[63]

There was tremendous hazard in this debate. Not only did it set nativists against one another—in fact, it was a major stumbling block to the unification of several of the nativist fraternities—but it put at risk the identity that the nativist movement sought to cultivate between nativism and republicanism. Once a case had been made that a republic could function satisfactorily with some people kept outside the circle of citizenship, it was hard to maintain that the republic could work only if all (white) men were equally independent. In fact, the idea suggested that some sort of "virtual representation" in which some people could be trusted to vote for the benefit of all would be sufficient to guarantee republican rights. Occasionally, nativist ideologues made this explicit, distinguishing between the "social rights" of the resident and the "political rights" of the citizen and noting that what they believed immigrants sought most—economic betterment and equal protection of the laws—did not require giving them political responsibilities.[64] Although it is now clear to us that civil and political rights are inseparable, this was still considered debatable in the mid-nineteenth century, and, of course, it would take almost a century of experience by black Americans following the Civil War to convince a majority of their countrymen of this truism. But nativist politicians were capable of pushing much further than this, distinguishing not between blacks and whites but between categories of white men, leaving open the possibility that not only immigrants but also "unqualified" natives might reasonably be kept from the vote. Although he was not alone in saying it, Thomas R. Whitney was probably the most articulate proponent of a sort of oligarchic republicanism in which political rights were limited to the "qualified." In his *Defense of the American Policy,* a book-length apologia for the Know Nothing campaign of 1856, Whitney boldly admitted, "As I understand the term, I am no democrat. If democrat implies universal suffrage . . . without regard to the intelligence, the morals, or the principles of the man." And, true to nativist dogma, the chief characteristics Whitney called for in the suitable voter were "righteous independence" and "becoming self-respect," "qualifications . . . rarely found in one trained to submission and inbred with the sense of his own inferiority." This distinction obviously could be used to set apart the native from the foreign-born, but it could be taken much further—and OUA

loyalists besides Whitney seemed to do just that, arguing that a "republic" was not a "democracy"; that taxation without representation was
acceptable so long as the whole community was subject to uniform tax
laws and "the men who impose the taxes are among those who pay the
taxes . . . , so that the party who does not vote for a representative is
protected through the interest of the representative himself"; and that
not equality but inequality was the genius of American institutions.[65]
The founders, Whitney wrote, did not declare "all men 'equals' in intelligence, genius, or morals; that all men are equally competent for self-
government or even self-protection." In fact, he went further, insisting
that "inequality" was what made American society and government
work: "inequality is the source of action; action is the source of life,
thought, fruition." Whitney was not alone in making such pronouncements. William C. Rives of Virginia used much the same language in
offering up American party "republicanism" as an antidote to the
"extravagances and corruptions of modern Democracy."[66] Words like
these were bound to sound discordant to the larger number of mid-
nineteenth-century Americans who worshipped at the altar of equality
(albeit equality for white men only), but they were a logical extension
of nativist ideology and showed how far some nativist ideologues were
willing to go to keep that logic intact.

Extreme efforts to maintain ideological consistency created other
problems for political nativism beyond alienating droves of potential
voters. For as soon as it was conceded that nativity was not the key
issue in suitability for political enfranchisement, it opened an opportunity for all sorts of discord within nativist ranks. For example, what
about native-born Roman Catholics? Was their intellectual independence assured by their being *American* Catholics, as Know Nothings
in Louisiana argued? By a close vote, the Know Nothing National
Council of 1856 said "yes," admitting native Catholics to membership
in the Know Nothing order. But to some key nativist leaders like Kenneth Rayner of North Carolina, this was nothing short of a surrender of
basic Know Nothing principles. Did the Protestant faith of many antebellum immigrants ensure their independence of character? Not only
could nativist leaders be found to argue that Protestant immigrants
"were an honor to the country that gave them birth and are equally an
honor to the country they have made their home," but some went so
far as to organize nativist pressure groups uniting native and foreign-
born Protestants, like New York state's American Protestant Assembly. In many locations, the American Protestant Association of Orange

Irish marched proudly with nativist fraternal orders in patriotic parades, and naturalized German and Irish Protestant voters sometimes cast nativist ballots in states from Pennsylvania to Wisconsin.[67] Nativists' embrace of native-born Catholics or the Protestant foreign-born is frequently treated by historians as little more than cynical jockeying for votes, but it was actually quite consistent with their ideology.

The willingness—even enthusiasm—of nativists to make distinctions among white men flew in the face of contemporary racial mores, according to which the most important differences were between "white" and "black," "yellow" and "red." Even more discordant were the efforts of some nativists to follow the logic of their arguments to show that African-Americans and Native Americans could be *more* suitable candidates for citizenship than white immigrants. The *Republic*, for example, repeatedly ran columns praising aboriginal Americans' natural independence and nobility and commended every evidence of their interest in learning from whites. In Congress, OUA's Whitney was an indefatigable critic of the efforts of the federal government to grab Indian land and consistently contrasted the "savage" behavior of supposedly civilized white frontiersmen with the civility of supposedly savage Indians.[68] During the late 1840s and early 1850s, George Copway, a Canadian-born Ojibway activist and sometime Methodist minister, made a career of lobbying for Know Nothing support for the true "natives" of the land and for his scheme for an American Indian candidate state. In 1851 he was admitted to OUA.[69]

The *Republic* even denounced the African colonization movement (which proposed to put an end to slavery and race relations by resettling freed slaves in Africa), editorializing that American-born blacks were much more naturally patriotic and even better suited for full citizenship than most foreign-born whites and deserved to remain in America. In 1850, Alfred Brewster Ely, OUA's grand sachem in Massachusetts, went so far as to proclaim, "With far better reason to our mind, might the aborigines of our native forests, and the slaves of our southern plantations, particularly the latter, be admitted to all the rights of citizenship, than the foreigner, who comes among us with habits of mind and body, formed and fixed under influences so totally different from those he will encounter here."[70] This remarkable polemic appeared just at a time when nativists were trying to court conservative Whigs of the "silver gray" faction, who were particularly interested in conciliating southerners anxious about growing antislavery sentiment in the north. It demonstrates just how important ideology was to nativist leaders and the lengths to which they would go to try to preserve its "logical" integrity. It may also help explain why nativists divided over the wisdom of expansionist schemes of the 1850s that proposed extending the United States into the Caribbean or across the Rio Grande. With equal "logic" nativists could argue that it was a mistake to try to absorb a Catholic, "dependent" people or that (as the nativist sympathizer Sam Houston insisted) it was essential for the United States to spread "republican government and Anglo-Saxon Christianity" to people who had been the "victims of Spanish superstition." It is not the case, as historians have sometimes surmised, that nativists "came naturally to a racist rejection of tropical expansion."[71] Distinctions based on race played little part in nativist ideology; in fact, nativists' unwillingness to make more of race was doubtless a source of political weakness and part of their vulnerability to southern charges of "abolitionism," despite the American party's efforts to avoid sectional issues.

Accounting for the Know Nothings' Decline

Ironically, the same factors that allowed the explosive growth of political nativism at midcentury also contributed to the abrupt demise of Know Nothingism. Devotion to the language of "independence," commitment to ideological consistency, and an organizational foundation of fraternal lodges proved to be sources of weakness as well as strength. It did not take long for both the strengths and the weaknesses to become apparent.

Astonishing political success at the local level between 1853 and 1855—especially in the north—encouraged the Know Nothings to prepare for a national presidential campaign in 1856. Although they drew support from both Democrats and Whigs, because of a historical gravitation of naturalized voters to the Democrats the Know Nothings inevitably became identified as an anti-Democratic party. This could only hasten the collapse of the Whig party in the north. Once southern Whigs found themselves without effective northern counterparts, it was logical for many to look to the upstart Know Nothings, who conveniently sought to avoid the issue of extending slavery and instead talked about "American" issues which could be embraced in both regions. The existence of at least a shell of nativist fraternities in the south facilitated this process, and a nationwide Know Nothing party emerged in a flash.[72] Significantly, in 1856 the president of the Know

Nothing order—which tried to maintain a fiction of separate identity from the American party—was a southerner, the Kentuckian E. B. Bartlett.

The Know Nothing National Council that Bartlett convened in February 1856 found it necessary to confront issues as a national organization that it had been able to avoid when the movement was just a coalition of local fraternal and political organizations. Sectional discord broke out over the retention of "section 12" of the Know Nothing platform of 1855, which declared Congress powerless to rule on the future of slavery in either the states or the territories of the United States. A compromise plank called for preservation of the Union, endorsed the concept of popular sovereignty, and vaguely referred to "unqualified recognition and maintenance of the reserved rights of the several states." At their national convention a few days later, American party delegates chose as their presidential ticket the former Whig president Millard Fillmore of New York and Andrew Jackson Donelson of Tennessee, although disappointed backers of an alternative ticket (George Law and Sam Houston) and opponents of extending slavery (who found the platform too evasive on this subject) walked out of the meeting.[73] There seemed to be much to commend Fillmore to the Know Nothings. He had a history of complaining about "the contest for the foreign vote . . . corrupting the ballot box"; his presidency had been notable for its economy and for restricting its foreign policy to opening up the world for American trade; and he was a champion of the Compromise of 1850, which had seemingly preserved intersectional peace. He appears to have begun positioning himself for a possible nativist presidential candidacy as early as the fall of 1854, and he joined a Know Nothing lodge in Buffalo early in 1855.[74]

Premonitions of disaster surfaced early, however. Fillmore's denunciation of the ticket of the new Republican party headed by John C. Fremont as purely sectional and calculated to split the Union seemed disproportionately pro-southern and alienated many potential supporters in the north. The vulnerability of the American party above the Mason-Dixon line made it much less valuable to southerners who felt that they needed to count on a truly national party to defend their interests in Congress and weakened southerners' loyalty to the Know Nothings. Some feared that ballots cast for Fillmore might not only fail to elect him but actually give the victory to Fremont by drawing away previously Democratic voters. Increasingly, Fillmore was tagged as the "no chance" candidate.[75]

The election results showed just how many voters in both the north and the south turned to other political alternatives. Votes for the American party dried up entirely in New England; fewer than 30,000 went for Fillmore. The American party ticket did little better in the western states, picking up only about 12 percent of the vote. In the north, only among the middle Atlantic states did Fillmore have a respectable showing, attracting almost a quarter of a million votes, roughly 20 percent of the total. In the south, the party did better, but it still collected only the electoral votes of Maryland, a border state. About 240,000 voters in the deep south and an equal number in the border states cast ballots for Fillmore; but in the deep south these votes constituted a losing 40 percent of the total and in the border region a closer but still losing 48 percent. Throughout much of the south, the defeats state by state were close—Alabama by 1,800 popular votes, Arkansas by a razor-thin 1,100—but so was the lone victory in Maryland: the margin there was 8,000. The election brought out large numbers of new voters—who did not vote Know Nothing. And old Know Nothing voters stayed home in droves.[76]

As a national political party, the Know Nothings were through. This was so apparent even to the party faithful at the Know Nothing National Council meeting in June 1857 that they resolved "that the American party in each State and Territory be authorized to adopt such a plan of organization as respectively may be best suited to the views of the party in their several localities" and adjourned without plans for a future meeting.[77] This, of course, allowed for the possibility that political nativism might survive at the local level, and the party had been fairly successful in some of the larger cities even in the face of the presidential debacle. But the signs were not good. Without hope of a national party or influence in Congress, there was no federal patronage to distribute, there were no higher offices for aspiring politicians, and there was certainly little hope that the party could provide a basis for intersectional unity.

If the Know Nothings seemed to have a future as a political party, it was in Maryland. Thomas Swann of the American party won the Baltimore mayoral election in October 1856, and in 1857 the party captured the governorship for Thomas Hicks, picking up 43 house seats and 15 senators in the state legislature. The Democrats seemed so cowed by the string of Know Nothing victories that they did not even run a regular state ticket in 1857, but self-described "reform" candidates earned the support of defectors from the American party and former Democrats who objected to the increasing violence between nativists and immigrants during the elections in Baltimore. Since upper-class Baltimoreans and well-to-do country planters were so visible in the leadership of reform politics, nativists tried to attack it as an elitist movement and refocus attention on themselves as the party of the "independent" honest workman. A nativist congressman, Henry Winter Davis, attracted much attention in October 1859 by addressing a mass meeting in Baltimore under the banner of a shoemaker's awl, a symbol of workers' autonomy. Despite a massive victory for the American party in Baltimore, statewide voting went against the Know Nothings in 1859 and the Know Nothings were reduced to a minority in the legislature. In early 1860, the Democratic legislative majority expelled Baltimore's American party members who had allegedly been elected with the help of violence and fraud.[78]

Elsewhere in the southern and border states there remained pockets of nativist political activity. The American party had won control of the New Orleans city government in the spring elections of 1856, and Fillmore subsequently carried the city by over 3,000 votes. Statewide, the American ticket won 14 parishes, a loss of only 2 parishes since the gubernatorial election in 1855. By 1858, however, it had become pretty evident that political nativism was in eclipse outside of New Orleans. Even in Baton Rouge, the state's second-largest city, Know Nothings could win only three of nine contested offices. Only in New Orleans did a nativist ticket continue to be successful in local elections as late as 1859 and 1860.[79] The American party organization in Tennessee won a quarter of the state senate seats in 1857 and 40 percent of the seats in the lower chamber, and as late as 1858 Missouri elected two nativist congressmen. The Alabama Know Nothings, styling themselves the "opposition," remained viable after 1857 only by taking what J. Mills Thornton has called the "extreme southern rights position."[80]

In the north, local political organization faded even more quickly. New York, long the center of nativist political organizing, sent only two American party representatives to Congress in 1856 and elected only eight Know Nothing state legislators. What survived in the north were only the cores of several of the nativist fraternities, including the Order of United Americans, which pointedly dissociated itself from the American party in 1857 and pledged to go on.[81] Local issues, however, could sometimes give nativism new political life. In California, a lurid political murder led to the reinvigoration of the 1851 vigilance committee with a membership which resembled and acted like the 1854-1855 Know Nothing organization.

To historians, the rapid demise of the American party cries out for explanation. The brief life of the organization encourages doubt that it ever had much of a serious following. But that is reading backward. In fact, this approach almost always finds its way back to the words of opponents of political nativism. These were hardly disinterested analysts, but they are often highly quotable—like Horace Greeley, who claimed as early as 1854 that the Know Nothings were "as devoid of the elements of persistence as an anti-cholera or anti-Potato Rot party." Contemporary and scholarly criticism falls into just three or four categories, all somewhat interrelated. In 1855, the *Lebanon (Pennsylvania) Courier* opined that the American party's championship of "new men" was flawed: "We beg to express our decided belief that new men . . . are not the best men to fill office."[82] And, to be sure, there is plenty of evidence of ineptitude by "new men" who were elevated to office on Know Nothing tickets. In Massachusetts, the legislature of 1855, dominated by the Know Nothings, was so full of men new to office that it took days and sometimes weeks merely to organize the two houses at the beginning of the session. New men in office had new ideas—often ill formed—and spent new money on activities that subsequently looked unwise. With the zeal of true believers, "new men" called for actions that were more symbol than substance and often had the appearance of foolishness. The Know Nothing governor of Massachusetts, Gardner, proposed that the legislature prohibit the teaching of foreign languages in the public schools and even remove the Latin inscription above the speaker's chair in the statehouse as a "foreign" affectation. A committee created to investigate the houses of Catholic women's orders to see that no one was being "deprived of liberty without due process of law" was so ludicrous that it was quickly dubbed the "smelling" committee (intent as it was on sniffing around).[83] In New York City, the Know Nothing Common Council of 1855 promoted an investigation of the police to eliminate allegedly excessive "foreign" influence. When it turned up numbers suggesting that the city's principal ethnic groups were represented on the force in just about the same proportion as they were in the population, a fair amount of ridicule was unleashed.[84]

Other opponents of the Know Nothings charged that the party's problems had less to do with inexperience than with overexperience. The accusation was that as soon as the party showed signs of success, it attracted "broken-down" political "hacks" and "office-seeking leeches" pursuing the main chance. Of course, any new party that drew both leaders and followers from older political affiliations was bound to encounter such charges. In 1856, Republicans argued that the American party was being used by Democrats in disguise to divide the northern vote, while Democrats insisted that it was a hiding place for antislavery Whigs. Since the party disintegrated and most of its participants wound up elsewhere, it is easy to assume that men came into the party never intending to stay.[85]

Both the "newness" and the "oldness" of party leadership, ironically, fueled claims that the Know Nothings lacked or had lost "principle." Allegedly, either they were new men more interested in self-promotion than in platform or worn-out refugees from other parties looking for a new lease on political life and willing to say anything to win votes. According to this argument, lacking a commitment to the principles that brought the party into existence, they ultimately lost the voters. Historians are attracted to these accusations because of what they take to be weak evidence of effective nativist legislation to achieve the movement's ostensible goals in naturalization and electoral reform.[86]

But to attribute the demise of political nativism entirely to these factors is to rely far too much on hindsight, to adopt far too uncritically the language of the Know Nothings' political adversaries and, most important, to discount the strength of the forces that gave rise to Know Nothingism in the first place. Actually, the success of political nativism in the 1850s is very closely tied to its ultimate failure. To a considerable extent, the failure of Know Nothingism *was* a product of its success. In states and cities where Know Nothings wielded substantial political power, the party did achieve objectives that were consistent with the ideology of the nativist movement. By the mid-1850s, nativists in Philadelphia had achieved direct election of school and health commissioners and even prison inspectors, giving voters more influence in government. The nativist council passed new safety codes for tenements and workplaces. On the surface, these effects may seem to have little to do with what is popularly taken to be the core of nativism, but in fact they were part and parcel of the nativists' insistence on promoting personal independence. In Pittsburgh, as in Philadelphia, the number of Irish-born political candidates fell as it temporarily became unfashionable for any party to aggressively seek out ethnic candidates.[87]

In Massachusetts, Dale Baum points out, "the reform-minded Know Nothing legislature passed measures recognizing the property rights of married women, requiring compulsory vaccination and attendance for public school children, and abolishing imprisonment for debt"—all of which conformed to the nativists' commitment to republican "independence." This, too, applied to the legislature's insistence that race, color, or religion not be used as a bar to children's admission to the public schools; to a mechanic's lien law to guarantee payment for labor; and to an exemption of an individual's homestead from a sheriff's sale for debt. As in Pennsylvania, new legislation expanded the number of offices elected by popular vote. And a Know Nothing act provided funds to each of the state charitable institutions for acquiring and maintaining a library for residents.[88]

Acts like these, which put into practice what nativists had been preaching, were legislated in state after state. Michigan and New York passed laws to ensure that the property of churches was held by lay trustees. Baltimore expanded its police force and provided for additional polling places to meet citizens' demands. In New York, preservation of the Maclay Act rather than new legislation seemed to satisfy Know Nothings' desire that public funding be restricted to public schools. Merely by coming into power and driving most naturalized voters into the Democratic party, the Know Nothings eliminated much of the most visible competitive partisan pursuit of ethnic voters that had been one of the issues that brought them into being.[89]

The point is that nativist mayors, councilmen, governors, and legislators did a good deal to implement nativist ideology. Only when we recognize that nativists had a broader agenda than naturalization reform (a subject, as we have seen, on which they were divided) is this apparent. "Success," however, brought apathy and disillusionment. Nativism was more of a cause than a party, and when it achieved a fair number of its objectives the wind went out of its sails. Moreover, its "successes" had less than a transforming effect on American politics and society, and this led to a sense of disappointment and futility among all but the most dedicated activists.

The Know Nothings also suffered from internal organizational problems connected to the party's roots in nativist secret societies. From the beginning, the fraternities were repellent to some potential converts to nativism, especially to those who came out of the anti-Masonic tradition which had been strong in the middle Atlantic states. On balance, secrecy had probably been a political asset during the early years of nativist political organization, allowing the fraternities to make surprise endorsements of political candidates. The emergence from the

Know Nothing order of a national party with its own candidates seemed to make secrecy unnecessary, and the National Council eliminated it in its own proceedings in 1855-1856. But in all likelihood, more was lost than gained by this development, for it blurred the distinction between the brethren and the general public. "Brotherhood" had been significant in nativist ideology, as had the ritual surrounding it, to say nothing of the practical benefits of the lodge. Moreover, the fraternities had been the glue which had allowed nativists to stick together enough to remain active between elections—more active than was usual in American politics. Brotherhood had also worked to limit membership to those who seemed to take the movement's goals fairly seriously and, as we have seen, created a mechanism for conducting a sort of local primary election, restrictive as that may have been. When Know Nothingism began to act like the other parties, it lost much of the attractiveness that had produced its dramatic growth, particularly the apparent harmony between ideology and organization.

There were other advantages and disadvantages in nativist fraternalism. Laden with grandiloquently titled offices and extravagant rituals, the fraternities had more than their share of opportunities for bickering, personal jealousy, and factionalization. As Ronald Walters has shown for the contemporaneous abolition movement, intramural conflict could have a highly ritualized function, helping to set true believers apart from outsiders and strengthening their commitment to the movement. This was certainly the case with nativism. But it also set the stage for battles over trivia that drove wedges into the movement and instilled a sort of institutional paranoia. " Treason in the Camp," trumpeted a headline in OUA's *Republic.* When the number of new applications for chapter charters from Pennsylvania and upstate New York fell, OUA's archchancery concluded that they must "have been suppressed, by some treasonous influence." The Know Nothing order itself, for a time, fell into an "Allen branch" and a "Barker branch"; this was partly a result of division over ideology and direction but to a considerable degree also a matter of personality and personal alliances.[90]

Then, too, as critics at the time pointed out, some men were attracted to nativist societies strictly by their novelty or by their practical lodge benefits. In time, of course, the novelty wore off, and the lodge benefits eventually became closely connected to the political success of nativism. When nativist organizations were growing, membership was a useful thing, and it became more useful as the orders spread across the country. When the organizations were shrinking, giving up membership was hastened simply by its lost utility. We can probably sce both phenomena at work in the rapid turnover that plagued most fraternal chapters. One study of a Know Nothing lodge in Worcester, Massachusetts, showed only 20 percent of the membership remaining from one year to the next, with new recruits following departures through a revolving door. As the fraternities grew, central control of local auxiliaries weakened, but membership turnover made even local leadership challenging. As is true in most voluntary organizations, leadership at all levels tended to fall into the hands of a dedicated few— an oligarchy—and this distanced leaders from followers.[91]

Finally, the nativist commitment to ideology and the efforts of key leaders to maintain ideological consistency were at least as important as departure from "principle" in leading to the political demise of antebellum nativism. As we have seen, ideologues like Thomas R. Whitney repeatedly found themselves taken by the logic of nativist ideas to positions that were sure to alienate a mass political audience. These positions ranged from denunciation of "democracy" to stated willingness to regard blacks and Indians as better candidates for citizenship than European-born whites. The point is not that most nativists held these positions but that they were visible enough to be used effectively against nativists in politics.

What enduring strengths there were in nativist organization and ideology were shrewdly borrowed by political rivals and used to build their share of the electorate. The new Republican party mimicked the fraternal form in "Wide-Awake" clubs that not only fostered a sense of masculine "brotherhood" but kept enthusiasm alive between elections. In some places, Republicans experimented with a kind of closed primary for "card-carrying" party members which would keep out disruptive interlopers. Before the Civil War, a Republican legislature would create a voter registry system for New York which would accomplish much of what nativists had sought in the way of electoral reform. In Massachusetts, a Republican-endorsed "two-year amendment" created a probationary period for naturalized citizens before they could exercise the franchise. The New York Democratic mayor Fernando Wood's work-relief program during the depression of the late 1850s, and Pennsylvania Republicans' hostility to lucrative public railway and streetcar franchises, revealed a populism reminiscent of nativists' criticism of domineering big business.[92]

The attractiveness of the nativists' stress on personal "independence" is underscored by the central role it continued to play in politics as sectional disharmony grew. In fact, the theme may have outgrown the movement, as voters found other ways of embracing it. Extreme southern nationalists, particularly, adopted the language of Know Nothingism—though with a twist. They actually played off Know Nothingism, charging that the main flaw in the movement was that it could not guarantee southern "independence." To some extent— because of words like Whitney's—they were able to link Know Nothingism to alleged northern "domination." Pro-secession Alabamians, J. Mills Thornton notes, were able to argue that northerners, "not satisfied 'with abolishing black slavery among themselves and instituting white slaves in their place,' now wished to extend the same class tyranny to southerners." Democrats called Know Nothingism a "new development of the aristocratic element of our society; that element can always be detected in any political organization which affects to treat the people as *children* to be deceived and humored, instead of as *brothers and equals in political rights.*"[93]

Thomas R. Whitney's claptrap about the limits of democracy did not play well in the south. There, what George M. Fredrickson has called "Herrenvolk democracy" had become well established in popular culture, promoting a pseudo-equality among all whites as a mechanism for defending white supremacy from both internal dissent and external assault. Southerners were outraged by the Massachusetts Know Nothing Alfred Ely's provocative assertion that native-born slaves were more suitable candidates for republican citizenship than foreign-born whites, and by George Copway's efforts to connect "native Americanism" with citizenship rights for aboriginal "native Americans." Daniel Walker Howe notes that a good part of Alexander Stephens's hostility to the Know Nothings was his objection to any kind of "discrimination against categories of white men."[94] (Stephens was later vice-president of the Confederacy.) The twilight days of Know Nothingism in the south before secession reflected all of these anxieties. The last major statewide Know Nothing campaign in Louisiana in 1857 turned into a contest with the Democrats over which party could best protect southern "independence." The fire-eater W. L. Yancey of Alabama blamed Know Nothingism for sacrificing southern autonomy by treating slavery as an "incidental" issue that did not require the party's whole attention. In Mississippi, John Quitman took the same line.[95]

By the late 1850s, commitment to "independence" had lost none of the appeal that had made it such an effective basis for nativist fraternalism and political activism, but in north and south alike many people had identified new threats to independence and had embraced new enthusiasms which promised to preserve it. In the south, personal autonomy had become bound up in popular thought with regional autonomy, and the Democratic party effectively snuffed out the Know Nothings by persuasively making the case that only a truly intersectional party in which southerners maintained veto power could preserve southern rights. When the fragmentation of the Democrats into rival regional factions in 1860 undercut this argument, secessionism itself took up the battle cry "independence." As Michael Holt has pointed out, secessionism had an eerie resemblance to nativism, with its denunciations of out-of-touch politicians, evasiveness in political party platforms, and corruption in high places. Moreover, it was driven by more than a fear of political subordination to growing northern Republicanism; there was also—in the words of the historian J. Mills Thornton—fear that in a modernizing capitalist society individuals were becoming increasingly entwined in a "national net of complex interrelationships" that threatened the end of treasured forms of personal autonomy.[96] In the south, secessionism displaced Know Nothingism.

Something not so very different took place in the late antebellum north. There, commitment to independence and autonomy increasingly became bound up with resistance to what was taken to be southern "dictation" and the need to preserve the unity of the republic. As Phillip Paludan has persuasively argued, the Union itself seemed the best bulwark against loss of individual autonomy in a region which, on the whole, had effective local democratic institutions in the form of town and township governments. Southern society, with its traditions of family alliances and dominance by planters, seemed to represent the greatest threat to republican autonomy. Better to preserve—and extend—the northern republican model of local democratic self-government than stand for the spread of a slaveholder "aristocracy." This outlook was particularly strong in the newly organized states and territories of the west, where, as Paluden points out, the recent experience of building communities on the frontier had given an unusually large proportion of the people personal knowledge of republican self-government. He notes that throughout the north, there was relatively little "roll-off" of voters in off-year elections, suggesting widespread satisfaction with—and participation in—local government. The threats of southern proslavery radicals seemed like challenges to a system which provided many opportunities to prove one's republican equality and independence.[97] Nativists, of course, tried to take advantage of this anxiety by casting themselves as the party of the Union, and no others could wax so poetic about the benefits of the American republic:

What is it that has peopled the wilderness? What is it that has substituted for the shrubbery of the wilderness fields of waving grain? What is it that has whitened with sails of commerce those lakes and rivers upon whose shores solitude has brooded for ages? What is it that has carried our literature, our science, our arts, our manufactures, our arms, from the shelving beach of the Atlantic to the beetling crags of the Pacific? It is the Union of these states.[98]

"Judgement and reason," argued OUA's Whitney in 1856, seemed no longer to appeal to secessionists, who would be better described as "factionists, fisionists, or sectionists," and he lamented that sectionalism was not only fracturing the harmony of the Protestant churches but becoming the key issue in even the most local politics. But in the end, it was the new Republican party which proved most capable of joining the themes of independence and Union by its attacks on the secession-bent "slave power."[99]

Conclusion: The Hard Core Survives

Although the political nativism of the 1850s flamed and went out, nativism was by no means dead as a social movement. The rapid rise of Know Nothingism was made possible by the preexistence of both ideologies and organizations that could be adapted to widely shared aspirations and anxieties. Neither the ideas nor the organizations completely disappeared when the American party did; they remained in waiting, to resurface when the cultural and political climate seemed encouraging. There is some temptation to reduce antebellum nativism to a series of mob eruptions, gang wars, election-day riots, street harangues, and comic opera political ineptitude. But, in fact, it had a much more enduring life in the "patriotic" fraternal and beneficiary societies and in assorted voluntarist "reform" organizations. It was these that made it possible for Know Nothingism to rise rapidly and, for a time, flourish. They also help explain its demise. For commitment to ideological purity and selective membership, which were essential to these small groups, did not suit a mass political party.

At the same time, the small-group basis of the nativist movement ensured that it outlasted the demise of Know Nothingism. Though skeletal, many of the nativist fraternities survived into the 1860s. The movement could live without central national organization. And some recent close analysis of the voting behavior of those who had cast Know Nothing ballots in the early and mid-1850s suggests that many did not shift their votes to either the Republicans or the Democrats but opted out of political participation entirely. Here was a constituency for further nativist activism.

Chapter Five

The Nativist Movement
in an Age of Organization

Henry Adams, the American historian and man of letters, spent much of the last two decades of the nineteenth century scrutinizing the future and looking back. Adams's *History of the United States of America during the Administrations of Thomas Jefferson and James Madison* (1889-1891) reviewed the challenges that had faced the young American republic and introduced what Adams took to be the organizing theme of United States history before the Civil War: "national unity." By this he meant the need for the United States to establish itself as a real nation in the face of "provincialism," "pluralism," and "sectionalism" exacerbated by rapid geographical expansion in a time of rudimentary transportation. This was very much like what Americans of the antebellum period had meant when they spoke in anxious tones about a "national character"—the ability of a people who lacked the familiar European attributes of nationhood to function and survive as a nation. In *Democracy,* a novel written in 1880, Adams offered his views on what Americans had to face up to in the postwar era. David Contosta, Adams's biographer, interprets the reaction of the novel's heroine, Madeline, to her discovery of the political corruption practiced by her fiancé, a United States senator, as follows: "At last she has 'got to the bottom of democratic government' only to discover that it was 'nothing more than government of any other kind.' The American people were no better and no worse than other people and systems; the country was not exempt from the laws of nature." In short, the United

States, having proved by its survival through its Civil War that it had the endurance of a nation, now had to establish "national character" in a different sense. What sort of a nation was it to be? What was its temper? What were its values? What kinds of people would hold the reins of power?[1]

Sharing such concerns, postbellum Americans of all classes directed their attention to organizations and to the practice of organization. For if there was a nation to be led or a national "character" to be established, it would be by men (and perhaps women, although there was disagreement over this) working together through organizations. The Civil War itself seemed to have established that—the way to get things done was through organizations. And if right-thinking folks did not organize to mold the national character, other, wrong-thinking people probably would. The late nineteenth century was, after all, the age of the corporation, the industrial "trust," the urban political "machine," the institutional church, the city social-work settlement house, and the "billion-dollar Congress." It was also the age of the rural Grange and the Farmers' Alliance, labor unions, urban reform leagues, ethnic fraternities, and insurance beneficiary societies. "Ultimately," observes John D. Buenker, "nearly everyone began to perceive that the only way to cope with his problems and to advance or protect his interests was to organize, for the new environment put a premium on large-scale enterprise." Alan Trachtenberg has expressed this another way by describing the late nineteenth century in America as an age of "incorporation"—in business, cultural, political, occupational, and social life. Bernard Weisberger, in *The New Industrial Society,* flips the coin over, reminding us that this was also an age of "counterorganization." According to Robert Wiebe, Americans remained concerned about autonomy, as in the antebellum period. But their focus shifted from autonomy sought individually to autonomy pursued as part of a community or an interest group. This provoked suspicion of other groups perceived to be intruding on self-determination and led to a broadening of the concept of "alien" to apply to "any distant, threatening power."[2]

All this ensured that there would be a place for organized nativist activism in post-Civil War America. Many Americans defining themselves as "native" would see a war at hand for the nation's soul or "character." Moreover, they would perceive the contestants as organized for battle. And, indeed, the apparent rivals were almost always portrayed as better organized. The Roman Catholic church, ethnic politicians, immigrant fraternalists—and a variety of the nativists' other traditional villains—all showed signs of having learned the lessons of organization and institutionalization, too. In the years following the Civil War, the nativist was one who saw suspicious, organized efforts everywhere to shape the nation's future. In nativist parlance, each one of these was in its own way "alien." Not surprisingly, nativists sought to achieve a higher state of organization themselves, although they never saw the irony in their reaction.

The Nativist Movement from Pre- to Post-Civil War

Over the last quarter of a century, historians have become increasingly skeptical about the idea that the Civil War was a watershed in all areas of American life; but a conviction persists that it neatly divides the nativist movement into two distinct phases. In much historical literature, the conventional analysis is that with the outbreak of intersectional violence, nativism as a distinctive social movement went into hibernation, not to come fully to life again until the emergence of the American Protective Association in the late 1880s. In fact, the typical argument is that the war killed off antebellum nativism by affecting both the native-born, Protestant community, which provided recruits for the nativist movement; and European immigrants, especially Catholics, who were the objects of nativists' suspicion. First of all, the argument runs, the conflict between sections brought people within sections together. "The crisis of the Union," Stephen Thernstrom has written, "heightened common loyalties and dissolved many of the suspicions of the fifties. The war seemed no respecter of persons. . . . Men fought and died independent of rank, of office, of social position." Earlier, Oscar Handlin had waxed poetic: "The war quickened understanding and sympathy. . . . In the armies of the field, men of all nativities fought a common battle. Living together, they came, for the first time, to know one another, and knowing each other, they insensibly drew closer together."[3] In the 1960s, John Higham used the Civil War as the point of departure for his theory that nativistic sensibilities in the American population rose and fell in fairly direct relation to the public's sense of well-being and confidence. Following Appomattox, Higham wrote, "there was no domestic cleavage deep enough to produce . . . anxieties and no nation-wide agitation to awaken the sleeping conscience of society. Untroubled by doubts of the success of their own institutions, Americans saw little reason to fear the influence of foreigners upon them. Confidence in the country's economic vitality extended, by and large, to its whole social order."[4]

The argument for the virtual demise of nativism during and after the war also runs the other way. Immigrants (and their children), historians have suggested, undercut their nativist detractors by proving their loyalty to the American nation. Of course, a cottage industry of filiopietistic praise for diverse ethnic groups' contributions to the war effort—north and south—sprang up before the last guns had fallen silent, but, surprisingly, it has survived in serious scholarship. A number of scholars have drawn the conclusion that by wedding themselves to national goals and proving their patriotism, immigrants put nativistic fears out of fashion. Phillip Paludan points out that "even the Catholic church" acquired new stature by supporting the war to save the Union.[5] One study of antebellum political nativism flatly insists that "nativism . . . died. . . . With the war foreigners were needed for labor and for soldiers, to work and die for the country and its principles. . . . The Know Nothing party was dead."[6]

This last statement, of course, is problematic, for it confounds nativism with Know Nothingism and the American party—which were dead, for all intents and purposes, before the outbreak of the war. But it is more surprising that so many historians see the organized nativist movement in its entirety fading from view—as David Bennett has recently put it in *Party of Fear*—only to "reappear at the end of the nineteenth century and in the first half of the twentieth century."[7] Some students concede, as Robert Remini does, that the "bigotry underpinning" the nativist movement survived during and after the Civil War, but surprisingly few have gone so far as Herbert Gutman, who has pointed out that "nativism neither died out during the Civil War nor awaited a rebirth under the auspices of the American Protective Association and the Immigration Restriction League."[8] Why should it have? Certainly its contemporaries, immigrant and native, doubted that it was gone.[9]

In fact, a discernible nativist movement never entirely disappeared during the Civil War or after. Nor did it survive only as an emotion—as popular bigotry—without organizational structure. The shells (or perhaps more accurately the cores) of a number of nativist societies of the 1850s endured, and individual activists persisted too. It really is not hard to see why. The sectional crisis may have blunted political nativism, but wartime created as many opportunities for native-foreign, Catholic-Protestant, and interethnic friction as for camaraderie and sympathy. This, after all, has been the American experience in times of war before and since. All of the ingredients were there to get a nativist movement through the Civil War.

Interethnic friction was certainly alive and well among the troops, particularly in the north, where the population was ethnically diverse. Among the most popular songs of march and camp in the Union army were some with sharp ethnic barbs. There was poor "Corporal Schnapps" who reluctantly went to war because his "fraulein" shamed him into it (and then faithlessly left with another man for "Zhermany"). "Dere's only von ting vot I fear, Ven pattling for der Eagle," commiserated a German-American volunteer in "I Goes to Fight mit Sigel": "I vont get not no lager beer." Other songs somewhat more harmlessly perpetuated old stereotypes—the German with his sauerkraut and the "Mick" with his potato. But not a few were dripping with contempt. A parody of "When This Cruel War Is Over" portrayed a reluctant Irish soldier pining for a substitute to take his place, finding no meaning in his occupation save the "paymaster's tin," and praying at the last for "When this cruel war is over . . . a good horn of gin."[10] Except that they are in verse, these do not sound much different from what the American party had said about immigrants a decade earlier.

To many soldiers, a German or an Irishman in blue (or gray) was still a suspect "foreigner," and immigrants were both the butt of jokes and scapegoats when the fortunes of war turned ugly. Stonewall Jackson's overrunning of German-American units at Chancellorsville provided an excuse for Anglo-Americans to impugn German manhood at every opportunity until the end of the war. Stung, German-born officers resigned, and enlistment of German-American troops never quite recovered. Officers were only too happy to blame breakdowns in discipline on stereotyped ethnic characteristics. One Union general reported to a congressional committee that he had little trouble with excessive drinking among his troops except for "the great many Irishmen, to whom a frolic is as necessary about once a month as dinner."[11] Enlisted men were not above perpetuating stereotypes, either, and Civil War diaries included descriptions of comrades like "lisping, light-haired Weibel, the German" and "Pat O'Toole, our wild Irishman," which appeared in a reminiscence published in 1864 while the war still raged.[12] At the top, civilian officials fretted about the tendencies of Catholic generals, and even the *New York Times* suspected that William Rosecrans's defeat at Chickamauga had something to do with his Catholicism. James Garfield—Rosecrans's brother officer and a future president—speculated on the same point.[13]

In the Civil War armies, hostility toward groups traditionally considered "alien" by nativists sometimes went well beyond words to outright violence. This was almost guaranteed by the assembling of two armies (north and south) of local volunteer units which took on the ethnic and religious character of the neighborhoods, workplaces, clubs, and even churches from which they were recruited. Confrontations between units in bivouac or on leave from the front often began as, or easily turned into, interethnic brawls. Neither German nor Irish troops were insensitive to what they took to be slights or actual maltreatment, and both publicly complained about it.[14]

Evidence of interethnic suspicion or at least tension reached far above the level of the troops, where it might be expected that bored, frightened, angry, and armed young men would lose their civility. In the north, official Washington often seemed not to go very far out of its way to make German- or Irish-born soldiers feel valued. In mid-1861, consternation was created in German-American communities when a War Department order seemed to prohibit the enlistment of non-English-speaking recruits. German-Americans were only partly reassured when it was explained that the order did not apply to whole ethnic units, where officers and men could understand one another.[15] The War Department was also slow to make provision for Catholic army chaplains and seemed to expect that Catholics in units composed of men of mixed religious backgrounds would be satisfied with Protestant clergymen. Gardiner Shattuck, author of a modern study of religion and Civil War soldiers, notes that after more than a year of war, "the proportion of Roman Catholic to Protestant soldiers was approximately one to six [but] only twenty-two priests served among the 472 Union chaplains then on duty." When Catholic chaplains did serve, they were almost always assigned to uniformly Catholic (usually Irish-American) units. The few instances in which Catholic chaplains appeared in mixed regiments produced opportunities for dramatic Protestant rebuffs.[16] Tellingly, when the Lincoln administration called on the United States Sanitary Commission "to make a study of the physical and moral condition of Federal troops" in the hope of better understanding the causes of the military debacle at First Bull Run, the investigators not only decided to measure the height, weight, girth, head shape, and facial angle of soldiers in different ethnic and racial categories but also supposed that these would indicate physical fitness for service and such qualities as "ability to learn tactics."[17] The underlying assumption was that ethnicity governed behavior. Benjamin

Apthorp Gould's *Investigations in the Military and Anthropological Statistics of American Soldiers,* published four years after the war, even went so far as to describe desertion from the battlefront as a "crime of foreign rather than native birth."[18]

This evidence of the endurance of old stereotypes and interethnic friction does not point, in and of itself, to the survival of the nativist movement through the war years. But it should give us pause before we accept the cheerful conclusion that nativism could not have lasted because the war created an atmosphere of interethnic harmony and a new appreciation of immigrants' value to the nation. Actually, wartime conditions exacerbated some of the prewar anxieties that had motivated nativist activists.

If prewar nativists worried about the threats to effective citizenship and thus to personal autonomy that they supposed were offered by the willingness of politicians to make special appeals to "alien" communities, there was little in the political experiences of wartime to give them much comfort. In a largely volunteer army raised at the state and local level, all ranks above sergeant were potentially political spoils. As William L. Burton put it in *Melting Pot Soldiers: The Union's Ethnic Regiments,* "Professional ethnic politicians turned into professional ethnic colonels—even generals." At the least, politicians of all ethnic backgrounds understood that they could please or alienate whole districts by their nominations to officers' commissions.[19] Likewise, if "Irish Guards" and "German Rifles" militia companies had produced high anxiety among antebellum nativists, imagine the effect created by whole ethnic regiments, let alone an "Irish Brigade" marching under a green flag. When the Irish Brigade's commander, General Michael Corcoran, was freed from a Confederate prison and made his way home to New York, he was greeted at each major city by large turnouts from Irish Catholic communities praising him as a true son of Ireland. This was the stuff that prewar nativism had thrived on.[20]

Certainly it was common enough during the war years, as it had been in the 1840s and 1850s, to charge the Irish with political unreliability—now given the more awful name "disloyalty." When a "List of Copperhead Voters" was published by the "loyal men of the town" in Hudson, Ohio, during 1863, it was pointed out that a third of the names belonged to foreign-born residents, all but two Irish.[21] Fernando Wood of New York City, a highly visible Peace Democrat elected mayor in the midst of the war, was popularly identified as the immigrants' candidate because of his open appeals to Irish and German voters. By no means were the ethnic communities of New York united in opposition to the war, but there were plenty of people around who were only too ready to see in Wood's political success evidence of the disloyalty nativists had attributed to immigrants in the 1840s and 1850s. It did not help that Lincoln's opponent in 1864, James B. McClellan, made a strong showing among Irish Catholic and German voters. Recent estimates suggest that up to a third of McClellan's votes in key states came from Irish-Americans.[22]

Certainly the war gave millions of immigrants and their children an opportunity to demonstrate their loyalty to the Union. But it required only a few exceptional cases to provide sufficient ammunition to keep a nativist movement alive. When German tailors in Philadelphia under contract to make uniforms struck after negotiations broke down over piecework pay, it was easy for some Anglo-Americans to interpret this not in class or economic terms but in nationalist and political terms— as treason. Later, at the end of the war, some people would make much of the fact that two accomplices in Lincoln's assassination—John and Mary Surratt—were Catholic.[23] While the tendency to impugn the loyalty of "aliens" was more common in the north (which had the largest immigrant populations and the strongest tradition of organized nativist activism), it was not unknown in the Confederacy. The political cartoonist Adalbert J. Volck produced biting images of German soldiers in federal uniforms pillaging southern property. When German gymnastic clubs—Turners—joined regular U.S. Army troops to protect a St. Louis government armory from pro-southern Missouri militia, it prompted enduring hostility, evident in a Confederate ballad which concluded: "The time for glory is coming. We yet shall see the time when all of us will shine. And drive the Dutch from this happy land of Canaan."[24]

To many, the draft riots of mid-1863 seemed a confirmation of nativists' direst predictions about the unreadiness of "un-American" immigrants for the responsibilities of republican citizenship. The great upheaval of July 13-17 in New York City and the smaller antidraft protests across the north were by no means ethnically exclusive. But public accounts of the riots and protests focused on the participation of Irish-Americans and emphasized that these were *organized* acts of resistance. This was equally true of reports of 3,000 to 4,000 blocking draft enrollment in Chicago's Third Ward (the Irish "Patch"), and of accounts of violent resistance among Irish-American quarrymen in Vermont.[25] In New York City, especially, the antidraft mob in July seemed to have specific targets and appeared to re-form as if under some direction each time it was dispersed by the police and troops. This inspired unsympathetic New Yorkers to seek causes while the bullets still flew and the fires burned. The fact that some rioters were heard cheering for Jeff Davis, and that antiwar Democrats publicly offered their sympathy, suggested political inspiration rather than the mix of labor, ethnic, and class grievances (as well as frustration over an unfair draft law that allowed money to buy exemption) that modern historians put at the root of the violence. The silence of the aging Catholic archbishop of New York, John Hughes, until late in the week of the riot was bound to convince some alumni of prewar nativism that there was a treasonous Irish-Catholic conspiracy afoot.[26] Glimmers of antebellum nativism were apparent when leading Philadelphians, fearful that the New York riots might spill over into their city, insisted that the Lincoln administration place in charge of civil defense the militia commander who in 1844 had suppressed the violence between Irish-Americans and nativists, the elderly General George Cadwalader.[27]

If the war itself created numerous opportunities for friction between the native-born and immigrants and Anglo-Americans and ethnic minorities, many of the economic and demographic conditions that had sustained a nativist movement during the two decades before the sectional conflict simply persisted. Antebellum nativism attracted some of its adherents by drawing attention to the loss of autonomy—and hence of republican independence—experienced by laborers in "sweated" pseudo-crafts and emergent mechanized industries. During the war years in the north, there was even more evidence of extraordinary profit and power coming into the hands of merchants and industrialists while inflation, running well ahead of wage increments, produced a greater sense of workers' dependence. Strong evidence of discontent among workers is to be found in the enthusiasm for labor organization during the war and the acceleration of strikes in 1863 and 1864. For workers anxious about stretched wages and retaliation by employers for work stoppages, the passage of an Emigrant Aid Act by Congress in 1864 to permit employers to import labor from abroad reminded them of complaints from the nativist organizations of the 1850s that politicians were ignoring native citizens in favor of immigrant voter blocs.[28]

Although the outbreak of the Civil War initially discouraged immigration (which had been declining anyway, from a peak in the mid-1850s), before the conflict was half over annual immigration was out of the doldrums. As Phillip Paludan succinctly puts it, the Union proved to be "a magnet even in the midst of war." Four-fifths of a million people landed in the United States during the war years. The newcomers' visibility was enhanced by their overrepresentation in cities. Philadelphia, for example, grew by 100,000 during the 1860s, and much of the increment was attributable to immigrants and their children.[29] The continuing development of institutions associated with ethnic minority populations also attracted attention. The Catholic school system of New York City grew by some 50 percent during the early 1860s. Similar if less dramatic growth in the parochial schools of Baltimore, Pittsburgh, Cincinnati, Boston, and Philadelphia made education a major item, in 1864, on the agenda of the American Catholic bishops' meeting, which took action to set standards of organization for church school systems.[30] The demise of Know Nothingism brought no end to the kind of random anti-Catholic violence and vandalism that had peppered the antebellum period. A year before Sumter, after 20 years of more or less underground existence, the Irish Catholic population of the northeastern Ohio community of Hudson (the village, heavily populated by New England Whig-Republicans, where the abolitionist John Brown grew up) erected a church. The native-born Protestant who had sold the building lot was threatened by neighbors, and the steeple cross almost immediately disappeared to vandals.[31]

Since so many of the conditions that contributed to the flourishing of antebellum nativism continued during and after the war, it should be little surprise that the institutional core of a nativist movement outlived the sectional bloodletting, despite an unpromising climate for the survival of voluntaristic organizations of many kinds. Without question, it was difficult for the fraternal societies that provided the basis for much nativist organizing to operate during the war years. A nonpolitical "patriotic" society which had inspired some of the nativist orders of the 1840s and 1850s and which had experienced its own internal ethnic fracture shortly after midcentury—the Improved Order of Red Men (IORM)—shows how challenging it was to carry on in the early 1860s. Because of the absence of key leaders in military service, its great council of the United States was unable to meet in 1862, although it resumed the following year. Worse, the grand sachem in IORM's home state, Pennsylvania, died in combat not long after his election. As early as 1861, IORM found it impossible to prepare accurate statistical reports of local chapters and members and gave up until 1866; and it was seriously in debt by 1865 because of its inability to collect regular dues. The overtly nativist fraternities, already embarrassed by the political failures of the late 1850s and by plummeting memberships, faced all of the same difficulties. The Order of United Americans' grand sachem not only went off to war but ended up in a Confederate prison. Circumstances like these made institutional continuity difficult.[32]

But institutional continuity there was in the nativist movement, enough to keep some old organizations alive and some old activists sufficiently energized to create new organizations at the end of the war.[33] In fact, the fraternities left a trail. The central command of the Order of United Americans, for example, continued to support speakers and publish tracts into the early stages of the war, giving business to the grand sachem Charles Gildersleeve, who was operating as a printer and stationer on William Street in lower Manhattan. These publications were full of self-justification, such as this commentary by the national arch grand sachem John Lloyd in December 1860, on secession: "More than sixteen years ago, the Order of United Americans was established to guard against such a state of things, and to warn our fellow citizens of the dangers with which they were surrounded, and to urge them to a more filial reverence for the Institutions of our Country, and the necessity for constant and active measures for their prevention and defense."[34] No doubt, Charles Gildersleeve was right when he remembered, around 1900, that in midwar the archchancery, made up of chapter representatives, was "so small, it could have met in one room."[35] But still, the really consequential thing is that some brethren did continue to meet and to place themselves in positions of public responsibility as the war wound down. Take Gildersleeve himself. Back from the war, he gravitated to management of the New York Fire Department (a traditional source of nativist recruits). By 1865, he was secretary to the commissioners.[36] Later, Gildersleeve—who at some point received training as an attorney—became a ward commissioner for New York City's Board of Education, which was locked in battle in the years after the Civil War over whether the school curriculum should be chosen by the Protestant school board leadership or according to the preferences of local (often Catholic) citizens.[37] Although OUA itself seems to have disappeared during 1866 (except perhaps as a social club for a few New York nativist veterans), it is much more important that individuals with nativist affiliations continued to believe in the power of organization.

OUA was not the only nativist society to make it through the war; actually, other survivors managed to last a good deal longer. The Patriotic Order, Sons of America, based in Pennsylvania, was not much heard of for a few years but was back publishing its semimonthly newsletter by 1866 and seeing to the annual succession of leadership.[38] The American Protestant Association elected grand masters annually without interruption throughout the war and demonstrated enough institutional continuity to boast in the late 1880s that its national convention had been held in the same Philadelphia hall since the end of the Civil War. In fact, the wartime organization had sufficient life in it to create a "Junior" auxiliary modeled after the Junior Order, United American Mechanics, in 1864.[39] In most nativist organizations, "Junior" identified not only an institution for younger men but also one designed to be more politically active. The 1860s—before, during, and after the war—were a fertile period for the introduction of new anti-Catholic, or at least aggressively Protestant, organizations. Although the Knights of Malta (an offshoot of the northern Protestant Irish society of the same name) was not officially chartered in the United States until 1870, local predecessors were in place by 1860. In fact, in 1859 a "Sons of Malta" chapter in Cleveland, Ohio, found itself under attack as a "Know-Nothing" fraternity. Another Protestant fraternity, the Knights of Pythias, was organized in 1864 under the direction of an activist in both the Masons and the Improved Order of Red Men (IORM).[40] The Red Men themselves continued to show signs of ethnic fissures. Just before the Civil War, IORM elected Paxon Coats as "great incohonee." Coats came to national leadership from Cincinnati's Miami Tribe 1, which had been involved in nativist politics earlier in the decade. IORM continued its vendetta against the German-American Independent Order of Red Men, which had broken away, rejecting proposals for reconciliation from 1869 into the mid-1870s. New bylaws for the Improved Order instituted in 1866 excluded anyone who had ever been affiliated with the Independent Order. Gradually, IORM lost what was left of its German membership. More decidedly Anglo-American and Protestant than ever, IORM began to grow again rapidly; at the end of the Civil War, only 3,500 members were counted in Pennsylvania, but within eight years there were nearly 20,000.[41]

Although not always successful in producing enduring postwar nativist organizations, old nativist activists and old nativist practices turned up frequently enough in the period immediately following the Civil War to ensure that they would be hard for anyone to forget. E. Z. C. Judson (better known by his pen name, Ned Buntline), one of the originators of the Patriotic Order, Sons of America, surfaced in California in the late 1860s as a newspaper editor, temperance organizer, and anti-Catholic lecturer. A few years later, he attracted attention and reminded contemporaries of the loose links between nativist fraternalism and the "patriotic" societies represented by the earliest Tammany organizations and the Red Men by turning up in Pennsylvania to pay homage at the supposed grave of Chief Tammany.[42] Likewise, James Barker, an early Know Nothing organizer, reportedly got involved again with insurance sales and nativist fraternalism not long before he died in 1869. The various Union League Clubs that appealed to wealthy Republicans and War Democrats during and after the Civil War celebrated all of the same occasions that were holy to the prewar nativist fraternities, especially Washington's birthday. With these sorts of folks floating about, it is no wonder that George Templeton Strong recorded signs of agitation among former Know Nothings in New York City in the aftermath of the 1863 draft riots.[43] While this evidence does not indicate the existence of a robust and politically consequential nativist movement in the years during and immediately following the Civil War, it is enough to warn us away from drawing hasty conclusions about the death of antebellum nativism, and from the temptation to isolate nativism in the postwar period from what went before.

As is shown by some of the wartime working-class discontent, by hostility to the appeals of the Peace Democrats to immigrant voters, by anxiety over possible organized support for the draft riots, and by the reaction to ethnic preferences in political and military appointments, there endured throughout the war years widespread concern about personal autonomy and the necessity of individual independence for true republican citizenship. If many Americans had worried during the 1840s and 1850s about the challenges posed to individual autonomy by the changing scale of manufacturing and trade and political forces which seemed to diminish the voice of the private citizen, there was little in the 1860s or 1870s to alleviate these concerns. In fact, one scholar of the Civil War, Phillip Shaw Paludan, has suggested that the conflict itself was produced by just this anxiety about autonomy, participation, and political voice. Fear of "outside" forces, political deals, and (depending on section) "slave power" or "black Republican" conspiracies drove citizens of both north and south toward a crisis. In this respect, the sectional crisis had taken the wind out of the sails of the nativist movement by demonstrating that it was not just (or even primarily) *foreigners* who threatened equal republican citizenship and the ability of the United States to function effectively as a nation.[44]

Redefining the "Alien" Threat

The Civil War encouraged many Americans to see autonomy—and threats to autonomy—in collective terms. Thirty years ago, George M. Fredrickson made a persuasive case that the Civil War was an important transitional period during which antebellum confidence in the power of the individual began to be replaced by appreciation for the effectiveness of collective action and formal organization coupled with recognition of limits on individual activity. Fredrickson suggested that the war machine itself—particularly in the north—demonstrated to a generation the power of combination, hierarchy, and central direction. Individual good works proved incapable of alleviating human suffering on the massive scale to be found on Civil War battlefields and in disease-ridden camps, making way for the United States Sanitary Commission, the YMCA, and other institutional forms of humanitarianism. In the political arena, organized patriotism was promoted by the proliferation of Union League Clubs and Loyal Publication Societies.[45] To turn Fredrickson's point around, Americans who came to appreciate the power and effectiveness of organized action to achieve their goals also became more sensitive about the power of organized opposition to thwart these goals.

More recently, the historian Anne Rose, in *Victorian America and the Civil War,* has argued that appreciation for "bureaucracies" and "process" was part of the postwar Victorian temper. Something like this is also the point Paludan makes in describing Charles Russell Lowell during his years as a soldier writing home "of his growing feeling that heroism consisted of something different from involvement in 'crude and stupid theories.'" The true hero was "mighty unpretending" and devoted himself to having a practical effect on society by doing jobs that needed doing and turning his back on the most self-centered pursuits of the prewar years. All this has persuaded Alan Trachtenberg to call the postwar period an age of incorporation, when "the ability to mobilize, to concentrate, to *incorporate,* counted for more than [individual] thrift and diligence."[46] Antebellum concerns about republican independence, autonomy, and equality persisted long after the Civil War, but they coexisted with a new sense that organizations were the vehicles for obtaining these ends—and that organized resistance would have to be overcome. The postwar appeal of nativism would be that it offered an organized approach to securing the "national character" and that it identified organized foes.

The Civil War had another important effect on the long-term future of the nativist movement by speaking directly to the question of "national character," which in prewar terms had meant the ability to function and survive as a unified nation without the traditional characteristics of European nation-states. Of course, the war brought this question to a head. Contemporaries often described the war for the Union as a test of "whether we have a government or not." "Preservation of self-government" is what Garry Wills calls the "great task" that President Lincoln laid out for the American people in his address at Gettysburg in late 1863. According to Wills, in fact, Lincoln's enduring rhetorical achievement was in "refounding" the nation by diverting attention away from the Constitution, which laid out a mechanical government of separated powers and balanced interests, and focusing instead on the Declaration of Independence—which held up lofty ideals that could pull Americans together.[47] Of course, the experience of war itself created a new shared history and new traditions. Even before the conflict was over, Ralph Waldo Emerson observed that "Before the War, our patriotism was a firework, a salute, a serenade for holidays and summer evenings. . . . Now the deaths of thousands and determination of millions of men and women show that it is real." According to Carl Degler, "The measure of that reality was the evocation of an emotional attachment to the nation—that is, the creation of a modern sense of nationhood."[48]

If the war proved that the United States was an enduring nation, it did not fully answer the question what sort of a nation that was. The very power of a restored Union suggested this question. What would be the nation's impact on the world? What, in a different sense from before, was its "character"? To what end did it tend? Who controlled its destiny? A new appreciation of the power of organized groups suggested to many Americans a need both for watchfulness and for combination with other "right-thinking" citizens to produce the America they wanted. This was an extraordinary stimulus for a resurgent nativist movement if "aliens" came to be perceived as better-organized than "natives" to shape the nation's future.

It did not take long for some natives to arrive at the conclusion that there were indeed powerfully organized "alien" forces operating in American life; it did not take longer than the Civil War itself. Although its military aspects had much of the character of comic opera, the Fenian movement for the liberation of Ireland from British rule that rippled through Irish America in the mid-1860s had a capacity to renew American nativism in an age sensitized to the power of organizations. Indeed, the basic premises of Fenianism were likely to provoke nativist reaction. It was—at least cosmetically—highly organized, boasting a constitution (political rather than associational, and supposedly ready for use in a free Ireland), a capitol (in a New York City mansion), a flag, and an "army." Organizationally, it regarded itself as sufficiently independent of American law to commission its own privateers to prey on British shipping. Moreover, it not only sought "extra-American" goals but proposed to shape American foreign policy to achieve its ends. This was precisely the sort of "character"-shaping organization that was sure to put nativist veterans and those they could recruit into a lather.[49]

The American Fenian organization (named for the Fianna, a warrior band in Celtic mythology) was founded in 1858, held its first national convention at Chicago in 1863, and picked up a sizable following in northeastern and Great Lakes urban centers between 1864 and 1866. It had a twofold appeal. It proposed that the American Irish could expect little respect until they could show a relation to an independent, democratic homeland. And it flattered the Irish-American army veteran, flaunting the prospect that a quarter of a million battle-tested soldiers under experienced Irish-American officers could bring Britain to its knees. But what most struck many non-Irish-Americans was that the Fenians apparently demonstrated (1) that Irish immigrants (and perhaps their children) remained more interested in Ireland than in the United States, (2) that the would-be revolutionaries were willing to involve the United States in a scrape with Britain if it would serve their ends, (3) that the whole movement was a cynical manipulation of wartime anti-British sentiment in the north, and (4) that here was an effort to take advantage of organization not to serve the nation but to manipulate it.[50]

Fenianism looked much more formidable than it actually turned out to be. Bumbling armed raids on Canada from Buffalo and upper New England in 1866 (and a second time from New England in 1870) should have revealed not only the divisions in Fenian leadership and the reluctance of veterans to take on another fight but also the determination of the United States government to have no part in the Fenians' plans. However, what many Americans thought they saw was different. They saw big picnics, parades, and fund-raising rallies. They saw politicians addressing Fenian gatherings in what they took to be fawning terms. And when Fenianism began to fragment after the failures of 1866, they saw internal Fenian divisions bleeding over into local politics. They were impressed when the police confiscated caches of Fenian arms and ammunition and angry when they thought that Fernando Wood of New York City had been elected to Congress because of his fierce rhetorical support for Fenian militancy. Conversely, a sensation was created in Illinois when an Irish-born candidate for the state legislature lost because immigrant voters took him to be anti-Fenian. This was the kind of ethnic voting that prewar nativists had denounced, as were the weird political alliances that emerged in the presidential election of 1866, which saw Irish Democrats denouncing Andrew Johnson for throwing American law against Fenian military adventurism and Republicans (seeking to embarrass the president) lauding the courage of Fenians captured in the raids on Canada. As Thomas N. Brown, a scholar of Irish-American nationalist movements, points out, one of the reasons for the breakup of Fenianism was the participants' admission that the organization was likely to be more useful for achieving *American* political goals than international goals. Although these goals turned out to be diverse and sometimes conflicting, this was just what American nativists feared—that organized "un-American" groups were influencing the nation's political life.[51]

While the military aspects of Fenianism produced more smoke than fire, the idea of organized Irish-Americans with guns in their hands was harrowing to Americans who chose to view it against the background of the wartime antidraft mobs. A few highly publicized incidents of ethnic and religious violence in the early postwar years fueled such fears. Violence could be counted on to accompany aggressive Protestant Irish celebrations of the Battle of the Boyne each July. A major confrontation with Irish Catholics occurred in New York City in 1869. A more serious affray resulted in 1870, leaving five dead and scores injured. About 50 were killed the following year, when militia guarding the Protestant marchers fired on unsympathetic onlookers. Boston, too, experienced a brawl in 1871.[52] Different in character but just as capable of provoking nativist sentiment was a riot in Memphis, Tennessee, in May 1866 directed at the freed-black community. It resulted in 46 deaths among African-Americans and the incineration of 100 homes, and it involved a large number of Irish-American Confederate veterans. While the freedmen could not expect quite the same outpouring of sympathy as white Protestant Orangemen, the riot did serve to remind contemporaries that organized violence could take place outside of wartime.[53]

Less dramatic than mob violence but probably more consequential for the resurgence of organized nativist activism was evidence of Irish-

American involvement in (or manipulation by) increasingly sophisticated urban political machines. "Boss" William Marcy Tweed's New York organization, Tammany Hall, was the most elaborate and best publicized of these. Although the contemporary press focused—as memory now focuses—on the fiscal corruption of the Tweed "ring," Thomas Archdeacon has put his finger on the elements of urban machines most likely to produce a nativist reaction: "The emergence of party machines that openly fostered group reaction rather than individual reflection in the making of political decisions offended middle-class Protestant sensibilities, as did the open exchange by the lower classes of ballots for social and economic benefits. Worse, from the natives' point of view, the effectiveness of the new politics threatened to put control of urban America in 'alien' hands at the very time that the cities were becoming the center of life in the United States."[54] Again, it was organization that produced anxiety and for, that matter, was a defining characteristic of "alien." The native-born Protestant bourgeoisie gave little thought to what we now recognize as the effectiveness of late-nineteenth-century urban machines in providing what working-class, often immigrant, city dwellers needed and were unable to get through other means. Voters traded their ballots for political recognition (their own version of republican equal citizenship), public and private employment, paid political careers for some, and organized charity that functioned in an age before unemployment benefits or survivors' insurance. A political machine that offered all this to its supporters was not likely to produce urban "progress" in a form that made sense to the middle or upper classes, but it appealed to working-class people who looked to local government for survival rather than "progress." What the "better sort" saw was not just corruption and expense but, more important, government that happened without them. Moreover, they saw "foreigners" organized for political purposes and took alarm whenever evidence of naturalization fraud in the service of the "bosses" was brought to their attention.[55]

The practical exchange between urban ethnic voters, ward politicians, and city officials suggested the growing power of politically organized first- and second-generation immigrants and brought Irish-American politicians into positions of visibility and leadership. The institutional muscularity demonstrated by the Roman Catholic church in the 1860s and 1870s provided further testimony to what people who were outcast and despised could achieve by organization. It was the evidence of organization itself as much as what organization accomplished that would provoke a nativist reaction in the post-bellum period. In the powerful Catholic archdiocese of New York, Archbishop John Hughes had not been idle during the Civil War years. He convened a church council in 1861 to build on the administrative centralization he had begun in the 1850s; a principal achievement of this conference was solidification of leadership of the spreading parochial school system. Hughes also took the lead in bringing together in 1864 a national bishops' council which established standards for the organization of Catholic schools. These developments alone were likely to rekindle the hostility of nativists who had spent much of the preceding quarter-century trumpeting secular (by which they meant conventionally Protestant) public education as the foundation of an independent-minded republican citizenry. At the same time, it was precisely the uncompromisingly Protestant nature of the public schools that had driven the largely immigrant Catholic population to create their own alternative educational system. By the end of the Civil War, it was clear what organized immigrants could achieve.[56]

Although more and more of the leadership of the Catholic church in the United States was American-born, events far away conspired to persuade American Protestants that Catholics remained under foreign dictation and to encourage a nativist reaction. The papal Syllabus of Errors of 1864, which criticized liberalism and secularism—including secular education—and the Vatican's articulation of papal moral and theological infallibility in 1870 could be interpreted as justifying all of antebellum nativists' direst warnings about the challenge of Roman Catholicism to American traditions of "independence." That an American Provincial Council of the Clergy found itself in 1866 in the position of having to support the Vatican's antimodernist positions at the same time that the Catholic church was coming under political attack in both Germany and Italy only reinforced nativists' argument that Americans were displaying weakness before a foreign "potentate." This allowed Americans who cast themselves as "native" (in "character" as well as in birth) to find what they took to be all sorts of examples of calculated "foreign" Catholic assaults on American public secular education. These included a highly publicized battle in Cincinnati in 1869 over the use of the King James Bible as a text in the schools which was interpreted as "defeat" of Protestants by an organized opposition. And Boss Tweed's successful promotion of a bill in New York's state legislature late in the same year providing for public assistance for nonpublic—hence, among others, Catholic—schools was easy for nativists to portray as evidence that Irish political clout was being put to the service of a Vatican-inspired effort to undermine "nonsectarian" public education.[57]

A series of court actions and legislative measures between 1873 and 1875 could give the appearance to the suspicious that a well-organized Roman Catholicism was a much more powerful threat to "American" institutions and practices than it had ever been in the antebellum period. The most anxious pointed to state supreme court cases in Ohio which upheld the exemption of church property—including parochial schools—from taxation and supported Catholic parents' contention that the King James Bible was sectarian and not suitable as a public school text. They also pointed to legislation in both Wisconsin and Ohio which authorized Catholic priests to serve as chaplains in prisons and state hospitals. Legislative "victories" for Catholic interests were regarded as especially threatening, since they were believed to reveal the consequences of ethnic bloc voting. The election of a Catholic priest to the public school board in Cleveland in 1874 caused a sensation. In 1875, Bible reading disappeared from Chicago schools.[58] All this gave special significance to the impressive public ceremonies that accompanied the dedication of St. Patrick's Cathedral in New York City in May 1879. For nativists, when 400 priests and 41 bishops proceeded up the aisle for the first mass, the organized power of a "foreign" church was on display. When the press reported the attendance of so many of the city's, state's, and nation's (mostly non-Catholic) elite, it was taken to mean that "Americans" were truckling to this power.[59]

Certainly the tendency for some Americans to see events like these in apocalyptic terms was exacerbated by the economic depression of 1873-1877. This unexpected crisis put a million or more out of work, cut the wages of the employed urban working class by as much as a fourth, and left food prices relatively high even though farmers were suffering. People looked for villains, and, as was characteristic of the postwar period, they tended to look for *corporate* villains. Workers suspected that the depression was a consequence of speculation by investors but also held up to special criticism a federal law of 1864 which facilitated recruitment of contract labor abroad. The National Labor Union, which had begun criticizing contract labor as early as 1870, raised the volume of its denunciations once the depression hit. Its rhetoric condemned not just immigrant labor but "organized" immigrant labor and not just business but business which organized itself to keep labor costs low by shopping abroad. When operators of bituminous coal mines in Pennsylvania contracted with a broker of Italian labor to provide substitute workers during a strike in 1874, the reaction was violent enough to leave three dead.[60]

Among the upper and middle classes, it was temptingly convenient to view depression-era labor unrest against a backdrop of the contemporaneous Paris Commune and to see in early labor organizations a seedbed for socialist revolution. It was especially easy so long as employers, managers, and professionals persisted in seeing labor activism as "foreign" and based in politics as much as economics. Like the workers themselves, though, they focused their attention as much on form as on substance. The form of labor unrest that caught their eye was allegedly *organized* unrest. For that reason, it was the Irish "Molly Maguires" of the Pennsylvania anthracite mining districts who attracted sustained and lurid attention in the newspapers, even though their activities were peripheral to the story of American labor activism.[61] In Chicago, what generated the most excitement was not the specific demands of labor regarding wages and working conditions but the existence of Irish and German working-class authorized and unauthorized militia units. The presence of these organizations led the *Chicago Tribune* to report that the police would have to be specially prepared to "thwart an insurrection of a whole continent."[62]

In order for anxiety about organized foreigners to turn nativistic, it had to be specifically associated with threats to the "national character." And a resurgent postwar nativist movement which made this connection could take its cue on how to respond from a host of highly organized approaches to contemporary social and political issues. The 1870s, for example, saw an explosion of "city reform" clubs and associations created to weaken the political "boss" and the "machine." Raymond Mohl notes that middle-class Philadelphians created their version in 1871 and Chicagoans created theirs in 1874. The Orange-Irish "riot" of 1871 and a fiscal crisis faced by New York City in the same year gave stimulus to an Executive Committee of the Citizens and Taxpayers for Financial Reform of the City. Typically, such organizations worked (with the help of state legislatures dominated by rural, Protestant, Anglo-American representatives) to secure new city charters which took powers away from city councils elected at the ward level and invested them in mayors elected at large, diluting the effect of the allegedly "foreign" vote.[63] Although urban reform coalitions were not entirely new to the postbellum period, their number and popularity were. So was their tendency to attribute flawed government to a "machine" and their conviction that the bosses could not be defeated at the ballot box through normal political means but that structural changes were required in city administration to thwart organized challenges to "good government."

The postwar temperance movement also saw a villain in organization. The antebellum movement had focused on reforming the drunkard; by contrast, temperance in the 1860s and 1870s focused on the suppliers of drink. In many respects, antebellum temperance had been a success; per capita alcohol consumption fell by almost 80 percent between 1830 and midcentury. But after the Civil War, beer consumption rose fivefold or more. The site of much beer drinking was the saloon, and it is estimated that by 1873 there were some 100,000 saloons, a number that would increase 50 percent more by the end of the decade. Beer was popularly regarded as an immigrants' drink, and associated largely with Germans. The new temperance societies of the postwar period, dominated by women, identified the saloon and the organized brewers that supplied it, rather than the drinker, as most worth their attention.[64]

Old nativists and new recruits had no difficulty determining what strings to pluck to get maximum public response to their warnings that well-organized "foreign" forces were poised to dictate the character of the postwar nation. A pronounced anti-Catholic theme in major party politics began manifesting itself in 1868 and grew stronger through the presidential election of 1876. The initial blow was struck when Congress passed a law discontinuing public funding for the 40-year-old American diplomatic mission to the Vatican. In Ohio, the Republican governor, Rutherford Hayes, successfully exploited anti-Catholic sentiment—exposed at least in part by a debate in Cleveland over imposing property taxes on Catholic schools—to win reelection in 1872. In 1875, Hayes actively campaigned against the Geghan Law, promoted by Ohio's Democratic party, which authorized Catholic priests to serve in state penal and charitable institutions. Hayes, who was about to run for president, seems to have concluded that popular anxiety about the institutional growth of the Roman Catholic church extended well beyond his home state. It took only until August 1876 for the United States House of Representatives to pass, overwhelmingly, a proposed sixteenth amendment to the Constitution banning the use of tax dollars for church-related schools. Although the bill fell just short of the required two-thirds majority in the Senate, Hayes—elected president in November 1876—went on to capitalize on anti-Catholic sentiment by appointing as secretary of the Treasury Richard Wigginton Thompson, who had just attracted attention for writing a nativistic tract entitled *The Papacy and the Civil Power.*[65]

The advantage that Hayes got out of exploiting anti-Catholicism in Ohio was available to politicians in other states, too. The Wisconsin Republican platform of 1875 called for no application of public money to parochial education. New York legislators fought year after year over the question of giving Catholic priests access to state prisons; and this right was not secured for Catholics in Massachusetts until the end of the decade. Although the proposed sixteenth amendment to the Constitution failed, parallel clauses were added to existing state constitutions or became part of the constitutions of new states formed in the west.[66] Hayes was quite explicit about what he took to be the value of fighting for a prohibition of public support for church schools, confiding to his diary in mid-1875 that the issue could be used to show Democrats' "subserviency to the Roman Catholic demands."[67]

The Nativist Self-Image: Counterorganizing

Under these circumstances it was not difficult for a new wave of nativist organizing to begin. Many of the organizations that emerged did not survive long, although by the standards of the nativist fraternities of the 1840s and 1850s they reached adulthood. Some left little trace, like two California orders, the Native Americans of 1872 and the Crescents of 1875. Some tried hard to reenlist old nativist activists, like the American Alliance, which ceremoniously elected a southern Know Nothing, Kenneth Rayner, to honorary membership in 1878. By far the most consequential were those that had been able to survive the Civil War with a core of loyalists. The American Protestant Association, which had a strong base among Scots-Irish Protestants, rode along through the war years and even flourished with the postwar formalization of the Orange Order in the United States, reporting 50,000 members in 300 lodges in the early 1870s. The Order of United American Mechanics (founded in the 1840s) and its Junior Order (founded in the 1850s) both survived the 1860s. Of the two, the Junior Order was the more thriving concern, strong enough to support a couple of spinoff nativist fraternities of its own besides assisting in the revival of the prewar Patriotic Order, Sons of America in 1874. Among the new organizations was the Order of the American Union in New York City—inspired, interestingly enough, by an original Know Nothing,

James W. Barker, who reappeared after the Civil War at the head of a short-lived organization called the Order of the American Shield. Another new venture was a women's auxiliary to the Junior OUAM, the Daughters of Liberty, which was organized in central Connecticut in 1875.[68]

The attraction of these new and surviving nativist orders was both utilitarian and ideological. The idea of fraternal benefits took on new life when dozens of modern insurance companies operating by actuarial principles failed in the financial panic accompanying the depression of the 1870s. The old principle of mutual assessment was easier for ordinary people to understand and kept friendly societies out of the unpredictable capital markets. Some modern estimates place the number of mutual-assessment fraternal organizations founded between 1870 and the first years of the twentieth century at well over 3,000. It was virtually inevitable that most of these went almost as rapidly as they came, brought down by unexpected claims and aging memberships. On the other hand, these very deficiencies caused them to clone "junior" orders at a rapid rate, keeping up the enthusiasm of the youngest and most active members. It is no surprise that most of the nativist orders that sprang up in the 1870s either operated entirely on the mutual-assessment principle or offered optional mutual-assessment insurance.[69] Historians have routinely noted that as the United States continued its expansion westward following the Civil War, fraternal organizations of all kinds took on enhanced practical value, whether for their mutual-assessment insurance, their guaranteed burials, their instant "brotherhood," or their business contacts. One scholar of western expansion observes that by the late 1860s Sacramento, California, could boast of chapters of "Good Templars, Druids, Knights of Honor, Knights of Pythias, United Workmen, Red Men, Janissaries of Light, Champions of the Red Cross—as well as . . . Masons and Odd Fellows."[70]

Ideologically, the nativist societies of the 1870s focused their attention on the supposed dangers of "foreign" organization to the national character. The Order of the American Union denounced evidence of the growing sophistication of "Roman hierarchy" in America and pitted itself against "religiopolitical" organizations which it saw as thwarting legislation to maintain the "nonsectarian" (read "Protestant") nature of public schools and charitable institutions. The Daughters of Liberty argued that it was the special prerogative of American womanhood to protect the public schools from ecclesiastical control and to ensure that the schools instilled authentic "American" values. This order, too, made it plain that it saw the Roman Catholic church, assisted by immigrant-based political "machines," as the chief threat.[71]

During the 15 years following the Civil War, a revised definition of "foreign" emerged, and with it a new definition of "native" and "nativist." Increasingly, anything of putatively immigrant origin that had an organizational character came to be taken as a "foreign" threat to the national character. The institutional Roman Catholic church, contract labor, ethnic fraternities, urban political machines, labor combinations, and ethnic militia companies—to name a few such organizations—assumed, to many "natives," this "foreign" character. It was the fact of organization itself that seemed threatening, for through organization the national character might be re-formed. "Native" also came to be associated as much with organization (or perhaps counterorganization) as with nativity. The true "native" American was one who organized—or participated in organizations—to resist foreign assaults on the national character. This, of course, tended to blur the definition of just what constituted a nativist organization. In the postbellum period, some nativist organizations continued to take the traditional fraternal form, but others did not. Some, like the Loyal Orange Order, were effectively ethnic fraternities themselves but seemed to nativists to be arrayed on the "right" side. Others were merely "patriotic," like the Improved Order of Red Men, but their patriotism was directed at maintaining the cultural status quo. Even the city reform leagues and the hugely popular Grand Army of the Republic (for Union Civil War veterans) had public agendas that put them on the fringes of the nativist movement.

The sort of nativism that emerged from the Civil War remained influential enough to transcend political parties and could bind old nativists together with new recruits. This was apparent across the nation but is no better documented anywhere than for Jersey City, New Jersey, the setting of Douglas V. Shaw's careful studies of nativist continuity. A stronghold of the Order of United Americans since the 1850s, Jersey City elected as its Republican mayor in 1867 an old OUA man who had the support of the OUA editor of the city's leading Democratic newspaper.[72]

What galvanized nativist veterans to action and brought new members into the nativist fold in Jersey City was the political success of the growing, organized Irish-American community. By the end of the Civil War it was powerful enough to extract from Democratic politicians a

number of positions on the police force more in keeping with its representation in the population. By 1870, the Irish political community was
in a position to gain a majority on the board of aldermen, place a
Catholic representative on the school board, and altogether take a
much more public role in the city. Within a year, old nativists of both
political parties had pulled enough new men into their orbit to work a
bill through the rural, Anglo-American, Protestant state legislature that
took most executive authority away from the local city council and
placed it in the hands of commissions appointed by the state. The commissioners—for police, fire, and public works—were frequently men of
time-tested nativist affiliations. Simultaneously, city voting districts
were rearranged to weaken the Irish vote within the city as a whole and
even within the Democratic party. Douglas Shaw notes that these
structural changes were so effective that "the Irish did not play a
prominent role in Jersey City politics again for another fifteen years."[73]

In a short time, followers of both political parties who had joined to
resist the effects of Irish political organization formed themselves into
a new nativist fraternity, the Order of the American Union, which
appeared in Jersey City in the mid-1870s. When it was opened up to
public scrutiny in a series of newspaper articles in 1876, the organization proved to have some 400 members, including much of the city's
political elite. It is clear that this organization understood its role as
resisting "foreign" organization of all kinds. In the same year, an affiliated newspaper even "lumped Catholic total abstinence societies in
with other 'treasonable secret organizations of the Papal church' that
sought to undermine American institutions."[74]

During the 20 years following the Civil War, the experience in Jersey City was repeated in cities and towns across the country, and this
indicates much about the nature of nativist organizing on the national
scale. The tattered remnants of antebellum nativist fraternities—or at
least a sizable number of men (and some women) who had been participants in them during their more robust days—offered a fragile but ser-
viceable skeleton for the growth of new societies which posed as
defenders of the "national character" against "alien" institutions perceived as dangerously more organized than in the past. Old nativists
particularly drew attention to the organizational maturity of the Roman
Catholic church in the United States (still largely an immigrant
church) to attract new recruits. In fact, the statistics of Catholic growth
were impressive. James H. Campbell notes that as late as 1869, the
Catholic church in Ohio was still considered weak enough to receive

missionary assistance from Europe but that by the early 1880s "Ohio had a population of about 249,000 Catholics, attending 544 churches and chapels. . . . At the same time, the church ran 238 parochial schools with an enrollment of about 48,446 students, eleven orphanages taking care of 1,454 children and nine hospitals." This was institutional muscularity, and it showed up elsewhere as well. By the end of the 1880s, the archdiocese of Boston had half a million parishioners supporting nearly 200 churches, and 30,000 children were enrolled in church schools.[75]

Nowhere was sensitivity about Catholic organizational development greater than among the churches and agencies of mainline Protestantism. Split by sectionalism and the Civil War, denominations like the Methodists, Baptists, and Presbyterians were also unsettled by the continuing westward expansion of population, the growth of large cities, and the accelerated postwar development of secular social welfare institutions that performed roles once monopolized by the church. Evidence of Catholic unity and growth, and what was taken to be Catholics' political influence, was unnerving and produced in Protestant church circles an anti-Catholic rhetoric that could rationalize nativist regrouping. Protestant anxiety, in fact, helped create provocations for nativistic bodies that not only portrayed themselves as counterorganizing to resist Catholic influence over the national character but also characteristically took a fraternal form that, ironically, seemed better able than the churches themselves to help meet members face the uncertainties of a mobile, more urban society.

Somewhat surprisingly, on the national level, one of the principal issues that politicized friction between Protestants and Catholics and kept it before the public, providing a new excuse for nativist organizing, was the question of how to handle the education of American Indians. As far back as the early 1870s, the Ulysses Grant administration had sought to regulate the relationship between missionaries and American Indians by assigning specific Indian agencies ("reservations") to specific Christian denominations. Although Catholic missionaries had established relationships with Indians at about 40 percent of the agencies, in the official distribution Catholics received a much smaller fraction of the assignments. Ten different Protestant churches divided up access to over 70 agencies. Despite Protestant dominance of Indian missions, there was great sensitivity among the Protestant denominations—which operated their mission enterprises separately—to the creation in 1874 of a Catholic Bureau of Indian Missions, which seemed to highlight the Catholics' organizational sophistication. A new source of controversy surfaced in 1880-1881, when the establishment of a Catholic mission just off the grounds of an agency assigned to a Protestant denomination caused Protestants to cry foul. The crisis passed when it became apparent that Protestant missionaries were doing the same thing, but one consequence was that official government mission assignments were rescinded in 1881. This, in turn, was attributed by Protestant leaders to Catholic meddling, a charge made more powerful by being disseminated from church pulpits across the land.[76]

Ten years later, interdenominational hostilities boiled over again. When it came to office in 1889, the Harrison administration appointed as Indian commissioner Thomas J. Morgan, an ordained Baptist minister and educational reformer armed with a conviction that public school education in the English language was the great equalizer in American society. His church background and his loud pronouncements in favor of compulsory public education were not likely to win him favor among Catholic education officials; but his selection of the Reverend Daniel Dorchester, who had published an anti-Catholic tract during the recent Boston school text controversy, as commissioner of Indian education provoked outright hostility. Also, the emergent policy of closing mission schools at bureau agencies and replacing them with government-run boarding schools was seen by Catholic educators as aggression aimed at eliminating the church from Indian education. By the early 1890s, relations between the director of the Catholic Bureau of Indian Missions and Commissioner Morgan had grown almost irretrievably rancorous, and for the next couple of years barbs were sent back and forth about the alleged misuse of Indian appropriations. Not only did these exchanges draw publicity; a few years later, they gave Benjamin Harrison's supporters an opportunity to blame the Republicans' loss in the 1892 presidential election on organized Catholic opposition.[77]

The prevalence of anti-Catholic rhetoric in the everyday discourse of Protestant churches as well as in local and national politics was reflected in the publications and practices of mass-membership fraternal benefit societies, which experienced a resurgence during the last two decades of the nineteenth century. Lynn Dumenil describes the treatment of Catholicism in such Masonic periodicals as the *Trestleboard* and the *American Tyler* as "shrill"; and the Knights of Malta listed among its purposes "to promote Protestant unity and to defend the Protestant faith." In this respect, the Knights of Malta was not far different from the Loyal Orange Institution of the United States, which rewrote its constitution in 1884 to specifically address contemporary issues, particularly the sanctity of "nonsectarian" public schools and the illegitimacy of any tendency of churches to "meddle" with government. This quasinativist society was particularly successful at mobilizing middle-class Protestant women on the schools issue, and it spun off a Ladies Loyal Orange Association in 1882. The Knights of Pythias and the Improved Order of Red Men (IORM) were not immune to these tendencies. At the time that the issue of English-language instruction in schools was heating up, the Knights of Pythias provoked the secession of its German-American members by refusing to continue publishing the order's ritual in German. IORM never did reconcile with the German-language Independent Order, and in 1890, it departed from its exclusively faux-Indian symbolism to identify itself more thoroughly with the Anglo-American heritage. Members of its exclusive Chieftain's League were outfitted in replicas of Washington's Continental Army uniform.[78]

There is every reason to think that the traditional fraternal orders found these heated issues of language and the schools helpful to their own growth. The Improved Order of Red Men, which—after a postwar spurt—had declined by 50 percent between 1874 and 1880, more than doubled in size over the next decade and then tripled again from 1890 to 1907. The Knights of Malta grew by half during the late 1890s alone. In fact, fraternalism peaked in popularity in this period, for a variety of reasons not unrelated to the impetus behind the nativist movement. Lynn Dumenil, a modern analyst of the Masonic order in late nineteenth and early twentieth centuries, argues that participation in fraternities like the Masons was not only a way for middle-class men—and men aspiring to the middle class—to advertise their respectability by buying into the Masons' "moral code of self-improvement through self-restraint" but also (despite the Masons' official nonsectarianism) a way of asserting Protestant Christian unity in the face of denominational division. Both Dumenil and another recent scholar of fraternalism, Mark Carnes, suggest that the costumes, paraphernalia, and rituals of the fraternities symbolically bound the brethren to one another and emphasized their distinctiveness from the divisive world outside the lodge. As the nation grew, as geographical mobility over long distances became even more common, and as business transactions came to be increasingly impersonal, the sheer economic value of lodge membership increased. The pioneering sociologist Max Weber, after his visit to the United States in the first years of the twentieth century, wrote that membership in a fraternal lodge announced, "I am a gentleman patented after investigation and probation and guaranteed by my membership."[79]

The popularity of fraternal orders was nothing short of remarkable. A contemporary noted that at the end of the century 19 million men shared between 5 and 6 million fraternal memberships in 70,000 local lodges, with nearly 1 million each in the Odd Fellows and the Masons and hundreds of thousands in groups like the Knights of Pythias and the Red Men. Mark Carnes calculates that from the Civil War to the end of the century the income of the Odd Fellows alone approached $200 million and that many millions were paid out to holders of fraternal insurance. He also perceptively observes that the cost of membership, while not exorbitant, had the effect of confining participation to those who had at least reached the lower rungs of the middle class. Moreover, these figures do not include the increasingly large numbers of Americans joining the women's and even children's off-shoots of the male fraternities. Nor does it dilute the force of these statistics to recall that it was typical for "joiners" to belong to more than one lodge at a time.[80]

With the divisions in Protestantism on display and the purported organizational strength of Catholicism "revealed," with a new wave of anxiety about the nation-building capability of the public schools, and with the enhanced attraction of fraternalism, it is little wonder that fraternal and quasifraternal organizations—representing themselves as a patriotic force ready to battle "foreign" organizations for control of the national character—experienced terrific growth. The antebellum nativist orders that had limped through the war years but were able to reorganize in the 1870s were the initial beneficiaries. The Brotherhood of the Union updated its organization in 1888, reaching out to men aged 16 to 50 with a range of fraternal insurance benefits. The American Protestant Association, still centered in Pennsylvania but with chapters throughout the northeast and the midwest and even in California, gleefully reported at its 1889 annual meeting at the mother hall in Philadelphia that it had gathered "with our broken ranks filled up." Although not an insurance society at the national level, the American Protestant Association authorized local chapters to offer survivors', unemployment, and funeral benefits. Opening its membership to Protestants of both native and foreign birth, it specifically identified the "foreign" challenge to the American character as the orchestrated "designs and intrusions of Popish mercenaries."[81]

The Patriotic Order, Sons of America, improved its "benefit fund" package in 1880 and in 1885 added a women's auxiliary, the Patriotic Daughters of America, which spun itself off a few years later as a new order for both sexes, the Patriotic Order of True Americans. The Sons' "Declaration of Principles" in 1886 focused on organized "foreign" threats: contract labor, land-grabbing "foreign capitalists," allegedly coordinated "anarchist" violence in Chicago and Milwaukee, and challenges to the culturally homogenizing role of the public schools. By 1889, it reported "districts" in 17 states and federal territories and more extensive state "camps" not only in Pennsylvania, Ohio, and Illinois but also in Colorado and Montana Territory. As in the case of other fraternities, the success of the order depended a great deal on local leadership. In 1889, the Ohio camp reported 70 local chapters, though it could document only 36 as active. Interestingly, of those, a dozen met in their own halls and half a dozen gathered in Odd Fellows temples, Knights of Pythias halls, or the facilities of other "friendly societies."[82]

By 1882, the Order of United American Mechanics (OUAM) had shed whatever remained of its original function as a mutual protection society for "native" workmen and took pains to assert that it had "no affiliation to that species of associations known as Trades' Unions." Now it emphasized its fraternal insurance benefits and its attractiveness to "speculative mechanics" (that is, businessmen). It defined the threat to "native" businesses and "native" institutions as "foreign combinations." A women's branch, the Daughters of Liberty, offered insurance for its members under the 1887 constitution of its national council. Roy Rosenzweig, who has assembled information about OUAM in the industrial city of Worcester, Massachusetts, observes that in the mid-1890s the local membership "split fairly evenly between blue- and white-collar workers (with most of them falling into the skilled blue-collar or the lower level white-collar categories); the most common single job was foreman." Significantly, it was in 1885 that the Junior Order of OUAM asserted its full independence from its parent, taking a more aggressive political posture. By the first years of the new century, it had twice the membership of the original order.[83]

The chosen objectives and enemies of these organizations highlight the distinction between "nativism" as a popular mood and "nativism" as an organized social movement. The mass-circulation press drew attention to the involvement of "foreigners" in what was taken to be political radicalism, acquainting the public with sinister-sounding words like "anarchism," "socialism," and "communism"; it boldly headlined dramatic incidents like the Haymarket bombing in Chicago; and it highlighted the participation of immigrant workers in strikes and labor violence. But the rhetoric of the nativist *movement,* as represented by its constituent organizations, overwhelmingly focused on perceived threats to the public schools and "sectarian" assaults on the public treasury. "Foreignness" or "un-Americanism" itself remained closely connected with organization, and no "radical" party, union, or cell was viewed as holding a candle to the traditional ethnic clubs and societies or "drilled" ward voting blocs, much less to the Roman Catholic church. In fact, the principal theme of the nativist *movement* continued to be anti-Catholicism.

This was evident not only in the language and objectives of the older nativist organizations that had survived the Civil War or emerged soon after, but also in most of the rich variety of new nativist fraternities, orders, leagues, and even parties that sprang up in the 1880s and 1890s. Several of these had especially predictable aims, for they were offshoots of or secessions from earlier nativist organizations. The Order of American Freemen (1884) in Pennsylvania and the Loyal Knights of America, founded in upstate New York two years later, were formed from chapters that had left the American Protestant Association, seeking a more fraternal style. Fraternal benefits were apparently also the goal of a new Junior American Protestant Association, limited to insurable men aged 18 to 45, which was one of the few societies to append to a long list of supposed Catholic outrages to true Americanism a catalogue of "foreign ideas" that included anarchism and socialism.[84]

Also predictable was the anti-Catholic theme of the large number of local nativist organizations which emerged in response to issues or incidents in particular cities or states. Sustained battles in Boston over appropriate texts in the public schools, which divided Protestants and Catholics from the mid-1880s to the mid-1890s, brought successive waves of nativist organizing in the area. Boston's Loyal Women of American Liberty emerged in 1888 as part of the political effort to keep Catholics off the school committee. The related Loyal Men of American Liberty took as their object "to call attention of the people to the aggressions of Romanism" and, in a reference to several currently popular anti-Catholic writers who claimed to be former church "insiders," urged members to "assist all excommunicated Roman Catholics." The pointedly named Order of the Little Red School House, formed in Boston in 1895 following violence between Protestant paraders and unsympathetic Irish bystanders, experienced a spurt of growth by promoting an "America for Americans" theme that was explicitly anti-Catholic. Not surprisingly, these sorts of organizations frequently did not long outlive the incidents that brought them into being, and, in fact, their purposes were often narrowly political, sometimes focused on winning a particular election.[85]

This was the case not only in Boston but in other communities, large and small. A controversy over the schools in Newburyport, Massachusetts, in 1889 produced a fraternal society, the Get-There Benefit Association, which (in a somewhat odd turn of phrase) charged that the aim of the Roman Catholic church was to "disrobe the native born citizens of the inculcated allegiance to God, Country, natural, and civil rights," blasting Catholic influence on the public schools and an alternative "parochial system" of church schools at the same time. The foreign threat was unmistakably organizational—not individual Catholics but a "Papistry with its vast local and national power." Seeking to mobilize Protestant voters for local elections, the Get-There Benefit Association did not survive long, despite its fraternal beneficiary features. In the environs of New York City and across the Hudson in New Jersey, a Templars of Liberty, founded in 1881, took much the same line and with much the same objectives. In St. Louis, a Protestant Knights of America took shape in the mid-1890s to counter the supposed strength of the Knights of Columbus.[86] Local organizations of a nativist hue were by no means only an eastern phenomenon; they turned up in the 1880s all the way over on the west coast. San Jose's United Order of Native Americans (1887) was open to native-born men and women who were "opposed to the union of church and state, and in favor of sustaining and upholding the Free Public Schools untrammeled by Sectarianism."[87]

While most of these organizations took their strength from the white-collar middle class, broadly construed, forms of nativist organizing appealed to higher and lower social strata. Chicago's United Order of Deputies (1886) attracted a more working-class membership with its calls for preferential employment of Protestants. The American Knights of Protection—which cropped up in Baltimore and Washington in 1894 as a result of efforts by men with experience in the Junior Order, United American Mechanics—sought to appeal across classes with a program that called for restraints on immigration to protect

American workers, tariff legislation to protect industry, and, as the glue which held all this together, defense of the public schools and the "sanctity of the franchise." Up from Texas through the midwest, a National Order of Videttes, founded in 1886, combined an appeal to rural people not unlike that of the contemporaneous Farmers' Alliances—opposition to "foreign influence" over land and money— with denunciation of contract immigrant "pauper" labor and conventional attacks on "sectarian influence" in local politics and the public schools.[88]

On the other hand, the 1880s and 1890s saw an outpouring of genteel nativist organizing in the form of "educational" and "patriotic" societies. Unlike the nativist orders that appealed to merchants, petty professionals, office workers, foremen, and skilled laborers, these orders rarely featured fraternal insurance. This is not to say that they had no "utilitarian" benefits for their members. In fact, membership was a kind of validation that one was a part of the true Anglo-American national core, and hence a mark of status. Not surprisingly, a number of these organizations had at least loose affiliations with groups like the Sons and Daughters of the American Revolution. That was certainly the case with the Young People's Society to Promote Practical Patriots (proposed in New York City in 1891 and perhaps a matter more of paper than of real activity) and probably with the roughly contemporaneous Patria Club. Both, in the words of the latter, sought to promote "patriotic studies and object lessons in our schools for immigrant children" and affirmed that public rather than parochial schools were the only way to ensure that foreign-born young people might become real "Americans."[89] The most elaborate organization of this type was the Order of the Red, White, and Blue, established in Rochester in 1888, which was restricted to people with at least two generations of American-born ancestors and led its members through three ranks, named for the colors of the national flag. It advertised as its goal the "protection" of Protestants from organized Catholic efforts to capture the nation—that is, the "national character."[90]

Conclusion: "Systems" versus "Systems"

"Nowadays," said Julian West, the main character of Edward Bellamy's famous novel *Looking Backward* (1887), "everybody is part of a system with a distinct place and function." In the novel, Julian is supposed to have been propelled into the future, but Bellamy was also offering a commentary on his own time. We might well borrow this notion to summarize the goal and accomplishment of the nativist movement from the Civil War up to the mid-1880s: getting and staying organized to contest with putatively alien "systems" to define the "character" of the nation. It also helps to remind us who nativist activists were. Into the early twentieth century, they remained the off-spring of the Civil War era, accustomed to organization as the way to get things done. On the one hand, this made them unusually sensitive to what they took to be "alien" organization. Virtually, to be *alien,* a threat to the "national character" had to be an organized threat. On the other hand, these were not people terrified of organization as such. In fact, their tendency was to respond to perceived threats with their own organizations, or what they would have described as counterorganizations. These agents of middle-class, Anglo-American Protestantism were often on the offensive in promoting cultural values which to them had become fused with the political existence of the nation. While fraternal and "patriotic" nativism would rise to higher levels of organizational and political sophistication before the nineteenth century ended, new developments in Anglo-American intellectual culture would also begin to lead some Americans away from requiring acculturation of immigrants and toward efforts to keep many of them out of the United States altogether.

Chapter Six

Forks in the Road: The American Protective Association and the Immigration Restriction League

In most respects, 1911 was an inauspicious year. For the nativist movement in the United States, it served as no watershed. Yet a succession of easily overlooked events will show how organized nativist activism had evolved since the beginning of the 1880s. On November 5, 1911, a back page of the *New York Times* carried the obituary of Charles E. Gildersleeve, last recorded grand sachem of the Order of United Americans (OUA) and repository of the brotherhood's institutional memory. It had been exactly 60 years before, in 1851, that Gildersleeve, then 23, had first attracted public notice as an officer of OUA's Washington's birthday celebration committee in New York City. Perhaps it was he who had something to do with decking out the "thirteen elegantly caparisoned white horses" that led the eye-catching parade.[1] The year 1911 was also the last of Henry Bowers who, in 1887 in Clinton, Iowa, had founded the American Protective Association (APA)—a political consortium of the nativist fraternities that had survived the Civil War, their immediate offspring, and a host of new fraternal and "patriotic" societies which proliferated during the 1880s and 1890s. Rattling its sabers at both local and national elections until the mid-1890s, the APA captured exaggerated attention from nativists and their detractors alike. Having established it, Bowers had also tried to keep it alive after its political capital was spent. With his death in 1911, there was nothing left.

By no means, however, did 1911 see an end to nativist organizing. After all, this was the year in which Wilbur Phelps began publishing an aggressive anti-Catholic periodical, *The Menace,* which grew to a weekly national circulation of 1.5 million in less than four years. Capitalizing on the attention grabbed by a Catholic-baiting series launched the preceding August with the publication of an article entitled "The Roman Catholic Hierarchy: The Deadliest Menace to Our Liberties and Our Civilization" in the Georgian Tom Watson's *Jeffersonian Magazine,* Phelps's *Menace* showed that the traditional themes of the nativist movement were very much alive.[2] It was not coincidental that Watson himself backed the founding in 1911 of a new nativist organization calling itself the Guardians of Liberty. Headed by Nelson A. Miles, an aging Civil War veteran who was a former chief of staff of the U.S. Army, and attracting the support of other retired military officers, the Guardians planned—not unlike the APA before them—to oppose any candidate for elective or appointive public office "who owes superior temporal allegiance to any power above his obligation to . . . the United States." The Guardians' literature demonstrated nativists' sustained concentration on organization as a defining characteristic of the "alien," and (along with *The Menace*) it expressed particular anxiety about the growth of the Roman Catholic Knights of Columbus. The Guardians' sympathizers were the kind of people bound to find in contemporary events, such as an effort by Irish-American legislators in Connecticut to repeal the state's Sunday blue laws, evidence that alien "organization" was paying off politically. Counterorganization remained the preferred response, producing the Connecticut Lord's Day League and the Christian Endeavor Union.[3]

Yet for all this evidence in 1911 that traditional themes in organized nativist activism endured, there were also signs of competition for the attention of "native" Americans whose fears included "foreigners." There were alternative ideas afloat that suggested a rather different definition of "native" (and, by implication, "foreign"), a definition which had little to do with either "character" or "organization" and everything to do with what had traditionally been called "blood" and was beginning to be called "race." Evidence can be found in two significant publications of 1911—one quite short and one very long—that were not products of the nativist movement but certainly had the capacity to send it off in some new directions if embraced by its orders and societies. The shorter publication was a scholarly article by the historian Frederick Jackson Turner, "Social Forces in American History." It sounded, in academic prose, what some of the nation's citizens took as a warning cry:

It is evident that the ethnic elements of the United States have undergone startling changes. . . . The composition of the labor class and its relation to wages and to the native American employer have been deeply influenced thereby, the sympathy of the employers with labor has been unfavorably affected by the pressure of great numbers of immigrants of alien nationality and lower standards of life.[4]

The longer publication was a report by a federal panel on immigration—the so-called Dillingham Commission—consisting of 42 volumes and resulting from four years of study and hearings. Publicly announced just before Congress's Christmas recess in 1910, the commission's recommendations gave official sanction to the ideas that there was a "new" immigration of eastern and southern Europeans which had largely replaced the "old" immigration from northwest Europe; that the "new" immigrants were less likely to have been pulled by the attractions of American political or religious liberty and more likely to have been pushed by economic disadvantage; and that strategies to limit the supply of unskilled immigrant labor were warranted by economic conditions in the United States. Moreover, the panel endorsed the concept that a way to limit the "new" immigration was by imposing a literacy test (or, as the report called it, an "illiteracy" test) for admission to residency.[5] In 1911, the nativist *movement* remained largely in the grip of traditional ideas about what constituted "native" and "alien." After 1911, organized nativist activism would have opportunities to choose between—or combine—new themes and old.

Continuities in Organized Nativist Activism

It is unusual to examine American nativism by taking a run from the mid-1880s—as this chapter will attempt—to the second decade of the twentieth century, probably because so much modern scholarship has focused on nativism not as an organized social movement but as a popular frame of mind. Looking at the ebb and flow of nativism as a broad, loosely shared outlook, historians have perceived the 1880s as a quiet time, the depression-scarred early 1890s as a time of high nativistic anxiety, the turn of the century as another period of nativism in retreat—followed by another resurgence of enthusiasm by 1910 or so. John Higham has worked up the most elaborate theoretical treatment, arguing that it was the rise and fall of national "confidence" that largely determined popular receptivity to nativistic notions.[6] From this perspective, there is not much to commend a summary of nativism across a stretch of 30 years or so which saw the economy rise and fall and war or threats of war come and go. Even organized nativist activism can appear a fragmented affair at first glance. The most notable nativist organization of the period—the American Protective Association (APA)—seems like a flash in the pan, rising and falling in a period of less than 10 years. Nor do the public policy achievements of the nativist movement really encourage treating the period from about 1885 to about 1910 as a whole. The "accomplishments" seem slim: repeated stabs at a restrictive literacy test for immigrants that did not get much of a boost until endorsed by the Dillingham Commission report.

But if we get away from the comings and goings of the popular mood and resist looking at immigration restriction (reached in the 1920s) as the inevitable end of the nativist story, we will get another picture. The relatively short-lived APA was actually part of a long-term accumulation of nativist organizations without which it could not have boomed. At its peak in the early 1890s, in fact, the APA was really a consortium of many nativist organizations that preceded it or grew up alongside it. And when it collapsed (for all intents and purposes by the middle to late 1890s), many of these survived. In part, they lived on for the same reason that some of the nativist brotherhoods were able to keep going through the collapse of the American party and the travail of the Civil War: they pursued "utilitarian" as well as public policy goals. Simply belonging had many personal benefits.

In fact, organized nativist activism did have public policy consequences in this period, but they are to be found in measures less dramatic than literacy tests. Stimulated by a Supreme Court ruling which prohibited state regulation of immigration in 1876 and by Congress's immigration act of 1882, which imposed more federal oversight, traditional nativist organizations like the Junior Order, United American Mechanics (JOUAM) lined up behind the Foran bill—passed by Congress in 1884—which outlawed some forms of prearranged foreign "contract" labor, denounced by nativists as *organized* and "unnatural" immigration.[7] The nativist societies were also interested in a congressional act of 1887 which barred aliens who had not declared their intention to become citizens from purchasing federal lands in the western territories. This was aimed less at immigrants arriving as individuals or families than at "organized" corporate landholders. The notion that immigration itself was somehow artificial and manipulated by organizations was also implicit in nativist enthusiasm for the immigration act that came out of Congress in 1891, holding shipping companies responsible for returning to their homelands immigrants who were inadmissible under the immigration laws in effect as well as arrivals who turned out within a year to require public charity. This was the same act which had the more famous consequence of centralizing the reception and inspection of immigrants at a new federal facility on Ellis Island in New York harbor.[8]

Equally popular among the nativist brethren was the bill that passed the House of Representatives in 1894, only to founder in the Senate, which provided for the examination of emigrants in their homelands by American consular officials before admission to the United States. Backed by JOUAM, this initiative fit perfectly with nativist rhetoric which held that the real issue in immigration was "character." Although the historian John Higham has argued that organizations like JOUAM, OUAM, and the Patriotic Order, Sons of America, shared in the 1880s and 1890s a phobia about foreign "anarchists" and "revolutionaries," it was not until the National Board of Trade weighed in on the side of a consular inspection bill, in the aftermath of an avowed anarchist's attempt on the life of the industrialist Henry Clay Frick, that the measure became associated with antiradicalism. In fact, despite the opportunities provided by labor violence connected with economic distress in the 1870s and 1890s and incidents like the Haymarket bombing in Chicago in 1886, attributed to foreign-born anarchists, antiradical themes remained muted in the rhetoric of the major nativist organizations. To nativist ideologues, political radicals were "foreign" enough but rarely seemed sufficiently organized to prove as threatening as the Catholic church or ethnic politicians and their "drilled" supporters.[9]

To participants in the mainstream nativist organizations, the literacy tests repeatedly brought before Congress from the mid-1890s on were just back-end versions of consular inspection. They would protect national character by screening out immigrants who were considered ill-prepared to exercise the independence of American citizens and who putatively had been sent ("dumped" was the preferred word) rather than drawn to America. The focus remained on the corrosive effect of foreign organizations, on holding organizations responsible for the hazards posed by foreigners, and on protecting the "national character" through counterorganization. Not surprisingly, in the three decades beginning with the 1880s, organized nativist activism found itself in relationships with other movements which portrayed their enemies in organizational terms, including temperance, urban Progressivism, women's suffrage, and even non-nativist benevolent fraternalism, which proposed an alternative to the alleged coldness and inhumanity of the modern urban, industrial "system."

While much scholarly attention has been paid to the increasing assertions in the 1890s and early 1900s that a "new" immigration was menacing the United States, organized nativists continued to be more excited by the "old" immigration and even by the American-born offspring of these "foreigners." In many ways, it was not the differences of those they defined as foreign that worried nativist activists, but the similarities to themselves. What made them fret were the observations like those of a newspaperman at an Irish Catholic temperance rally in the mid-1890s who pointed out that the attendees "did not look Irish." Worse, they were organized; they had adopted an American way of doing things; they were indistinguishable from "real" Americans—and yet they still thought of themselves in some way as "Irish." When, in 1895, Theodore Roosevelt, as Alexander DeConde puts it, "inveighed against the hyphenated American—the German-American, the Irish-American, and others," he made them sound much more sinister to nativist ears than if he had simply criticized Germans or the Irish.[10]

Anti-Catholicism and Nativism

In the 1880s, Josiah Strong's *Our Country: Its Possible Future and Its Present Crisis* had much the same effect in stimulating nativist activism as had Henry Ward Beecher's *Plea for the West* half a century earlier. Like Beecher, Strong portrayed the United States as facing an apocalyptic moment, a fleeting time when the nation's course would be set for an age. And, like Beecher, Strong suggested that the battle lines would be drawn in the west as the population filled up the land from sea to sea. On one side would be the true Americans, who represented traditional Anglo-American Protestantism, and on the other side inebriates, socialists, and greedy capitalists—but especially Catholics, immigrants, and sons and daughters of immigrants well organized to create their version of the national character, which Strong presumed was "un-American".[11] Josiah Strong, secretary of the Evangelical Society of the United States, was the most famous of a flock of contemporary alarmists; and though he was not closely identified with avowedly nativist organizations, many of the others were. Reverend Justin D. Fuller of Boston, for example, had published *Outlook of Freedom, or, The Roman Catholic Element in American History* at the height of the Know Nothing movement in 1856. His two new books of the 1880s, *Rome in America* (1887) and *Washington in the Lap of Rome* (1888), updated the nativist message by focusing on the increasing organizational sophistication of the Roman Catholic Church and its ability to influence American education and government. Fuller put great stock in a recent decision to build the Catholic University of America not in Baltimore, the historical center of the church in the United States, but in the nation's capital, the heart of political power.[12]

Sometimes, the alarmists made it difficult to distinguish between what was and was not a nativist organization. Certainly agencies of mainstream Protestant churches often moved close to the line. "The balance of power in this State," according to a speaker at the annual convention of Wisconsin Baptists in 1880, "is easily held by the foreign element in our population and nine-tenths of that is infidel and Catholic, and these are united in one thing—to reduce our secular education to the extreme of godlessness and disbelief." Contemporary Congregational publications, too, denounced the dangers to national character of a "bad church" ruled from abroad. The 1880s saw a new run of publications not unlike those of the 1830s, purporting to be revelations of the workings of Catholicism from the inside by former priests and nuns.[13]

Perhaps it is not surprising that the rhetoric of institutional Protestantism and organized nativism sometimes came close to converging in the late nineteenth and early twentieth centuries. Leaders and activists from both traditions seemed overwhelmed by what they took to be the massive organizational front of Roman Catholicism. No doubt this had something to do with the fact that American Protestantism appeared to be *dis*organized and its influence waning. Even the "social gospel" movement, the principal development and in many respects the chief success of mainline Protestantism in this era, had a defensive character—especially in its insistence that the church needed to be involved in helping the urban poor. It grew from a sense that the churches doing business as usual were no longer reaching the teeming populations of the big cities, and it was guided by a sense of urgency, a feeling that much of the American people might somehow be "lost."

Defensiveness was encouraged by divisiveness within major Protestant denominations, which weakened churches and created outright schisms. Among Baptists, the "Landmark" controversy, which had erupted before the Civil War, peaked by the 1890s. Landmarkers recast Christian history to render Baptist churches the only original, true churches. This not only created debate and division within Baptist circles but made it difficult for Landmark Baptists to participate in any kind of ecumenical dialogue, much less cooperate with other denominations in social or moral reform. American Methodism went through its own fractious period from the 1880s into the early twentieth century. First, "Holiness" associations emerged which purported to rekindle the evangelical fire of early Methodism and loudly denounced the spiritual deadness of serene, middle-class churches. These denunciations intensified when Holiness devotees began to depart entirely from the denomination in the mid-1890s. By 1901, the secessions that would lead eventually to the foundation of the Assemblies of God (just before World War I) had taken place. In 1908, the Church of the Nazarene grew out of another secessionist strain.

With the two major Protestant denominations—which had had the greatest evangelical success in America over the preceding century—beset with such internal difficulties, it is no wonder that Protestant leaders doubted their own organizational strength and feared the strength of the church they took as their rival: Roman Catholicism. Institutional Protestantism would take one more hit around 1910 when the first of 12 volumes of the theologically conservative *The Fundamentals* began to be distributed (at the expense of the California millionaires Lyman and Milton Steward) to Protestant leaders of all denominations across the country. Controversial in content, they helped bring into everyday parlance the term "fundamentalism," which would bedevil the mainline churches thereafter.[14]

Divisions—real and imagined—in institutional Protestantism magnified the impression that Catholicism was united and powerful. To be sure, the numbers associated with Catholic growth were stunning.

Numbering something like 650,000 in 1840, Roman Catholics in the
United States totaled about 12 million by 1910. By 1890, the church
was already the largest religious denomination in the nation. The
United States census calculated 6.3 million Catholics, while the
church itself estimated between 7.8 and 10 million.[15] But it was not the
numbers that provoked a nativistic response so much as the evidence
of effective church organization. It was organization—the capacity to
effect change in the "national character"—that struck nativist activists
as "un-American."

Ironically, the very success of American Catholics at adopting the
fraternal form of organization preferred by nativists, as a way to promote supportive community and good "Catholic citizenship," drove
nativists to near-frenzy. Founded in 1881 as a local fraternal benefit
society for young Catholic men in New Haven, Connecticut, the
Knights of Columbus gradually won over a skeptical clergy and
became a national fixture in time for the great Christopher Columbus
anniversary celebrations of 1892. Although, according to the Knights'
recent chronicler Christopher Kauffman, the organization's consistent
theme in this period was "proclaiming the nobility of the American-
Catholic experience and . . . conspicuously avoiding any association
with the Old World," what nativists took to be un-American was simply
the high level of organization achieved by a "foreign" institution.[16]

The contrast between the weakness nativists thought they detected
in "American" Protestantism and the new organizational robustness of
"foreign" Catholicism in the United States was given a sharp edge by
well-publicized contemporary Catholic commentary. In the early 1880s,
the Catholic scholar John Gilmary Shea and Bishop Bernard McQuaid
of Rochester both published widely circulated articles proclaiming the
decline of Protestantism and the ascension of Catholicism in America.
McQuaid's piece appeared in the *North American Review* in 1883 under
the provocative title "The Decay of Protestantism." Such predictions
did not go away; 15 years later Archbishop John Ireland was still writing about Protestant weakness.[17] Moreover, this was exactly the time
when the Catholic church in America was publicly addressing issues of
institutional growth. The Third Plenary Council of Catholic Bishops,
meeting in 1884, was the first to call for the creation of parochial
schools in every parish and to attempt to mandate that Catholic parents
send their children to church schools. This, of course, played to
nativists' fears about a demanding church, a pliable—heavily immigrant—flock, and a war for the minds of youth.

Actually, American Catholicism was facing its own intramural conflicts. These had to do with a phenomenon that came to be known as "Cahenslyism," after a German priest who encouraged the retention of ethnic-specific Catholic parishes in the United States. Calling for the preservation of key elements of congregational activity in European languages and for the provision of priests who could work in immigrants' tongues, clergymen who supported the movement—especially Germans—founded their own societies in the 1880s to challenge the church hierarchy's apparent enthusiasm for "Americanization." Though the movement achieved some temporary successes in preserving local autonomy, its more enduring effect was to leave central authority in the church in the hands of largely Irish-American clergy.[18] This magnified nativists' perception of the church's unity and centralization.

The Cahensly, or "nationality," controversy also produced its own literature, some of which was sure to provoke nativists. Probably the most inflammatory was a book by Anton Walburg, the priest of a German-American parish in Cincinnati: *The Question of Nationality in Its Relation to the Catholic Church in the United States* (1889). In the course of criticizing Anglicizers and Americanizers in the Catholic hierarchy, Walburg made unflattering comments about Anglo-American culture and the English language and argued that it was futile to try to keep nationality separate from religion. There was plenty of grist for nativist literature in remarks like these: "The American nationality, when tried by the test of true Americanism, will be found wanting. It is often the hotbed of fanaticism, intolerance, and radical, ultra views on matters of politics and religion. All the vagaries of spiritualism, Mormonism, free-loveism, prohibition, infidelity, and materialism generally breed in the American nationality." The same could be said of his assertion that the Catholic church would have to grow primarily by the addition of newcomers from abroad who would pass both their faith and their "nationality" on to their American-born offspring.[19] In some respects, the Catholic Americanizers' efforts to blunt the effect of such rhetoric did not help much—at least with nativists. When Cardinal Gibbons got President Benjamin Harrison to make a public statement supporting the Americanizers' position, nativists simply took it as another sign of the growing influence of the "political" church on American politics.[20]

Given their sensitivity to symbols, nativists found plenty to react to in the 1890s. The celebration of Columbus Day in 1892 was taken by

American Catholics—especially the "Americanizers"—as an opportunity to show the integral place of Catholicism in American culture, confirming nativists' worst fears. In January 1893, an apostolic delegate from the Vatican to the United States, Francis Satolli, took up his post in Washington. The nativist (as well as the Protestant denominational) press constantly reported his comings and goings with legislators and followed his travels across the country, noting especially whenever he made speeches in Italian. Satolli could thus be portrayed as both a surrogate pope representing organized Catholicism and an alien appealing to unassimilated immigrants. After Satolli's first year in the country, an Episcopal bishop, A. Cleveland Coxe, denounced him in an article in one of the nation's leading popular periodicals as a dangerous meddler.[21]

A "parliament of religions" at the World's Columbian Exposition in Chicago in 1893 produced as an unintended consequence backlash from conservatives in both the American and the European Catholic church against the ecumenism of leading Americanist clergy. A papal letter to the American church which followed in early 1895 not only disappointed many Catholics but discomforted suspicious Protestants and antagonized outright nativists. While lauding the maturation of the church in America, Pope Leo XIII doubted that the American case was a good example for Catholics everywhere and expressed skepticism about the separation of church and state. Papal condemnation of the Masons, the Knights of Pythias, the Odd Fellows, and the Sons of Temperance for their secrecy and their oath-laden rituals obviously irritated not only nativist activists but brethren of Protestant fraternal and "patriotic" societies who were prime recruits for nativist orders. The nativist press had a field day with the circumstances surrounding the assassination of Chicago's mayor at the world's fair, gleefully pointing out that the assassin was a Catholic. In fact, this event spawned a new enthusiasm for conspiracy theories connecting immigrant Catholics to everything from the death of Lincoln to the desertion rate in the Union army during the Civil War.[22]

With this level of anxiety about supposed Protestant weakness and Catholic power, it is not surprising that nativists and prospective nativists were on the lookout for evidence that the church was throwing its weight around in local politics. This exaggerated sense of anticipation led to an eruption of nativist organizing in Boston between 1886 and 1888. Complaints of Catholic parents about the treatment of church doctrine in a standard public school history text (and about teachers who taught from it) led the city School Committee to drop the book. Charging that this was a sign that the School Committee had come under the sway of Catholics, nativists played a role in the organization of a "Committee of 100" pledged to return a Protestant school board at the next election. Among the committee's backers was the recently formed British-American Association, largely composed of Protestant Irish-Americans.[23]

The enfranchisement of women in school elections in some locales (this was deemed suitable to their "natural" motherly concerns) created a special opportunity for nativists to call for the organization of Protestant women to counteract the organization of "foreigners." One women's group growing out of the Boston controversy, the Independent Women Voters, was particularly cooperative with out-and-out nativist organizations like the Loyal Women of American Liberty. The strength of this coalition was sufficient not only to seat a Protestant majority on the Boston School Committee but also to ensure that the city's first Irish Catholic mayor, elected in 1884, would be the last until the turn of the century. One significant consequence of this was a new enthusiasm for women's suffrage among nativists, who suddenly discovered that there was a large untapped pool of prospective political supporters among middle-class and upper-middle-class Protestant women. Moreover, this kind of local success was bound to persuade many nativists that conditions were again ripe for political activity on a national scale.[24]

Nativists were given special encouragement to think that their time had arrived politically by contemporary developments in the midwest. The Bennett Law of Wisconsin and the Edwards Law of Illinois, both passed at the end of the 1880s, required children to attend schools where the principal subjects were taught in English. These laws were not specifically anti-Catholic (in fact, German Lutheran schools were among the chief targets). What really attracted nativists' attention was the political fallout from these measures. In both states, Republicans associated with the laws paid a political price by alienating both German Protestants and Catholics, who feared more state intrusion into parochial schools. This backlash seemed a modern example of organized political action by "foreigners," and nativists believed that aggrieved Republican voters might respond to a nativistic appeal. They also sought to take advantage of a controversy that was taking place in Faribault, Minnesota, at about the same time. Faribault, a community unable to support a public school, struck a deal with the local Catholic parish school to offer free public instruction. This was the kind of event that nativists could exploit as evidence of a Catholic "takeover."[25]

But this was fraught with hazard. Republicans might draw quite another conclusion: that offending an ethnic community could prove politically costly. In fact, developments in New York politics about the same time showed the advantage of wooing rather than denouncing ethnic minorities. When the acting mayor of New York City allowed the flag of Ireland to be flown on public buildings for St. Patrick's Day in the early 1890s, not only nativists howled—so did representatives of other immigrant communities. In the local elections of 1894, the Irish Catholic vote lined up pretty solidly behind the Democrats, but the Republicans won the mayoral race by putting up a reform ticket which took advantage of anti-Tammany, anti-Catholic, and anti-Irish rhetoric but also by pursuing other ethnic voters. This did not bode well for any nativist attempt to capture the Republicans.[26]

Ethnic issues were a highly visible—if confusing—part of national politics throughout the 1880s and 1890s. It was actually this confusion that gave them nativistic potential. The Democrats' candidate for the presidency in 1884, Governor Grover Cleveland of New York, had come to be regarded in some quarters as anti-Catholic and anti-Irish. As a fiscal conservative, he had vetoed New York state legislation sharing public funds with religious charities; and as a representative of upstate, he had warred with the political "spoilsmen" of New York City. In a turnabout of popular perceptions, the candidate of the Republicans—the party usually identified with the Protestant, Anglo-American establishment—Senator James G. Blaine, was taken to be a friend to Catholics because of his coziness with Irish-American politicians. The election saw unusual realignments of voters, with some Irish-American Democrats temporarily abandoning their party and some traditional Republican voters casting ballots for Cleveland. That more Irish-Americans and Catholics did not vote for Blaine may have been a result of a widely recounted diatribe by a Republican Presbyterian minister just before the election: he called the Democrats the party of "rum, Romanism, and rebellion," prompting last-minute second thoughts among some potential Democratic defectors. There was plenty of rhetorical resource material for nativists in all this. On the one hand, there was evidence that both parties were wooing "foreign" voters. On the other, it could be made out that foreigners were moving in supposedly organized "blocs." President Cleveland's nomination of a Catholic, Senator Edward White of Louisiana, for the Supreme Court played into the hands of nativist ideologues, who asserted that Cleveland had duped "native" voters.[27]

The Nativists Reenter National Politics

Since by the late 1880s Protestant-Catholic issues had taken a place on the national political stage, there was a clear temptation for nativist activists to organize for maximum nationwide political effect. One of the consequences of the debate over the role of denominational mission agencies in American Indian education was a proposal for a sixteenth amendment to the Constitution of the United States which would outlaw any application of public funds to "sectarian purposes"— a not very subtle code for Catholic agencies. This provided an opportunity for nativist organizing that would transcend local issues and bring pressure on both political parties. In New York City, two such organizations sprang up at the very end of 1889. The first, an American Patriotic League, not only endorsed the proposed sixteenth amendment and made the usual emotional appeals on behalf of "one General Non-Sectarian American Free School System" but also called for "extension of the time required for Naturalization," "an Educational Qualification for every voter," and even "Restriction of Immigration." It used time-tested definitions of the threats to American national character as organized threats, even though, by the last decade of the century, some of these appeared anachronistic. Manipulated "pauper labor," religious (read Roman Catholic) "sectarianism," and boss-bought immigrant voters were the essence of "foreignness" itself. By 1891, the American Patriotic League claimed to be represented in at least five states.[28]

A second "league," the National League for the Protection of American Institutions, took nearly the same line. The soul of bourgeois respectability, this organization traded on the names of a corps of honorary vice presidents constituting a veritable biographical dictionary of leading Protestant clergymen, college presidents, and professors. In 1890, from the same block of New York City's Nassau Street that had housed Thomas R. Whitney's *Republic* as well as a number of other antebellum nativist publications, the National League issued a "Protest and Petition" which called for exclusion of Catholic schools from the Indian Department appropriations bill. The next year it attacked a New York State "freedom of worship" bill which would have ended the monopoly of Protestant chaplains in state prisons, asylums, and hospi-

tals, arguing that the bill would threaten the "existence of the nonsectarian institutions engaged in the benevolent and reformatory work of
the state." In 1892, it exerted pressure on behalf of a sixteenth amendment bill introduced in Congress by Senator Platt of Connecticut.[29]

Of course, this volume of nativist organizational activity was bound
to persuade some activists that the time was ripe to vigorously press
shared objects politically. There seemed to be two ways to take advantage of the organizational richness of the late 1880s and 1890s. One
was to emulate the nativist orders of the 1840s and 1850s and declare
an independent party to challenge or at least threaten the Democrats
and Republicans. Somewhat surprisingly, given the disaster of 1856,
the name that kept cropping up was "American party." In August 1887,
an executive committee of a party styling itself in this way met in
Philadelphia and called for a national convention in September.
Clearly, these political activists sought to build on perceived institutional strength, offering a special invitation to "representatives and
members of the following organizations . . . viz. The Patriotic Order of
United Sons of America [*sic*], the Order of United American Mechanics, the Junior Order of United American Mechanics, the Order of
Deputies, the Sons of the Revolutionary Sires, the Political Alliance, the
United Minute Men, the various societies and all other organizations
whose principles and sentiments will enable them to work in the American party on the foregoing basis." The "foregoing basis" included 11
platform articles which were nearly all traditional nativist boilerplate,
the only exceptions being the seventh, "to abolish polygamy in the
United States immediately," a slap at Mormons; and the second, which
boldly called for the "restriction of immigration."[30] But there was far
more old here than new, a point made clearer at the party's second
national convention in Washington in 1888 by a platform speaker who
read out a list of organized threats to American national character:
"modern" political organization; the "threatening attitude of the Roman
Catholic Church," poised for "invasion of our system of common
schools"; and "corporations and foreign holders" who endangered
"true" Americans' possession of their own land. Providing more evidence that these were traditional goals, S. E. Church emphasized that
these "causes have forced into renewed life and fresh activity, the ever-
existing, and, when aroused, ever triumphant American Party."
Rebuffed in its initial attempts to find an attractive candidate for the
presidential election of 1888, the party limped along for a short time
thereafter.[31]

Alternatively, the organizational robustness of the nativist movement could be used to advantage not by combining the leagues and orders into a single political party but by creating an umbrella under which all could operate. This was the theory behind the National Council of Patriotic Organizations assembled by Henry Baldwin of New Jersey. Baldwin began corresponding with nativist organizations like the American Protestant Association as early as 1887 and by 1889 had scheduled an initial conference in New York City. Donald Kinzer notes that by the third annual meeting in 1891, almost 60 societies from two dozen states took part." The public goals of the National Council were virtually identical to those of the short-lived American party. The National Council, however, had the virtue of allowing members of constituent units to retain their old political affiliations while putting pressure on both parties. Moreover, it permitted all kinds of nativist organizations with different structures, rituals, and benefits to coexist while cooperating. Conspicuously absent from the first conferences was a new organization, the American Protective Association, founded in Clinton, Iowa, in 1887. But by 1893 it was one of just ten societies still active in the Council, and by 1895 it was one of five. By that time, this society growing out of the midwest had emerged as a new and more aggressive umbrella itself, driving the National Council of Patriotic Organizations into obsolescence.[32]

The sustained focus of *organized* nativism on such traditional objects of nativist hostility as the Roman Catholic church and the voting strength of ethnic (no longer necessarily immigrant) communities suggests that the course of immigration itself in the late nineteenth and early twentieth centuries had relatively little to do with either the waxing or the waning of nativism as a social movement. So long as the nativist index of "foreignism" was capacity for organized or institutional impact on American life, it was not the numbers or origins of immigrants that nativists would find most provocative. The numbers were large, of course; more than 18 million newcomers arrived in the 30 years between 1890 and 1920—about four times the number that had arrived over a similar span before 1860 and 80 percent more than those who came in the period 1860-1890. Yet raw numbers are deceptive. John Higham puts them into perspective: "In 1860 the proportion of foreign-born to the total population of the United States was already about what it would remain through 1920, and most of the immigrants were concentrated in urban areas. Indeed, the twenty-five principal cities had a higher percentage of foreign-born residents in 1860 than they have had since." There was even some tendency for immigrants to spread out as the nation grew and transportation improvements provided speedier access to a wider variety of places. New York state's population, 24 percent foreign-born in 1860, was only 16 percent foreign-born 30 years later. The proportion of immigrants in the populations of Massachusetts, Pennsylvania, Illinois, and Ohio dropped markedly, too, if not quite so dramatically. It was just such calculations that encouraged Higham, over 30 years ago, to conclude that popular nativistic attitudes had to be related to something other than simply the ebb and flow of immigration.[33]

Yet if the putatively "foreign" rather than just the foreign-born were what galvanized organized nativist activism, then some other numbers are probably relevant. The proportion of immigrants *and their children* in many places continued to grow substantially in the late nineteenth and early twentieth centuries. In 1900, three-quarters of the population of Minnesota were of first- or second-generation immigrant background, and states as disparate as Utah, Massachusetts, Wisconsin, and Rhode Island all had proportions between 62 and 71 percent. As early as 1880, 87 percent of Chicago's population was made up of immigrants or the children of immigrants, and the proportion in Milwaukee, Detroit, New York, and Cleveland was also above 80 percent; in St. Louis and San Francisco, it was only slightly lower. Such percentages amounted to very large numbers: New York City in 1910 was home to 2 million of the foreign-born and 2 million more born of immigrant parents. Nor was this a phenomenon only of the biggest cities. Arthur Mann rightly observes that "Popular opinion does not usually associate immigration with Iowa, Nebraska, Idaho, or Washington, but in the decades after the Civil War the foreign stock in each of those states never fell below 35 percent." Moreover, immigrants (and their children) were new to more places as more of the continent opened up to settlement in the late 1800s.[34]

For all that, there were significant continuities in immigration and the characteristics of "foreign-stock" populations. This was, to be sure, the period in which the sources of European immigration were broadening. Immigrants from northern and western Europe continued to come, but they were joined by an enlarged flow from central, southern, and eastern Europe that actually began to outnumber them in 1896. One scholar notes that "by 1907, for every person entering from the old areas, four were being admitted from the new. A quarter-century earlier, when the first signs appeared that a major demographic shift was in the making, the ratio had been just the reverse."[35] There is no question that this was noticed at the time. Many of the newcomers looked different, sounded different, and conducted their lives differently, not just from "native" Anglo-Americans, but even from previous generations of immigrants. Still, it would be a serious mistake to assume that what would come to be called the "old" immigration was replaced by the "new" or that it ceased to have an impact on the sources of organized nativist activism. The historian Timothy Meagher, for example, points out that "Forty years after the Famine immigration of the 1840s and 1850s, the Irish born population was still growing. Until 1890, the institutionalization of emigration in Ireland sent more than enough Irish newcomers to the United States to replace the dying members of the Famine era migration." In fact, he shows that the absolute number of the Irish-born in America increased by nearly a third during the last two decades of the century, noting that the cultural impact of the arrivals was magnified by the fact that "almost all of these new Irish immigrants were adults, while a large proportion of the second generation counted in the census were children or adolescents."[36]

There are, then, many ways to count immigrants in the nineteenth century and to measure their impact, but what moved nativists was the newcomers' capacity to reinforce "foreign" organizations. Nativists found evidence enough of that in the three decades after the 1880s. This was a golden age of ethnic fraternalism, as it was of nativist or "patriotic" fraternalism. Between 1880 and the early 1890s, Poles, Portuguese, Danes, Lithuanians, Hungarians, Slovaks, Russians, and Swedes all formed major fraternal benefit societies. It has been repeatedly pointed out by scholars that linguistic and occupational assimilation and the advent of an American-born generation actually promoted such organization, as ethnic groups worked *harder* to preserve (or create) a sense of identity and belonging.[37] This helps explain a whole new wave of ethnic organizing and reorganizing in the early twentieth century, including the creation of the Sons of Italy and renewed enthusiasm for the Ancient Order of Hibernians. Roy Rosenzweig, a scholar of late-nineteenth-century working-class life, also argues that "ethnic communities with elaborate organizational infrastructures—churches, clubs, kinship networks, saloons" were creating "alternative" cultures which preserved a sense of individual and group autonomy in industrial settings where investors and managers (often Protestant Anglo-Americans) seemed to call the shots during work hours.[38]

Over time, leaders in many ethnic communities came to argue that loyalty to homeland was best displayed not so much by engagement in the affairs of the old country as by making a collective impact on American political life which could both promote group welfare and advance group recognition. After the Civil War, no American ethnic group embraced this so enthusiastically or practiced it so effectively as the Irish, especially after the fizzle of Fenianism. Although there were periodic setbacks, the Irish in Massachusetts were instrumental in electing a sympathetic Democratic governor in 1882 and rejoiced in the election of Boston's first Irish Catholic mayor two years later (following closely on the heels of the first Irish Catholic mayors elected in the industrial cities of Lawrence and Lowell).[39] Barbara Miller Solomon estimates by that the end of the decade "Irish politicians controlled the government of sixty-eight Massachusetts cities and towns." In 1880, William R. Grace took office as New York City's first Irish-American mayor. Irish-Americans were able to use this political clout to defend group interests. This showed up in Ohio in successful resistance to legislation that would have provided free textbooks to students in public schools but not in church-related schools, and in Michigan in rejection of bills that would have stripped legal control of church property from Catholic bishops.[40]

The concentration of immigrants in certain kinds of industrial employment could convey the impression (to those who were looking for it) of "foreign" aggregation if not outright organization. The United States Bureau of Labor reported in the mid-1880s that while less than one-seventh of all Americans were foreign-born, almost a third of all of the workers in manufacturing and mining were immigrants. Since these were the areas in which labor organizing was most advanced, there was also a tendency—right or wrong—among middle-class folk to equate immigrants with unionization, as well as with the strikes and other activities the bourgeoisie associated with workers' organizations.[41]

Sensitivity to "foreign organization" reached near-hysteria in some locales in response to the perceived appearance of international criminal combines. By the 1890s, the American press was full of reports about the Italian "mafia." Although it was probably connected more with Louisiana politics than with anything else, the shooting of the New Orleans chief of police in 1890 was laid at the door of imported "organized" Italian violence. In March 1891, a mob assaulted the parish prison and lynched 11 Italians arrested during the investigation of the case.[42] Yet this dramatic incident smacked more of "popular" nativism than of organized nativist activism. The nativist movement found legitimate "foreign organizations"—churches, fraternal societies, and political networks—far more threatening than illegitimate ones. Because of this, the nativist movement had a capacity to blend its aims with those of other interest groups. This, of course, could provide a funnel for a constant flow of new members into nativist organizations. Within the American organized labor movement of the late nineteenth and early twentieth centuries, for example, there remained much expressed fear of allegedly imported "contract" labor. This showed up in the rhetoric of the Federation of Organized Trades and Labor Unions—a predecessor of the American Federation of Labor (AFL)— from its founding in 1881, and in the platforms of the Knights of Labor beginning with its annual convention in 1883. Hostility to "pauper immigration," exacerbated by workers' distress in an economic downturn that lasted from 1883 to 1886, showed up in such new organizations as a New York Independent Labor party, which called for a heavy head tax on immigrants. Prompted by a complaint of one of its key constituent craft unions, the Window Glass Workers, that employers were trying to break the union by bringing in cheap labor from abroad, the Knights of Labor called for federal legislation in 1884 which would ban "contract" labor. The resulting Foran Act was passed by Congress early in 1885 with little resistance. For the most part, industry had little reason to oppose the bill, since "contract labor" was more illusion than reality, and even conservatives were able to equate tariffs which protected industry from foreign competition with putatively protective legislation for workers.[43]

Although evidence was thin that industry was contracting for foreign labor, and although the Foran Act had been passed, denunciation of contract labor continued to be a convenient way of attacking irresponsible corporate power. Terrence Powderly of the Knights of Labor came increasingly to tie what he took to be immigration-related problems of all kinds to activities of the "agents of American employers."[44] Samuel Gompers of the American Federation of Labor kept up charges that the Foran Act was widely violated by industry. At the AFL annual convention of 1891, Gompers decried immigrant "dumping" and blamed challenges to American labor on a combination of European senders and American receivers, all of them in turn "combinations" of some sort. Robert Parmet notes that there is not much evidence that contract labor was regarded as a critical concern at the local union level, but "contract and assisted emigrants" remained an issue at AFL national conventions through 1897. In that year, Gompers was finally able to marshal enough floor support to pass a resolution favoring a literacy test for immigrants seeking admission to the United States. Still, agitation about organized, "imported" immigration would not go away; it was an issue in several southern states—then in the process of industrialization—through 1910.[45]

Overlap was also evident between nativist anxiety about organized, "foreign" threats to American national character and the belief of the temperance movement that intemperance (and resistance to the temperance movement itself) was neither native nor personal but "foreign" and organized. In fact, in the late nineteenth century, the villain of the temperance movement was the "saloon," which temperance advocates had no problem describing as an "alien" institution. A publication of the Women's Christian Temperance Union (WCTU) put the number of saloonkeepers who were "foreigners" at 87 percent. WCTU charged not just that saloonkeepers conspired to keep their victims in the thrall of alcohol but that they wielded illegitimate but highly orchestrated political power through the distribution of funds to political candidates. Ruth Bordin, a scholar of women in nineteenth-century temperance activism, identifies one state WCTU president who bemoaned the surrender of the political system to the "hands of a foreign mob." Despite active temperance forces within the Roman Catholic church, the church's defense of the cultural autonomy of its members put it—in the eyes of many temperance advocates—among the organized forces of resistance to moral and political rectitude.[46]

Identifying the sources of intemperance this way was a powerful stimulus for counterorganization. The Anti-Saloon League, established in northern Ohio in the early 1890s, held its first national meeting by the middle of the decade. It was able to capitalize, as Roy Rosenzweig has pointed out, not only on the seemingly organized threat of the saloon network but on middle-class apprehensions about the "alternative" culture of the industrial working class which seemed to center—at least for men—on the community of the saloon.[47] An antitemperance parade in Chicago in 1906, which drew some 80,000 marchers—largely first- and second-generation immigrants—only magnified temperance advocates' worst fears and propelled them further from individual moral appeals toward legislated prohibition. In this, they achieved much success. Raymond Mohl summarizes it: "Between 1895 and 1913, some thirty-one states, ten of them predominantly urban, enacted local option laws. By 1917 alcohol had been prohibited entirely in twenty-six. . . . In 1911, the Anti-Saloon League identified fifty-two American cities which had abolished the saloon. . . . In Chicago, where a no-license option applied down to the precinct level, half of the city was dry by 1908."[48]

Like education, temperance brought women to the forefront of public debate, and the politicization of the temperance movement led logically to demands by participating women that gender should be no disqualification for voting. Beginning as early as the late 1870s, the founder of WCTU, Francis Willard, called for improvement of "the quality of voting by admitting intelligent women." Once the foes of temperance had been identified as organized foreigners, it was not a big leap to the position that politics could be reformed by letting "intelligent women" into the franchise and keeping "ignorant foreigners" out. The success of mobilized Protestant women voters in the local Boston school elections of 1888 seemed to recommend extending the suffrage; and by the mid-1890s, in states like Massachusetts, temperance organizations, women's voting-rights leagues, and outright nativist societies were involved in cooperative lobbying efforts. Increasingly, these efforts took the form of extending the franchise to women, in connection with an education or literacy test for voters of both sexes. The disappointing turnout of working-class Catholic women in the Boston school balloting of the late 1880s discouraged church support for an expanded franchise, setting it up in the eyes of many women's rights activists as an organized "foreign" foe.[49]

Just as temperance activism spilled over into women's rights, the movement for woman's suffrage spilled over into the kinds of municipal reform initiatives which constituted part of the turn-of-the-century Progressive movement. This was evident in the connection of the women's franchise with an educational requirement which would put the vote in the hands of the "right sort" of people of either gender and help break the power of the political bosses, who were believed to trade on the ballots of the "ignorant." In its early stages, Progressive political reform focused on eliminating perceived corruption in the distribution of public employment. The assassination of President Garfield by a disappointed office-seeker in 1881 initially focused public attention on civil service reform. By the 1890s, urban Progressivism had transformed itself into the so-called "good government" movement. Activists—or "goo goos," as they were sometimes termed—increasingly sought structural changes in municipal government that would reduce the power of the "uneducated" masses, often of immigrant origin, and increase the influence of educated experts and the middle-class voter who would keep them in charge. These changes included, for instance, municipal services commissions and the substitution of offices elected at large for ward-level representation.[50]

The American Protective Association

The proliferation of nativist fraternal orders and societies, united by the conviction that there were organized foreign threats to American national character, and the indistinct boundaries between nativism and other social and political movements of the late nineteenth and early twentieth centuries paved the way for the emergence of the most attention-getting—and in some ways most potent—nativist organization since the 1850s, the American Protective Association (APA). APA was founded in the Mississippi River town of Clinton, Iowa, in 1887 by Henry Bowers. A protégé of Bowers's, the incumbent mayor Arnold Walker, had been defeated in the election of 1887. The actual circumstances of the election are not entirely clear, but Bowers seems to have blamed Walker's defeat on the opposition of local organized labor, which he took to be both Irish and Catholic. Bowers himself was a kind of walking history lesson, and this perhaps helps to explain why he responded to political disappointment by forming APA. A man of about 50, he had been born in Maryland but moved west with his mother in the late 1850s as a young adult. There is no evidence that he was involved with antebellum nativism, but he certainly was well aware of it, leaving behind a hotbed of organized nativism in Maryland and emigrating to a section of Iowa where it was notably strong. He was Methodist and active in the Masonic order. He seems to have conceived of APA as a Masonic-like brotherhood that would resist what he took to be the growing power of organized foreigners over American institutions.[51]

During 1887-1888, Bowers established chapters of his new order in Iowa and the adjacent states of Illinois and Nebraska. By 1890, the year of its first national council, APA had spread as far as Wisconsin and eastern Michigan. Up to this point, it might have been just another of the short-lived nativist societies of the time, but from its Detroit chapter it acquired an aggressive organizer, William Traynor, who took it to another level. Traynor was not new to nativism. He was involved with the Order of the American Union, the American Patriotic

League, and the Crescents and was the publisher of the Orange order's *Patriotic American*. Initially head of APA in Michigan, he replaced Bowers as supreme president in 1893. Donald Kinzer summarizes Traynor's impact by pointing out that his "contribution to the career of the APA was his attempted diversion of it from its negative anti-Catholicism, which found 'victory' in defeating Catholics and their sympathizers for office, into a positive vehicle for electing men to office who would put its program into effect."[52]

The statement of principles publicized by the American Protective Association in 1894 read entirely like that of a dozen kindred orders and, like the others, addressed what were treated as *organized* threats to the "national character." APA called for loyalty to "true Americanism," defined as opposition to foreign "ecclesiastical power"; support for "nonsectarian" public schools; resistance to distribution of funds to denominational agencies; support for public inspection of church-related institutions (something of a throwback to the convent inspections of the Know Nothing period); and rejection of "preferential legislation," on either the state or the federal level, for any religious denomination. It called for tighter measures to keep out "pauper" and imported labor and had three planks regarding naturalization: repeal of naturalization for minors, imposition of an English-language requirement for the vote, and addition of seven years' residence (after an immigrant's official declaration of intention to become a citizen) before naturalization. These were offered as specific antidotes to naturalization "frauds" perpetrated by organized political factions and parties.[53] APA also added a new twist—or, at least one not much seen since the 1850s: exclusion of the foreign-born from the armed forces and state militias. As a secret order, APA was also able to set behavioral standards for its members, and through ritual pledges it attempted to discourage members from employing Catholics, joining with Catholics in strikes or other labor actions, or getting involved with any Catholic institutions.

All of this was pretty traditional stuff, and APA picked up public support from both established nativist activists and those who had been on the fringes of the movement. Among the most notable of the latter was the former United States Indian Commissioner, Thomas J. Morgan, who had been at the forefront of the controversy over denominational mission schools. The rapid growth of APA between 1893 and 1895 (including its penetration of both the far west and New England) is often attributed to frustrations resulting from the economic depression that had begun in 1893. But given its grounding on already well-established nativist organizations and its ability to take advantage of contemporary controversies (like Indian missions and the arrival of the papal legate Satolli), it is not surprising that APA's aggressive leadership was able to gain quick attention.[54]

The American Protective Association was also able to take advantage of the rage for benevolent fraternalism. Modern scholars of the organization often make too little of this aspect, but it had much to do with APA's appeal. Even before APA had expanded beyond its midwestern roots, planning took place for adding a fraternal insurance plan, and by the end of 1895 a program was in place, accessed through membership in a suborganization, the American Minute Men. Significantly, the insurance was backed by an established insurer that handled programs for the Masonic Order and the Knights Templars—an instance of the blurriness at the fringes of the nativist movement. APA also had all of the regalia and fraternal paraphernalia that had made groups like the Order of United Americans popular half a century before. Progress through offices in local chapters as well as within state and national bodies brought active members more elaborate robes and fraternal jewelry. Symbolism was heavy-handed: the colors of the national standard, the "little red schoolhouse," the eagle, and the Bible were recurrent icons. Officers had grandiloquent titles (all of the national officials were "supreme"), and a hierarchy of membership oaths created an aura of mystery.[55]

The organizers of APA revealed their background in both nativist and non-nativist fraternalism. By requiring that new chapters enlist at least 25 members to earn a charter, they showed that they had learned that undersized fraternal cells had poor staying power and that recruitment was easiest before the first blush of novelty had worn off. As early as 1891, a women's auxiliary, the Women's APA, was founded by an activist in the Loyal Orange Institution. With the addition of a Junior APA for 14- to 21-year-olds in 1895, APA leadership had established opportunities for the whole family to be involved. In the late 1890s, when its political influence had withered, APA reemphasized the order's fraternal benefits in order to stay alive.[56]

The American Protective Association combined the organizational features that attracted people to nativist societies for utilitarian reasons with an aggressive political agenda which proposed to force both major parties to pay attention to issues dear to the nativist movement. Just as size and broad geographical coverage made APA more useful to prospective members as a fraternal beneficiary society, successful expansion gave it more political clout. Initially, it was not entirely unwelcome to either the Republican or the Democratic party, but for different reasons. Donald Kinzer explains it this way: "The test of the importance of the APA to Republicans was whether it brought them votes that the party had not had; the importance of the order to the Democrats was that, by opposing it and making sure that Republicans were tagged with responsibility for it, Catholics would be kept from slipping into Republican columns." That APA could make more headway among Republican voters than Democratic—and that the Democrats, in fact, were inclined to use APA as a foil—was made apparent by the presidential election of 1892 and was reinforced by the congressional elections two years later.[57]

On the whole, APA probably played a greater role in solidifying the Democrats' hold on immigrants and Catholics than in adding new voters to Republican tallies. This showed up in local as well as national elections. In New Britain, Connecticut, ethnic and religious division over APA and its goals shattered what had been an alliance between Protestant and Catholic temperance advocates. In Chicago, growing Republican opinion that APA was not needed, and the emerging appeal of the Democrats as the anti-APA party, contributed to a particularly embarrassing defeat when APA tried to run its own ticket in the city and county races of 1894.[58] Other incipient third parties viewed APA as a threat. In the upper midwest, publicists for the Populist movement of the mid-1890s attacked APA, fearing an exacerbation of ethnic and religious divisions among voters whom they wished to build into a third party. This was particularly a problem in a state like Minnesota, where German and Scandinavian Lutherans were made nervous by indiscriminate APA attacks on parochial schools. By the same token, labor organizations from Massachusetts to Missouri criticized APA for splitting the working class.[59]

APA's Traynor did not see the handwriting on the wall, however, and overplayed his hand. As the election of 1896 approached, Traynor sought to bring the influence of a whole bloc of APA delegates to bear at the Republican national convention. APA particularly wanted a platform calling for legislation barring the use of federal funds for "sectarian purposes." However, when Traynor denounced the leading candidate, William McKinley, as pro-Catholic, he outraged so many Republicans in the APA ranks that he was driven out of the leadership of his own organization in May. By then, any hope of influencing the

Republicans was lost, and the party's platform of 1896 proved to be the first in 20 years with no plank supporting the public schools. In fact, in the presidential campaign that followed, individual APA councils took opposing sides in the debate over currency (gold standard versus gold and silver standard) that divided much of the electorate. As if to thumb his nose at APA and display his confidence that most of its constituency was firmly in the Republican camp, the president-elect nominated a Catholic judge to his cabinet.[60]

The disappointment of 1896 pretty much killed off APA as a political movement. Its national magazine folded in the summer of 1897, and Traynor's public call for the formation of a new "American party" that same year fell flat. State councils faded away, though some local chapters continued to meet, perhaps buoyed by the restoration of APA's founder, Henry Bowers, to its presidency in 1898. Although the organization survived on paper until Bowers's death in 1911, its last functional gasp was a national meeting in 1900 which reiterated its original principles.[61]

APA failed politically because the Republicans found that they did not need its support to attract anti-Catholic voters, and that it was a liability at a time when the party thought it might be able to reach out to some recently arrived immigrant groups. In some areas, APA caused defections from the Democrats, but for the most part the Democratic party was able to make political capital of APA's opposition. As in the case of antebellum nativism, political disappointment led to organizational shrinkage, which in turn made APA membership less valuable.[62]

At the same time, APA lost some of its most potent issues. Somewhat like the Know Nothings, it experienced—not necessarily through its own actions—too much "success." Emergent voting reform undercut the traditional nativist complaint that illegal naturalizations were taking place on the eve of elections. Individual states began to add legislation lengthening the period before an immigrant could cast a vote. Several states also sought from Congress a national commitment to the principle of naturalization as a condition for voting. School board elections in a number of major cities seemed to show that Protestants were firmly in command and the Catholic "threat" to the schools had been exaggerated. In New York state, where it was an agitated issue, the legislature upheld a ban on state assistance to parochial schools. Congress took steps to eliminate the contracting of schools for American Indians to denominational agencies (the contract schools disappeared entirely before long).[63] The spread of women's suffrage at the state and local level—because of the higher turnout rates among middle-class, native-born, Protestant women—had the effect of quieting the fears of many actual and potential nativists. Even one of APA's wilder wishes—that employment preference be given to the native-born—took partial shape in the form of laws in Pennsylvania and New York in the mid-1890s which excluded aliens from public works jobs. On the tamer side, there was a spate of state laws requiring "patriotic" education and flying the American flag in schoolrooms. Another aspect of this was legislation, in such states as Ohio and Illinois, prohibiting flying other nations' flags on public buildings—a slap at St. Patrick's Day celebrations in particular.[64] In Connecticut, the voters approved an expansion on a Know-Nothing era constitutional amendment requiring not just that prospective voters be able to read English but that they be able to read from the state statutes or constitution. By the early 1900s, almost two dozen states had passed legislation requiring that major subjects in schools of all kinds be taught in English.[65]

In 1895, APA was embarrassed by an exposé (made much of by historians) revealing that the organization never had anywhere near as many members as it claimed. A former activist, Walter Sims, charged that at a time when APA claimed 1 million members, he had a hard time accounting for a tenth that number. Consequently, it is tempting to write off the import of APA as exaggerated. But that is missing the point.[66] Built on a foundation of nativist societies, APA really functioned as an umbrella for these organizations, some of which lost their identity during the period of its growth but many of which lived through its rise and decline. Many people who were actually in the Junior Order, United American Mechanics, or the Loyal Orange Institution thought of themselves as part of APA, attended APA rallies, and responded to its rhetoric but never actually became members. When APA faltered, some fellow travelers denied any connection with it, choosing to emphasize their other nativist connections. Samuel T. McSeveney even identifies a nativist political activist in New Britain, Connecticut, who denied being in APA but admitted to old Know Nothing connections.[67]

Two conditions created the impression—and for a while the reality—of APA's strength. One was its broad view of membership. It welcomed all adult male Protestants, whether native or foreign-born (befitting contemporary nativists' definition of "alien" as an *organized* challenge to their version of the "national character") and was happy to count members of other, sympathetic orders as part of its constituency.

Initially, this broad-mindedness probably made working relationships with some other "patriotic" societies difficult. The National Council of Patriotic Organizations, which at the outset tended to represent the more exclusive and sometimes ancestral societies, initially ignored APA. But over time, APA's flexibility proved an asset. There was open cooperation between the APA and more solidly "middle" middle-class nativist organizations like the Junior Order, United American Mechanics and the Patriotic Order, Sons of America. APA may even have brought back into the nativist camp more of the skilled workers that groups like the Order of United American Mechanics had been trying so hard to disassociate from "respectable" nativism. Certainly APA's speakers and publicists went out of their way to emphasize the ordinariness of its membership and harped on the virtues of being a "plain American."[68]

The second condition was APA's willingness to push a political agenda without resorting to a futile third-party challenge, as the doomed American party had done just a few years before. In fact, the evidence suggests that APA picked up many members from the other "patriotic" orders who were dissatisfied with their own organizations' political inaction. This was not just at the national level but also local. In many cities, APA members were particularly active in endorsing school board candidates or whole slates of municipal officials. Donald Kinzer notes that this reputation for political activity allowed APA to take disproportionate credit for political pressure brought to bear mainly by other nativist societies.[69]

In the long run, it is possible that APA's position as a sort of nativist "umbrella" accelerated its demise. When APA's political ambitions came up short, it was easy enough for many members to slip back into the longer-lived nativist orders without withdrawing entirely from nativist activism. These societies remained active alongside APA in many places and operated alone in other places, called "APA" by press and public alike. Along the east coast, the Junior Order, United American Mechanics, remained particularly active at the turn of the century.[70] The very traditionalism of APA encouraged this: it made little effort to distinguish itself from half a century of nativist activism before it. An APA periodical in New York state went so far as to call itself the *Republic,* harking back to Thomas R. Whitney's antebellum journal. No wonder a widely reprinted newspaper article of 1893 from the *Providence [Rhode Island] Journal* held that APA could best be regarded as a reappearance of Know Nothingism:

Those whose memory runs back forty years or more, and those of a younger generation who are superficially acquainted with the political history of the United States, are well aware, of course, from what has been publicly made known of late regarding the APA, or the OUD, that this organization is, in all essentials, almost an exact reproduction of the old native American movement, which under the popular name of Know-Nothingism, troubled the politicians along the early fifties. . . . In principles, purposes and methods the APA today are the old Know-Nothings galvanized into temporary activity once more.[71]

Just as APA was losing its allure, international events conspired to give the nativist movement a new opportunity to broadcast its message. The Venezuelan border crisis of 1895, which grew from Great Britain's saber-rattling response to a dispute over the boundaries of British Guiana, initially provoked a threatening response from the Cleveland administration in defense of the Monroe Doctrine. But in the long run it paved the way for a British-American rapprochement and more rosy expressions of fraternal affection than theretofore had been common. The American business community—to say nothing of British-American fraternal groups—was horrified by any hint of transatlantic hostilities and moved quickly to give new emphasis to bonds of language and history. The inverse of this proposition was an implication that "native" and "Anglo-American" were related adjectives. The nativist press had a field day suggesting that organized Irish Catholic (even "Jesuit") forces had conspired to bring about enmity between the United States and Britain in the first place. Hostility between the United States and Spain, which escalated to war in 1898, reinforced the tendency among some nativists to emphasize what they took to be the nation's Anglo-Protestant tradition, contrasting it with the "medievalism" of Catholic Spain.[72]

The Immigration Restriction League

International developments created conditions under which the largely middle-class nativist orders that undergirded and in some cases survived the American Protective Association achieved a measure of tactical alliance with a decidedly elitist organization, the Immigration Restriction League, by linking Anglo-Saxonism, Protestantism, and Americanism. But no actual ideological convergence, much less institutional assimilation, ever took place. Although they influenced each other, the Immigration Restriction League moved into the twentieth century focusing on what it took to be the Anglo-Saxon character of "true" American nationality, while the middle-class fraternal mainstream of the nativist movement continued to draw attention to what it interpreted as organized "foreignism," the chief example of which continued to be the Roman Catholic church. Still, sympathetic relations between the two elements introduced some new ideas to the nativist movement that would have consequences in following decades.

The Immigration Restriction League emerged indirectly from the "good government, good citizenship" movement which appeared in major northeastern cities in the middle to late 1880s. This was an upper-class, even patrician movement, operating through "patriotic" clubs and societies that promoted education as the best long-term hope for good government in an increasingly diverse society with universal (at least white) manhood suffrage. These groups, like the Massachusetts Society for Promoting Good Citizenship, operated largely by sponsoring lectures and distributing tracts.[73] Over time, these activities seemed to some a tepid response to a pressing civic concern. It was not a long leap to the conclusion that some of the human material having arrived and currently arriving in the United States was uneducable to the standards necessary to sustain a self-governing republic. In academic circles, this drew reinforcement from the contemporary enthusiasm for tracing democratic political traditions back to northern European "Teutonic" sources. For some, this geographical link between the United States and Saxon or Anglo-Saxon Europe became an ethnic link, suggesting that Anglo-Saxons alone could carry on the American political tradition.[74]

This idea drew support from both American and English academic circles. Francis A. Walker, a famous professor of political economy at Yale and director of the United States Census who became president of the Massachusetts Institute of Technology in 1881, began publicizing, as early as the mid-1870s, his concern that the "traditional" elements of the American population were being outpaced by descendants of other ethnic groups. Barbara Miller Solomon notes that Walker was dubious about even non-English northern European immigrants and their offspring, wondering whether second-generation Irish- and German-Americans were not "home-made foreigners." He was particularly anxious about evidence that the birthrate among old-stock Americans had drifted below that of newcomers.[75] Those who shared Walker's views were made more nervous in the early 1890s by the implications of the "closing" of the American western frontier, described by the historian Frederick Jackson Turner in his celebrated paper presented to the American Historical Association, "The Significance of the Frontier in American History." For Turner argued that "the frontier promoted the formation of a composite nationality for the American people. . . . In the crucible of the frontier the immigrants were Americanized, liberated, and fused into a mixed race, English in neither nationality nor characteristics." But if the frontier was gone—or almost gone—would "Americanization" and "liberation" still take place?[76] The international developments which served to draw the United States and Britain together also created a more sympathetic audience for British scholarship, including writings like Charles Pearson's *National Life and Character* of 1893, which gloomily predicted that the biological range of the "higher races" in the temperate zones would dictate their ultimate eclipse in the competition for world mastery.[77]

Filled with ideas like these, three young Harvard graduates whose sense of civic activism was not satisfied by distributing "good citizenship" literature met in the spring of 1894 to found an organization that quickly grew into the Immigration Restriction League (IRL) of Boston. While not necessarily committed to cutting off immigration entirely, the organization—as its name implied—from the beginning sought mechanisms to alter contemporary patterns of minimally regulated immigration to the United States. And it sought to do so in ways that, presumably, would admit only the "best" prospects for citizenship and exclude others. A leading American academic, John Fiske, was persuaded to take the presidency of this organization, and it attracted other notables, including Teutonist scholars, to leadership positions. Within a year, counterparts had sprung up across the northeast and midwest and even into the far west and deep south. Ultimately, a national umbrella was called for, a national Association of Immigration Restriction Leagues.[78]

Even before the advent of the Immigration Restriction League, federal immigration policy had begun to pay more attention to the physical characteristics of immigrants. Legislation authorizing the immigration reception station at Ellis Island in New York harbor, which opened in 1892, allowed federal inspectors to exclude immigrants for an expanded number of physical debilities and illnesses. Although the evidence suggests that immigrants turned away for these reasons did not exceed more than about 1 percent of arrivals over the next two decades, the development could only give encouragement to those who thought that entire groups of people were genetically handicapped for effective republican citizenship. The stratagem pursued by the Immigration Restriction League to limit immigration to the "right sort" was not altogether new: a literacy test. It had the attraction of not seeming to outlaw whole ethnic groups entirely on the basis of descent while in fact it worked against the admission of people from southern and eastern Europe, who were an increasing proportion of immigrant arrivals. When the test was first promoted by the League in 1895, it was able to garner support from organized labor, just then looking for any means of slowing immigration in a time of economic depression. From the first, its principal legislative champion was the Republican senator Henry Cabot Lodge of Massachusetts.[79]

A literacy test bill was introduced into both houses of Congress in mid-1896. It quickly passed the House but then languished in the Senate as, with a presidential election approaching, both parties grew wary of a negative response from ethnic voters. When it was finally passed by the Senate in 1897, the bill was vetoed by President Cleveland. Reintroduced in 1897-1898, it ran into better-organized public opposition from representatives of even old, established ethnic groups like the Irish and Germans. A bill did pass the Senate in 1898 but was tabled in the House and not resurrected when the Spanish-American War intervened. Subsequent efforts to pass a literacy test bill in 1902, 1903, and 1904 also failed.[80]

Over time, the Immigration Restriction League attracted some support from traditional nativist orders. The historian Barbara Miller Solomon notes that the Junior Order, United American Mechanics, backed the effort to move a literacy test bill through Congress in 1897 with a petition to lawmakers and pledged some funding for continued lobbying during the first decade of the twentieth century. But, overall, the older nativist orders were only halfhearted about the "racial" fears that seemed to motivate the intellectuals of IRL; and IRL itself was not very supportive of traditional anti-Catholicism, which paid little attention to "racial" descent.[81] In fact, most of the institutional constituents of the nativist movement continued to show more interest in what members took to be evidence of organized threats to the national character than they did to the intellect or physique of individual immigrants. The sort of thing that still excited these nativists was any sign of imported, "contract" labor or managed, fraudulent naturalization and "bought" votes. A local chapter of the Order of United Mechanics in western

Pennsylvania, for instance, sprang into action in 1904 to attack what it took to be manipulated "pauper" labor from southeastern Europe. After the assassination of President McKinley in 1901, the disapproval of the Philadelphia Union League fell on all immigrants who failed to take steps to secure naturalization, suspecting that this was not simply inertia but orchestrated resistance to Americanization.[82]

Actually, many nativist activists were not enthusiastic about the implications of "racial" exclusionism. One symptom was the increasing sympathy of the Immigration Restriction League crowd for "old" immigrant groups like the Irish. "In 1892," Barbara Miller Solomon observes, "[Francis A.] Walker altered his rationalization [for immigration restriction] in one significant respect by suppressing his hostility to the Irish Americans. Retracting much of his harsh description of the alien invasion . . . since the 1850s, he admitted that after a time the Irish had improved their standard of living and worked hard for the decencies of life." Other backers of IRL waxed even more enthusiastic about how the Irish had adapted to American life, especially political life.[83] But this energetic involvement in American politics was just what traditional nativists feared about the Irish. These nativists were much more excited by the attention the Supreme Court brought to several naturalization fraud cases in 1903 and, especially, when the Naturalization Act of 1906 established federal standards and procedures for making citizens of immigrants. The Naturalization Act was a long-standing nativist goal, and its achievement took much wind out of the movement's sails—or at least made it more difficult for nativists to find new outrages at election time. John Higham argues that the act marked "the separation between nativism and municipal reform." This was bound to rob the nativist organizations that remained of much of the respectability they had gained by keeping company with the "good government" activists.[84]

Nativism, Racism, and Anti-Semitism

Not surprisingly, the "racial" sensitivities of Immigration Restriction League activists and fellow travelers made them considerably more sympathetic than the fraternal and "patriotic" societies that made up the mainstream of the nativist movement to contemporaneous anti-Semitism and popular anxiety about Asian immigration—the fear of the "yellow peril" of Chinese, then Japanese, immigration that sometimes worked itself up into virtual hysteria. In fact, there was no more dramatic evidence of the shift of the center of European emigration from western to east central Europe in the last decades of the nineteenth century and the first of the twentieth than the patterns of Jewish immigration to the United States. Arthur Goren estimates that of approximately 250,000 Jews in the United States in 1880, fewer than 50,000 had roots outside western Europe, whereas by the end of the First World War, well over 3 million out of a total of 4 million American Jews were of eastern European derivation.[85] Not only could IRL types use this as symbolic of the shift from an "old" to a "new" immigration, but they could tap wells of traditional anti-Semitism to reinforce their argument that the "new" was less desirable.

There is a growing consensus among historians that American anti-Semitism is something other than just a brand of nativism, even when nativism is interpreted in the broadest sense as a set of popular attitudes. This is apparent in the repeated scholarly evaluations of the work of John Higham. On the whole, these have given rather more emphasis than Higham to the continuities between European and American anti-Semitism and rather less to the specific role in promoting anti-Semitic outbursts of what Higham called America's nineteenth-century "agrarian tradition."[86] A new generation of scholars doubt both the softening of anti-Semitism predicted by the demise of the agrarian tradition—which questioned urbanization, industrial capitalism, and cosmopolitanism—and the necessity of Higham's formulation to explain the potential for anti-Semitism that seems to have endured from the colonial period of American history into the twentieth century. Edward S. Shapiro captures the drift of much modern scholarship in arguing that "American anti-Semitism was part of a transnational mindset, not merely a response to American conditions"—a point made slightly differently by David A. Gerber, who suggests that anti-Semitism in America has been a response "not merely to Jews as foreigners, but to Jews as Jews."[87] It was the very "transnationality" of anti-Semitism that set it apart from conventional nativism. Anti-Semitic stereotypes portrayed Jews as a threat not to the American nation but to *international* Christianity or *international* finance or the *international* Anglo-Saxon "race."

There is plenty of evidence that anti-Semitism has had a peculiarly long life in America and that it has repeatedly quickened in the absence of the particular conditions of the late nineteenth century, when defenders of the "agrarian tradition" seemed under siege and, as Higham puts its, a "middle class scramble for prestige" was unleashed by a modernizing economy. The latent strength of anti-Semitism in the European cultural baggage of generations of emigrants to North America is, in fact, underscored by the very amicability of Jewish-gentile relations throughout most of the colonial period and on into the 1800s. Jewish Americans turned up in leadership positions in fraternal orders, tradesmen's societies, and secular (even church-related) charitable organizations both before and after the birth of the American republic. The tendency of both colonists and citizens of the new nation to conceive of their enterprise—often in frankly religious terms—as a "new Israel" encouraged them to at least accept and often respect the small number of Jews among them, something encouraged by most Protestant Americans' accommodation to denominational pluralism by the end of the eighteenth century. If a characteristic response of American churchgoers to Jewish neighbors during the first half of the nineteenth century was repeated calls for their conversion, it seems not to have been a matter of religious disrespect so much as a conviction that this was the intended fulfillment of Jewish history. Interestingly, this attitude could coexist with Christian agreeableness and even financial support for the forming of Jewish congregations and the building of synagogues. Few eyebrows were raised when a rabbi was asked to give the opening prayer before Congress in 1860.[88]

But *some* eyebrows were raised at this incident, and it drew enough criticism to provide clear evidence that anti-Semitic notions had survived the sea voyage from Europe intact. Jonathon Sarna, who has closely examined the substantial antebellum Jewish community in Cincinnati, is certainly right in saying that most mid-nineteenth-century anti-Semitism was "rhetorical," but rhetorical or not, it had considerable ability to cause pain and rationalize discrimination. John Higham reminds us that the "earliest published plays [in America] containing Jewish characters (1794, 1823) portrayed Shylock types, and by the 1840s the verb 'to Jew,' meaning to cheat by sharp practice, was becoming a more or less common ingredient of American slang."[89] Judah P. Benjamin's premature departure from Yale College in the late 1820s dogged him for decades: there were stereotyped rumors that he had been exposed as a thief. Benjamin (who had been raised in South Carolina) would be elected to the United States Senate from Louisiana in the 1850s and would serve in key posts in the Confederate cabinet in the next decade; but when the war began to turn against the south, there were increasingly snide comments about his Jewish background. These came on the heels of speculation in the northern press at the time of secession that Benjamin's resignation from the United States Congress might somehow represent a larger pattern of Jewish unreliability (which brought an anguished outcry from northern Jewish leaders). Latent anti-Semitism came into the open in the north during the war, when Ulysses Grant, then a regional commander in the west, responded to General William T. Sherman's complaints about cotton speculators descending on the recently captured Mississippi port of Memphis by summarily banishing Jews from the state of Tennessee. This arbitrary General Order 11 of December 1862 was triggered by old stereotypes rather than any particular personal animus on Grant's part, and it was disallowed by President Lincoln, but it was symptomatic of disturbing incidents of rhetorical prejudice that popped up again as scapegoating under the strains of wartime.[90]

Consequently, during the 20 years following the Civil War there was nothing very remarkable when Jews were blackballed by a bar association or turned away from a college fraternity or spurned by a resort hotel. Nor was it surprising that incidents like these coexisted with sympathetic portrayals of Jews in literature or public outrage over vicious Russian pogroms in the 1880s and 1890s. Anti-Semitism remained a matter of very old and fundamentally imported stereotypes that were fully capable of bubbling up when a layer of civility was scratched deeply enough.[91]

One thing is quite clear, however: Anti-Semitism was not central to either the prewar or the postwar nativist movement. Jews never constituted a large enough minority or seemed anywhere near organized enough to be taken as a threat to the "national character" in the antebellum or the postbellum sense. The very diversity of their national origins—which increased over time—and their emerging denominational richness (ultimately represented by Orthodox, Conservative, and Reform branches of Judaism) militated against seeing Jews as agents of another nation or a monolithic religious institution. Antebellum nativists, if anything, seem to have preferred to advertise Jewish Americans as an example of the loyalty to traditional values and to the "founding fathers" that they wished to promote in republican citizens. It was the future American party Presidential candidate Millard Fillmore who, as one of his last acts as a Whig president in 1852, offered a Supreme Court seat to Judah P. Benjamin; and it was Mordecai Noah of New York, architect of a plan for a gathering point for Jews in the new world near Niagara Falls, to be called "Ararat," who published a nativist-aligned newspaper and proved a special favorite of the Order of United Americans' Thomas R. Whitney.[92]

There is little to indicate that there was anything very special about the eruptions of anti-Semitism in the 1890s and at the turn of the century, except for another set of circumstances that in some quarters of society set off a search for scapegoats and took advantage of traditional stereotypes. Clearly, the economic depression that began in 1893 was made for this. Old money under financial pressure (Henry Adams is an example that historians like to use) was only too happy to blame its troubles on "Shylocks" with names like Rothschild and Belmont. Enthusiasts of the southern and western Populist movement, too, were happy to find ready-made symbols for distant bankers, inscrutable merchants, and "goldbugs" in the stereotyped rhetoric of anti-Semitism. It would be wrong, though, to see American anti-Semitism in this period as only a matter of words. In the north, it led to a new round of social discrimination against wealthy Jews; in the south, there were nasty incidents of night-riding and burned-out Jewish businesses.[93] Still, as in an earlier period, these were juxtaposed with oft-repeated defense of and praise for American Jews among their gentile neighbors, especially from the same camp of evangelical Protestants that was most closely aligned with the nativist movement because of shared hostility to Roman Catholicism.[94]

Anti-Semitism, then, was alive and well in America with or without the nativist movement—but usually without. It is a separate phenomenon from nativism and deserves independent analysis. Anti-Semitic stereotypes could be put into service by "racial" immigration restrictionists of the type to which the Immigration Restriction League appealed but were scarcely essential to the IRL's program, much less at the root of its formation. The best evidence that anti-Semitism was latent across a much wider population was its cynical manipulation by the Georgia Democrat Tom Watson, who discovered that the circulation of his *Jeffersonian Magazine* soared when he took a strong anti-Semitic editorial line in 1915, in the midst of the controversy over the commutation of Leo Frank's sentence for murder.[95]

Likewise, hostility to Chinese and Japanese immigration—for that matter, all Asian immigration—in the late nineteenth and early twentieth centuries was not on the agenda of the mainstream nativist societies and orders, and it was peripheral even to IRL. Prejudice against Asians seems to have had very little to do with nativism and was much more akin to the racism directed against blacks in the United States or the racism directed by white frontiersmen against American Indians. "Chinamen" (and later the Japanese) were regarded as racially outside the pale of American "peoplehood," and it was widely presumed that they had few rights which whites were bound to respect. Little was required in the way of organized interest-group activity, much less an organized social movement, to exclude the Chinese by law in 1882 and (by subsequent extensions of the law) to effectively exclude the Japanese a quarter of a century later.

From their first arrival on the west coast at the end of the 1840s, the Chinese were put into stereotyped pigeonholes conditioned more by the way white Americans thought of African immigrants than by the way they thought of Europeans. Beginning in the 1850s, there was anxiety in the hotbeds of antislavery sentiment in the northeast that Chinese immigration was just another form of the slave trade. The fact that the passage across the Pacific was arranged by Chinese commercial societies, or "companies," only reinforced fears that Chinese migration was not voluntary. The end of the Civil War reenergized these anxieties, and lurid stories about the hardships of the Pacific crossing replaced stories about the "middle passage" from Africa favored in antislavery literature. Occasional incidents—like a merchants' and planters' convention in Memphis in 1869 at which the adaptability of Chinese labor to cotton fields and cloth mills was discussed, coming hard on the heels of the Burlingame Treaty in 1868, which permitted unrestricted Chinese immigration to the United States—provoked exaggerated apprehensions that a new domestic "slave power" was in the making.[96]

On the west coast itself, where most—but not all—Chinese immigrants came to live in the 1850s, 1860s, and 1870s, there was already a considerable heritage of hostility to African-Americans and dark-skinned Mexicans and a smattering of South Americans. Robert Parmet sees the anti-Mexican hostility of white miners and laborers of the late 1840s as rolling seamlessly into opposition to the first large-scale Chinese immigration of the early 1850s. This was more than just competition for jobs. Hostility grew even as the proportion (though not the absolute number) of Chinese in the population of California declined. Rather, the "anticoolie societies" of both skilled craftsmen and journeymen laborers which harassed Chinese workers and their employers in the 1860s seem to have calculated that the general popular disfavor toward the Chinese was a powerful lever for organizing white labor and using it to achieve conventional workplace goals. A decade later, in the late 1870s, Denis Kearney of California found that popular prejudice against the Chinese was powerful enough to use as a basis for a political organization (the Workingman's party) that could challenge the two-party system in the state.[97]

Alexander Saxton showed pretty clearly a generation ago that the sentiments that led to a legislated conclusion to most Chinese immigration in 1882 were more than regional; they expressed a national consensus. "By 1876," Saxton noted, "both major parties had adopted anti-Chinese clauses in their national platforms." Renegotiation of the Burlingame Treaty just a couple of years later allowed the United States to regulate Chinese immigration, and the act of 1882 which suspended the immigration of Chinese labor for a 10-year period (and subsequently renewed, ultimately—in 1904—indefinitely) passed Congress with unanimous western support, by a 4-to-1 margin among midwestern legislators, and by more than 2 to 1 among northeasterners.[98]

At the heart of this consensus, which came about without much hint of a movement to promote it, was what Saxton has called "anti-coolieism," another way of saying unabashed racism. In the south and the west, the Chinese came to share as "colored" people the animus directed at blacks, in some ways sharpened after the Civil War by the most intense racists' resentment of a society in which "inferior races" could live in at least statutory freedom. In the north, the same working-class fears directed at free blacks, who were believed to compete for jobs on unequal terms because of their low-cost, "animalistic" lifestyles, were easily transferred to the Chinese, some of whom began to show up east of the Mississippi. The popularization of early forms of the germ theory of disease in the late 1860s and 1870s arrived just in time to make prejudiced white Americans exceptionally wary of people who looked different, smelled different, and ate differently. The overwhelmingly male demographics of emigration from China, calculated to excite rumors and fears about sexual conduct anyway, fueled a hysterical notion that the Chinese were bound to cause an epidemic of venereal disease. Among few Americans does there seem to have been the slightest idea that such a different people could actually become fully participating citizens. If there was a question, it was only whether they should be permitted on American soil at all.[99] The exclusion—or, properly, "restriction"—act of 1882 only reinforced the notion that the Chinese had no place in the United States.

Still, there simply was not enough about Chinese immigration to excite the nativist movement. There was no popular expectation that they could become citizens. There was no fear of their ability to organize politically. Moreover, out-and-out nativists were reluctant to get into bed with some of the most outspoken detractors of the Chinese—the American Irish. In the aftermath of the Civil War and black emancipation, Irish-Americans worked harder than ever to show that they were part of the "superior" community of whites. Stuart Creighton Miller notes that Irish denunciations of the Chinese sounded uncannily like the barbs the Irish themselves had received from Anglo-Americans over the preceding 50 years or more. John Higham has observed that "the anti-Chinese movement in California seemed to have helped the Irish feel at home there."[100]

Because of the legislation of 1882, the Chinese question was nearly gone by the time that the racialism on which the Immigration Restriction League thrived came into vogue. "Scientific" racialism was in place, however, by the time popular attention—and anxiety—turned to the Japanese shortly after the turn of the century. While Japanese began migrating in some numbers after the doors were closed to Chinese, what gave their arrival at least nativistic potential was sudden anxiety about the military prowess of the Japanese nation after its defeat of Russia in 1905. Already seen in racial terms as an inferior "colored" people, like the Chinese, the Japanese now came to be associated with what was taken to be a powerful and aggressive homeland. This appeared just as American—and European—racialists were beginning to bemoan more publicly a supposed loss of fertility and drive among the Nordic, Teutonic, or Anglo-Saxon peoples. However, anti-Japanese initiatives never became central to any branch of organized nativist activism. An Asiatic Exclusion League sprang up almost overnight on the west coast in 1905, seeking exclusion of the Japanese on the same terms as the Chinese, and in short order local public agencies like the San Francisco School Board moved to segregate Japanese children. Mindful of the consequences of such local affronts in international relations, during 1907 President Roosevelt exchanged notes with Japan constituting a "gentlemen's agreement" by which Japan pledged to withhold new migrants so long as those already in the United States did not become the objects of official, legislated discrimination. All of this occurred so quickly and with so little opposition that it offered scant opportunity—if there was any inclination—for nativist activists to get involved.[101]

At the very least, "racial" immigration restrictionism moved off one way as the nineteenth century turned into the twentieth, and "traditional" nativism moved off in another. The former waxed enthusiastic about the "science" of William Z. Ripley, whose *The Races of Europe* ushered out the old century by introducing the notions that the Europeans consisted of three "racial" types—the Nordics, the Alpines, and the Mediterreaneans—and that immigration to the United States had shifted from the first two to the third—and not for the better. In the early twentieth century, social scientists like John Commons and E. A. Ross took these ideas further, worrying that high birthrates among "new " immigrant groups and falling birthrates among old-stock Anglo-Americans or even "old" immigrant ethnic groups were leading to, in Ross's words, "race suicide" for Nordics. The biologist David Starr Jordan, president of Stanford University, was just one of many academics whose enthusiasm for the "science" of eugenics led him to draw wild conclusions about the dilution of the genetic strength of old-stock Americans through "interbreeding" with inferior newcomers. The end product of these speculations was Madison Grant's *The Passing of the Great Race,* published in 1916, just as "Nordics" were busy slaughtering one another in the trenches of eastern France. Grant predicted that northern Europe's offspring would be overwhelmed by more "productive" races.[102] In fact, what continued to distinguish this kind of racialism from mainstream nativism was its transnational concern for "Nordics" or "Anglo-Saxons" as types. By definition, nativism had always been concerned about threats to American "national character" specifically. The mainstream of the nativist movement was nationalist; the academic racialism of the Immigration Restriction League enthusiasts was internationalist.

In fact, nativists of the old school continued to see the same old dangers in the same old enemies. The papal declaration of 1908 that the Catholic Church in the United States was no longer a missionary church but a full-fledged national church could have been construed by nativists as evidence that they had exaggerated the extent of Rome's control over American Catholics. But they preferred to see it as a sign of the threatening strength of international Catholicism in the United States.[103] They were especially troubled by such developments as the expansion of the Knights of Columbus into the southern Protestant Bible belt in the first years of the century. (The fraternity's 1909 annual convention was held in Mobile, Alabama.) The dedication of a new Knights national headquarters building in New Haven, Connecticut, in

1906 was just the sort of event to drive traditional nativists mad. Located within a stone's throw of Yale University—symbol of the Puritan, Protestant tradition in America—the headquarters was opened in a ceremony which brought Cardinal Gibbons into Yale's Woolsey Hall and, as the Knights of Columbus historian Christopher Kauffman points out, the president of the university credited Yale and the Knights with a common purpose—education. A new fourth degree in the Knights' ritual, added in 1899, contained words bound to stick in a nativist's craw: "Proud in the olden days was the boast, 'I am a Roman Catholic'; prouder yet today is the boast, 'I am an American citizen'; but the proudest boast of all times is ours to make, 'I am an American Catholic citizen.'" Showing its institutional muscularity, the order could count a chapter in every state by the fifth year of the new century. Outposts of the Knights in Canada, Mexico, and the Philippines only reinforced nativist fears about Catholic extranationalism.[104]

Just as nativists tended to put a negative interpretation on the institutional maturation of the Catholic church in America, they chose to view with alarm the consequences of the eroding Irish monopoly of the church. As Timothy Meagher has shown so effectively in his close studies of Worcester, Massachusetts, once the weight of Catholic Poles, Lithuanians, Italians, Quebecois and other newcomers could no longer be ignored, Irish Catholics began to transform their institutions from narrowly ethnic ones into broader Catholic ones. In fact, the years after 1910 witnessed the beginnings of the pan-Catholic "ethnic" group that Will Herberg was to write about in the 1950s in *Protestant, Catholic, Jew.* This did not remove Irish-Americans from disproportionate representation in the church hierarchy or completely erase the fears of other Catholics that they were being coopted by the Irish. But it did create a stronger undergirding for Catholic institutions, including parochial schools, fraternal orders, service societies, missions, and youth organizations. Meagher even argues that it promoted Catholic militancy by allowing Catholics to more easily opt out of Protestant-dominated institutions.

These developments in American Catholicism were likely to provoke a nativist response, and they did. The Junior Order, United American Mechanics, for example, experienced an increase in membership of more than 50 percent in the decade before the First World War, reaching nearly 250,000 members. Nativist orders were able to take advantage of another wave of enthusiasm for fraternalism that began to sweep over the United States in the first years of the new century and continued unabated into the 1920s.[105] The fissure between traditional nativists and racialists of the Immigration Restriction League type did little to help the crusade for a literacy test, which was beset with other divisions as well. The business community, in particular—major bene-factors of the Republican party, where sentiment for the literacy test was strongest—blew hot and cold on the issue, depending on the state of the economy and the demand for labor. Modest support in the mid-1890s gave way to outright opposition a decade later. In 1907, the National Association of Manufacturers called for more immigration, not less. "Old" immigrant groups—perhaps encouraged by growing Catholic unity—took little comfort in the racialism of the most fervent supporters of the literacy test. German-Americans and Irish-Americans organized to oppose the literacy test. Even with a sympathetic presi-dent, Theodore Roosevelt, in the White House, the Republican con-gressional hierarchy, led by Speaker Joe Cannon, resisted passage of a literacy test for fear of alienating too many ethnic voters, particularly the newer arrivals who were not yet strongly affiliated with the Democ-rats.[106]

Conclusion: Nativism's Mixed Goals

Confronting new and potentially divisive ideas within and finding only mixed support without, the nativist-restrictionist front had to be satis-fied with a new immigration bill that gave a little to many and a lot to none. It created an impression of modest restraint on immigration by doubling the head tax on new arrivals to $4, yet it appeased business by giving the secretary of Commerce and Labor greater authority to permit exceptions to excluded groups. It addressed the growing popu-lar (but not particularly nativist) anxiety about Asian immigration by permitting the president to negotiate individual agreements regulat-ing migration with foreign nations. And in a move calculated to offend no one but increase expectancy in all, it created a Federal Immigration Commission to gather information and report on immigration and its consequences. This commission came under the chairmanship of Senator William Dillingham of Vermont, whose name became associ-ated with it. Whatever it reported, it was bound not to please all. The Immigration Restriction League; the Junior Order, United American Mechanics; and others sought to make their weight felt by the commission from the beginning. But on the question of what was "alien" and what (or who) threatened the national character, they remained far from united.[107] No wonder that over the next 15 years nativism would pursue so many goals, from "Americanization days" to immigration restriction, and that it would take so many forms—from "100 percent Americanizers" to the Ku Klux Klan.

Chapter Seven

Twentieth-Century Nativism and the Irony of Immigration Restriction

The parade, it was reported, filled the streets of the nation's capital with thousands of marchers, most dressed in the regalia of their orders. They represented local chapters with names like "Liberty Bell" and "Old Glory." "Miss One Hundred Percent American" graced one float. Another float carried a replica of a "little red schoolhouse," around which an honor guard hovered protectively. In 1851, the Order of United Americans (OUA) had organized just such a public spectacle in New York City. But now the year was 1925, and OUA had been gone for over half a century. This parade, staged in the month of August, was a production of the Knights of the Ku Klux Klan.[1] The similarities between this event and others which had been associated with organized nativist activism over the preceding century were not lost on contemporaries. Americans within and outside the Klan sometimes specifically acknowledged this hooded order's ideological descent from organizations like the Guardians of Liberty and the American Protective Association, and from there it was not an unthinkable reach back to OUA and the Know Nothings.[2] Much of what had motivated OUA and its kind was still alive in the 1920s: interwoven longings for secure personal, group, and national identity (a "national character") and anxieties about perceived barriers to equal participation in republican self-government.

"Victorian" Nativism in Doubt

It is ironic that the "achievement" most commonly connected with nativism in the United States came not as a triumph of the nativist movement, the culmination of a century of social organizing and political action, but almost as an act of despair—a mood that nativists shared with many others in the early 1920s. In many respects, federal legislation restricting immigration was not so much an achievement of the nativist movement as a repudiation of it. The years in which national immigration restriction was put into place by law—first the Provisional Act of 1921 and then the National Origins Act of 1924— were a time of widespread questioning of the premises on which organized nativist activism had been based since the mid-nineteenth century. The historian Anne Rose argues that the early 1920s saw the demise of "Victorianism": "faith in the significance of human efforts in an image of the Civil War." Victorianism had been the backbone of the nativist movement, manifested in the notion that through organized activity of right-thinking citizens, a *national character* could be preserved. (Perhaps what nativists were really saying was "created"— harmoniously Anglo-American, Protestant, and protective of personal independence.) *Organized* nativist activism, moreover, was driven by a suspicion that other, well-prepared forces were at work to thwart nationalists: cultural "hyphenates," "foreign potentates," and dependent, compliant "naturalized foreigners."

Victorianism was surely at the heart of the nativist fraternal orders that peppered the last third of the nineteenth century; it was evident not only in their ideology but in their very structure. Their devotees confidently assumed that organization could meet members' diverse personal needs—for sociability and belonging, for insurance or relief, for a business reference or a job—as well as achieve important public policy objectives. Thus arose fraternities that operated with all the self-assurance (and many of the personnel) of the soldiers' aid societies of the Civil War or the good-government coalitions of the early Progressive era. The immigrant could be Americanized, the ethnic voter could be freed from the city "boss," and the Catholic—if not converted— could at least be made independent of Rome.

Victorianism was also plainly at work in the Immigration Restriction League, the turn-of-the-century elitist organization that was peripheral to, but sometimes allied with, the mainstream of the nativist movement. It had what Robert H. Wiebe has called a "bureaucratic orientation" which was part and parcel of the Victorian outlook.³ Having identified what it took to be a problem of national importance, it sought a "scientific" basis for it and created what was advertised as an orderly mechanism for resolving it. In the early twentieth century, this approach to social issues had broad appeal. As scholars from J. Joseph Huthmacher to Samuel Hays and John D. Buenker have made clear, the Victorian style reached far beyond the middle class which spawned it to become, as Buenker puts it, "the response of Americans from nearly all walks of life to the conditions wrought by industrialization, urbanization, and immigration."⁴

Immigration restriction achieved through a literacy test—the chief object of the Immigration Restriction League and a staple of congressional debate from the 1890s up into the First World War—was a typically bureaucratic, Victorian device and was repeatedly kept from becoming law by presidents, both Republican and Democratic, who saw it as bad politics. By the time it was finally legislated under the extraordinary conditions of the First World War, even its fiercest supporters had come to doubt that it would really solve the immigration "problem" anyway. It could keep a certain number of newcomers out, but it offered no assurance that immigrants or their descendants who were already in would embrace the "national character" that nativists endorsed. Consequently, even before a literacy test for immigrants was passed by Congress over President Wilson's veto in 1917, many backers of the measure had turned their attention to an alternative approach to traditional nativist goals: "Americanization." As bureaucratic and "Victorian" as the literacy test, Americanization was a movement for cultural conformity that sought to organize the resources of the schools, popular entertainment, and even employers to "dehyphenate" not only immigrants but the offspring of earlier generations of immigrants. As Robert Wiebe has pointed out, it was a movement which initially was voluntaristic but which "gravitated almost by nature toward coercion, replacing the earlier paternalism with demands to cast off all foreign ways at once."⁵ Both Americanization itself and its coercive applications were given encouragement by the approach of the First World War.

The big casualty of the war and the peace that followed was Victorianism itself. Americans of all classes seemed more doubtful than before that organized human effort could always be counted on to produce social progress. To many, the war seemed to be organization running amok, producing unprecedented slaughter. During the 1920s there would be a wave of speculation that the war had been unnecessary, that it had been manipulated into being by private interests (significantly, in this view, organized, monopolistic big business) in order to serve finance and trade. And then the peace, though elaborately orchestrated in the Victorian tradition, seemed driven more by competitive nationalism than by an attempt to preserve world harmony. Domestic Victorian achievements made possible by the war, like Prohibition, seemed to many not to have the consequences long advertised by their advocates. Overly aggressive governmental response to the postwar "red scare" struck some as worse than the disease of radicalism it was supposed to eradicate. In fact, by the early 1920s, a popular backlash against Victorianism was developing: the idea that organized, bureaucratized action—particularly action involving government enforcement—was intrusion, sapping individual independence and consequently offending the American "national character."[6]

Legislated immigration restriction—which actually came about in several stages from 1921 until nearly the end of the 1920s—emerged from disappointment with the bureaucratic defense of the "national character" through "Americanization." Frustrated by the political maneuvering which had been apparent in the prolonged debate over the literacy test and uncertain of the motives and methods behind "Americanization," participants in organized nativist activism as well as non-nativists (even some antinativists) could agree on wanting an end to the whole immigration question. Closing the gates seemed the simplest way of ending or at least shrinking whatever "problem" there might be with immigration and ethnic diversity. As it came about over the course of the 1920s, immigration restriction scarcely needed the support of organized nativist activism. It had much more widespread appeal.

The nativist movement, in fact, headed off in another direction, a direction quite consistent with its historical roots. The Ku Klux Klan was its most visible—although not exclusive—representative. Impatient with bureaucratic measures and more than a little suspicious of people in power, Klansmen (and women) turned their attention to individual "moral" regeneration to produce a harmonious national character and a society of equal republican citizens. Of course, participants in the movement sought to define just what "moral" was, and they used a mirror to find out. The assumption was that "if everyone could be like us," problems of society and national identity would pretty well take care of themselves. The Klan was briefly a cultural and political power to be reckoned with, but it fizzled when its participants discovered that the "us" they had in mind was something far more complex than they had ever imagined. By then, the effects of immigration restriction had taken the wind out of nativism's sails, and the movement never really recovered its momentum.

Nativist Opportunism before World War I

It is easy to overlook the nativist movement in the period immediately preceding the United States' entry into World War I. During this span of half a dozen years or so, the imprint of major nativist organizations was indeed slighter than it had been in the immediate past. But it is possible to read too much into this—as John Higham, for example, may have done. Higham made much of the brevity of the anti-Catholic career of *The Menace* and concluded, in *Strangers in the Land,* that "the anti-Catholic movement shrank like a pricked balloon in 1915."[7] An alternative reading may be that anti-Catholic themes had become so commonplace in American popular culture that they were no longer grist for journalistic sensationalism and did not require much aggressive reinforcement from nativistic organizations. Certainly politicians in many areas recognized that there were plenty of Protestant voters who, having adopted as cultural dogma that institutional Catholicism inherently threatened American "nationality," would respond reflexively to charges of "foreign" ecclesiastical aggression. The sometime Populist Tom Watson, of Georgia, cynically exploited anti-Catholicism in his political comeback around 1915. He skillfully attacked not individual Catholics but the "foreign" institutional church, and he made political capital out of the church's effort to organize a boycott of businesses that advertised in his political magazine. In New York state, a discredited Democratic ex-governor, William Sulzer, picked up surprising support among voters in 1914 by organizing an "American" party that trotted out time-tested messages about priest-led, foreign-born Catholic voters and the influence of New York City's Tammany-connected politicians. In this atmosphere, nativist activists did not so much have to press their case as simply wait to take advantage of promising circumstances.[8]

Likewise, it took little effort on the part of nativist organizations to provoke aggressiveness among native-born Protestants on a number of "cultural" issues. They needed only to jump in after popular passions had been inflamed. This was the case in Rhode Island, where there were battles over whether to declare Good Friday a public holiday (or, if not, whether to excuse Catholic children from the public schools to attend religious holiday services). It was also the case in New York (with echoes in Ohio and Massachusetts), where the legislature debated the legality of Sunday professional baseball off and on between 1910 and 1920 (old divisions reopened between pietistic, generally Anglo-American Protestants and adherents of a more relaxed "continental Sunday," who were often of other ethnic origins and frequently Roman Catholic.) In Massachusetts, there was an effort to amend the state constitution to cut off any possibility that public funds could be used to assist Catholic parochial schools. Again in New York, bills came before the legislature to withhold the franchise for 10 years after naturalization and even to restrict eligibility for public office to the native-born. In Chicago, in 1915, there was such rumbling among Protestants about the number of Catholic women taking teaching posts in the public schools that the school superintendent sought to limit Catholic enrollment in teacher training at Chicago Normal School. Episodes like these offered opportunities for nativist organizations like the Junior Order, United American Mechanics, and the Guardians of Liberty to attract public attention but did not require them to take a leading role.[9]

In the deep south, 1910-1920 witnessed the same kind of anti-Catholic aggressiveness that had been played out much earlier in the north and midwest. To some extent, this was a function of the increasing mobility of the population in the early automobile age and the spread of foreign-born and Catholic populations. Between 1913 and 1915, the Florida legislature debated bills reminiscent of the experience of Massachusetts in the 1850s: one to ban the wearing of any religious (read "Catholic") symbols (such as jewelry) by public school teachers; another calling for "inspection" of public and private "institutions"; a third (aimed at Catholic women's teaching orders) prohibiting whites from serving as teachers of African-American children and blacks from teaching whites; and even a measure making Bible reading compulsory in schools. Nativist societies like the Guardians of Liberty, previously confined to the north, took these issues as an opportunity to expand well beyond their original haunts, although they had by no means originated the issues.[10]

Anti-Catholicism played a central role in the Florida gubernatorial election of 1916. The candidate of the Prohibitionist party was Sidney Catts, whose rhetoric had a decidedly nativistic flavor, focusing on the alleged intrusion into politics of a Roman Catholic hierarchy "receiving its orders from Rome" and intent on destroying "our public schools, the freedom of the press and free speech," and usurping the "rights of all our free institutions."[11] The historian David P. Page notes that Democratic legislators became so unnerved by the appearance of the Guardians of Liberty in Florida that they inadvertently gave Catts new ammunition by passing party resolutions denying the vote in the primary elections to those "who would refuse to swear that they were not influenced by nor affiliated with such secret societies."[12] Catts, of course, was able to turn this into a charge that Catholic pressure was being used to strip Americans of their right of association and political organization. Catts was elected, and as governor he called on the legislature to tax church property, open religious facilities to public inspection, and require state examination of both private and public school teachers. Legislators actually did pass an inspection bill which, though scarcely enforced, stayed on the statute books for almost 20 years. With less drama than Florida, other southern states—like neighboring Alabama—considered similar measures. In Birmingham, a slate of municipal candidates rode into office on a nativistic ticket and removed Catholic city employees.[13]

Across the nation from 1912 to 1917, nativist organizations took advantage of developments which seemed to offer an opportunity to remain in the public eye. Four hundred and twenty years after Christopher Columbus's landing in the new world, a congressionally funded statue of Columbus was unveiled near the base of Capitol Hill. President Taft spoke at the dedication, as did the chief officer of Washington's Catholic University and a former National Director of the Knights of Columbus currently serving as a Justice of the New York supreme court. An accompanying parade featured both military groups and units of the Knights of Columbus. The outcry provoked from militant Protestants, who took this event as symbolizing the influence that Roman Catholicism had gained over public institutions, rippled through the rest of the decade as the Knights of Columbus took the lead in promoting the official recognition of Columbus Day state by state.[14]

In the same fashion, established nativist orders sought to make much of the fund-raising visit of the Irish republican Roger Casement to the United States in the summer of 1914, implying that Catholics and Irish-Americans were conspiring to involve the United States in what seemed to be an impending armed revolt of the Irish against

British rule. When a "Committee to Celebrate One Hundred Years of Peace Between English Speaking People" sought the endorsement of Governor Edward F. Dunne of Illinois, an Irish-American, his refusal to comply until the body was retitled the "Peace Centenary Committee" (removing any reference to "English") provoked a new round of charges that "foreign" events were intruding on American life.[15] Fissures between Protestants and Catholics were also an exploitable byproduct of the continuing prewar temperance crusade. Oklahoma's passage of "bone-dry" legislation in 1916 was initially challenged by a Catholic priest seeking sacramental wine. The court battles that followed saw conventional Protestant church groups aligned with militant nativists only too happy to take advantage of the issue.[16] Episodes like these provided just enough sustenance to keep the nativist orders in business, though they lacked the public prominence they had sometimes previously enjoyed. The Junior Order, United American Mechanics, which had grown by over 50 percent between 1905 and 1910, managed to hold onto most of that increase over the next five years (despite a schism in 1913 that took a number of members away to form a Fraternal Order of Patriotic Americans) and was poised for another period of dramatic growth that would come on the heels of the First World War. The continuing organizational strength of nativist activism was one impetus for the creation of a Commission on Religious Prejudices by the Catholic Knights of Columbus in late 1914.[17]

Although the traditional fraternal and "patriotic" orders that had for so long been the mainstream of the nativist movement seemed content to exploit popular prejudices during the prewar period, they achieved at least as much public visibility and success on their own terms as the elitist immigration restrictionist organizations that linked themselves with other "progressive" social and political initiatives. In the years that followed the report of the congressional Dillingham Commission, enthusiasm for the "scientific" preservation of the alleged American genetic rootstock passed from the Immigration Restriction League to a variety of "professional" and "reform" organizations such as the Immigration Committee of the American Medico-Psychological Association and the Commission of the Alien Insane.[18] These found much comfort (or perhaps anxiety) in the continuing findings of sympathetic social scientists that social problems were traceable to weaknesses in imported human material. *The Old World in the New* (1914), a contribution to the Anglo-Saxon preservationist outlook by Edward A. Ross of the University of Wisconsin, for example, purported to show that immigrants from eastern and southern Europe could live at wage levels that would line the pockets of greedy capitalists while undercutting respectable American workers.

R. Fred Wacker, a scholar of the history of race theory, notes that contemporary American social science continued to be dominated by what he calls "neo-Lamarckianism," the idea that "adaptations to physical and environmental forces were transmitted to later generations through hereditary mechanisms." Consequently, culture and "national character" were taken to be a matter of "race."[19] These attitudes managed to creep beyond the confines of the universities where they were nurtured by "progressive" scholars anxious about what they believed to be widening class fissures in the United States. Such attitudes circulated, for example, in popular culture through such new media as motion pictures. In an exploration of silent films of the prewar years, Steven J. Ross found repeated portrayals of "foreign-born agitators who relied on violence and duped good but dim-witted workers into serving their own selfish ends . . . East European foreigners with disheveled hair, wild beards, and bulging eyes that shine with madness." Such images were so pervasive that even the conservative American Federation of Labor—which had a rather jaundiced view of immigration—joined more radical labor groups in condemning the early film industry.[20]

Still, activists for immigration restriction had little to crow about when it came to actual public policy. It did not take long for Congress to pass a measure calling for a literacy test—the Dillingham-Burnett Bill—on the heels of the Immigration Commission report; but when President Taft vetoed it at the beginning of 1913, there were not enough votes in the House to override. A similar measure met the same fate at the hands of President Wilson two years later. In both cases, the literacy test was rejected by the White House for a combination of practical and ideological reasons: reluctance to offend nationality groups that were already well represented among the American citizenry and were likely to be affected; doubt that it would actually exclude the supposedly most troublesome immigrants; and hesitancy to tamper with the American tradition of openness to newcomers. A literacy test act was finally legislated over Wilson's second veto, but only after the election of 1916 was safely behind both of the major parties and the war in Europe had sent many Americans—and certainly many politicians—into a frenzy of "Americanization."[21]

"Americanization"

The enactment of the literacy test owed little to the nativist movement. Enthusiasm for a literacy test had always been peripheral to the nativist mainstream anyway. American nativism as a social movement had consistently been more about self-definition than about the mechanics of exclusion. Nativist activists saw themselves less as sentinels at the gate than as cultural instructors and evaluators. Exclusionist initiatives, in fact, threatened to put nativist activism—and the organizations that sustained it—out of business by suggesting that the national character was all a matter of who was let in. If it was not swept up in the same enthusiasm for the literacy test that had captured elements of the Progressive movement, the populist center of the nativist movement was stirred by the excitement over Americanization which virtually made the literacy test obsolete. All at once the question was not whether newcomers were suited by either intelligence or education for admission to the United States but whether anyone—native or foreign-born—was loyal and "one of us."

In fact, in terms of the popular attention it generated, the "Americanization" movement that emerged in the years immediately before the United States' entry into the First World War quite overshadowed the debate over the literacy test. Although it had little to do with legislation (which to the literacy test movement had been everything), "Americanization" as it was prosecuted both before and after the United States declared war on Germany was every bit as much a "Victorian," bureaucratized approach to "reform" as the restrictionist movement. The Americanization campaign made the same assumption as the immigration restriction movement: that there was a core culture (largely Protestant and Anglo-American) on which the successful operation of republican government must be based. But Americanization proposed that most immigrants and their offspring could become part of that core if their environment was properly arranged through education, training, and supervision. This was the sort of approach that President Woodrow Wilson, a progressive, could enthusiastically support—and so could the nativist movement. Addressing an audience at a naturalization ceremony during his first term, Wilson attacked "hyphenism": "You cannot become Americans if you think of yourselves in groups. America does not consist of groups."[22] The hallmark of Americanization, however, was not rhetoric but managed, structured experiences.

Like Progressivism (and Victorianism), Americanization was pursued by a partnership of public agencies and private organizations. In this lay an opportunity for old elements of the nativist movement to reassert themselves as well as for new bodies assuming nativist features to emerge. A Committee for Immigrants in America, which grew out of the New York chapter of the North American Civic League, took the lead in pressing for a Division of Immigrant Education as part of the United States Bureau of Education in 1915. The focus of this agency was less on the "three R's" than on a combination of cultural indoctrination, patriotic political science, and English language instruction. Filtering down to the local level, pressure for cultural conformity took the form of "Americanization days" in cities across the country which stressed the colorfulness but superficiality of ethnic diversity.[23] Business and business groups got into the act, too. The most famous initiative in this area was the Ford School, which instructed some thousands of automobile workers in English and "Americanism." Gerd Korman notes that in Ford classrooms "the first thing the immigrant learned to say was 'I am an American.'" According to Korman, "the immigrant student was expected to attend classes for six to eight months before or after his work shift. At the end of his course of seventy-two lessons, a printed diploma qualified him for his first naturalization papers without further examination by federal authorities."[24] There was little doubt among those who organized this private-public partnership that such domestic cultural missionary activity would transform its subjects and preserve the "national character."

The war that broke out in Europe in 1914, and the likelihood of American participation, gave urgency to the efforts of the Americanizers while reinforcing their bureaucratized, "Victorian" character. Frances Kellor, a leading Americanizer and editor of *Immigrants in America Review,* the journal of the Committee for Immigrants in America, set the magazine on a course from its beginning in 1915 which demanded from right-thinking citizens a "conscious effort to forge the people of this country into an American race that will stand together for America in time of peace and war."[25] This was the sort of effort taken up by organizations which formed just before and during the war: for example, the National Security League (1914); the American Defense Society (a 1915 offshoot of the NSL); and the American Protective League (a private but quasi-official ally of the federal government's Bureau of Investigation, founded on the eve of the United States' entry into the war in 1917).[26] During the period of enthusiasm over "preparedness" for national defense—during 1914, 1915, 1916, and early 1917—such bodies argued the merits of compulsory military service as training in Americanism for "hyphenates" and denounced the divisive influences of "foreign" organizations, whether ethnic lodges or "radical" labor unions.[27]

American entry into the war in the spring of 1917 temporarily redirected the nationalist and preparedness organizations toward focusing their energies on ensuring the loyalty of German-Americans and rooting out potential saboteurs. In the years preceding the United States' entry into the war, German-American organizations had shown some hostility toward the American tilt in favor of the Allies; nevertheless, disloyalty—let alone sabotage—turned out to be a nonissue. There were, of course, what now seem ludicrous efforts to eliminate even the most harmless references to German culture in American life—like renaming sauerkraut "liberty cabbage" and suspending German-language instruction in schools—but these could not absorb highly charged wartime energies for long.

But if suspicion of German-Americans fizzled for lack of provocation, the private and quasi-public preparedness organizations had no difficulty finding other sources of anxiety which turned them in nativistic directions. Attention was transferred from finding "those who are against us" to identifying "those who are for us" or maybe just "us," the classic nativist objective. What is clear is that the war unleashed much more aggressive demands for cultural conformity, aimed indiscriminately at individuals or groups that were in the eyes of the Americanizers in any way "foreign." While non-German immigrant populations were praised as a strategic asset (labor for the war effort) and were given opportunities to demonstrate their American patriotism, the price demanded of them was an even higher degree of "Anglo-conformity" than before.[28] Public and private agencies concerned with war propaganda devoted nearly as much energy to dehyphenizing Italians or Greeks or Slavs as to demonizing the German "Hun." An article of faith of the Federal Committee on Public Information's Division of Work with the Foreign-Born was that "whoever is homesick for another country is lost for America."[29] Midway through the war, Congress provided for the naturalization of noncitizens enlisting in the armed forces, less as a recruiting incentive than out of the conviction that military service would be a powerful socializing and Americanizing mechanism. The American Federation of Labor, which lashed out at the socialist wing of the labor movement as "foreign" and dangerously

unenthusiastic about the war, went so far as to call for mandatory naturalization of resident aliens. Suspicion was directed especially at political organizations that seemed outside the mainstream, and the Sedition Act of 1918 actually criminalized public criticism of the American
form of government, supplementing an Immigration Act of 1917 that
made it possible to deport immigrants who had expressed "revolutionary" views. All this, John McClymer has argued, was close to classic
nativism, a "campaign to fix the public meaning of Americanism."[30]
Although one of the chief publicists for the exclusion of immigrants on
"racial" grounds, Madison Grant, was among the trustees of the American Defense Society, the popularization of Americanization gave more
immediate comfort to old-style nativist lodges like the Junior Order,
United American Mechanics, which promoted cultural conformity
and—as we shall see—a new generation of organizations built around
the denunciation of everyone "not like us."

Because Americanization was more in harmony with the aims of the
traditional nativist and "patriotic" lodges than with those of the "racial"
exclusionists, it should be no surprise that even "old" immigrant ethnic
groups came under fire. Both cultural Anglophilia and anti-Catholicism
were aroused by Irish-Americans' sympathy for Irish republican
nationalism. To those who believed that an Anglo-American core culture was at the heart of American "national character," militant Irish
nationalism in the midst of war was nothing short of disloyalty, and
Irish-American support for it was evidence of incomplete Americanization. For those with long-held suspicions about the supposed power of
an international Catholic hierarchy, the Irish clergy's support for widespread public resistance to British rule in the aftermath of the violent
Easter uprising in Dublin in 1916, and the willingness of some American clergy to open their pulpits to Irish nationalist fund-raisers, could
be construed as signs of some unholy transatlantic alliance.[31] In either
case, there was suspicion that "Americanization" was incomplete, even
among such "old" immigrants as the Irish. (In general, Americanizers
were always on the lookout for evidence of "hyphenism." When in
1916—just as the wartime preparedness campaign was really gaining
steam—a strike in the Youngstown, Ohio, steel industry turned violent,
public attention was directed by Americanizers to the fact that the overwhelming majority of arrested strikers were non-citizens of eastern and
southern European origin.[32] Efforts of wartime Americanizers and traditional nativists to capitalize on such episodes put them very nearly on
the same road.)

Ironically, the efforts of American Catholics to demonstrate their patriotism and to support the war in 1917 and 1918 served to provide propaganda that traditional nativist organizations could use to sustain anti-Catholicism through the decade. The war brought an abrupt end to a controversy which had disturbed the American Catholic church for a quarter of a century: the wisdom of maintaining distinctively ethnic parishes. Eager to unify for the war effort and to demonstrate that the church in the United States was authentically American, church leadership suspended the creation of new "national" parishes catering to non-English-speakers. Faced with meeting the need for Catholic chaplains in the armed forces, organizing the laity to support their kinsmen and neighbors in uniform, and addressing home-front social issues, the bishops of the American church created a Catholic War Council in Washington to coordinate the work of Catholic parishes, charitable agencies, and lay organizations. Together, these developments reinforced a growing tendency of the sons and daughters of immigrants to think of themselves more as American Catholics and less as ethnics and to affiliate more comfortably with church-related institutions than with ethnic institutions. The historian Martin Towey has shown, for example, that even before the war the decline of "purely Irish organizations" in St. Louis was paralleled by the growth of the multiethnic Knights of Columbus.[33] Given new responsibilities for organizing the faithful during the war, the Knights continued to gain strength. People with preexisting hostility toward the Catholic church viewed these developments with alarm, for they highlighted Catholic unity and organizational effectiveness. Some were inspired to connect all manner of international events to alleged Catholic power. Pope Benedict XV's call for an armistice and negotiated settlement of the war in August 1917, for example, was denounced by the American ambassador in London, Robert Page—an Anglophile—as a "Catholic peace conspiracy," aimed at saving Catholic Austria-Hungary from certain defeat.[34]

"Americanizers" took all of this as reason to redouble their efforts, even as the war came to a close. In 1918, a proposal was floated in Washington to create a federal Department of Education to set nationwide standards for schools. Subsequent public debate typically found evangelical Protestants and Catholics taking opposing sides. The National Catholic War Council (reconfigured in 1919 as the National Catholic Welfare Council to address postwar domestic issues) criticized the proposal as an assault on the autonomy and perhaps the very existence of parochial schools. Conversely, organizations with a tradition of anti-Catholicism like the Masons actively promoted the measure and interpreted Catholic opposition as another sign of the church's resistance to Americanization itself.[35]

If "old" immigrant communities unexpectedly endured a new wave of anti-Catholicism, "new" immigrants ran afoul of the anxieties Americanizers felt about Russia's bolshevik revolution and the emergence of a Soviet Union which promoted itself as the herald of worldwide socialism. There was already a long tradition in the United States of labeling socialism and communism "foreign" ideas, represented in America only by virtue of immigration—though, as we have seen, this rarely became the central message of organized nativist activism. The nexus of war and revolution turned such "foreign" ideologies from curiosities, more or less, into objects of fear. Initially—before the upheaval in Russia—there was a tendency to equate political radicalism with the German threat, on the assumption that political divisiveness, like ethnic diversity, translated into national weakness. Thus, one of the popular names for the International Workers of the World, or IWW, was "Imperial Wilhelm's Warriors." This concept of the political left was reinforced when the new bolshevik government in Moscow took Russia out of the First World War, releasing German and Austrian armies for service on other fronts. Coming just after the widely publicized successes of American socialists in New York City and New York state elections in 1917 (Socialist party candidates showed particular strength in New York City's heavily immigrant Lower East Side), this generated a new wave of criticism of "hyphenism" as damaging to the war effort.[36]

By early 1919, however, attention had shifted from Russia's role in the war to the supposed interest of the new Soviet Union in promoting worldwide communist revolution. Lenin's letter "To the American Workers" and the multilingual publicity of the Comintern also captured the attention of the Americanizers, who charged that these were direct appeals to unassimilated and underassimilated ethnic Americans. While the American left did derive some energy from the excitement generated by the Soviet experiment, American socialists reacted so differently to the question of what to do next that two rival communist parties emerged (alongside more moderate socialist groups). The split, however, gave no comfort to the Americanizers, who continued to treat any sympathy for socialism as a foreign import and a sign of incomplete Americanization.[37] On the whole, political radicalism remained a bugaboo more of the federal government's Americanization apparatus than of the private organizations that were part of or near the nativist movement.

There was nothing in the wartime experience to discourage a bureaucratized, Victorian (or Progressive, if you will) approach to social issues. In fact, Americans entered the postwar world with a variety of bureaucratic initiatives under way. First among these was Prohibition. Devised in steps during wartime to conserve resources and maintain both social and military order, Prohibition was codified in an Eighteenth Amendment to the Constitution and ratified by enough states to become law in early 1919. Clearly it harmonized with Americanization, which conceived of most alcoholic beverages as a foreign affectation. Scarcely an innovation, nationwide Prohibition—and its enforcement mechanism, the Volstead Act—built on state and local restrictions that had become commonplace before the war. Norman Clark reminds us: "When Congress and the states approved the 18th Amendment, they did so after a century's experience in local regulation and at a time when a majority of the people in a majority of the states wanted this truly national effort to influence national morality." In fact, there was substantial continuity between the leaders of all sorts of bureaucratic, "progressive" social and political reform of the early twentieth century and the enthusiasts of nationwide Prohibition. Prohibition also enlisted supporters from among the native-born, Protestant, Anglo-American middle class which had been the mainstay of temperance movements since the mid-1800s and now saw prohibitory legislation in terms of "Americanization."[38]

The Americanization movement of the war period also gave new prominence to the notion that education could rechannel lives. Just before, during, and after the war, states redoubled their efforts to enforce school attendance laws, a development that was at once part and parcel of the Americanizers' experiments in cultural retraining and of progressive reformers' concern that children be kept from exploitative labor.[39] Public schools—like the military—could be cultural blenders, spreading core values while flattening out the rough spots of diversity. This was also the age in which a new enthusiasm emerged among educators for testing, screening, and classifying. Psychologists and school administrators, encouraged by the "intelligence" testing of soldiers, saw testing as a means of sorting young people and placing them on educational and career tracks appropriate to their supposedly "natural" abilities. Although this was the same testing that immigration restrictionists thought verified the unassimilability of various European ethnic stocks, for the most part it was taken as reinforcement of the idea that the schools could provide a rational, organized way to integrate and Americanize all comers.[40] This optimism was firmly in the Victorian tradition of public policy as it had emerged from the Civil War half a century earlier.

From "Americanization" to Immigration Restriction

Something like the disillusionment that Europeans came to feel about World War I itself infected American bureaucratic reform once the excitement of the return to peace was past. Prohibition did not work out as expected; even many of its fervent supporters could agree on that. Enforcement was irregular—lax in some times and places and overdone elsewhere. Whole new industries arose to supply the undampened demand for alcohol, most of them operating outside the law, encouraging gaudy crimes and quiet corruption. Prohibition failed to bring about the moral reform or cultural harmony envisioned by some. To more and more people, the effort to sustain it seemed like bureaucracy out of control.

Education reform proved in many respects equally disappointing, becoming a political battleground, first at the federal and then at the state level. The Smith-Towner Bill proposed the creation of a federal education agency which would conduct educational research, set national teaching standards, and channel funds to improve teachers' salaries. It also called for a national minimum of 24 weeks' schooling for all children between the ages of seven and fourteen, with the principal subjects taught *in English.* Proponents anticipated widespread enthusiasm for a measure that they believed would serve the national interest in the tradition of wartime Americanization. In fact, many of the enthusiasts of Americanization did line up behind the bill: the Masons, the Daughters of the American Revolution, and the General Federation of Women's Clubs. So did the (Protestant) Federal Council of Churches and even the American Federation of Labor. But other Americans denounced it, beginning with many Catholics and Lutheran Protestants who feared that it was the beginning of an assault on the autonomy of church-affiliated schools. Still others then took up the criticism, including many old Progressives. "Standardization and bureaucratization, bolshevism and paternalism" were among the epithets hurled at the proposed "department of religion," observes the historian

Lynn Dumenil. The red tape involved in federal expansion into a traditionally local activity was criticized, as was the supposed intrusion of federal power. With such varied opposition, the education bill did not even make it to the floor of both houses of Congress for a vote.[41]

Similar battles broke out at the state level in the war's aftermath. When a Massachusetts commission recommended state assistance to local school districts in order to establish a more uniform standard of education, it brought a blistering response from Boston's Cardinal O'Connell, elaborating on themes which had come to the fore in the opposition to the federal department of education: "The medical inspection of schools, the physical examination of school children, the supplying of food for the indigent pupil, free dispensation of treatment for the defective, and similar provisions which have been added to the educational program of the State, are all signs of the spirit of machine centralization and control." Lest we write this off as rhetorical exaggeration, Joseph Huthmacher observes that at least some of the education reformers probably did hope through regulation to make it so difficult for parochial schools to compete with public education that they would be driven out of existence.[42] At about the same time, in 1920, an effort to undercut religious schools through an amendment to the state constitution did reach the voters of Michigan, but it was rejected at the polls. It had drawn the ire not only of Catholics and of Scandinavian Lutherans but of others who thought the measure smacked of excessive state intrusion in local and private affairs. On the other hand, supporters of the amendment included Scottish Rite Masons, who had fused Americanization and anti-Catholicism during the war years.[43] Gary Gerstle describes an analogous situation in Rhode Island: "The state legislature authorized the establishment of an Americanization division in the department of education to promote Americanization training among prospective teachers. Civics and American history classes occupied more and more space in the school curriculum. . . . And since the state's parochial school population lay beyond the reach of public school authority, the State Assembly, in 1922, passed the Peck Laws mandating that the required subjects of the public school— American history, civics, math, and English—be taught in English at all parochial schools in the state."[44]

The most dramatic confrontation came in Oregon. There, in 1922, voters actually did approve a law virtually restricting the education of children between eight and sixteen to public institutions by taking advantage of a "Progressive" reform: initiative. A Federation of Patriotic Societies took a visible part in promoting this legislation, pulling in the membership not only of organizations like the Orange lodges (which had a history, for over 50 years, of identifying "Americanism" with Protestantism) but also brethren of fraternities such as the Odd Fellows and the Knights of Pythias (which had hung about the fringes of the nativist movement for almost as long). Once again, Masons—especially of the Scottish Rite—were conspicuous for their support. An organization which had come to public attention only much more recently—the Ku Klux Klan—was also deeply involved in promoting the measure. Catholics were joined by others in attacking the law as involving "monopoly" and "state hegemony." When the law was finally struck down by the United States Supreme Court in 1925, the justices specifically cited the misuse of the "power of the state to standardize its children."[45] It was not just the substance of educational reform—or for that matter, of Prohibition—that came under attack. By the early 1920s, the optimistic, bureaucratized "Victorian" approach to social issues itself was falling into disrepute.

For those who still believed that the United States was threatened by "hyphenism," this spelled disaster. They certainly had no difficulty pointing a finger at what they took to be evidence that loyalty to the old world was taking precedence over effective American citizenship. A remarkable amount of finger-pointing was in the direction of "old" immigrants, particularly the Irish. It is no surprise that American sympathizers with Irish independence from Great Britain took seriously President Woodrow Wilson's rhetoric, at the end of the war, promoting national self-determination in Europe. The Friends of Irish Freedom sought to capitalize on it by staging their own events during a nationwide "Self-Determination Week" in December 1918, as did the sponsors of the Sinn Fein leader Eamon de Valera's visit to the United States in the summer of 1919. While many Irish-Americans saw this as nothing more than holding their government to a uniform standard of commitment to nationalist aspirations throughout Europe, nativist and anti-Catholic organizations claimed to see something much more sinister. They leaped to remarkable conclusions. They were disturbed by the fact that the Friends of Irish Freedom chose a Catholic priest as its president during the last year of the war, and they saw an international conspiracy in a petition by Catholic clergy to President Wilson on behalf of Irish independence half a year later. Protestant ministerial alliances were whipped to a frenzy in some places over the appearance of Irish nationalist speakers in their communities. The

Orange Order in the United States took advantage of this situation to play host to Protestant ministers from Ireland who predicted Catholic oppression in a self-governing Ireland. In Massachusetts, a new organization calling itself the Loyal Coalition emerged in 1920 specifically to support the Orange critique of the Irish Free State. Significantly, its leading figures included not only secular notables but prominent Protestant clergymen who treated the struggle over the future of Ireland as a battle for souls.[46] This was the explicit message of a national Masonic publication, too, which editorialized in early 1921 that "the Irish question is 85 per cent a religious question."[47]

To scratch the rhetoric of the critics of Irish nationalism in the United States, in fact, is to discover that the hostilities expressed were really about not foreign but domestic affairs. Masonic organizations, which had a tradition of mild anti-Catholicism and had not infrequently shared members with out-and-out nativist bodies, emerged from the war years offering much louder and sharper criticism of the Knights of Columbus, now portrayed as a rival. Lynn Dumenil points out that Masons read much into the federal government's rebuff of their proposal to establish soldiers' canteens behind the battlefront in France and its acceptance of a similar program advanced by the Knights.[48] All of the old nativist themes were evoked: exclusion from full participation, access to government power, and "foreign" organization. To be sure, wartime activities showcased the size and organization of the American Catholic church, which had almost doubled in size in the quarter-century before the United States entered World War I. The postwar National Catholic Welfare Council and descendants such as the National Council of Catholic Women and the National Council of Catholic Men proved that the church, bolstered by immigration-related growth, intended to take on the challenges of peacetime with as much organization as it had taken on those of the war. So reinvigorated was nativist energy that less than three years after the Armistice the Knights of Columbus created a Historical Commission that was intended to prove Catholics' loyal Americanism and refute nativist attacks.[49]

Significantly, the principal point of the nativistic Loyal Coalition was that the contest in Ireland was "not a proper concern of any department of the Government of the United States" and therefore that lobbying to generate American diplomatic activity on behalf of a free Ireland was "un-American." Now, this was nativist boilerplate, and it captured the frustration of Americanizers that, in their view, all of the orchestrated programs for patriotic education had failed, even with the most established ethnic minorities. They were particularly distraught when not just Irish-Americans but Americans born in or descended from Italy and the emergent Yugoslavia sparred over just whose national claims the United States would support in a remade Europe.[50] Discouragement with the achievements of Americanization grew when Mayor "Big Bill" Thompson of Chicago took advantage of anti-British rhetoric to solidify his base among the Irish in a reelection campaign in 1919. Later that year, President Wilson began to complain that the competing demands of "hyphens" were undercutting his drive to enlist American support for the League of Nations. And, indeed, ethnic politics played a visible role in the presidential election of 1920. Although the Republican candidate, Harding, criticized Irish-American nationalist militancy, "hyphenism," and the perceived role of ethnic issues in politics, there were significant defections of traditionally Democratic voters in some key states, provoked by the offense some ethnic communities took at Wilson's perceived lack of support for particular national aspirations in Europe. The Democratic candidate, James M. Cox, at least, complained that he had been done in by "un-American" issues. How voting patterns shook out, however, was less important than the conviction among many old-stock Americans that the old world was intruding on the affairs of the new world and that Americanization—for all of its sophisticated, "Victorian" organization—had not worked.[51]

Nothing promoted cynicism about the effectiveness of "Americanization" more than the postwar "red scare." The demobilization of the war economy was not painless. In some industries, workers' prewar aspirations regarding pay or hours or working conditions, having been set aside during the war, reasserted themselves just as management was confronting anticipated changes in a postwar market. Elsewhere, workers sought to maintain gains achieved during the war itself. In early 1919, a shipyard strike in Seattle idled 60,000 workers. Six months later, two dozen steelworkers' unions went on strike over wages and hours, ultimately taking 350,000 to 400,000 workers out of plants across the country. About as many coal miners also took to picket lines before the end of the year. A strike by Boston police over union recognition and a "general strike" in Lawrence, Massachusetts, which cut across industries and trades, were novelties to the American experience. Taking place in an atmosphere of economic uncertainty, these events were bound to be seen by some people as unsettling. Moreover, since ethnic minorities were so well represented among blue-collar workers in general and the troubled industries in particular, there was every opportunity for the response to take on a nativistic character.[52]

But not only economic tension was in the air. Compounding the vague ill ease some Americans felt with the way the rearrangement of Europe and the European empires was taking place in the postwar period was uncertainty about the meaning of the bolshevik revolution in Russia and the emergence of the Soviet Union. Americans' unpreparedness for an international development of this magnitude compounded their fear that things were happening beyond their ken or control and that conspiracies might be operating under their very noses. Certainly the federal government did little to defuse such anxieties. Caught as much by surprise as the public, the Wilson administration quickly transferred the machinery of anti-German propaganda to antibolshevism. It did nothing to refute even the wildest rumors connecting revolution in Russia, American socialists, left-wing labor groups, and immigrant communities—especially those of eastern European derivation. Still, despite this background of anxiety and suspicion, it took political opportunism of the first order to produce the "red scare" of 1919-1920.

A series of actual and attempted bombings, including explosives sent to the mayor of Seattle, Ole Hanson, during the shipyard strike, played into the hands of the United States attorney general, A. Mitchell Palmer. Palmer was strongly energized after his own residence was victimized in June 1919, and he and the Justice Department's Bureau of Investigation, led by the young J. Edgar Hoover, pursued a program that admitted no doubt that there was a radical conspiracy, controlled from abroad, afoot in the United States. This conspiracy was seen behind all domestic labor unrest. The centerpiece of Palmer's program became rounding up self-described anarchists and others on the left who were of foreign birth—the so-called "Palmer raids"—and taking advantage of the Alien Law of 1918 to deport them on the ground that they at least tacitly supported the violent overthrow of the United States government.[53]

Like the Americanization campaign that preceded and to some extent accompanied it, the "red scare" was prosecuted by a combination of public and private organizations, although its hub was Palmer's federal department. In New York, the Union League Club pressured the state legislature to investigate "seditious" political activity among immigrant populations. The wartime National Security League and

American Defense Society redirected their energies from exposing a German threat to unmasking "radical" subversion. An "Americanism Committee" of the Motion Picture Industry of the United States was formed, as Steven J. Ross explains it, to utilize popular films to "promote true Americanism and awaken a nation to the 'seriousness of the Bolshevistic' threat." Actually, the "red scare" brought about something like a fusion of Americanization and nativism, in which "foreign" and "un-American" became interchangeable. It was also nearly the last gasp of the Victorian, bureaucratized approach to issues surrounding immigration and national identity, holding that the nation actually could be cleansed of elements that created political discord.[54] It was this very bureaucratization that the public—or at least influential elements within it—repudiated within a year. When the intrusiveness of Palmer's and Hoover's agents began to seem too high a cost, when it became evident that political dissent outlived the deportation of a few hundred aliens, and when Palmer resorted to near-hysterical predictions of more bombings to keep his campaign and all of its bureaucratic apparatus alive, the "red scare" lost too much of its constituency to be sustained.[55]

Confronted with the rebuff of the Department of Education Bill (the ultimate bureaucratization of the Americanization campaign), disappointed that nationwide Prohibition failed to produce cultural reformation, disillusioned by the comic opera conclusion of the "red scare," and surprised by the apparent vitality of ethnic politics in the election of 1920, the largely Protestant middle classes of northwestern European descent eventually lost patience with half a century of Victorian, or Progressive, reform aimed at "Americanizing" the immigrant or restricting immigration to those who putatively could be "Americanized." Thus they also turned their backs on the nativist movement, for nativist organizations and activists had always posed as gatekeepers, tutors, and monitors. Although over a century and a half the understanding of "national character" had changed markedly, evolving from a political objective to a cultural standard, nativist activists consistently promoted themselves as its most reliable defenders. They would not only set the standards for what constituted authentic American citizenship but would also measure the progress of those who sought to attain it. This sense of purpose—an almost missionary purpose—gave organized nativism much of its appeal. It also suggests why outright opposition to immigration or even exclusion of broad national or "racial" categories of the foreign-born had little appeal for nativist activists. To survive as organizations and preserve for their participants all of the benefits of organization, the nativist fraternities and related "reform" societies had to retain a mission, and to do that they had to preserve the notion that "true" Americanism was something sought and earned. In turning its back on bureaucratized Americanization, the political public of the early 1920s turned its back on this notion too. What did it embrace instead? Immigration restriction.

Immigration Restriction

Fundamentally, federal immigration restriction was an act of impatience, even frustration. Restricting immigration by congressional legislation was not an entirely new idea. Throughout the last quarter of the nineteenth century, successive immigration laws had made ineligible for admission individuals charged with certain crimes or believed to carry communicable diseases. But these measures were really more in the way of regulation than restriction and never had much impact on overall numbers of immigrants. Moreover, they focused entirely on individuals rather than on national or ethnic groups. It was in the meeting rooms of the immigration restriction leagues of the 1890s, which operated on the periphery of the nativist movement, that a rationale began to emerge for withholding admission to the United States from whole classes of people on the basis of their descent. It was in these almost "academic" salons that the notions began to circulate that "true Americanism" was obtainable only by selected peoples around the world who had an inherent capacity for it, and that nationality was associated with what activists in the Immigration Restriction League began to call "race." Although the League's promotion of a literacy test as a requirement for admission to the United States seemed aimed at individuals, the presupposition behind it was that literacy was a commodity rationed by heredity and that a test would therefore discriminate against "inferior" stock.

By putting into the language of public debate the concepts of "old" northwestern European immigrants and "new" southern and eastern European immigrants, the Dillingham Commission report of 1910-1911 gave both legitimacy and visibility to the idea that suitability for citizenship was somehow related to ethnicity. World War I created the conditions that permitted Congress to finally legislate and sustain a literacy test; though by dividing the "Anglo-Saxon" world into friends and foes the war temporarily made difficult an ethnic construction of American nationality. And the war was scarcely over before the public was exposed to a new assault of academic (or quasi-academic) polemics predicting dire consequences for the United States from continued mixture of "inferior" peoples through unrestricted immigration. Perhaps the war itself—in hindsight—was a context that provided an enlarged readership for this material. The armed forces gave "official" endorsement to the concept of "intelligence" testing, and the widely publicized results of military testing purported to show that "IQ" was related to ethnicity. The Harvard psychologist William McDougall published a compendium of his lectures in 1921, entitled *Is America Safe for Democracy?* His answer was "no," so long as the population continued to grow more diverse. In 1920 Lothrop Stoddard brought out *The Rising Tide of Color,* which suggested that the real tragedy of the war was that it had turned the "superior" Nordic race on itself. In this postwar atmosphere, an earlier work, *The Passing of the Great Race in America* (1916), by Stoddard's mentor, Madison Grant, experienced sales that it had not achieved before the American declaration of war. By mid-1920, when European entrants at Ellis Island had built up again to some 5,000 a day, there was plenty of ideological sustenance for a public policy approach to immigration which would not look to Victorian "Americanization" but which would remove a controversial issue simply by putting something nearly like an end to it.[56]

As it happened, it was not so much ideology as economics which started the ball rolling toward federal immigration restriction. Before the end of 1918, a committee of the American Federation of Labor, examining the prospect of postwar layoffs, called for a two-year moratorium on further immigration. Prodded by labor union officials, the House Committee on Immigration reported out a bill in early 1919 that actually included a four-year suspension. Although it was not acted on by the full Congress, the moratorium bill was the talk of the AFL annual meeting in June 1919. This was the kind of public support that Congressman Albert Johnson of Washington state, a longtime supporter of immigration restriction, had been looking for in vain since well before World War I. Now, newly installed as chairman of the House Committee on Immigration, Johnson made his first goal in the fall of 1920 the movement to the House floor of a two-year moratorium on immigration. This was passed in modified form by the House as a simple one-year suspension, but it was killed in the Senate under heavy lobbying from business groups worried about the long-term labor supply.

Once started, the restriction bandwagon was hard to stop, and other interests took precedence over those which had initiated congressional consideration of the matter. Senator Dillingham proposed not a moratorium, which was labor's interest, but a nationality-based plan that would give primacy to the admission of "good" ethnic stocks. Although this was not really what organized labor had wanted, it was something, and it was more acceptable to business because it left the door open to some immigration. After retooling in the House of Representatives, the legislation that passed both houses and was signed into law by the newly elected Republican president, Warren G. Harding, in May 1921 set annual limits for the admission of new immigrants by nationality, based on 3 percent of the number of foreign-born of that group counted in the federal census of 1910. Not only would the act restrict immigration to a maximum of about 350,000 annually (less than half the 1919-1920 rate and far below the prewar experience), but it would discriminate in favor of immigrants from the north and west of Europe.[57]

Outside the circles of academic "race" theorists and patricians of the old Immigration Restriction League school, the attraction of immigration restriction was that it was *not* classic bureaucratized progressive or Victorian reform. It promised no expansion of state or federal power, no Americanization campaigns or education agencies. Instead, it seemed to offer to shrink a divisive public issue. It was also appealing because it did not seem to surrender to mainstream nativism.

Perhaps this appeal is why there was enough public support for a permanent restriction law on the heels of this "provisional" legislation—even though the initiative fell entirely into the hands of the Anglo-Saxonist crowd, which had a much different agenda from the protection of labor or the rejection of bureaucracy. Seeking to redirect immigration as well as to shrink it, Albert Johnson in the House and David A. Reed of Pennsylvania in the Senate, advised by some of the nation's highest-profile Anglo-Saxonist racial theorists, worked between 1921 and 1923 to come up with legislation that would reinforce the supposedly Anglo-Saxon character (with an emphasis on "Anglo") of the American population. With the visible support of President Calvin Coolidge, the Johnson-Reed Act passed Congress in April 1924 and was signed into law. It, too, was a quota law, but its percentages were based on ethnic *stocks* (not just the foreign-born) as counted in the census of 1890, before much of the immigration from southern and eastern Europe had begun. Two percent of each national stock would be allowed in annually until 1927 (this was later postponed until 1929). Thereafter, the total annual limit would be 150,000, with national allotments recalculated to fit this total and with the census of 1920 as a base. Moreover, the act simply excluded Asians—save Filipinos—by giving them no quota at all, undoing even the fiction of the 1907 "gentlemen's agreement" with Japan. Under the impact of the new law, immigration shrank to about 300,000 per year in the mid-1920s.[58]

Fraternalism, Nativism, and the Ku Klux Klan

That immigration restriction as legislated was not in the tradition of mainstream nativism (although nativist activists could scarcely oppose it) is demonstrated by the continued efforts of nativist organizations and those with a nativist tinge to operate in the Victorian manner. Although the term fell into disuse, something like the "Americanization" campaign was kept up by these organizations into the mid-1920s. Robert A. Murray ticks them off: the Better America Foundation, the Allied Patriotic Societies, the National Patriotic Council, the United States Patriotic Society—all founded between 1920 and 1925. "Americanization" remained in the vocabulary of the American Legion, the veterans' organization founded in 1919. Established in the tradition of the Civil War's Grand Army of the Republic, it attempted to fuse the veteran's individual identity as an American with an organizational identity as a defender of true Americanism. Enrolling nearly 1 million members in its first year, the American Legion demonstrated the sustained appeal of old-fashioned Victorianism by organizing itself to offer lectures, publications, and school curricula that would combat "foreign" bolshevism and political radicalism. By 1923, it had moved far enough in a nativistic direction that some delegates to its national meeting openly questioned the suitability of a candidate for Legion leadership who was a Catholic.[59] For a time, this was the approach of the Masons, too. As Lynn Dumenil points out, Masons came out of the war years with an increased appreciation for the power of organization. No group used it more enthusiastically than the Masons in promoting a federal education department or state legislation implicitly undermining Catholic schools.[60]

Over the course of the 1920s, though, the assumptions behind Masonic civic activism evolved. No longer confident that "their kind"— Protestant, predominantly native-born, and bourgeois—had a monopoly on social or cultural authority, Masonic leaders, Dumenil correctly argues, increasingly drew "attention to the lack of organization of the middle class" in the face of "noisy minorities and scheming groups." This captured all the old nativist themes: fear of exclusion from public effectiveness, loss of participatory citizenship, powerlessness in the face of superior "foreign" organization. Here was a kind of nativism which could easily survive—at least for a while—even in the aftermath of immigration restriction. It was a kind of nativism which could identify a threat to national and individual identity in the diverse, increasingly urban society (and most Masonic lodges, Dumenil notes, were urban) of the 1920s.[61] The Masons, in short, struck a well of popular sympathy when they discovered that their order could represent itself as the champion of the "forgotten" native-born, Protestant middle class.

But there were inherent limits to the Masons' exploitation of this sympathy. Despite all of its offshoots for men, women, and young people of both sexes, the Masonic order remained a selective fraternity, not a mass movement. Moreover, its own ideological traditions stressing nonsectarianism and even secularism—as well as a dose of internationalism—prevented it from portraying itself convincingly as a representative of native American Protestantism. For that, another sort of organization was needed. Enter the Ku Klux Klan, the principal bearer of organized nativist activism into the 1920s.

Although it did not make a big splash until the early 1920s, the Klan, at least indirectly, had a long lineage. The founder of the twentieth-century Klan, William J. Simmons, liked to say that its inspiration had been the post-Civil War southern night riders and vigilantes who had sought to intimidate free blacks and white Republicans. Actually, the Klan of 1915 had much more immediately to do with nativist and "patriotic" fraternities of the turn of the century. Simmons himself was a discredited Methodist preacher who had been rejected by the institutional church in 1912. His time in the ministry in Alabama, however, had coincided with an excitation of anti-Catholicism in southeastern Protestantism, a furor over the growth of the Knights of Columbus, the intrusion of the issue of public versus parochial schools into regional politics, and the spread southward of some overtly nativist societies of the northeast. Significantly, after the Methodist Episcopal Church, South, denied him another appointment, Simmons became a promoter and recruiter for fraternal orders. A "joiner," he participated in a number of Masonic organizations, including the Knights Templar, and was an officer of the

Spanish-American War Veterans. He made his living as a district manager for the Woodmen of the World.[62]

The Reconstruction Klan provided Simmons with an image; but the Masons, Odd Fellows, and Elks—to say nothing of the Guardians of Liberty or the Order of the Little Red School House—provided him with organizational and even ideological models. Inspired by current events or, as a veteran organizer, craftily timing his activities to coincide with them, Simmons brought his new order into being in Atlanta, Georgia, simultaneously with the anti-Semitic episode of Leo Frank's lynching and the release of the pathbreaking motion picture *The Birth of a Nation*. This film provided the imagery that Simmons exploited when he led a small band to Stone Mountain, outside Atlanta, and inducted it into an order which adopted the name, the costume, and some of the symbols of the post-Civil War Klan romanticized in the film. By Simmons's own description, the Klan was to be fraternal and beneficiary in the tradition of the Masons and similar orders.[63] William D. Jenkins, a recent scholar of the Klan in northeastern Ohio, describes its criteria for membership, which should seem familiar: "the new charter limited membership to a 'white male Gentile person, a native-born citizen of the United States of America,' and 'a believer in the tenets of the Christian religion.' " Additionally, Jenkins notes, "The provision that members could not owe any allegiance 'of any nature or degree whatsoever to any foreign government, nation, institution, sect, ruler, prince, potentate, people or person' served as bar to Catholics."[64] The Klan excluded neither Catholics nor Jews by name but represented itself (in the nativist tradition) as the defender of Protestant Christianity.

Simmons's Ku Klux Klan did not grow explosively; in fact, it might have remained a local curiosity if not for the hyperpatriotic atmosphere that accompanied the United States' entry into World War I. But the Americanization campaign and the exaggerated antisabotage vigilance movement helped the fledgling Klan earn itself a place in the network of "patriotic" organizations and gave its membership a sense of status and achievement.[65] This simultaneously gave encouragement to Simmons and made the Klan attractive to professional organizers who were more skilled than he. By the end of the decade, Simmons had teamed up with Edward Y. Clarke and Elizabeth ("Bessie") Tyler of the Southern Publicity Association to take the Klan nationwide. What may have helped build the Klan more than anything else was a serialized "exposé" in the *New York World* which ran from October 1920 well into 1921.

Visibility and growth were accompanied by the emergence of local leaders with bolder vision and more aggressive styles than either Simmons or Clarke. Headed by Hiram Wesley Evans, a dentist from Dallas; and David Curtis ("Steve") Stephenson, a Klansman from Indiana, the new leadership essentially bought Simmons's retirement and took advantage of scandal surrounding Clarke and Tyler to maneuver them out of control.[66] Like Simmons, Evans—who took the titles "emperor" and "imperial wizard"—had a background in fraternal and patriotic lodges. And he made more explicit the Klan's roots in the nativist tradition. Under Evans's leadership (and in Evans's own words) the Klan declared its "loyalty to the white race, to the traditions of America, and to the spirit of Protestantism, which has been an essential part of Americanism ever since the days of Roanoke and Plymouth Rock. They are condensed into the Klan slogan: Native, white, Protestant supremacy!"[67] Defining Americanism in terms of race and religion as well as nativity was an ideology that could easily outlive restriction of immigration.

Clearly, Evans had struck a chord. By 1922, the Klan claimed chapters from Oregon to Massachusetts. Everywhere it could count on kinship with preexisting fraternal and "patriotic" groups, and gradually it would supplant not a few of them. J. Joseph Huthmacher, a scholar of New England politics, notes that the "king kleagle" of the Maine Klan was none other than the former leader of the "Loyal Coalition," formed in 1920 from the most vocal critics of Irish-American nationalism; as a Klansman, he built his rhetoric on the same theme, denunciation of "hyphenates." M. Paul Holsinger, who has studied the schools controversy in Oregon in the early 1920s, observes that the Klan-sponsored Good Government League in that state attracted the Odd Fellows, Orange Lodges, and Knights of Pythias and cooperated with the Federation of Patriotic Societies, made up of some of the old nativist orders.[68] A women's affiliate, the Ladies of the Invisible Empire (LOTIE), established in Oregon in 1923, found it convenient to meet in the Redmen's Hall; and according to Kathleen Blee, a historian of women in the Klan movement, involvement in "political, civic, or fraternal organizations" was the typical path for women into LOTIE and into its successor, the Women of the Ku Klux Klan.[69]

To understand the Klan of the 1920s and its place in the nativist tradition, it is not particularly helpful to think in terms of the Klans of the 1860s or of the 1950s and 1960s, even though they shared a name and regalia. It is more useful to think of the late-nineteenth-century and early-twentieth-century fraternal orders from which the Klan took inspiration and many members. Almost from the earliest days, the Klan leadership demonstrated that it had a keen grasp of the "utilitarian" benefits of membership, apart from any ideological appeal. These leaders promoted new chapters and recruitment by creating financial incentives for commissioned agents, and a pyramidal structure which brought greater rewards for those promoted upward while building the organization below. The Klan created a veritable industry for the manufacture and sale of institutional regalia and chapter supplies; in addition, it operated its own press, turning out not only publications and propaganda but routine forms and handbooks for the conduct of chapter business. For the individual member at the grassroots, there were, as David Chalmers has pointed out, the pleasures of "mass initiations, masks and robes, parades, picnics, barbecues, and other ceremonies," the stuff that made the Odd Fellows go—and also the Order of United Americans and even the American Protective Association. The participation of the early Klan in the wartime vigilance movement encouraged its adoption of secret signs and passwords, and this—along with the hooded robes inspired by the Reconstruction-era Klan as represented in *Birth of a Nation*—enhanced the aura of romance and excitement and reinforced members' sense of belonging.[70]

Not surprisingly, the Klan appealed to traditional "joiners," and many of its members were likely also to be members of outright nativist lodges like the Orange Order, of "Protestant" fraternities such as the Knights of Pythias, or—perhaps most often—of Masonic organizations. In his study of the powerful Indiana Klan, *Citizen Klansmen,* Leonard J. Moore concludes that the "typical Klan meeting, far from resembling a secret gathering of conspiring vigilantes, followed the unremarkable pattern of other voluntary organizations. Chapter officials, usually the only members dressed in full regalia, began each session with designated ceremonies from the Klan's national handbook *Klaoran.* Chapter business, future social events, and during the election campaigns, politics dominated discussions." For men and for women (who not only participated in Klan "family" activities but created their own Women of the Ku Klux Klan), sociability was an appealing aspect of the Klan, which sponsored parties, picnics, and charity shows. William Jenkins and Robert Goldberg, who have taken a look at the Ohio and Colorado Klans respectively, observe that many chapters never did much more than this.[71]

Clearly there was more to the Klan than social, fraternal, and commercial attractions, although the importance of these should not be overlooked. Ironically, it took well over half a century for historians to agree on a truth about the Klan that had been captured by H. L. Mencken and George Jean Nathan in an editorial for *Smart Set* in the spring of 1923:

Not a single solitary sound reason has yet been advanced for putting the Ku Klux Klan out of business. If the Klan is against the Jews, so are half of the good hotels of the Republic and three-quarters of the good clubs. If the Klan is against the foreign-born or the hyphenated citizen, so is the National Institute of Arts and Letters. If the Klan is against the Negro, so are all of the states south of the Mason-Dixon line. If the Klan is for damnation and persecution, so is the Methodist church. If the Klan is bent upon political control, so are the American Legion and Tammany Hall. If the Klan wears grotesque uniforms, so do the Knights of Pythias and the Mystic Shriners.[72]

Back in the late 1950s, the historian J. Joseph Huthmacher made the same point by drawing attention to the fact that both major political parties were so impressed by the size of the Klan's following in the early 1920s that the Republican party scrupulously avoided any criticism of the Klan at its national convention in 1924, and that even the Democrats, traditional home of established ethnic constituencies, agreed to a resolution denouncing the Klan by only one vote at a convention of well over 1,000 delegates.[73]

If there has been a central theme to the state-by-state studies of the Klan of the 1920s that have been completed over the past 15 years, it is—to use the formulation of a scholar of the Indiana Klan, Leonard J. Moore—that the Klan "represented mainstream social and political concerns, not those of a disaffected fringe group."[74] This is not so much flattering to the Klan as unflattering to a society that was increasingly, as some scholars have put it, "tribal." Earlier evaluations of the Klan tended to locate its center in small-town and rural America and, accordingly, attributed its attractiveness to a protest against urbanism and cosmopolitanism. But more recent studies have found little to distinguish the Klan of the countryside from the Klan of the city and suburbs and much in common between the Klan of the farm belt and the Klan of the industrial states. Moore concludes that the postwar Klan can best be thought of as a "populist" movement "promoting the ability of average citizens to influence the workings of society and government." If so, this places the Ku Klux Klan squarely in the tradition of the Order of United Americans or the American Protective Association, especially since the Klan was adept at finding "foreign" peoples and powers interfering with "true" popular self-government. Moore, in fact, identifies the Klan with "ethnic nationalism," the real stuff of American nativism, which persistently sought to equate the United States' success as a nation with the hegemony of what was essentially an ethnic, Anglo-American culture. Nancy MacLean's close study of the Klan in Clarke County, Georgia, led her to conclude that the "right to full citizenship" was the most cherished goal of the farm proprietors, shopkeepers, clerks, and lower-level managers who made up so much of its membership. In the "republican" tradition, they interpreted "full citizenship" as the ability to participate and be heard in government, something they thought was threatened by both elitist bureaucrats and corrupted politicians, susceptible to the ballots of "alien" voters or the money of "alien" rum-runners.[75]

Like nativist organizations throughout American history, the Ku Klux Klan was preoccupied with *self*-definition (taking it for granted that in defining itself it was defining the basis of *real* Americanism); and it derived its definition of others (consequently, inauthentic Americans) from that. Like nativist orders before it, the Klan thrived on the notion that it was, in the historian David Chalmers's words, an "embattled minority." The nation was turning away from its roots, the argument ran; but if only more people would "be like us," the national character would be made safe. The primacy given to self-definition prevented the Klan from becoming dependent on opposition to any one particular "alien" group and permitted it to craft different appeals for different locales. This allowed the Klan to thrive in states where immigrants were few, powerful ethnic minorities were indiscernible, or "foreign" churches were thinly scattered. It may even help explain the Klan's relative inattention to the movement for legislated immigration restriction, which peaked just as the Klan was experiencing its most rapid growth. At best, the Klan's investment in the federal bills of 1921 and 1924 was rhetorical. Defining and empowering the "real" Americans who were *in* seemed more important than keeping anyone in particular *out*.[76] By carefully examining local Klan membership rosters in Indiana, Leonard Moore has found that children of immigrants often found the Klan as appealing as those with a long American ancestry. Likewise, William D. Jenkins, the modern scholar of the Klan in northeastern Ohio, has observed that Klansmen and -women could even be persuaded that Roman Catholics were "real Americans" under certain circumstances. Where the Klan set up Catholics as aggressors against true Americanism, it took advantage of environments in which anti-Catholicism was already well established—as in Indiana or Oregon. Elsewhere, the Klan was likely to identify other challengers—in Utah, for example, the Mormon church.[77]

As an "embattled minority," the Klan—entirely in the populist nativist tradition—perceived itself not only as the conservator of "American" cultural values but as a victim of a political culture which paid little attention to moral character and overlooked local community standards. "At a time when organizations like the Rotary Club, Chambers of Commerce, and the Indiana Farm Bureau had emerged to advocate a definition of community based almost exclusively on the idea of business success," writes Leonard Moore, "the Klan drew together a powerful cross section of community social groups that were devoted to the primacy of a more traditional value system." The historian of the Klan in Indiana sees the movement as in part a backlash against the "segmentation, impersonalization, and the concentration of authority in civic affairs," observing that the decline in voting since 1890 suggests that the Klan might have struck a responsive chord among citizens alienated from the political process. In fact, the Klan seems to have targeted business and political elites as among its chief enemies and held up failures to enforce Prohibition and to prevent crime as evidence that the politicians and business boosters had different priorities from "the people."[78] Prohibition and its enforcement, Norman Clark reminds us, were as much as anything "ceremonial and ritualistic, validation of a lifestyle or of cultural values possible in America," and perceived deficiencies in their administration were easily translated as an assault on the underlying values themselves. The kind of community-based political activism that the Klan promoted was not the stuff of reactionaries seeking a refuge from social change. Instead, it was activism in the populistic nativist vein. The historian William Jenkins has made the observation that the Klan appealed less to people associated with the conservative "fundamentalist" movement in American Protestantism than to people connected with social activist denominations like the Methodists.[79]

The appeal of the Ku Klux Klan lay in its fusion of "true Americanism" with a set of moral values that it claimed were central to the historical national character. Clearly, it was possible to warp commitment to these values into a crude racism that held entire peoples to be without virtue, but on the whole the Klan seemed more interested in trumpeting the alleged moral superiority of its own members, whom it elevated to saviors of the nation.[80] In an often quoted article which appeared in the *North American Review* in 1926, "The Klan's Fight for Americanism," Imperial Wizard Hiram Wesley Evans spouted:

Americans for the last generation have found themselves increasingly uncomfortable and finally deeply distressed. There appeared first confusion in thought and opinion, a groping hesitancy about national affairs and private life alike. . . . There was futility in religion, too, which was in many ways even more distressing. . . . Finally came the moral breakdown that has been going on for two decades. One by one all our traditional moral standards went by the boards, or were so disregarded that they ceased to be binding. . . . Those who maintained the old standards did so only in the face of constant ridicule. . . . We are a movement of the plain people. . . . We are demanding . . . a return to power into the hands of the everyday, not highly cultured, not overly intellectualized, but entirely unspoiled and not de-Americanized, average citizen of the old stock.[81]

Mainstream institutions like the Masons and even the principal Protestant churches were making similar pronouncements, but the Klan proved particularly successful in appealing to a cross-section of Americans of middling status and in conveying the impression that there was something on the order of a conspiracy that was pushing the "plain people" to the periphery of political effectiveness.[82]

Although the most recent scholarship on the Klan of the 1920s emphasizes the regional and local differences that permeated what became for awhile a vast national organization, there is almost complete agreement among the historians that the attractiveness of the Klan lay not so much in bemoaning that native-born, Protestant, middle-class, white Americans now wielded too little influence as in insisting that this influence could be regained. The Ku Klux Klan promised a crusade—and for dues of a few dollars, ordinary men and women could become crusaders while reaping all of the usual benefits of participation in a fraternal social society (and, at that, an unusually large one in many locales). Of the order in Colorado, Robert Goldberg writes: "The Klan offered Protestants an opportunity to enlist in a cause to save a nation, a faith, and a way of life from their detractors . . . any man or woman in any community could battle the forces of evil." The Ohio Klan, notes William D. Jenkins, combined— through its social events, ceremonies, and political rallies—a consciousness of being "with one's own kind" and "the good feeling of being associated with a noble cause." The analyst of the Indiana Klan, Leonard J. Moore, reports that "typically, the Klan acted as a social and civic organization, reinvigorating the sense of unity and cohesiveness in community life. . . . Even more importantly, it became a means through which average citizens could express their dissatisfaction with the political establishment."[83] Each of these scholars concludes that the backbone of the Klan was composed not of economically marginalized men and women, alienated from the emerging urbanized, industrialized society of the early twentieth century, but of doers— involved members of churches, fraternal orders, and civic organizations who saw in the Klan an opportunity to reassert their claim to political and cultural significance. Jenkins notes that the Klan in metropolitan Youngstown, Ohio, at one point enlisted up to a third of the Methodists and almost a quarter of the Presbyterians—mainline "liberal" Protestant denominations. In Indiana, the Klan was so popular in the early 1920s that it may have embraced nearly a third of *all* native-born white males. Likewise, the Women of the Ku Klux Klan attracted members who had already staked a claim to a public voice through participation in the temperance movement, church activism, school issues, and the women's suffrage movement. Although the Ku Klux Klan was uneasy about some aspects of women's liberation from the home and hesitant to see "dependents" gain full citizenship rights, the capacity of Klan women (and other Protestant women) to provide a winning margin for the Klan's political candidates was hard to resist.[84]

In the years following the First World War, the Klan's political strategy was dictated by its self-image as "real" Americans organized for battle, its diagnosis of the nation's ills as fundamentally moral, and its own remarkable growth. The Klan did not trouble itself with complex platforms or debates on public policy issues but seemed satisfied that if enough Klansmen were elected to office, these citizens of the "right sort" would see to it that communities, states, and the nation itself would be restored to the proper moral and political track. Election of its own, consequently, became the central tenet of Klan politics. In office, these forthrightly "American" officials were expected to enforce Prohibition, Sunday closing laws ("blue" laws), and the regulation of public entertainment.[85] In many locales—and sometimes in whole states—the Klan was remarkably successful in bringing its candidates to office.

However, the simplicity of the Klan's political program played a large role in its rapid political demise. Public officials elected with Klan support often found it both difficult and impolitic to enforce legislated morality with the single-minded vengeance that their backers expected of them. Even when they tried to do so, the results were often disappointing. Their supporters took them to be failures or, worse, sellouts. Also, an organization with a platform of putting new men into office attracted political opportunists with little regard for what passed as Klan ideology. Once in office, they proved impossible to control. In many places, the Klan found itself bringing to power the very career politicians that it claimed to despise. In most states, moreover, the Klan never gained sufficient influence in state government to be able to stand up against established officeholders who regarded it as dangerously unpredictable and a threat to the major parties. What passed for Klan public policy were vague nostrums about enforcing the law and cleaning up crime. These were broad enough goals for any public official to pursue, and it was easy for the Klan's opponents to take away votes by publicizing "reform."[86]

The Klan also suffered from the same ills as other "secret" fraternities. It was prone to schisms and fights between individual chapters and higher levels of organization. Heavily dependent on the charisma of the recruiters who organized chapters, it easily fell victim to personal disputes among leaders. Since personal profit itself lay at the root of most recruiters' success, greed was always just a little below the surface and was bound to break out here and there, to the disgust of members who took the order's moral pronouncements seriously. The worst blow to the Klan's image was the highly publicized trial of the Indiana Klan leader "Steve" Stephenson in 1925 for a rape and brutalization of a female state employee which led to her grisly suicide. One historian has also made the useful point that the Klan placed such a premium on organizing the "real" people that at some point saturation of a local community was reached and there was no goal left. Half of the excitement of belonging to the order was in building it—in bringing one's neighbors into the fold. Once they were all in, the thrill was gone; and, faced with disappointments in politics and leadership, members began to drain away.[87]

In Texas, which became a focal point of Klan organizing, attracting perhaps almost 500,000 participants in the early 1920s, a disastrous defeat for the Klan-backed candidate in the gubernatorial election of 1924 took the bloom off the bush for many members who had expected the order to reform politics. By 1926, the order in Texas had lost about 80 percent of its peak membership. The Indiana Klan, rocked by Stephenson's trial and conviction, came unglued in 1927 when Stephenson, in prison, was denied a quick pardon by the governor, who had been supported by the Klan. Stephenson took out his fury by publicizing evidence of campaign finance fraud. Although it survived longer in Oklahoma and the deep south, the Klan was so weakened politically by 1928 that it was not even able to put much of a dent in southern support for the nomination of Al Smith of New York—a "wet" Catholic—as the Democratic party's candidate for president.[88]

In an effort to save itself, the Klan fell back on benevolent fraternalism. It experimented with new insurance benefits. It announced a second degree—the Knights Kamelia—with its own ceremony and regalia. In 1928, with a fanfare, it lifted its masks while introducing a third fraternal degree.[89] But ideologically it was becoming less and less appealing to a mass membership. In this period of decline, mainly the true believers stayed on, and they took their chapters in more extremist directions. By 1927, Klan-backed bills had been introduced into state legislatures to ban the Catholic Knights of Columbus, to make illegal the Catholic requirement that parties to a church-sanctioned marriage agree to raise their children in the faith, and to prohibit interracial marriages. These immoderate measures drove many early members away. In fact, William D. Jenkins argues that there were "two Klans" in the 1920s. The one that was lost was the one made up of a mass membership which "sought Protestant moral dominance only, not Protestant hegemony."[90] The one that survived was shrinking to a core of bitter radicals by the end of the decade.

As the Klan contracted, it lost, by stages, its specifically nativist character. Its ideologues talked not about moral or cultural challenges to American "national character" but about threats to a "superior race"—variously styled white, Caucasian, Anglo-Saxon, and Nordic—which was extranational. They increasingly made league with non-nativist racists concerned about the international "purity" of the Nordic type. One dimension of this changing emphasis was the growing importance of anti-Semitism in Klan rhetoric. In part, this was opportunistic on the part of Klan leadership, for in the 1920 they could tap into strong currents of anti-Semitism at several levels of American society. In May 1920, Henry Ford's newspaper, the *Dearborn Independent,* launched a sustained attack on "international Zionism." By the mid-1920s, national circulation of this paper reached almost 750,000. From the first, it was internationalist rather than nationalist. In fact, its initial anti-Semitic article was entitled "The International Jew: The World's Problem," and its editors gobbled up tidbits thrown to them by foreign as well as domestic anti-Semites. The challenge of the Jews was allegedly not so much to American "national character" as to the stability of international finance and the safety of worldwide Christianity (the *Independent* held Jewish intellectual subversives responsible for spreading doubts about the scriptures by promoting scholarly "higher criticism" of the Bible). The paper went so far as to put the "Jewish conspiracy" in league with other allegedly historical international troublemakers like the Masons and the Bavarian Illuminati.[91]

The strength of anti-Semitism in American culture in the 1920s is underscored by a growing pattern of excluding Jews from institutions as diverse as middle-class civic service clubs and elite private colleges. In none of these cases were the expressed concerns nationalistic or nativistic. Rather, they echoed the sentiment expressed by Henry Pratt Fairchild—a leading eugenicist—in his *Melting Pot Mistake* (1926) that "a people" were responsible for protecting their inherent character from adulteration. When the president of Harvard, A. Lawrence Lowell, examined the Jewish-Gentile composition of his student body in 1922, he said he was concerned about what he called the "race distribution." This, too, was the point of view carried into the 1930s by the last remnants of the Immigration Restriction League, which sought to make the immigration restriction acts of the 1920s even more restrictive by excluding Hispanic immigrants from the Americas and denounced any softheartedness which might facilitate the admission of Jewish refugees from Nazi Germany.[92]

The Nativist Movement in Decline

For all intents and purposes, the Ku Klux Klan of the 1920s was the last gasp of organized nativist activism; and over time, it sacrificed the larger portion of its nativist credentials. Even the presidential election of 1928, which featured a Catholic Democratic candidate—Governor Al Smith of New York—did not restore the vitality of the nativist movement. To be sure, there was plenty of anti-Catholicism evident in the campaign rhetoric and in ultimate voting behavior. But this was actually so commonplace that it offered little room for nativist activists to make a special appeal or assume leadership. In fact, by demonstrating that there was little likelihood for some time to come that a Catholic would be elected president, the election undermined traditional nativist scare rhetoric.

Another reason why the nativist movement went into a sustained decline was that its customary vehicle of organization—the fraternal order—became an anachronism and lost its attractiveness. The fraternal form had served the nativist movement well: it offered practical benefits along with public purpose, and it neatly represented, in microcosm, the "nationality" that nativists claimed to be pursuing—a "nation" of participatory, autonomous citizens defending through righteous organization a shared culture against organized "aliens" who would violate this "character." But the last traditional major nativist fraternity, the Junior Order, United American Mechanics, reached its twentieth-century membership peak in the middle to late 1920s and then went into permanent decline.[93] Over the course of the next decade, it would lose two-thirds of its members. Its experience was shared by fraternal orders of all kinds. The decline of the Improved Order of Red Men was precipitous, and even the vast Masonic fraternal confederacy passed its apex. Ironically, ethnic fraternal organizations of immigrants and their descendants—among the nativist movement's chief bogeymen—were also undermined. Lynn Dumenil and Mark Carnes explain this decline in terms of an eclipse of fraternal benefits by modern insurance, a financial strain imposed by aging brethren, the increasing absurdity of nineteenth-century rituals in the age of the automobile and the airplane, changes in gender roles which kept young husbands and fathers closer to home, and the attractive alternative represented by "modern" civic service clubs like Rotary, Kiwanis, and the Lions.[94]

Ultimately, legislated immigration restriction itself sapped the nativist movement. While the core of the nativist movement had never been real enthusiasts for the kind of broad restrictions, based on national origin, that were finally operational by the end of the 1920s, the movement had clearly benefited from the support or at least the connivance of people who were. Many people who in the past might have been nativist recruits or hangers-on were satisfied in the aftermath of immigration restriction that the important questions about immigrants and aliens had been resolved. With ethnic minorities in the United States now cut off from sustained reinforcement from abroad, it was increasingly difficult to make the traditional nativistic case that immigrant aliens were just an advance party for foreign intrusion into American life. Without question, the immigration restriction acts did put an end to mass immigration from Europe as it had existed for 100 years. When all the details of the national-origins plan were finally worked out in 1929, 154,000 entrants were allowed annually. But the Quota Board calculated from the 1920 census that over 43 percent of Americans were of "colonial stock" and thus gave three-quarters of all available admissions to "old" immigrant population centers in northern and western Europe. In many years, these slots went unfilled and immigration dropped below its statutory maximum.

John Higham has nicely catalogued some of the consequences of restriction that ate away at the ideological foundations of the nativist movement. Without large numbers of newcomers, ethnic minority populations grew less apparently "foreign," even if they sustained a distinctive cultural style. Provocative symbols of putative "hyphenism" like the foreign-language press and ethnic clubs gradually declined. A larger and larger proportion of the foreign-born became naturalized citizens. In some respects cut off from their origins—or at least from new arrivals who would restore their memories—even some first-generation immigrants began to think of themselves as distinctively different from people remaining in their country of origin who might wish to follow them. Higham has astutely pointed out that by the late 1930s ethnic diversity had come to seem so safe that the public "meaning" of the Statue of Liberty began to shift from an abstract political concept to a symbol of a "golden door" of opportunity for generations of immigrants—a change represented by the popular rediscovery of Emma Lazarus's poem of 1883, "The New Colossus," in which the goddess beckons to newcomers.[95]

None of this means that ethnic variety or its manifestation in community cultures in the United States was extinguished in the 1930s. But developments in the aftermath of immigration restriction did make it more difficult for a nativist movement to sustain itself by charging that there was an orchestrated "foreign" threat to American national character and that immigrants were its shock troops. There were even some changes in the nature and meaning of ethnic diversity itself in this period which made it appear more "American" and less "foreign." Robert Wiebe, for example, makes a persuasive case that ethnic identity came to seem more important to many people and was sustained in political behavior precisely because tightly knit ethnic communities unraveled as a result of social and geographical mobility. Dennis Clark has done a masterful job of showing how these new ethnic identities had as much to do with shared experience in America as with "old world" traditions.[96] In either case, this was a domesticated ethnic diversity which gave little sustenance to charges of "hyphenism," a nativist mainstay. Interethnic friction and overt hostility remained in the United States, but it was increasingly difficult after 1929 to regenerate the themes that had formed the ideological superstructure of the nativist movement: effective, uncoerced participation in public affairs as the measure of republican citizenship and the need to organize to fight a war with an orchestrated "foreign" challenge to the national character.

Thomas Archdeacon reminds us not to confuse the decline of the powerful Ku Klux Klan of the 1920s with the "demise of the bigotry it represented."[97] Actually, we also have to be careful not to confuse decline with disappearance. Bits and pieces of the Klan survived, of course, to resurface during the 1950s and 1960s with an agenda of racial hatred that focused primarily on African-Americans. The Junior Order, United American Mechanics, much shrunken, was still asking initiates to defend the "free public school system" in the mid-1930s and was still predicting the malign affects from "an unrestricted horde of undesirable aliens." Other organizations which had sometimes acted on the fringes of the nativist movement continued to announce positions that had a superficially familiar ring. In 1938, the Great Council of the United States of the Improved Order of Red Men openly opposed "admittance of political refugees from Europe." And the American Legion, not satisfied that the Japanese were excluded from the national-origins system of immigrant quotas, kept up a rhetorical assault on the "Japanese menace."[98] But in voicing these concerns, such organizations were really demonstrating how far they had strayed from the nativist path. For in most cases, the alleged danger was cast as a product of "race." Whereas it had been characteristic of nativist ideology to treat American character as an individual achievement, the language of race imputed suitability for American citizenship to whole genetic categories or whole categories of skin color. Nativists proposed to differentiate between "real" and "false" Americans, whether of native or foreign birth; this is what gave a rationale to nativist organizations and a sense of importance to individual activists. But "race" and racism threatened to make "true" Americanism automatic. In the 1930s, this was a popular outlook, which showed up in an administrative crackdown on Mexican immigration at the beginning of the decade and in increasing outbursts of violence on the west coast against Filipinos—or the "Malay race," as California legislators put it when adding them to the state's miscegenation codes. The way was being paved for the wildly differential treatment of German and Italian aliens and (in General John L. DeWitt's words) the Japanese "alien race" once the United States entered the Second World War.[99]

The 1930s were characterized by the emergence not of new nativist organizations but of new racist organizations. Father Coughlin, the "radio priest," may have begun with assaults on alleged religious affronts by Judaism to Christianity, but it was not long before he and his supporters—the Christian Front—were indulging in much cruder stereotypes of Jews and holding the Jewish "race" responsible for a host of international economic and political ills. Even greater racist extremism was displayed by William Dudley Pelley's Silver Shirts and the Nazi sympathizers of the German-American Bund. The internationalist (rather than nationalist) outlook of these groups was evident in their appeal to some of the very ethnic minorities that nativists had traditionally accounted dangerously alien.

In short, by the mid-1930s, the old themes that had sustained a nativist movement for a century had become so weakened that the movement for all intents and purposes disappeared. Pursuit and protection of the "national character" no longer had a meaning that excited partisans. That the United States had the "character of a nation"—that it could function as a nation even without the history and common "peoplehood" of the traditional European nations—had been pretty much established by the end of the Civil War. Questions of what it meant to be an American citizen (at least for whites) had been largely removed by successive generations of naturalization and franchise reform and by the elimination of economic and gender barriers to participation in republican government. Personal autonomy—though still valued—no longer had the same meaning in an age in which individuals increasingly believed that the way to move ahead economically and socially was to make use of large organizations. The nativist plaint of the late nineteenth and early twentieth centuries that "aliens" were well-organized to wrest control of the cultural and moral character of the nation away from "Americans" also had an archaic ring by the third decade of the new century. The Great Depression brought into question whether "character" had much to do with either personal or national achievement, and the organizations that seemed to matter had less to do with culture than with economics and politics—corporations, labor unions, industrial associations, and structured interest groups. The nativist movement had much to do with the anxieties of, first, a new nation, and, later, a nation in the throes of modernization; but did not have much to say to a mature nation.

Conclusion: A New Nativism?

Six decades have passed since the expiration of the nativist movement in the United States. Now, in the 1990s, the mass media are again filled with reports about immigration and signs of hostility to immigration. Immigrants—documented and undocumented—are entering the country at rates not experienced in three-quarters of a century. Debates over the regulation of borders and the rights of unnaturalized aliens are the stuff of political discourse. Is there evidence of a reemergence of a nativist movement? Probably not just now. Present-day anxieties about immigrants seem to have less to do with nationalism than with private grievances. In place of classic nativist discourse about threats to the "national character," participatory citizenship, or cultural values we now hear plaints about the cost of social services for newcomers, the resources directed to the education of their children, and the funding of the welfare safety net for those in need—all putatively drains on the pocketbooks of individual taxpayers. Often among the most powerless members of contemporary society, immigrants can scarcely be portrayed as an "organized" threat to the "national character."

To be sure, the exact nature of any "native" hostility toward immigrants is clouded by the geographical reorientation of immigration since the 1920s. Europe has been supplanted as the source of new arrivals by Pacific Asia, the middle east, Latin America, and the Caribbean. This makes it difficult to distinguish evidence of nativism— which, historically, was intentionally choosy in its identification of "aliens" and "real" Americans—from evidence of racism, which tars with a broader brush. Certainly there is good reason to suspect racism at work in the lack of sympathy for black Haitian immigration, in contrast to a studied inattention to the considerable flow of "illegals" from white Ireland; as well as in a tendency to treat Hispanic bilingualism as a sort of new "hyphenism" despite impressive evidence that Hispanic immigrants are queuing up to learn English whenever they can. And while there are few signs of an institution-based nativist movement, there are plenty of examples of well-organized racist hatemongers. Historians, though, are leery of saying "never." A danger perhaps remains that some Americans who see themselves as powerless—in the government, the economy, and the culture—will attribute this to exclusion from the full privileges of "Americanism" and will somehow lay it all at the feet of "aliens." In just such a joining of personal and national identity was the nativist movement born.

Bibliographic Essay

One rationale for a modern study of organized nativist activism in the United States—a nativist movement—is that the available literature providing an overview of the subject is thin. But another rationale is that a wealth of useful scholarship is available, touching on different aspects of the topic, and that an effort to synthesize secondary material with original research should therefore be profitable. The following is an abbreviated listing and discussion of some of the key secondary works that an interested reader might wish to consult for more detail on the nativist movement and to get a better sense of how the thesis of the present study has been informed by existing scholarship. It does not pretend to be a complete list of all the works examined in the preparation of this book, or even of all the works cited in the notes, and it excludes primary source materials entirely.

Although dated, Ray Allen Billington's *The Protestant Crusade, 1800-1860: A Study in the Origins of American Nativism* (New York: Rinehart, 1938) is still the place for a student of the nativist movement to begin. Treating nativism as an Anglo-American cultural inheritance and the practice of the demagogue and the mob, it nonetheless provides close coverage of key events, organizations, and individuals. John Higham's *Strangers in the Land: Patterns of American Nativism, 1860-1925* (New Brunswick: Rutgers University Press, 1963) takes up chronologically where Billington left off, but with a very different interpretive slant. In this work and in a collection of important essays, *Send These to Me: Jews and Other Immigrants in Urban America* (New York: Atheneum, 1975), Higham treats nativism as a broad, popular mood and uses it to trace national anxieties. A fascinating retrospective on Higham's work and influence—including articles by Leonard Dinner-

stein and David Reimers, Howard Palmer, Alan M. Kraut, Roger
Daniels, Ronald H. Bayor, Milton Himmelfarb, Edward S. Shapiro, and
John Higham himself—appears in *American Jewish History* 76 (December 1986). More recently, in *The Party of Fear: From Nativist Movements to the New Right in American History* (Chapel Hill: University of
North Carolina Press, 1988), David H. Bennett has tried to place
nativism in what he views as a larger pattern of right-wing political
extremism. By its very nature, this study is drawn away from a tight
focus on nativism as a specific social movement.

Thomas J. Archdeacon's *Becoming American: An Ethnic History*
(New York: Free Press, 1983) not only does a fine job of setting the
context of American immigration in which the nativist movement operated but provides a helpful understanding of the contractual nature of
citizenship and nationality that emerged from the United States' revolutionary origins. *Individualism and Nationalism in American Ideology*
(Cambridge: Harvard University Press, 1964), by Jehoshua Arieli; and
This Sacred Trust: American Nationality, 1798-1898 (New York:
Oxford University Press, 1971), by Paul C. Nagel, both make a strong
case that citizenship was basic to membership in the American
national community. Both authors are misled, however, into thinking
that the Know Nothings of the 1850s attempted to substitute a romantic notion of Anglo-American "racial" peoplehood. Dale T. Knobel's
Paddy and the Republic: Ethnicity and Nationality in Antebellum America (Middletown, Conn.: Wesleyan University Press, 1985) clarifies
that Anglo-Americanism was popular in the years around midcentury
but did not particularly appeal to out-and-out nativists, who found it
threatening to the very existence of their movement. John Murrin's "A
Roof without Walls: The Dilemma of American National Identity," in
*Beyond Confederation: Origins of the Constitution and American
National Identity,* ed. Richard Beeman, Stephen Botein, and Edward C.
Carter II (Chapel Hill: University of North Carolina Press, 1987),
explains why Americans found it unpalatable to take their identity from
the British imperial past.

Much nearer to being a primary source than a secondary source,
Albert C. Stevens, *The Cyclopedia of Fraternities* (New York: Treet,
1907), offers fascinating vignettes on most of the fraternal orders that
made up the nativist movement in the nineteenth century. Often
based on interviews with contemporary or former activists, the *Cyclopedia* needs to be handled with care and tested against other sources
of information. Although not apparently having anything directly to do

with nativism, Lynn Dumenil's *Freemasonry and American Culture,
1880-1930* (Princeton: Princeton University Press, 1984) helps us
understand much better the rewards of participation in fraternal organizations like so many of those that formed the backbone of the
nativist movement. *The Social Order of a Frontier Community: Jack-
sonville, Illinois, 1825-1870* (Urbana: University of Illinois Press,
1978), by Don Harrison Doyle, gives a good idea of the meaning of
membership in fraternal and voluntary organizations in the context of
nineteenth-century communities. Mark C. Carnes, *Secret Ritual and
Manhood in Victorian America* (New Haven: Yale University Press,
1989) not only describes the symbolic elements in lodge membership
but suggests why fraternalism went out of fashion in the early twentieth century, sapping one of the nativist movement's traditional
sources of strength. In "To Be an American: Ethnicity, Fraternity, and
the Improved Order of Red Men," *Journal of American Ethnic History*
4 (Fall 1984), I have explored some of the connections between non-
nativist and nativist fraternalism.

In *Chants Democratic: New York City and the Rise of the American
Working Class, 1778-1850* (New York: Oxford University Press, 1984),
Sean Wilentz traces the rise of the commitment to personal autonomy
and equality in working-class culture and its role in the nativist American
Republican movement of the 1840s. Wilentz focuses on New York; but
these themes were previously explored effectively for Philadelphia by
David Montgomery, "The Shuttle and the Cross: Weavers and Artisans
in the Kensington Riots of 1844," *Journal of Social History* 5 (1972), and
Bruce Laurie, "'Nothing on Compulsion': Life Styles of Philadelphia Arti-
sans, 1820-1850," *Labor History* 15 (1974). Elliott J. Gorn's article, "'Good-
Bye Boys, I Die a True American': Homicide, Nativism, and Working-
Class Culture in Antebellum New York City," *Journal of American
History* 74 (September 1987), examines how working-class anxiety about
personal independence could bring men into the nativist organizations,
political and fraternal, of the 1850s. Validating my sense that before the
Civil War "autonomy" was popularly perceived as the essence of citizenship—and hence of nationality itself—J. Mills Thornton III, *Politics and
Power in a Slave Society, Alabama, 1800-1860* (Baton Rouge: Louisiana
State University Press, 1978), and Phillip Shaw Paludan, *'A People's Contest': The Union and Civil War, 1861-1865* (New York: Harper & Row,
1988), show how concern about personal and local independence and
civic participation contributed, on the one hand, to southern secessionism and, on the other, to northern commitment to the Union.

For two large, modern works that cover in detail the "whats," "wheres," and "whens" of Protestant-Catholic sparring (in a major venue for such conflict—New York City and New York state) over public policy issues in a context broader than the nativist movement itself, see John Webb Pratt, *Religion, Politics, and Diversity: The Church-State Theme in New York History* (Ithaca: Cornell University Press, 1967), and Diane Ravitch, *The Great School Wars: New York City, 1805-1973: A History of the Public Schools as Battlefield of Social Change* (New York: Basic Books, 1974). The eruption of denominational issues in politics in the 1840s and 1850s is thoroughly treated by Leonard Tabachnik, "Origins of the Know-Nothing Party: A Study of the Native American Party in Philadelphia, 1844-1852" (Ph.D. dissertation, Columbia University, 1973), and Ira M. Leonard, "The Rise and Fall of the American Republican Party in New York City, 1843-1845," *New York Historical Society Quarterly* 50 (April 1966).

Very old and interpretively very suspect, but useful in an encyclopedic way as an introduction to the tangled web of mid-nineteenth-century nativist organizations and alliances, is Louis Dow Scisco's *Political Nativism in New York State* (New York: Columbia University Press, 1901). Scisco had access to paper collections—and Know Nothing survivors—now gone. A modern, scholarly plowing of much the same ground is provided by Thomas J. Curran, "Know Nothings of New York" (Ph.D. dissertation, Columbia University, 1963). In "'Co-Laborers in the Cause': Women in the Ante-Bellum Nativist Movement," *Civil War History* 25 (June 1979), Jean Gould Hales not only explains the role of the female auxiliaries to the nativist fraternities but shows what the nativists' commitment to individual "autonomy" meant to working-class women. In a fine dissertation, "The Making of an Immigrant City: Ethnic and Cultural Conflict in Jersey City, New Jersey, 1850-1877" (University of Rochester, 1972), and a subsequent article, "Political Leadership in the Industrial City: Irish Development and Nativist Response in Jersey City," in *Immigrants in Industrial America, 1850-1920,* ed. Richard L. Ehrlich (Charlottesville: University Press of Virginia, 1977), Douglas V. Shaw traces the survival of the core of the nativist movement through the Civil War into the 1870s.

In *The Political Crisis of the 1850s* (New York: Wiley, 1978), Michael F. Holt paints a clear picture of mid-nineteenth-century Americans' fear that the Whig and Democratic parties had ceased to be effective guarantors of their personal independence; but I think he overstates nativist activists' aversion to political parties in general. There are a wealth of useful studies of the American party, in the form of books, articles, and dissertations. Unfortunately—for the purpose of understanding the nativist movement—the larger number have gotten bogged down in a debate over whether the Republican party was born because of political nativism or in spite of it. William E. Gienapp, *Origins of the Republic Party, 1852-1856* (New York: Oxford University Press, 1987), takes the position that Republicanism by and large absorbed Know Nothingism. Dale Baum, *The Civil War Party System: The Case of Massachusetts, 1848-1876* (Chapel Hill: University of North Carolina Press, 1984), argues that the Republicans had no need to make concessions to Know Nothing issues in order to replace the Whigs. Recently, Tyler Anbinder, *Nativism and Slavery: The Northern Know Nothings and the Politics of the 1850s* (New York: Oxford University Press, 1992), has made a case that the American party, for a time, carried forward both a nativistic and an antislavery message. For an interesting view of nativist organizing far away from New York and Massachusetts, see Ronald R. Matthias, "The Know-Nothing Movement in Iowa" (Ph.D. dissertation, University of Chicago, 1965).

There is also extensive scholarship concerning southern Know Nothingism. The traditional account is provided by W. Darrell Overdyke, *The Know Nothing Party in the South* (Baton Rouge: Louisiana State University Press, 1954). It is encyclopedic but has the flaw of seeing nativism as a catchall for every discontent of the region—at best a half-truth. Jean Baker, author of *Ambivalent Americans: The Know Nothing Party in Maryland* (Baltimore: Johns Hopkins University Press, 1977), properly understands nativism as a movement of the "dedicated few and the casual many" but confuses Know Nothing hostility to the existing political parties with "anti-partyism" in the abstract. Several state experiences with political nativism are dealt with by modern dissertations, including Marius Michael Carriere Jr., "The Know Nothing Movement in Louisiana" (Louisiana State University, 1977), Cecil S. H. Ross, "Dying Hard, Dying Fast: The Know-Nothing Experience in Mississippi" (University of Notre Dame, 1982); and Harry August Volz III, "Party, State, and Nation: Kentucky and the Coming of the American Civil War" (University of Virginia, 1982). Gregg Cantrell, in *Kenneth and John B. Rayner and the Limits of Southern Dissent* (Urbana: University of Illinois Press, 1993), understands the seriousness with which nativist activists took their ideology and the problems they had with their effort to maintain ideological consistency.

Five important books have helped me understand post-Civil War Americans' appreciation for the power of organization, an appreciation that was at the root of nativist fears in the late nineteenth and early twentieth centuries and at the center of their organizational efforts to respond to those fears: George M. Fredrickson, *The Inner Civil War: Northern Intellectuals and the Crisis of the Union* (Cambridge: Harvard University Press, 1965); Anne C. Rose, *Victorian America and the Civil War* (Cambridge, England: Cambridge University Press, 1992); Robert H. Wiebe, *The Search for Order, 1877-1920* (New York: Hill & Wang, 1967); John D. Buenker, *Urban Liberalism and Progressive Reform* (New York: Norton, 1973); and Alan Trachtenberg, *The Incorporation of America: Culture and Society in the Gilded Age* (New York: Hill & Wang, 1982). In "'The Insatiable Maw of Bureaucracy': Antistatism and Education Reform in the 1920s," *Journal of American History* 77 (September 1990), Lynn Dumenil offers some insight into the demise of Victorian enthusiasm for organization and homogeneity. This last point is also made by Lloyd P. Jorgenson in "The Oregon School Law of 1922: Passage and Sequel," *American Catholic Historical Review* 54 (October 1968), which shows how fraternities like the Odd Fellows, the Knights of Pythias, and the Masons hovered around the fringes of the nativist movement.

For a number of years, the standard modern work on the American Protective Association was Donald L. Kinzer, *An Episode in Anti-Catholicism: The American Protective Association* (Seattle: University of Washington Press, 1964). Just a few years ago, Les Wallace published *The Rhetoric of Anti-Catholicism: The American Protective Association, 1887-1911* (New York: Garland, 1990), which attributes to APA a more populist appeal and devotes more attention to its fraternal aspects. Barbara Miller Solomon, *Ancestors and Immigrants: A Changing New England Tradition* (Chicago: University of Chicago Press, 1956), remains the key study of the Immigration Restriction League. It is somewhat misleading in implying that the racialists and anti-Semites of IRL represented the mainstream of nativist activism. R. Fred Wacker, *Ethnicity, Pluralism, and Race: Race Relations Theory in America before Myrdal* (Westport, Conn., Greenwood, 1983), describes the academic racialists who lent ideological support to immigration restriction as well as those who came to oppose it. *Ethnicity, Race, and American Foreign Policy: A History* (Boston: Northeastern University Press, 1992), by Alexander DeConde, shows how international events exacerbated domestic anxieties about organized "foreigners."

Robert K. Murray's *Red Scare: A Study in National Hysteria, 1919-1920* (New York: McGraw-Hill, 1964) provides a link between the "Americanization" campaigning of the World War I years and the Klan of the 1920s. While the American Legion is not typically thought of as a nativist organization, William Pencak's *For God and Country: The American Legion, 1919-1941* (Boston: Northeastern University Press, 1989) shows that it had its nativistic aspects—like the Grand Army of the Republic before it.

Edward Cuddy, "The Irish Question and the Revival of Anti-Catholicism in the 1920s," *American Catholic Historical Review* 67 (April 1981), explores how Irish-American support for the republican movement in Ireland provoked nativistic fears of Catholic organization at a time of divisiveness among American Protestants. Timothy J. Meagher, "Irish, American, Catholic: Irish-American Identity in Worcester, Massachusetts, 1880 to 1920," in *From Paddy to Studs: Irish-American Communities in the Turn-of-the-Century Era, 1880 to 1920,* ed. Timothy J. Meagher (Westport, Conn.: Greenwood, 1986), discusses the ascendancy of pan-Catholic identity over traditional ethnic identities, a development that nativists found menacing; as does Lynn Dumenil in "The Tribal Twenties: 'Assimilated Catholics' Response to Anti-Catholicism in the 1920s," *Journal of American Ethnic History* 11 (Fall 1991). Robert B. Rackleff, "Anti-Catholicism and the Florida Legislature, 1911-1919," *Florida Historical Quarterly* 50 (April 1971), gives examples of continuing nativist fears of "foreign" organization in the early twentieth century.

No historiography has been changing more rapidly than that of the Ku Klux Klan. In "Historical Interpretations of the 1920s Klan: The Traditional View and the Populist Revision," *Journal of Social History* 24 (Fall 1990), Leonard J. Moore shows how recent scholarship has placed the Klan closer to the mainstream of middle-class civic activism and discusses it in terms of populism rather than as a movement of a disaffected social fringe. Moore is wrong, though, in thinking that as a populist movement the 1920s Klan was not nativist. In fact, its populism is partly what made it central to the nativist movement. For examples of new studies of the Klan, see William D. Jenkins, *Steel Valley Klan: The Ku Klux Klan in Ohio's Mahoning Valley* (Kent, Ohio: Kent State University Press, 1990); Leonard J. Moore, *Citizen Klansmen: The Ku Klux Klan in Indiana, 1921-1928* (Chapel Hill: University of North Carolina Press, 1991); Richard K. Tucker, *The Dragon and the Cross: The Rise and Fall of the Ku Klux Klan in Middle America* (Hamden, Conn.:

Archon, 1991); Robert Alan Goldberg, *Hooded Empire: The Ku Klux Klan in Colorado* (Urbana: University Of Illinois Press, 1981); and Nancy MacLean, *Behind the Mask of Chivalry: The Making of the Second Ku Klux Klan* (New York: Oxford University Press, 1994). Kathleen M. Blee reinforces this emerging consensus about the Klan by looking specifically at the role of women in the Klan movement in *Women of the Klan: Race and Gender in the 1920s* (Berkeley: University of California Press, 1991).

Notes and References

Preface

1. Richard Lacayo, "Down on the Downtrodden," *Time,* December 19, 1994, 30-32.

2. Jeff Jacoby, "Immigrant Bashing Is an American Tradition," *Bryan/College Station [Texas] Eagle,* November 19, 1994; "Nationline: Three Republicans Urge Immigration Caution," *USA Today,* November 22, 1994; James C. Harrington, "Texas at Last Pulling Itself from Disgraceful Era That Spawned Alamo Myth," *Houston Chronicle,* April 24, 1994.

Introduction

1. See *Proceedings of the United States Anti-Masonic Convention, Philadelphia, September 11, 1830* (New York: n.p., 1830), 118.

2. Alice Felt Tyler, in her magisterial social history *Freedom's Ferment,* even consigns nativism to a special chapter on reform entitled "Denials of Democratic Principles." See *Freedom's Ferment: Phases in American Social History from the Colonial Period to the Outbreak of the Civil War* (Minneapolis: University of Minnesota Press, 1944; New York: Harper & Row, 1962), 351.

3. Gunnar Myrdal, *An American Dilemma: The Negro in a White Nation,* 2 vols. (New York: Harper & Row, 1944).

4. Abraham Lincoln to Joshua Speed, August 24, 1855, in *Abraham Lincoln's Speeches and Letters, 1832-1865,* ed. Paul M. Angle (London: Bodley Head, 1957), 64.

5. "Washington's Birthday," *Republic* 3 (March 1852): 156.

6. Albert C. Stevens, *The Cyclopedia of Fraternities,* rev. ed. (New York: Treet, 1907), xviii, xvi.

7. See Lawrence Goodwyn, *The Populist Moment: A Short History of the Agrarian Revolt in America* (New York: Oxford University Press, 1978), xvii-xviii; and Sean Wilentz, *Chants Democratic: New York City and the Rise of the American Working Class, 1778-1850* (New York: Oxford University Press, 1984).

8. Samuel H. Barnes, for example, uses this attribution to make a similar point in "Ideology and the Organization of Conflict: On the Relation between Political Thought and Behavior," *Journal of Politics* 28 (August 1966): 522.

9. See, for example, Ray Allen Billington, *The Protestant Crusade, 1800-1860: A Study in the Origins of American Nativism* (New York: Rinehart, 1938). Billington was trained in the progressive tradition to see prejudices and social discrimination as weapons of organized group interest, but he also labored under the shadow of Nazism, which drew particular attention to ethnic and religious fanaticism. Oscar Handlin, in *Boston's Immigrants: A Study in Acculturation* (Cambridge: Harvard University Press, 1941), was less inclined to see nativism as the work of fanatics than as an outgrowth of concrete interethnic rivalries but remained convinced that it was an organized representation of group interest.

10. John Higham, *Strangers in the Land: Patterns of American Nativism, 1860-1925,* 2d ed. (New York: Atheneum, 1970), i.

11. David H. Bennett, *The Party of Fear: From Nativist Movements to the New Right in American History* (Chapel Hill: University of North Carolina Press, 1988), ix, 6, 13.

12. See, for example, Joel Silbey, *The Transformation of American Politics, 1840-1860* (Englewood Cliffs, N.J.: Prentice-Hall, 1967); Tyler Anbinder, *Nativism and Slavery: The Northern Know Nothings and the Politics of the 1850s* (New York: Oxford University Press, 1992). Anbinder takes much more seriously the gut-level appeal of the nativist message to a mass electorate. But, as he puts it, his primary concern in this study was to explain why very few "voters made nativism a priority when they went to the polls," and not to explain the institutional development of the mid-nineteenth-century nativist movement (237).

13. Higham, *Strangers in the Land,* 223-24.

14. Ronald Walters, *The Antislavery Appeal: American Abolitionism after 1830* (New York: Norton, 1984), xi.

15. See Barnes, "Ideology," 514-15.

16. Jean Baker, *Ambivalent Americans: The Know-Nothing Party in Maryland* (Baltimore: Johns Hopkins University Press, 1977), 153.

17. For a discussion of mass movement building, see Goodwyn, *Populist Moment,* xvii-xviii.

18. Walters, *Antislavery Appeal,* 143-44.

19. David Knoke and David Prensky, "What Relevance Do Organizational Theories Have for Voluntary Associations?" *Social Science Quarterly* 65 (March 1984): 4-5, 12.

Chapter 1

1. Thomas R. Whitney, "OUA," *Republic* 1 (January 1851): 44.

2. *Constitution, By-Laws, Rules of Order, and Discipline of Fredonia Council #52 of the Order of United American Mechanics, Pennsylvania* (Philadelphia, 1853), 3; *Patriotic Order, Sons of America, Pennsylvania State Camp* (Philadelphia, 1889), 6.

3. Isaac McCoy, *Remarks on the Practicability of Indian Reform, Embracing Their Colonization; With an Appendix,* 2d ed. (New York, 1829), 10; see also Robert J. Breckinridge, "The Black Race," *African Repository* 27 (February 1851): 144. Breckinridge called the Africans "a race without nationality."

4. Joseph J. Ellis, *After the Revolution: Profiles of Early American Culture* (New York: Norton, 1979), 194; Robert H. Wiebe, *The Opening of American Society: From the Adoption of the Constitution to the Eve of Disunion* (New York: Knopf, 1984), 19.

5. Daniel Walker Howe, *The Political Culture of the American Whigs* (Chicago: University of Chicago Press, 1979), 229-30.

6. John Murrin, "A Roof without Walls: The Dilemma of American National Identity," in *Beyond Confederation: Origins of the Constitution and American National Identity,* ed. Richard Beeman, Stephen Botein, and Edward C. Carter (Chapel Hill: University of North Carolina Press, 1987), 343-44.

7. Ibid., 342.

8. Ibid., 341.

9. Samuel Harris, *Our Country's Claim* (Bangor, Maine, 1861), 10.

10. Alexander McKay, *The Western World; or, Travels in the United States in 1846-1847* (London, 1850), 3.

11. See Henry Flanders, "British Strictures on Republican Institutions," *North American Review* 89 (July 1859): 104-7.

12. Howard Palmer, *Patterns of Prejudice: A History of Nativism in Alberta* (Toronto: McClelland and Stewart, 1982), 8.

13. John Adams to Mercy Warren, January 8, 1776. *Warren-Adams Letters, Being Chiefly a Correspondence among John Adams, Samuel Adams, and James Warren,* Massachusetts Historical Society, *Collections* 72, 2 vols. (Boston: 1917, 1925), 1:201-2; Alexander Stephens in Howe, *American Whigs,* 82.

14. For some discussion, see Howe, *American Whigs,* 82.

15. Some of the traditional discussions of early American "republicanism" and its origins remain the most succinct and useful. See, for example, Gordon Wood, "Rhetoric and Reality in the American Revolution," *William and Mary Quarterly* (3d series) 23 (1966): 3-32; Isaac Kramnick, "Republican Revisionism Revisited," *American Historical Review* 87 (June 1982): 629-64; Joyce Appleby, "The Social Origins of American Revolutionary Ideology," *Journal of American History* 64 (March 1978): 935-58; Robert E. Shalhope, "Toward a Republican Synthesis: The Emergence of an Understanding of Republicanism in American Historiography," *William and Mary Quarterly* (3d series) 29 (January 1972): 49-80.

16. Thomas J. Archdeacon, *Becoming American: An Ethnic History* (New York: Free Press, 1983), 22.

17. Neil Harris, *The Artist in American Society: The Formative Years, 1790-1860* (New York: Clarion, 1970), 28; Gordon Wood, "Conspiracy and the Paranoid Style: Causality and Deceit in the Eighteenth Century," *William and Mary Quarterly* 39 (July 1982): 413.

18. Wood, "Conspiracy and the Paranoid Style," 440.

19. Richard D. Brown, "The Emergence of Urban Society in Rural Massachusetts, 1760-1820," *Journal of American History* 61 (June 1974): 46.

20. Ronald H. Walters, *American Reformers, 1815-1860* (New York: Hill & Wang, 1978), 16; Wood, "Conspiracy and the Paranoid Style," 417; James H. Moorhead, "Between Progress and the Apocalypse: A Reassessment of Millenialism in American Religious Thought, 1800-1880," *Journal of American History* 71 (December 1984): 529.

21. Quoted in Wiebe, *Opening of American Society,* 4.

22. Walters, *American Reformers,* 11; David Brion Davis, *The Slave Power Conspiracy and the Paranoid Style* (Baton Rouge: Louisiana State University Press, 1969), 11; Wiebe, *Opening of American Society,* 8.

23. See Howe, *American Whigs,* 79-80.

24. Howe, *American Whigs,* 79-80; Wood, "Conspiracy and the Paranoid Style," 410.

25. Walters, *American Reformers,* 10-11; Wood, "Conspiracy and the Paranoid Style," 409, 411, 425.

26. George Will, "Americans Happiest Pursuing Happiness," *Bryan/College Station [Texas] Eagle,* July 13, 1992.

27. These points were eloquently made by Hannah Arendt in *On Revolution* (New York: Viking, 1965), 115, 124. Garry Wills has more recently made a strongly supportive case through his careful study of Jefferson's authorship of the Declaration of Independence; see *Inventing America: Jefferson's Declaration of Independence* (New York: Vintage, 1979), 252-53. Jefferson was far from alone in describing public happiness this way. In *The Federalist* Madison (#14) and Hamilton (#84) used the turn of phrase the same way. See Alexander Hamilton, John Jay, and James Madison, *The Federalist: A Commentary on the Constitution of the United States,* ed. Edward Mead Earle (New York: Modern Library, 1937), 84-85, 564.

28. See Edmund Morgan, *The Meaning of Independence: John Adams, George Washington, and Thomas Jefferson* (New York: Norton, 1976), 33, 36, 9-10, 16; and John Adams, *Discourses on Davilla,* in *Works of John Adams,* 10 vols., ed. Charles Francis Adams (Boston, 1850-1856), 6:232.

29. Gordon S. Wood, *The Creation of the American Republic, 1776-1787* (New York: Norton, 1972), 79.

30. Charles S. Sydnor, *American Revolutionaries in the Making: Political Practices in Washington's Virginia* (New York: Free Press, 1965), 34.

31. Michael Zuckerman, *Peaceable Kingdoms: New England Towns in the Eighteenth Century* (New York: Norton, 1978), 196; Robert A. Gross, *The Minutemen and Their World* (New York: Hill & Wang, 1976), 58; Richard L. Bushman, *From Puritan to Yankee: Character and the Social Order in Connecticut, 1690-1765* (New York: Norton, 1970), 265, 267, 281.

32. Hector St. John de Crèvecoeur, *Letters from an American Farmer,* in *The American Tradition in Literature,* 3d ed., 2 vols., ed. Sculley Bradley, Richmond Croom Beatty, and E. Hudson Long (New York: Norton, 1967), 1:193-94; Alexis de Tocqueville, *Democracy in America,* 2 vols., ed. Phillips Bradley (New York: Vintage, 1945), 1:250-52.

33. Murrin, "Roof without Walls," 343.

34. Thomas Jefferson, *Notes on the State of Virginia,* in *The Writings of Thomas Jefferson,* ed. Henry A. Washington (New York: Taylor & Maury, 1861), 3:93; Henry Cabot Lodge, ed., *The Works of Alexander Hamilton,* 12 vols. (New York, 1894), 8:288, 217.

35. Harry L. Watson, *Jacksonian Politics and Community Conflict: The Emergence of the Second American Party System in Cumberland County, North Carolina* (Baton Rouge: Louisiana State University Press, 1981), 162.

36. Historians often overlook the presence of a proto-nativism before 1820. See, for example, David H. Bennett's recent volume, *The Party of Fear: From Nativist Movements to the New Right in American History* (Chapel Hill: University of North Carolina Press, 1988), 22.

37. Wiebe, *Opening of American Society,* 112, 62-63, 97, 91.

38. U.S. Congress, Senate, *Citizens of Vergennes (Addison County), Vermont, to the President and Congress, May 30, 1798,* 5th Cong., 1st sess., Box 10 of Petitions and Memorials.

39. Wiebe, *Opening of American Society,* 73; Richard Buel Jr., *Securing the Revolution: Ideology in American Politics, 1789-1815* (Ithaca: Cornell University Press, 1972), 180.

40. James Morton Smith, "The Sedition Law, Free Speech, and the American Political Process," *William and Mary Quarterly* 9 (October 1952): 497.

41. Ibid., 497, 500, 510; Archdeacon, *Becoming American,* 61-62.

42. Michael F. Holt, *The Political Crisis of the 1850s* (New York: Wiley, 1978), 8; Wiebe, *Opening of American Society,* 93.

43. James M. Banner Jr., *To the Hartford Convention: The Federalists and the Origins of Party Politics in Massachusetts, 1789-1815* (New York: Knopf, 1969), 97nn.; David Hackett Fischer, *The Revolution of American Conservatism: The Federalist Party in the Era of Jeffersonian Democracy* (New York: Harper & Row, 1965), 163.

44. Banner, *To the Hartford Convention,* 95.

45. Wiebe, *Opening of American Society,* 62.

46. For a good, short summary of the main elements of classical republican thought, see Wilentz, *Chants Democratic,* 14-15.

47. Arendt, *On Revolution,* 115.

48. Richard L. Bushman, "'This New Man': Dependence and Independence, 1776," in *Uprooted Americans: Essays to Honor Oscar Handlin,* ed. Richard L. Bushman et al. (Boston: Little, Brown, 1979), 91; Rowland Berthoff, "Peasants and Artisans, Puritans and Republi-

cans: Personal Liberty and Communal Equality in American History," *Journal of American History* 69 (December 1982): 579.

49. *Lowell [Massachusetts] Journal,* May 4, 1827.

50. Quoted in Lois W. Banner, "Religious Benevolence as Social Control: A Critique of an Interpretation," *Journal of American History* 60 (June 1973): 39.

51. See Buel, *Securing the Revolution,* 100-101.

52. See Isaac Kramnick, "Republican Revisionism Revisited," *American Historical Review* 87 (June 1982): 662; Linda K. Kerber, "The Republican Ideology of the Revolutionary Generation," *American Quarterly* 37 (Fall 1985): 494; Jacqueline S. Reiner, "Rearing the Republican Child: Attitudes and Practices in Post-Revolutionary Philadelphia," *William and Mary Quarterly* 39 (January 1982): 154; Berthoff, "Peasants and Artisans," 585; David J. Rothman, *The Discovery of the Asylum: Social Order and Disorder in the New Republic* (Boston: Little, Brown, 1971), 252.

53. Ellis, *After the Revolution,* ix.

54. John R. Howe Jr., "Republican Thought and the Political Violence of the 1790s," *American Quarterly* 19 (Summer 1967): 156; Ernest Lee Tuveson, *Redeemer Nation: The Idea of America's Millennial Role* (Chicago: University of Chicago Press, 1968), 171.

55. Cathy Matson and Peter Onuf, "Toward a Republican Empire: Interest and Ideology in Revolutionary America," *American Quarterly* 37 (Fall 1985): 500; Banner, "Religious Benevolence," 35-37; Bushman, "This New Man," 92.

56. Watson, *Jacksonian Politics and Community Conflict,* 73; James Sterling Young, *The Washington Community, 1800-1828* (New York: Harcourt, Brace & World, 1966), 59, 63.

57. Rowland Berthoff, *An Unsettled People: Social Order and Disorder in American History* (New York: Harper & Row, 1971), 255-56.

58. Reiner, "Republican Child," 157; Jean Baker, "From Belief into Culture: Republicanism in the Antebellum North," *American Quarterly* 37 (Fall 1985): 539.

59. Baker, "From Belief into Culture," 540-41; Reiner, "Republican Child," 156.

60. Wilentz, *Chants Democratic,* 95; John Patrick Diggins, "Comrades and Citizens: New Mythologies in American Historiography," *American Historical Review* 90 (June 1985): 634-35, 628.

61. Wilentz properly notes the centrality of "independence" among artisans' goals but inexplicably stereotypes it as another

manifestation of self-denying "commonwealth." Yet individual autonomy itself was an established republican goal. See Sean Wilentz, "Artisan Republican Festivals and the Rise of Class Conflict in New York City, 1788-1837," in *Essays on Labor, Community, and American Society,* ed. Michael H. Frisch and Daniel J. Walkowitz (Urbana: University of Illinois Press, 1983), 49.

62. For more detail on New York, see Wilentz, *Chants Democratic,* 38; Alfred F. Young, "The Mechanics and the Jeffersonians: New York, 1789-1801," *Labor History* 5 (1964): 252, 258; and Staughton Lynd, "The Mechanics and New York City Politics, 1774-1785," *Labor History* 5 (1964): 242. On Baltimore, see Charles G. Steffen, *The Mechanics of Baltimore: Workers and Politics in the Age of Revolution, 1763-1812* (Urbana: University of Illinois Press, 1984), 53, 143, 146, 229.

63. See Alfred F. Young, *The Democratic Republicans of New York: The Origins, 1763-1797* (Chapel Hill: University of North Carolina Press, 1976), 202-3, 252-53, 272-73, 398-99.

64. William Utter, "Saint Tammany in Ohio: A Study in Frontier Politics," *Mississippi Valley Historical Review* 15 (1928): 326-28, 339-40.

65. Richard G. Miller, "The Federal City, 1783-1800," in *Philadelphia: A 300-Year History,* ed. Russell F. Weigley (New York: Norton, 1982), 201; Philip S. Foner, ed., *The Democratic-Republican Societies, 1790-1800: A Documentary Sourcebook of Constitutions, Declarations, Addresses, Resolutions, and Toasts* (Westport, Conn.: Greenwood Press, 1976), 7; Buel, *Securing the Revolution,* 97-98.

66. Buel, *Securing the Revolution,* 103-4, 98; Young, *Democratic Republicans of New York,* 392.

67. Foner, *Democratic-Republican Societies,* 35.

68. Foner, *Democratic-Republican Societies,* 9; Young, *Democratic Republicans of New York,* 393-95; Young, "Mechanics and Jeffersonians," 257.

69. Foner, *Democratic-Republican Societies,* 13, 38; Fischer, *American Conservativism,* 111; Young, *Democratic Republicans of New York,* 398.

70. Fischer, *American Conservativism,* 114, 116.

71. Howard B. Rock, "The American Revolution and the Mechanics of New York City: One Generation Later," *New York History* 57 (1976): 386-87; Howard B. Rock, *Artisans of the New Republic: The Tradesmen of New York City in the Age of Jefferson* (New York: New York University Press, 1979), 83-84.

72. Fischer, *American Conservativism,* 121.

73. Rock, *Artisans of the New Republic,* 89; Rock, "Mechanics and the Jeffersonians," 384-85; Fischer, *American Conservativism,* 128.

74. New Light Presbyterian minister Levi Hart quoted in Ruth Bloch, *Visionary Republic: Millennial Themes in American Thought, 1756-1800* (Cambridge: Harvard University Press, 1985), 62.

75. Richard D. Brown, "The Emergence of Urban Society in Rural Massachusetts, 1760-1820," *Journal of American History* 61 (June 1974): 38-39; Richard D. Brown, "Modernization and the Modern Personality in Early America, 1600-1865: A Sketch of a Synthesis," *Journal of Interdisciplinary History* 2 (Winter 1972): 218; Banner, "Religious Benevolence," 39-40.

76. Lawrence Kohl, "The Concept of Social Control and the History of Jacksonian America," *Journal of the Early Republic* 5 (Spring 1985): 31-32; Walters, *Antislavery Appeal,* 54.

77. Brown, "Emergence of Urban Society," 49; Don Harrison Doyle, *The Social Order of a Frontier Community,* (Urbana: University of Illinois Press, 1978), 156-57.

78. Ian R. Tyrell, *Sobering Up: From Temperance to Prohibition in Antebellum America, 1800-1860* (Westport, Conn.: Greenwood Press, 1979), 55; Doyle, *Social Order of a Frontier Community,* 189.

79. Brown, "Emergence of Urban Society," 39, 42-43.

80. Doyle, *Social Order of a Frontier Community,* 188; Lynn Dumenil, *Freemasonry and American Culture, 1880-1930* (Princeton: Princeton University Press, 1984), 101; Richard Brown, "The Emergence of Voluntary Associations in Massachusetts, 1760-1830," *Journal of Voluntary Action Research* 2 (April 1973): 68.

81. For some extended discussion of this from different points of view, see Lois Banner, "Religion and Reform in the Early Republic: The Role of Youth," *American Quarterly* 23 (December 1971): 678, 684; M. J. Heale, "From City Fathers to Social Critics: Humanitarianism and Government in New York City, 1790-1860," *Journal of American History* 63 (June 1976): 26; Doyle, *Social Order of a Frontier Community,* 182.

82. Paul A. Gilje, *The Road to Mobocracy: Popular Disorder in New York City, 1763-1834* (Chapel Hill: University of North Carolina Press, 1987), 129-30; Graham Russell Hodges, *New York City Cartmen, 1667-1850* (New York: New York University Press, 1986), 136-37.

83. Paul Goodman, *The Democratic-Republicans of Massachusetts: Politics in a Young Republic* (Cambridge: Harvard University Press,

1964), 91-92; William Brownlow Posey, *Religious Strife on the Southern Frontier* (Baton Rouge: Louisiana State University Press, 1965), 78.

84. For some discussion, see Richard L. McCormick, *The Party Period and American Public Policy: American Politics from the Age of Jackson to the Progressive Era* (New York: Oxford University Press, 1986), 135.

85. For a discussion of similar elements in antebellum Freemasonry, see Paul Goodman, *Towards a Christian Republic: Antimasonry and the Great Transition in New England, 1826-1836* (New York: Oxford University Press, 1988), 13, 40, 14.

86. Gregory Singleton has made just this point about the apparent consonance between the inclusive rhetoric of these groups and their actual conduct. See "Protestant Voluntary Associations and the Shaping of Victorian America," *American Quarterly* 27 (December 1975): 557.

87. Howe, *American Whigs,* 2-3.

88. Doyle, *Social Order,* 60.

89. Patriotic Order, Sons of America—Camp of Pennsylvania, *Something about the Order* (Philadelphia, 1888), 15; *Proceedings of the Right Worthy Grand Lodge of the American Protestant Association of the United States at Its 39th Annual Session* (Philadelphia, 1889), 69.

90. Don H. Doyle, "The Social Functions of Voluntary Associations in a Nineteenth-Century American Town," *Social Science History* 1 (Spring 1977): 345, 343-44; Goodman, *Christian Republic,* 12.

91. Doyle, "Voluntary Associations," 347-48; Goodman, *Christian Republic,* 16.

92. Walter S. Glazer, "Participation and Power: Voluntary Associations and the Functional Organization of Cincinnati in 1840," *Historical Methods Newsletter* 5 (September 1972): 151; Doyle, "Voluntary Associations," 335; Dumenil, *Freemasonry,* 110-11.

93. Doyle, *Social Order,* 186-87.

94. For a discussion of this, see Steven Watts, *The Republic Reborn: War and the Making of Liberal America, 1790-1820* (Baltimore: Johns Hopkins University Press), 290-92, 297, 321.

Chapter 2

1. Amy Bridges, *A City in the Republic: Antebellum New York and the Origins of Machine Politics* (Cambridge, England: Cambridge University Press, 1984), 13.

2. Douglas T. Miller, *The Birth of Modern American, 1820-1850* (New York: Pegasus, 1970), 39; Wilentz, *Chants Democratic,* 109-10; Edward K. Spann, *The New Metropolis: New York City, 1840-1857* (New York: Columbia University Press, 1981), 48.

3. Paul Boyer, *Urban Masses and Moral Order in America, 1820-1920* (Cambridge: Harvard University Press, 1978), 67.

4. For a helpful discussion of the changing relationship between employers and employees in antebellum America, see Paul E. Johnson, *A Shopkeeper's Millennium: Society and Revivals in Rochester, New York, 1815-1837* (New York: Hill & Wang, 1978).

5. Kenneth J. Winkle, *The Politics of Community: Migration and Politics in Antebellum Ohio* (Cambridge, England: Cambridge University Press, 1988), 95, 59.

6. Philip Hone, *Diary of Philip Hone, 1828-1851,* ed. Allan Nevins (New York: Dodd, Mead, 1936), 655.

7. Watson, *Jacksonian Politics and Community Conflict,* 162.

8. U.S. Bureau of the Census, *Historical Statistics of the United States: Colonial Times to 1957* (Washington, D.C.: Government Printing Office, 1960), 57.

9. See Bridges, *City in the Republic,* 39; Archdeacon, *Becoming American,* 46-47; Spann, *New Metropolis,* 23-25.

10. Bennett, *Party of Fear,* 141; Archdeacon, *Becoming American,* 47.

11. Leo Hershkowitz, *Tweed's New York: Another Look* (New York: Anchor, 1977), 47; Bridges, *City in the Republic,* 43.

12. Richard J. Purcell and John F. Poole, "Political Nativism in Brooklyn," *Journal of the American Irish Historical Society* 32 (1941): 12.

13. Frank Gerrity, "The Disruption of the Philadelphia Whigocracy: Joseph R. Chandler, Anti-Catholicism, and the Congressional Election of 1854," *Pennsylvania Magazine of History and Biography* 61 (April 1987): 168.

14. Elliott J. Gorn, "'Good-Bye Boys, I Die a True American': Homicide, Nativism, and Working-Class Culture in Antebellum New York City," *Journal of American History* 74 (September 1987): 394. Gorn places 60 percent of the New York Irish in these occupations by the mid-1850s.

15. Wilentz, *Chants Democratic,* 115. Wilentz calculates that by the mid-1850s three-quarters of the workers in New York's largest trades were immigrants and that half of the New York City Irish

were involved in the consumer finishing trades. See also Bennett, *Party of Fear,* 83. Bennett notes that by 1852 foreign-born manufacturing workers exceeded native in New York, Pennsylvania, and Ohio.

16. Spann, *New Metropolis,* 28, and Michael Feldberg, *The Philadelphia Riots: A Study of Ethnic Conflict* (Westport, Conn.: Greenwood Press, 1975), 34, both make this point.

17. Bennett, *Party of Fear,* 83.

18. Gilje, *Road to Mobocracy,* 137, 134.

19. Thomas J. Curran, *Xenophobia and Immigration, 1820-1930* (Boston: Twayne, 1975), 28-29.

20. Wilentz, *Chants Democratic,* 269-70.

21. Hershkowitz, *Tweed's New York,* 10.

22. Wilentz, *Chants Democratic,* 266-27, 269; Curran, *Xenophobia and Immigration,* 29-30.

23. Purcell and Poole, "Nativism in Brooklyn," 25.

24. Hershkowitz, *Tweed's New York,* 9-10; Ira M. Leonard, "The Rise and Fall of the American Republican Party in New York City, 1843-1845," *New-York Historical Society Quarterly* 50 (April 1966): 154.

25. See Joseph G. Mannard, "The 1839 Baltimore Nunnery Riot: An Episode in Jacksonian Nativism and Social Violence," *Maryland Historian* 11 (Spring 1980): 15-16.

26. William H. and Jane H. Pease, *The Web of Progress: Private Values and Public Styles in Boston and Charleston, 1828-1843* (New York: Oxford University Press, 1985), 157-58.

27. Mannard, "Baltimore Nunnery Riot," 22. Ironically, the NADA included several prominent Roman Catholics among its members.

28. Herbert Ershkowitz, "Race and the Origins of the Democratic Party, 1834-1870" (paper delivered at the annual meeting of the American Historical Association, Chicago, December 1984).

29. Wilentz, *Chants Democratic,* 299.

30. John Webb Pratt, *Religion, Politics, and Diversity: The Church-State Theme in New York History* (Ithaca: Cornell University Press, 1967), 171, 190; Karl F. Kaestle, *The Evolution of an Urban School System: New York City, 1750-1850* (Cambridge: Harvard University Press, 1973), 153.

31. See Wilentz, *Chants Democratic,* 315-18.

32. Pratt, *Religion, Politics, and Diversity,* 182-83.

33. Ibid., 183-84; Bridges, *City in the Republic,* 86-87.

34. Thomas J. Curran, "The Know Nothings of New York" (Ph.D. dissertation, Columbia University, 1963), 52-53, 25.

35. Leonard Tabachnik, "Origins of the Know-Nothing Party: A Study of the Native American Party in Philadelphia, 1844-1852" (Ph.D. dissertation, Columbia University, 1973), 74.

36. Feldberg, *Philadelphia Riots,* 31.

37. By the summer of 1842, distressed economic conditions had destroyed the multiethnic General Trades Union and many of the individual tradesmen's societies; self-help and self-improvement societies began to take their places. See David Montgomery, "The Shuttle and the Cross: Weavers and Artisans in the Kensington Riots of 1844," *Journal of Social History* 5 (1972): 421-22.

38. Montgomery, "Shuttle and the Cross," 433-34; Feldberg, *Philadelphia Riots,* 28, 30.

39. Montgomery, "Shuttle and the Cross," 51, 54-55; Gerrity, "Disruption of the Philadelphia Whigocracy," 128.

40. Feldberg, *Philadelphia Riots,* 87; Montgomery, "Shuttle and the Cross," 61-62; Tabachnik, "Origins of the Know-Nothing Party," 22; *Philadelphia Protestant Banner,* January 14, 1843.

41. Montgomery, "Shuttle and the Cross," 435-36.

42. Vincent P. Lannie and Bernard C. Diethorn, "For the Honor and the Glory of God: The Philadelphia Bible Riots of 1840," *History of Education Quarterly* 8 (Spring 1968): 67; Feldberg, *Philadelphia Riots,* 95-96.

43. Lannie and Diethorn, "Honor and Glory of God," 67, 72-74.

44. Gerrity, "Disruption of the Philadelphia Whigocracy," 131.

45. Feldberg, *Philadelphia Riots,* 18-19.

46. Montgomery, "Shuttle and the Cross," 436-37.

47. Tabachnik, "Origins of the Know-Nothing Party," 88.

48. See *Philadelphia Native American,* July 29, 1844.

49. Tabachnik, "Origins of the Know-Nothing Party," 48-50.

50. Ibid., 70.

51. Ibid., 54-55.

52. Feldberg, *Philadelphia Riots,* 63; Tabachnik, "Origins of the Know-Nothing Party," 13.

53. See Feldberg, *Philadelphia Riots,* 51, 55, 58; and Montgomery, "Shuttle and the Cross," 428-29.

54. Montgomery, "Shuttle and the Cross," 429.

55. See Stevens, *Cyclopedia of Fraternities;* and Dumenil, *Freemasonry,* 7.

56. Bridges, *City in the Republic,* 50.

57. Jed Dannenbaum, *Drink and Disorder: Temperance Reform in Cincinnati from the Washingtonian Revival to the WCTU* (Urbana: University of Illinois Press, 1984), 24, 26, 59-60.

58. Ibid., 55, 57. Dannenbaum notes that the Cincinnati New School Presbytery denounced the Sons of Temperance in the spring of 1847.

59. David Brion Davis, ed., *Antebellum American Culture: An Interpretive Anthology* (Lexington, Mass.: Heath, 1979), 184.

60. Arthur M. Schlesinger Sr., "Biography of a Nation of Joiners," *American Historical Review* 50 (October 1944): 15. For a more thorough discussion of the IORM, see Dale T. Knobel, "To Be an American: Ethnicity, Fraternity, and the Improved Order of Red Men," *Journal of American Ethnic History* 4 (Fall 1984): 62-87.

61. See Stevens, *Cyclopedia of Fraternities,* 324; Elijah M. Haines, *The American Indian* (Chicago: Mas-sin-na-gan, 1888), 657-67; Frank Gerrity, "The Masons, the Anti-Masons, and the Pennsylvania Legislature, 1834-1836," *Pennsylvania Magazine of History and Biography* 49 (April 1975): 201, 184, 206.

62. Alvin J. Schmidt, *Fraternal Organizations* (Westport, Conn.: Greenwood Press, 1980), 287; Stevens, *Cyclopedia of Fraternities,* 239-45; Haines, *American Indian,* 657-67; IORM, *Proceedings of the Great Council of the United States from its Organization to the End of the Annual Session 5616* (Baltimore, 1856), 14 (1847), 68 (1850).

63. Morris H. Gorham, *The History of the Improved Order of Red Men,* ed. William G. Hollis (Philadelphia, 1894), 277-78.

64. Charles H. Litchman, *Official History of the Improved Order of Red Men* (Boston, 1856), 45, 250; Gorham, *History of the IORM,* 279-82, 357; IORM, *A History of the Great Council of Pennsylvania,* comp. Thomas K. Donnalley (Philadelphia, 1908), 75.

65. Feldberg (*Philadelphia Riots,* 71) notes that the OUA counted among its founders men with experience in both the IORM and the General Trades Union.

66. Bruce Laurie, *Working People of Philadelphia, 1800-1850* (Philadelphia: Temple University Press, 1980), 174-75, 177.

67. Stevens, *Cyclopedia of Fraternities,* 311-12.

68. Laurie, *Working People of Philadelphia,* 314.

69. Ibid., 314-15, 174.

70. Jean Gould Hales, "'Co-Laborers in the Cause': Women in the Ante-Bellum Nativist Movement," *Civil War History* 25 (June 1979): 120-21.

71. Ibid., 123-24, 126-27, 136.

72. See Mary P. Ryan, *Cradle of the Middle Class: The Family in Oneida County, New York, 1790-1865* (Cambridge, England: Cambridge University Press, 1981), 654-54. Ryan notes that in Oneida County up to 60 percent of business organizations took the form of partnerships in which personal relationships were all-important and credit remained a function of personal reputation.

73. Ibid., 143; Doyle, "Voluntary Associations," 13.

74. See Ryan, *Cradle of the Middle Class,* 137-38; Davis, *Antebellum Culture,* 184; Dumenil, *Freemasonry,* 17.

75. See Diggins, "Comrades and Citizens," 624.

76. *Cleveland Daily True Democrat,* November 16, 1848.

77. Davis, *Antebellum American Culture,* 184.

78. David A. Gerber, "Cutting out Shylock: Elite Anti-Semitism and the Quest for Moral Order in the Mid-Nineteenth-Century American Market Place," *Journal of American History* 69 (December 1982): 634-35; for an extended discussion of the resistance of nativist rhetoric to popular Anglo-Saxonism in the mid-nineteenth century, see Dale T. Knobel, *Paddy and the Republic: Ethnicity and Nationality in Antebellum America* (Middletown, Conn.: Wesleyan University Press, 1986).

79. Leonard, "American Republican Party in New York City," 153, 157.

80. See Wilentz, *Chants Democratic,* 316-17; Leonard, "American Republican Party in New York City," 162; Curran, *Xenophobia and Immigration,* 36.

81. Leonard, "American Republican Party in New York City," 163-64; Curran, *Xenophobia and Immigration,* 36.

82. Bridges, *City in the Republic,* 90-95; Wilentz, *Chants Democratic,* 317; Tabachnik, "Origins of the Know-Nothing Party," 86.

83. Leonard, "American Republican Party in New York City," 166.

84. Wilentz (*Chants Democratic,* 317-18) discusses Harper's self-image; Tabachnik ("Origins of the Know-Nothing Party," 120) notes that Harper was supported by the tax-sensitive Anti-Assessment League.

85. Leonard, "American Republican Party in New York City," 167.

86. Ibid., 173-74.

87. For discussions of the difficulties of the Harper administration, see Wilentz, *Chants Democratic,* 322-23; and Tabachnik, "Origins of the Know-Nothing Party," 144.

88. See James Harper, "Proclamation," June 1844, in Harper Papers, New-York Historical Society.

89. Leonard, "American Republican Party in New York City," 181; Wilentz, *Chants Democratic,* 322-23; Purcell and Poole, "Nativism in Brooklyn," 29.

90. See Leonard, "American Republican Party in New York City," 188, 190-91.

91. For an insider's description of the origins of the order, see *OUA,* November 18, 1848.

92. This connection seems fairly obvious and was commented on by Stevens, who, at the end of the nineteenth century, still had access to some of the OUA founders; see Stevens, *Cyclopedia of Fraternities,* 318. Actually, the relation may have been to the original Red Men rather than the Improved Order. While IORM had an early presence in Brooklyn and Albany, it had no successful New York City tribes until 1848. At that time, it found remnants of "Tribes of the 'Order of Red Men'" still in the city. Given the competition offered by the nativist fraternities, IORM found the penetration of New York City difficult. A state Great Council was formed at the end of the 1840s but was defunct after a year. Only one tribe survived as long as 1852; see Litchman, *Official History,* 428-29, and Gorham, *History of the IORM,* 338.

93. See *Directory, Alpha Chapter 1, OUA* (New York, 1848) in the collection of the New York Public Library. Shopkeepers and self-employed tradesmen dominated among the more than 200 members listed.

94. For a treatment of Whitney family history, see Stephen Whitney Phoenix, *The Whitney Family of Connecticut and Its Affiliations . . . from 1649 to 1878,* 3 vols. (New York, 1878), esp. 1:383, 139, 50, 24.

95. See *Doggett's New York City Directory,* 1845-1846 and 1847-1848; *Wilson's Business Directory of New York City,* 1848 and 1852; *Rode's New York City Directory,* 1850-1851, 1851-1852, and 1854-1855. All are available in the collections of the New York Public Library.

96. For a list of OUA grand sachems, see Louis Dow Scisco, *Political Nativism in New York State* (New York: Columbia University Press, 1901), 75.

97. See *Republic* 1 (January 1851): 284.

98. See "Application for a Charter," *Republic* 1 (January 1851): 284; *Republic* 2 (November 1851): 237; "Seventh Anniversary of the Order of United Americans," *Republic* 2 (December 1851): 282-83; "Chapter Prosperity," *Republic* 4 (August 1852): 88; "The Widows and Orphans," *Republic* 4 (August 1852): 103.

99. "Ordinance No. 6, Establishing a Funeral Service, and Regulating Its Performance throughout the Order," *Republic* 1 (February 1851): 142-43; "Duties of Chaplains of the Order," *Republic* 3 (June 1852): 321.

100. See "Constitution of the Order of United Americans," *Republic* 4 (August 1852); "The Order—Its Fraternizing Influence," *Republic* 1 (June 1851): 284.

101. See the endorsement of the clothier Elias Combs in the *Republic* 3 (January 1852): 53; and "Chapter Rooms," *Republic* 3 (January 1852): 51.

102. Leonard, "American Republican Party in New York City," 173.

103. See Spann, *New Metropolis,* 47-48, 55, 75, 133-34.

104. Wilentz, *Chants Democratic,* 344-45.

105. For a typical denunciation of the "flood of immigrants" and its alleged consequences, see *Champion of American Labor,* April 3, 1847.

106. Robert Ernst, "Economic Nativism in New York City during the 1840s," *New York History* 29 (April 1948): 177, 179, 180, 182.

107. Curran, "Know Nothings of New York," 72-75.

108. See *Republic* 2 (July 1851): 45.

109. *OUA,* April 14, 1849. This fraternal organ was later renamed the *Continental*; Curran, "Know Nothings of New York," 75.

110. See Curran, "Know Nothings of New York," 42-45.

111. Feldberg, *Philadelphia Riots,* 169-71; Laurie, *Working People of Philadelphia,* 88.

112. *Philadelphia Native Eagle and American Advocate,* July 17, 1846.

113. *Philadelphia Sun,* March 11, 1847, and April 13, 1848.

114. Tabachnik, "Origins of the Know-Nothing Party," 162.

115. Laurie, *Working People of Philadelphia,* 195-96; Feldberg,

Philadelphia Riots, 171-72; Tabachnik, "Origins of the Know-Nothing Party," 190.

116. See Stevens, *Cyclopedia of Fraternities,* 318-20.

117. Tabachnik, "Origins of the Know-Nothing Party," 182-84, 208, 223.

118. See Wilentz, *Chants Democratic,* 367; and Stevens, *Cyclopedia of Fraternities,* 300-301.

119. See Martin G. Towey, "Kerry Patch Revisited: Irish Americans in St. Louis in the Turn-of-the-Century Era," in *From Paddy to Studs: Irish-American Communities in the Turn-of-the-Century Era, 1880-1920,* ed. Timothy J. Meagher (Westport, Conn.: Greenwood Press, 1986), 142-43.

120. Kathleen Neils Conzen, *Immigrant Milwaukee, 1836-1860: Accommodation and Community in a Frontier City* (Cambridge: Harvard University Press, 1976), 195-99.

121. *Baltimore Clipper,* November 5, 1844, March 12 and 13, 1845, and October 2, 1845.

Chapter 3

1. See Thomas R. Whitney to Millard Fillmore, July 25, 1856, Millard Fillmore Papers, State University of New York at Oswego; Thomas R. Whitney, *The Union of States: An Oration* (New York: William B. Weiss, 1855), 17; Thomas R. Whitney, *A Defense of the American Policy as Opposed to the Encroachments of Foreign Influence* (New York, 1856), 299.

2. Whitney, *Defense of the American Policy,* 272-73; Curran, "Know Nothings of New York," 76; Curran, *Xenophobia and Immigration,* 46-48; Scisco, *Nativism in New York State,* 78; "Peculiar Education," *Republic* 1 (January 1851): 41; "The Free School Law," *Republic* 1 (May 1851): 229; "An Incident of the 22nd," *Republic* 1 (April 1851): 189; "Proscription—what is it?", *Republic* 2 (November 1851): 228-29; "The Order of United Americans," *Republic* 4 (July 1852): 52-53; "General Henry Storms," *Republic* 2 (October 1851): 185.

3. Spann, *New Metropolis,* 299-300, 319; Scisco, *Nativism in New York State,* 81-82; "The Municipal Party," *Republic* 4 (September 1852): 152-53; "Municipal Reform," *Republic* 4 (October 1852): 214.

4. Curran, "Know Nothings of New York," 89; Bridges, *City in the Republic,* 137-39; James F. Richardson, *The New York Police: Colonial Times to 1901* (New York: Oxford University Press, 1970), 76;

Spann, *New Metropolis,* 324, 330; Scisco, *Nativism in New York State,* 87; "The Fifth Congressional District," *Republic* 4 (November 1852): 266; "Foreign Influence with a Vengeance," *Republic* 4 (December 1852): 321; "The First Assembly District," *Republic* 4 (December 1852): 329.
   5. Tabachnik, "Origins of the Know-Nothing Party," 223, 234, 240; Michael F. Holt, *Forging a Majority: The Formation of the Republican Party in Pittsburgh, 1848-1860* (New Haven: Yale University Press, 1969), 111-12.
   6. John R. Mulkern, "The Know-Nothing Party in Massachusetts" (Ph.D. dissertation, Boston University, 1963), 40; Dale Baum, *The Civil War Party System: The Case of Massachusetts, 1848-1876* (Chapel Hill: University of North Carolina Press, 1984), 29; Robert F. Dalzell, *Enterprising Elite: The Boston Associates and the World They Made* (Cambridge: Harvard University Press, 1987), 212-13.
   7. "Visit of the President," *Republic* 1 (June 1851): 276-77; "Parties," *Republic* 3 (March 1852): 131; "An American Convention," *Republic* 3 (January 1852): 46-47; "Is It a Political Institution?" *Republic* 3 (April 1852), 214; "A Third Party," *Republic* 3 (June 1852): 310; see also Scisco, *Nativism in New York State,* 81.
   8. Tabachnik, "Origins of the Know-Nothing Party," 251, 253-54; Curran, *Xenophobia and Immigration,* 49; Curran, "Know Nothings of New York," 83; "The Nominations," *Republic* 4 (July 1852): 40; "Conservative Common Sense," *Republic* 4 (October 1852): 208; "The Death of Daniel Webster," *Republic* 4 (November 1852): 264; "The Defeat of General Scott," *Republic* 4 (December 1852): 319-20; "A New Party," *Republic* 4 (December 1852), 328.
   9. Curran, "Know Nothings of New York," 86, 107; Curran, *Xenophobia and Immigration,* 51, 54; Scisco, *Nativism in New York State,* 88.
   10. See Scisco, *Nativism in New York State,* 98, 105-6, 111, 205, 207-8.
   11. Bennett, *Party of Fear,* 115; Curran, "Know Nothings of New York," 141, 151, 168; Scisco, *Nativism in New York State,* 129, 163.
   12. Mulkern, "Know-Nothing Party in Massachusetts," 113; Paul Goodman, "The Politics of Industrialism in Massachusetts, 1830-1870," in Bushman, *Uprooted Americans,* 187, 193; Baum, *Civil War Party System,* 27-28, 30, 33.
   13. Gerrity, "Disruption of the Philadelphia Whigocracy," 172-73; Tabachnik, "Origins of the Know-Nothing Party," 255-56; Holt, *Forging a Majority,* 145; William E. Gienapp, "Nebraska, Nativism, and

Rum: The Failure of Fusion in Pennsylvania, 1854," *Pennsylvania Magazine of History and Biography* 59 (October 1985): 444-45.

14. Ronald R. Matthias, "The Know-Nothing Movement in Iowa" (Ph.D. dissertation, University of Chicago, 1965), 1-6, 12, 15, 25, 28, 85, 103, 123; Ronald P. Formisano, *The Birth of Mass Political Parties, Michigan, 1827-1861* (Princeton: Princeton University Press, 1971), 261, 251-52, 249.

15. "Know Somethings," *Cleveland True Democrat*, September 30, 1854; *Cleveland True Democrat*, October 2, 1854; *Cleveland Plain Dealer*, October 19, 1855.

16. See Robert M. Senkewicz, *Vigilantes in Gold Rush San Francisco* (Stanford: Stanford University Press, 1985), 84-89, 107-13, 134-47; "California," *Republic* 2 (September 1851): 136; "California," *Republic* 3 (May 1852): 268.

17. Gary L. Browne, *Baltimore in the Nation, 1789-1861* (Chapel Hill: University of North Carolina Press, 1980), 204; *Baltimore Clipper*, March 15 and August 19, 1853; William J. Evitts, *A Matter of Allegiances: Maryland from 1850 to 1861* (Baltimore: Johns Hopkins University Press, 1974), 65, 72-73; W. Darrell Overdyke, *The Know Nothing Party in the South* (Baton Rouge: Louisiana State University Press, 1954), 58; Jean Baker, "Political Nativism: The Maryland Know-Nothings as a Case Study," in *Law, Society, and Politics in Early Maryland,* ed. Aubrey Land et al. (Baltimore: Johns Hopkins University Press, 1974), 318-19.

18. Harry August Volz III, "Party, State, and Nation: Kentucky and the Coming of the American Civil War" (Ph.D. dissertation, University of Virginia, 1982), 150-51, 92-94, 154, 175, 216, 185.

19. Overdyke, *Know Nothing Party in the South,* 59-60; *New Orleans Daily Crescent*, March 28, 1854; Marius Michael Carriere Jr., "The Know Nothing Movement in Louisiana" (Ph.D. dissertation, Louisiana State University, 1977), 77-79, 65; Gregg Cantrell, *Kenneth and John B. Rayner and the Limits of Southern Dissent* (Urbana: University of Illinois Press, 1993), 83.

20. See Overdyke, *Know Nothing Party in the South,* 69, 102-3; Cantrell, *Rayner,* 86; Cecil S. H. Ross, "Dying Hard, Dying Fast: The Know-Nothing Experience in Mississippi" (Ph.D. dissertation, University of Notre Dame, 1982), 56, 99; Robert E. May, *John A. Quitman: Old South Crusader* (Baton Rouge: Louisiana State University Press, 1985), 297-98; Harold T. Smith, "The Know-Nothing Party in Arkansas," *Arkansas Historical Quarterly* 34 (Winter 1975): 294;

J. Mills Thornton III, *Politics and Power in a Slave Society: Alabama, 1800-1860* (Baton Rouge: Louisiana State University Press, 1978), 352-53, 358; Alan S. Thompson, "Southern Rights and Nativism as Issues in Mobile Politics, 1850-1861," *Alabama Review* 35 (April 1982): 136-38.

21. Curran, *Xenophobia and Immigration,* 60; Scisco, *Nativism in New York State,* 135-37.

22. Scisco, *Nativism in New York State,* 156-57; for contemporary reports, see *New York Times,* June 15, 1855, and *New York Tribune,* June 9, 1855.

23. Curran, "Know Nothings of New York," 248; Curran, *Xenophobia and Immigration,* 64-65. Individual state Know Nothing councils also backed off of fraternal secrecy; see David A. Keller, "Nativism and Sectionalism: A History of the Know-Nothing Party in Lancaster, Pennsylvania," *Journal of the Lancaster County Historical Society* 75 (1971): 71; and Carriere, "Know Nothing Movement in Louisiana," 129.

24. Curran, "Know Nothings of New York," 131. See also *New York Herald,* September 22, 1855, and *New York Times,* September 25, 1855.

25. Bennett, *Party of Fear,* 124; Mulkern, "Know-Nothing Party in Massachusetts," 120; William E. Gienapp, "Nativism and the Creation of a Republican Majority in the North before the Civil War," *Journal of American History* 72 (December 1985): 547; Keller, "Nativism or Sectionalism," 84; Holt, *Political Crisis of the 1850s,* 148.

26. Baker, "Political Nativism," 326.

27. See Thornton, *Politics and Power,* 444-45; and Robert F. Berkhofer, *The White Man's Indian* (New York: Knopf, 1978), 154.

28. Thornton, *Politics and Power,* 443-44; see also Wiebe, *Opening of American Society,* 368.

29. Goodman, "Politics of Industrialism," 166-67; Susan E. Hirsch, *Roots of the American Working Class: The Industrialization of Crafts in Newark, 1800-1860* (Philadelphia: University of Pennsylvania Press, 1978), 42; Spann, *New Metropolis,* 244; Carville Earle and Ronald Hoffman, "The Foundation of the Modern Economy: Agriculture and the Costs of Labor in the United States and England, 1800-1860," *American Historical Review* 85 (December 1980): 1073.

30. George W. Van Vleck, *The Panic of 1857: An Analytical Study* (New York, 1943; reprint, New York: AMS Press, 1967), 62-64, 74-79; Spann, *New Metropolis,* 307-10, 322; Gorn, "'Good-Bye Boys,'" 393.

31. Davis, *Antebellum American Culture,* 184; Hirsch, *Roots of the American Working Class,* 101; IORM, *Great Council of the United States,* 458; *Diary and Letters of Rutherford Birchard Hayes,* ed. Charles R. Williams (Columbus, Ohio: Batton, 1922), entry for November 4, 1850.

32. Dannenbaum, *Drink and Disorder,* 10.

33. Temperance banner, item 86.410.1 in Collection of the Abby Aldrich Rockefeller Folk Art Center, Williamsburg, Va.; for a look inside a local chapter of the Sons of Temperance, see Robert L. Hempel, *Temperance and Prohibition in Massachusetts, 1851-1852* (Ann Arbor: University of Michigan Press, 1982), 132-33.

34. Whitney, *Defense of the American Policy,* 186. Hirsch (*Roots of the American Working Class,* 41, 50) describes the debasement of traditional apprenticeship.

35. John Hancock Lee, *The Origin and Progress of the American Party in Politics* (Philadelphia, 1855), 233-34.

36. Whitney, *Defense of the American Policy,* 170.

37. Wiebe, *Opening of American Society,* 335.

38. For examples of the beneficiary features of OUA and affiliates, see "Anniversary Celebration of Alpha Chapter," *Republic* 2 (December 1851): 282; "United Daughters of America—New York Chapter, No. 7," *Republic* 1 (June 1851): 283; "The Ball of the Washington Association," *Republic* 1 (March 1851): 138; "Free Membership to the Aged," *Republic* 2 (November 1851): 237.

39. "Duties of Chaplains of the Order," *Republic* 3 (June 1852): 321-22; "Funeral of Chancellor Beals," *Republic* 3 (May 1852): 267; "A Monument to Washington by the Order of United Americans," *Republic* 3 (February 1852): 102-4; "The Order—Its Fraternizing Influence," *Republic* 1 (June 1851): 284.

40. "Business Notices," *Republic* 4 (November 1852): 271-72; "Regalia and Jewels," *Republic* 3 (January 1852): 53; "Regalia," *Republic* 1 (March 1851): 140; "Certificates of Membership," *Republic* 4 (July 1852): 55; *New York Times,* June 14, 1855; "A Valuable Invention," *Republic* 2 (December 1851): 276.

41. For a sample of a withdrawal card and evidence of its utility, see "Cards of Withdrawal," *Republic* 3 (May 1852): 269; "Ordinances," *Republic* 3 (January 1852): 54; "Growth of the Order," *Republic* 1 (June 1851): 284.

42. Whitney, *Defense of the American Policy,* 260-61;

Chicago Daily True Democrat, September 5, 1853, and June 9, 1849; Scisco, *Nativism in New York State,* 118; *Cleveland Leader,* August 11, 1856.

43. Jay Monaghan, *The Great Rascal: The Life and Adventures of Ned Buntline* (Boston: Little, Brown, 1952), 162; Baker, "Political Nativism," 323; Matthias, "Know-Nothing Movement in Iowa," 81 n. 1; Keller, "Nativism or Sectionalism," 91; Overdyke, *Know Nothing Party in the South,* 84.

44. "Correspondence," *Republic* 3 (May 1852): 262; *Cincinnati Daily Enquirer,* April 3, 1851; Mulkern, "Know-Nothing Party in Massachusetts," 55.

45. Gienapp, "Nebraska, Nativism, and Rum," 443; Holt, *Political Crisis of the 1850s,* 141, 123-25.

46. Holt, *Political Crisis of the 1850s,* 125-26; "Short Memories," *Republic* 3 (April 1852): 210; "Foreign Demands for Public office— Intimidation of Parties," *Republic* 4 (December 1852): 324; Gorn, "'Good-Bye Boys,'" 399; Keller, "Nativism or Sectionalism," 67.

47. Douglas V. Shaw, "The Making of an Immigrant City: Ethnic and Cultural Conflict in Jersey City, New Jersey, 1850-1877" (Ph.D. dissertation, University of Rochester, 1972), 62; "The Spread of Our Principles," *Republic* 3 (February 1852): 106; "Funeral of Henry Gibson," *Republic* 3 (April 1852): 213-14.

48. See *Paducah [Kentucky] Weekly American,* August 8, 1855; Cantrell, *Rayner,* 88; James L. Huston, "The Demise of the Pennsylvania American Party," *Pennsylvania Magazine of History and Biography* 59 (October 1985): 492-93.

49. Letter to the editor, "The Primary Elections," *Republic* 4 (September 1852): 152. For a similar point of view, see Lee, *American Party in Politics,* 201-2.

50. For some treatments of the nativist attack on the nominating system, see Spann, *New Metropolis,* 327-29; Scisco, *Nativism in New York State,* 80; Gerrity, "Disruption of the Philadelphia Whigocracy," 174-75; Mulkern, "Know-Nothing Party in Massachusetts," 67-68; Holt, *Political Crisis of the 1850s,* 167-68.

51. *Congressional Globe,* 34th Cong., 1st sess., December 19, 1855, and January 21, 1856, 52-55, 281.

52. Whitney, *Defense of the American Policy,* 68; "The Future of Our Country," *Republic* 3 (April 1852): 207-8; "American Liberties," *Republic* 3 (March 152): 149.

53. Kenneth Rayner to Daniel Ullman, March 7, 1855, Daniel Ullman Papers, New-York Historical Society.

54. See Holt, *Political Crisis of the 1850s,* 62-63, 95-98, 104-12, 127-29, 154-55.

55. Ibid., 136.

56. Whitney, *Defense of the American Policy,* 224; Gienapp, "Nebraska, Nativism, and Rum," 449, 446; Keller, "Nativism or Sectionalism," 60, 46; Curran, "Know Nothings of New York," 201; Shaw, "Making of an Immigrant City," 56.

57. Spann, *New Metropolis,* 40-41; Gregory S. Kealey, *Toronto Workers Respond to Industrial Capitalism, 1867-1892* (Toronto: University of Toronto Press, 1980), 109; Ryan, *Cradle of the Middle Class,* 147; Volz, "Party, State, and Nation," 224.

58. For state-by-state discussions of the nativists' "new men" in politics, see Mark W. Summers, *The Plundering Generation: Corruption and the Crisis of the Union, 1849-1861* (New York: Oxford University Press, 1987), 35; Formisano, *Birth of Mass Political Parties,* 236, 258; Baker, "Political Nativism," 322-23; Jean Baker, *The Politics of Continuity: Maryland Political Parties from 1858 to 1870* (Baltimore: Johns Hopkins University Press, 1973), 32-33; Mulkern, "Know-Nothing Party in Massachusetts," 121; Holt, *Forging a Majority,*155; Ross, "Dying Hard, Dying Fast," 83; Shaw, "Making of an Immigrant City," 53; Evitts, *Matter of Allegiances,* 81-82.

59. "Chapter Rooms," *Republic* 3 (January 1852): 51; "Lectures," *Republic* 1 (March 1851): 138.

60. "A Word of Caution," *Republic* 3 (May 1852): 269; "Natives—Whigs—Democrats," *Republic* 4 (December 1852): 327.

Chapter 4

1. "A Hint for Our Statesmen—Prospects of the American Republic," *Republic* 3 (May 1852): 255-57.

2. "A Notice," *Republic* 4 (September 1852): 156-57; "General Scott in the Field," *Republic* 2 (August 1851): 82.

3. Thornton, *Politics and Power,* 445-46, 312; *Congressional Globe,* 34th Cong., 3d sess., December 30, 1856, 214; *Congressional Globe,* 34th Cong., 2d sess., April 9, 1856, 843.

4. "The Land Robbery Bill," *Republic* 4 (July 1852): 40-41; *Congressional Globe,* 34th Cong., 2d sess., May 14, 1856, 1221; "The

Times and Messenger," *Republic* 3 March 1852): 154.

5. Editorial, *Republic* 4 (October 1852): 216; "Agrarian Laws," *Republic* 3 (April 1852): 186-87; "The Public Land Scheme," *Republic* 1 (February 1851): 85.

6. *Congressional Globe,* 34th Cong., 3d sess., January 31, 1857, 519-21; *Congressional Globe,* 34th Cong., 2d sess., June 24, 1856, 1455; "Where Shall We Land?" *Republic* 1 (April 1851): 178.

7. Whitney, *Defense of the American Policy,* 47, 59; "City Library," *Republic* 1 (June 1851): 274-75; Tabachnik, "Origins of the Know Nothing Party," 244.

8. "The Pulpit and Politics," *Republic* 1 (June 1851): 274; "Taxation of Church Property" [letter to the editor], *Republic* 1 (April 1851): 190; "Public Support of Private Institutions of Learning," *Republic* 3 (April 1852): 204-5.

9. *Williamsburg [New York] Daily Times,* March 29, 1854.

10. For developments in different states, see Doyle, *Social Order,* 30; Berthoff, *Unsettled People,* 261; Formisano, *Birth of Mass Political Parties,* 224; Holt, *Political Crisis of the 1850s,* 132.

11. *Brooklyn Eagle,* December 17, 1853; see also Curran, *Xenophobia and Immigration,* 54.

12. Hershkowitz, *Tweed's New York,* 67-68; Overdyke, *Know Nothing Party in the South;* Senkewicz, *Vigilantes,* 142.

13. Formisano, *Birth of Mass Political Parties,* 219-24; Wiebe, *Opening of American Society,* 336.

14. Ross, "Dying Hard, Dying Fast," 51-53; *Jackson Mississippian,* February 11, 1853.

15. Holt, *Political Crisis of the 1850s,* 162; Whitney, *Defense of the American Policy,* 121.

16. Goodman, "Politics of Industrialism," 169; Ross, "Dying Hard, Dying Fast," 53.

17. Philip Wayne Kennedy, "The Know Nothing Movement in Kentucky: Role of M. M. Spalding, Catholic Bishop of Louisville," *Filson Club Quarterly* 38 (January 1956): 20; *Congressional Globe,* 34th Cong., 1st sess., July 28, 1856, January 5, 1856, 967-69, and 152-53; Whitney, *Defense of the American Policy,* 104; "Romanism," *Republic* 1 (March 1851): 136.

18. "Foreign Convicts," *Republic* 1 (March 1851): 134-45; "Foreign Impertinence," *Republic* 1 (June 1851): 275.

19. For a typical tribute to Washington, see Kenneth Rayner, *An Address Delivered before the North Carolina Agricultural Society* (Raleigh, 1854).

20. "Chit Chat with Readers," *Republic* 1 (April 1851): 181.

21. "Henry Clay on Intervention," *Republic* 3 (February 1852): 98-99; "Kossuth," *Republic* 2 (November 1851): 212; Uriah H. Judah, "One Thousand Dollars for Kossuth," *Republic* 3 (February 1852): 74-76.

22. C. D. Stuart, "Mazzini: A Sketch," *Republic* 2 (August 1851): 74-77; "Thomas Francis Meagher," *Republic* 4 (July 1852): 45-46.

23. "The Cuban Project," *Republic* 1 (June 1851): 275; C. D. Stuart, "Cuba and the Cubans," *Republic* 2 (September 1851): 104-10.

24. Whitney. *Defense of the American Policy,* 30-31; "European Republics," *Republic* 2 (December 1851): 276.

25. See Millard Fillmore, "Third Annual Message to Congress," in *A Compilation of the Messages and Papers of the Presidents, 1789-1902,* 10 vols., ed. James D. Richardson (Washington, D.C.: Bureau of National Literature and Art, 1903), 5:180; "Japan," *Republic* 3 (May 1852): 259-60. Thomas Whitney's editorial on Fillmore's letter to the emperor of Japan particularly lauded the fact that the ends of American contact were confined to secular trade and did not involve concessions for Christian missionaries.

26. "Coming to the Point," *Republic* 3 (March 1852): 155; "European Organizations," *Republic* 4 (August 1852): 102; "Kossuth. By the Editor," *Republic* 4 (September 1852): 132-33.

27. Wallace S. Hutcheon Jr., "The Louisville Riots of August 1855," *Register of the Kentucky Historical Society* 69 (April 1971):152; Overdyke, *Know Nothing Party in the South,* 28.

28. "The Sons of America," *Republic* 4 (July 1852): 52; "A Mare's Nest—War with Russia," *Republic* 3 (March 1852): 148-49; "Despotism versus Civil Liberty," *Republic* 2 (July 1851): 38; "Foreign Influence," *Republic* 1 (January 1851): 38; Curran, "Know Nothings of New York," 193.

29. "Desecration of the Sabbath," *Republic* 4 (July 1852): 41-42.

30. Hershkowitz, *Tweed's New York,* 17.

31. Dannenbaum, *Drink and Disorder,* 166; Formisano, *Birth of Mass Political Parties,* 233; Gienapp, "Nebraska, Nativism, and Rum," 469; Evitts, *Matter of Allegiances,* 878; Baum, *Civil War Party System,* 32.

32. Tyrell, *Sobering Up,* 260-61, 280; Holt, *Political Crisis of the 1850s,* 122-23.

33. For the opinion of a nativist politician on this point, see John Bowen, letter of October 30, 1854, in Ullman Papers.

34. For a report on Rayner defying temperance enthusiasts, see *North Carolina Standard,* August 25, 1855; "Chit Chat with Readers," *Republic* 1 (March 1851): 137; Mulkern, "Know-Nothing Party in Massachusetts," 151-52.

35. C. D. Stuart, "Society Reforms," *Republic* 4 (October 1852): 194-95; "The Anti-Gambling Law," *Republic* 2 (August 1851): 81; "Barnum's Museum," *Republic* 3 (February 1852): 101.

36. Volz, ""Party, State, and Nation," 194; Curran, "Know Nothings of New York," 117; Scisco, *Nativism in New York State,* 167; Matthias, "Know Nothing Movement in Iowa," 41.

37. May, *Quitman,* 302.

38. See *Rode's New York City Directory for 1848-1849* and *Directory, Alpha Chapter 1, Order of United Americans, August 1848* (New York: Root and Anthony, 1848).

39. Baker, "Political Nativism," 325-36; Matthias, "Know Nothing Movement in Iowa," 81 n. 1.

40. Lee, *American Party in Politics,* 198-99; Mulkern, "Know-Nothing Party in Massachusetts," 127-28; James L. Huston, *The Panic of 1857 and the Coming of the Civil War* (Baton Rouge: Louisiana State University Press, 1987), 156; "A Voice from Ireland," *Republic* 3 (February 1852): 96.

41. "The Press," *Republic* 1 (January 1851): 40; "National Academy of Design," *Republic* 1 (May 1851): 232; "The American Drama," *Republic* 1 (March 1851): 133; Lee, *American Party in Politics,* 199-200.

42. "Our First Volume," *Republic* 1 (June 1851): 273; "The Art Union," *Republic* 3 (January 1852): 38-39; *Congressional Globe,* 34th Cong., 3d sess., January 15 and 14, 1857, 342 and 317; "Amusements, Broadway Theater," *Republic* 3 (June 1852): 315.

43. *Constitution, By-Laws, Rules of Order, and Discipline of Fredonia Council 52 of the Order of United American Mechanics of the State of Pennsylvania* (Philadelphia: Klonegar, 1853), 5; Laurie, *Working People of Philadelphia,* 174–75.

44. Stevens, *Cyclopedia of Fraternities,* 322-23; Bruce Laurie, "Nothing on Compulsion: Life Styles of Philadelphia Artisans, 1820-1850," in *The Private Side of American History,* 3d ed., 2 vols., ed. Gary Nash (New York: Harcourt, Brace, Jovanovich, 1983), 1:314-15; Laurie, *Working People of Philadelphia,* 174-77, 184-85.

45. Elizabeth M. Geffen, "Violence in Philadelphia in the 1840s and 1850s," *Pennsylvania History* 36 (October 1969): 396; Wilentz, *Chants Democratic,* 367.

46. Hales, "'Co-Laborers in the Cause,'" 120-27, 130, 136.

47. See, for example, "The United Daughters of America," *Republic* 3 (May 1852): 267-69.

48. Letter to the editor, *Republic* 1 (March 1851): 141; "American Convention," *Republic* 2 (October 1851): 186; "New York Council, No. 10," *Republic* 2 (July 1851): 38; "The Union of the American Orders," *Republic* 4 (October 1852): 219; letter from the editor of the *Philadelphia American Banner, Republic* 3 (January 1852): 42; "Proposition from the United American Mechanics," *Republic* 4 (August 1852): 106.

49. "The Way Men Build Marble Palaces," *Republic* 4 (August 1852): 103; "Chit Chat with Readers," *Republic* 2 (July 1851): 39; Tabachnik, "Origins of the Know-Nothing Party," 245.

50. Hirsch, *Roots of the American Working Class,* 51, 56-57.

51. Spann, *New Metropolis,* 26.

52. Monaghan, *The Great Rascal,* 213; "The American Rifles," *Republic* 3 (May 1852): 261; Curran, *Xenophobia and Immigration,* 63-64.

53. Spann, *New Metropolis,* 135-36; Robert Ernst, "Economic Nativism in New York City during the 1840s," *New York History* 29 (April 1948): 172.

54. "Sound Doctrine," *Republic* 1 (March 1851): 135; Lee, *American Party in Politics,* 198; Whitney, *Defense of the American Policy,* 318; see American Party Platform of 1856, in *National Party Platforms,* ed. Donald Bruce Johnson (Urbana: University of Illinois Press, 1978); *Congressional Globe,* 34th Cong., 1st sess., March 25, 1856; "Order of United Americans," *Republic* 3 (May 1852): 266.

55. "National Pride," *Republic* 3 (April 1852): 208-9.

56. Lee, *American Party in Politics,* 204-5; "What Is the Value of the Oath of Allegiance?" *Republic* 3 (June 1852): 266-67; "Foreign Military Organizations," *Republic* 3 (February 1852): 100.

57. "Foreign Organizations," *Republic* 2 (September 1851): 134; *Jersey City Daily Sentinel and Advertiser,* April 4, 1854.

58. Whitney, *Defense of the American Policy,* 165.

59. Samuel C. Busey, *Immigration: Its Evils and Consequences* (New York, 1856), 88; M. W. Cluskey, *The Political Text-Book or Encyclopedia* (Philadelphia, 1858), 56.

60. "Organized Propagandism," *Republic* 3 (March 1852): 153; *Congressional Quarterly, National Party Conventions,* 13-14.

61. Whitney, *Defense of the American Policy,* 135.

62. See speech of Cong. H. W. Hoffman of Maryland in *Congressional Globe,* 34th Cong., 1st sess., July 29, 1856, Appendix: 1214; "What We Would Say to the Naturalized Citizen," *Republic* 3 (May 1852): 259; "Native Americanism," *Republic* 3 (June 1852): 308-9; "The Native American National Convention," *Republic* 4 (August 1852): 96; see also statement of principles of the New York City American Republican party in *New York Journal of Commerce,* November 4, 1843.

63. "Social Rights versus Political Rights," *Republic* 4 (September 1852): 157; Whitney, *Defense of the American Policy,* 140.

64. "Social Rights versus Political Rights," *Republic* 4 (September 1852): 157; Whitney, *Defense of the American Policy,* 140; Hoffman speech, *Congressional Globe,* 34th Cong., 1st sess., July 29, 1856, Appendix: 1214.

65. Whitney, *Defense of the American Policy,* 42, 126, 38-39; "To the Editor of the *Republic:* Public Men and Private Virtue. An Epistolary Essay," *Republic* 4 (July 1852): 11-13.

66. Whitney, *Defense of the American Policy,* 33-35; Rives quoted in Holt, *Political Crisis of the 1850s,* 239.

67. Curran, *Xenophobia and Immigration,* 66-68; Gienapp, "Nebraska, Nativism, and Rum," 447, 463; Holt, *Forging a Majority,* 146-47; Henry A. Murray, *Lands of the Slave and Free; or, Cuba, the United States, and Canada,* 2 vols. (London: J. W. Parker, 1855), 1:388-89.

68. "The Aztec Children," *Republic* 3 (January 1852): 39; *Congressional Globe,* 34th Cong., 3d sess., February 26, March 2, and January 20, 1857, 916-19, 963, 387.

69. George Copway, "Indian Pastimes," *Republic* 2 (May 1851): 221-22. For more detail on Copway's interest in nativist activism and nativists' interest in Copway, see Dale T. Knobel, "Know-Nothings and Indians: Strange Bedfellows?" *Western Historical Quarterly* 15 (April 1984).

70. Alfred Brewster Ely, *American Liberty: Its Sources, Its Dangers, and the Means of Its Preservation* (New York, 1850), 23.

71. Howe, *American Whigs,* 38-40; Robert F. May, *The Southern Dream of a Caribbean Empire* (Baton Rouge: Louisiana State University Press, 1973), 199.

72. Thornton, *Politics and Power,* 354; William J. Cooper Jr., *Liberty and Slavery: Southern Politics to 1860* (New York: Knopf, 1983), 244.

73. Curran, *Xenophobia and Immigration,* 66, 70.

74. Millard Fillmore to Isaac Newton, January 1, 1855, Fillmore Papers; Gilbert Haven to Millard Fillmore, April 24, 1856, Fillmore Papers; Curran, "Know Nothings of New York," 208-9.

75. See I. T. Williams to Millard Fillmore, November 2, 1856, Fillmore Papers; Curran, *Xenophobia and Immigration,* 71; Overdyke, *Know Nothing Party in the South,* 147.

76. See Overdyke, *Know Nothing Party in the South,* 154-55.

77. Evitts, *Matter of Allegiances,* 99.

78. Thomas Scharf, *History of Maryland from the Earliest Period to the Present Day,* 3 vols. (Baltimore, 1879), 3:265, 250; Evitts, *Matter of Allegiances,* 121, 128-29, 102, 132; Overdyke, *Know Nothing Party in the South,* 287; Carriere, "Know Nothing Movement in Louisiana," 158.

79. Carriere, ibid., 158, 178, 226.

80. Overdyke, *Know Nothing Party in the South,* 266, 281; Thornton, *Politics and Power,* 418.

81. Scisco, *Nativism in New York State,* 190; Senkewicz, *Vigilantes,* 167-74; Curran, *Xenophobia and Immigration,* 73.

82. See Horace Greeley, *Whig Almanac for 1854* (New York, 1854), 10; and *Lebanon [Pennsylvania] Courier,* May 11, 1855.

83. Mulkern, "Know-Nothing Party in Massachusetts," 125-36, 146, 162; Goodman, "Politics of Industrialism," 198.

84. Spann, *New Metropolis,* 375, 379; Richardson, *New York Police,* 70.

85. Summers, *Plundering Generation,* 66, 241; Holt, *Political Crisis of the 1850s,* 174.

86. Volz, "Party, State, and Nation," 194, 233; Holt, *Political Crisis of the 1850s,* 173.

87. Tabachnik, "Origins of the Know-Nothing Party," 258-59; Holt, *Forging a Majority,* 186.

88. Baum, *Civil War Party System,* 31; Mulkern, "Know-Nothing Party in Massachusetts, 143-46, 153.

89. Formisano, *Birth of Mass Political Parties,* 256; Baker, "Political Nativism," 321; Scisco, *Nativism in New York State,* 141; Curran, "Know Nothings of New York," 166.

90. "Treason in the Camp," *Republic* 1 (May 1851): 238; *New York Tribune,* September 5, 1855; *New York Times,* September 5, 1855.

91. Holt, *Political Crisis of the 1850s,* 172-73; for a discussion of oligarchy in fraternal organizations, see Dumenil, *Freemasonry,* 28.

92. Holt, *Forging a Majority,* 261-64; Curran, "Know Nothings of New York," 278; Eric Foner, *Free Soil, Free Labor, Free Men: The Ideology of the Republican Party before the Civil War* (New York: Oxford University Press, 1970), 252; Gienapp, "Creation of a Republican Majority," 550; Bridges, *City in the Republic,* 123.

93. Thornton, *Politics and Power,* 356-57.

94. Howe, *American Whigs,* 249.

95. Carriere, "Know Nothing Movement in Louisiana," 195; Overdyke, *Know Nothing Party in the South,* 205; May, *Quitman,* 298.

96. See Holt, *Political Crisis of the 1850s,* 240, 221; and Thornton, *Politics and Power,* 445-46.

97. Phillip S. Paludan, "The American Civil War Considered as a Crisis in Law and Order," *American Historical Review* 77 (October 1972): 1020-21, 1025-27, 1031.

98. Kenneth Rayner speaking at a Philadelphia Know Nothing rally, *New York Tribune,* June 9, 1855.

99. Whitney, *Defense of the American Policy,* 123, 211, 217-21.

Chapter 5

1. David Contosta, *Henry Adams and the American Experiment* (Boston: Little, Brown, 1980), 89; for another view of heightened concern about "character" in the nation, see Alan Trachtenberg, *The Incorporation of America: Culture and Society in the Gilded Age* (New York: Hill & Wang, 1982), 180.

2. John D. Buenker, *Urban Liberalism and Progressive Reform* (New York: Norton, 1973), 219; Bernard A. Weisberger, *The New Industrial Society* (New York: Wiley, 1969), 8; Robert H. Wiebe, *The Search for Order,* 1877–1920 (New York: Hill & Wang, 1967), 52-55.

3. Stephen Thernstrom, *Poverty and Progress: Social Mobility in a Nineteenth-Century City* (New York: Atheneum, 1971), 174; Handlin, *Boston's Immigrants,* 210.

4. Higham, *Strangers in the Land,* 18; this point more recently has been picked up and restated by David Bennett in *Party of Fear,* 159.

5. Handlin, *Boston's Immigrants,* 209; Philip Shaw Paludan, *A People's Contest: The Union and the Civil War, 1861-1865* (New York: Harper & Row, 1988), 22, 346.

6. Purcell and Poole, "Nativism in Brooklyn," 56.

7. Bennett, *Party of Fear,* 155.

8. Robert Remini [review of *Nativism and Slavery: The Northern Know Nothings and the Politics of the 1850s* by Tyler Anbinder], *New York Times Book Review* 97 (18 October 1992): 15-16; Herbert G. Gutman, "Work, Culture, and Society in Industrializing America, 1815-1919," *American Historical Review* 78 (June 1973): 584.

9. See Robert H. Lord, John E. Sexton, and Edward T. Harrington, *History of the Archdiocese of Boston . . . 1604 to 1943,* 3 vols. (New York: Sheed & Ward, 1944), 3:64-69.

10. Henry Clay Work, "Corporal Schnapps," F. Poole, "I Goes to Fight mit Sigel," and [anonymous], "The Army Bean," in *Singing Soldiers: A History of the Civil War in Song,* ed. Paul Glass and Louis C. Singer (New York: Da Capo, 1975), 115-17, 118-19, 168-69; William L. Burton, *Melting Pot Soldiers: The Union's Ethnic Regiments* (Ames: Iowa State University Press, 1988), 182.

11. Burton, *Melting Pot Soldiers,* 100, 153.

12. James K. Hospmer, *The Color Guard, Being a Corporal's Notes of Military Service in the Nineteenth Army Corps* (Boston, 1864), 25, 104.

13. Gardiner H. Shattuck Jr., *A Shield and a Hiding Place: The Religious Life of Civil War Armies* (Macon, Ga.: Mercer University Press, 1987), 79; Anne C. Rose, *Victorian America and the Civil War* (Cambridge, England: Cambridge University Press, 1992), 66.

14. See, for example, J. Matthew Gallman, *Mastering Wartime: A Social History of Philadelphia during the Civil War* (Cambridge, England: Cambridge University Press, 1990), 206; and Burton, *Melting Pot Soldiers,* 204.

15. Ella Lonn, *Foreigners in the Union Army and Navy* (Baton Rouge: Louisiana State University Press, 1951), 162-63.

16. Rose, *Victorian America,* 63; Shattuck, *A Shield and a Hiding Place,* 54-55.

17. See John S. Haller, "Civil War Anthropometry: The Making of a Racial Ideology," *Civil War History* 16 (December 1970): 309.

18. Benjamin Apthorp Gould, *Investigations in the Military and Anthropological Statistics of American Soldiers* (New York, 1869), 29.

19. Burton, *Melting Pot Soldiers,* 209.

20. Gallman, *Mastering Wartime,* 106.

21. "List of Copperhead Voters," 1863, Hudson (Ohio) Library and Historical Society.

22. Jerome Mushkat, *Fernando Wood: A Political Biography* (Kent, Ohio: Kent State University Press, 1990), 122, 123, 138; Baum, *Civil War Party System,* 95.

23. See Gallman, *Mastering Wartime,* 241.

24. Burton, *Melting Pot Soldiers,* 194; Towey, "Kerry Patch Revisited," 144.

25. See Paludan, *People's Contest,* 191-92; Gallman, *Mastering Wartime,* 27.

26. James McCague, *The Second Rebellion: The Story of the New York City Draft Riots* (New York: Dial, 1958), 123, 18, 174, 127.

27. Gallman, *Mastering Wartime,* 186.

28. See Paludan, *People's Contest,* 181, 186-87.

29. Paludan, *People's Contest,* 284; Gallman, *Mastering Wartime,* 333.

30. Vincent P. Lannie, "Catholics, Protestants, and Public Education," in *Catholicism in America,* ed. Philip Gleason (New York: Harper & Row, 1970), 55.

31. See George F. Houck, *A History of Catholicity in Northern Ohio and the Diocese of Cleveland from 1849 to 1900,* 2 vols. (Cleveland, 1903), 1:454.

32. See Thomas K. Donnalley, *Handbook of Tribal Names of Pennsylvania* (Philadelphia, 1908), 219; IORM, *Proceedings of the Great Council of the United States,* 317-18; 323; *New York Times,* November 5, 1911; for a discussion of the ethnic fracturing of the IORM that took place coincidentally with the rise of the nativist fraternities in the early 1850s, see Knobel, "To Be an American," 62-87.

33. The tendency of some historians to call all the prenativist organizations dead along with the American party and the OSSB (the Know Nothings) rests on a flimsy base: three late nineteenth- and early twentieth-century chroniclers who seem to have taken much of their information from one another—Humphrey Desmond, Louis Dow Scisco, and Albert C. Stevens. See Desmond, *The Know Nothing Party: A Sketch* (Washington, D.C.: New Century Press, 1912), 150; Scisco, *Nativism in New York State,* 225; and Stevens, *Cyclopedia of Fraternities,* 318.

34. OUA, *Address of Arch Chancery to the Order throughout the*

United States, February 22, 1860 (New York: Charles E. Gildersleeve, 1860); *An Oration Delivered before the Order of United Americans at Niblo's Garden, New York, February 22, 1861, on the Celebration of the Birthday of Washington* (New York: Charles E. Gildersleeve, 1861); *Message of John Lloyd, Arch Grand Sachem, OUA, December 1860* (New York: Charles E. Gildersleeve, 1860), 6.

35. Desmond, *Know Nothing Party,* 5.

36. See "Commemorative Program for the Reception of Commissioner Joshua G. Abbe at the Metropolitan Fire Department, September 4, 1865," collection of New-York Historical Society; "The Fire Department," *New York Times,* September 5, 1865.

37. [Obituary of Charles E. Gildersleeve], *New York Times,* November 5, 1911.

38. Patriotic Order, Sons of America, Camp of Pennsylvania, *Something about the Order* (Philadelphia, 1889), 3.

39. American Protestant Association of the United States, *Proceedings of the Right Worthy Grand Lodge . . . at Its 39th Annual Session* (Philadelphia: William Quinn, 1889); Stevens, *Cyclopedia of Fraternities,* 298-99.

40. See Stevens, *Cyclopedia of Fraternities,* 273; *Cleveland Leader,* July 19, 1859; Alvin J. Schmidt, *Oligarchy in Fraternal Organizations* (Detroit: Gale, 1973), 37-38.

41. Gorham, *History of the IORM,* 457, 317-18, 323, 342-54, 508-9; IORM, *Great Council of Pennsylvania,* 219, 109-10, 185-86.

42. Monaghan, *The Great Rascal,* 253-55, 266.

43. Scisco, *Nativism in New York State,* 175-76; Gallman, *Mastering Wartime,* 95; Allan Nevins and Milton Halsey Thomas, eds., *The Diary of George Templeton Strong,* abr. ed. (Seattle: University of Washington Press, 1988), 245, diary entry for July 20, 1863.

44. Paludan, *People's Contest,* 10-11.

45. See George M. Fredrickson, *The Inner Civil War: Northern Intellectuals and the Crisis of the Union* (New York: Harper & Row, 1965), 98, 131, 175-76.

46. Rose, *Victorian America,* 38, 8; Paludan, *People's Contest,* 311; Trachtenberg, *Incorporation of America,* 81.

47. Paludan, *People's Contest,* 12; Garry Wills, *Lincoln at Gettysburg: The Words That Remade America* (New York: Simon & Schuster, 1992), 101, 90, 40.

48. Carl N. Degler, "Northern and Southern Ways of Life and the Civil War," in *The Development of an American Culture,* 2d ed., ed.

Stanley Coben and Lorman Ratner (New York: St. Martin's Press, 1983), 127, 129.

49. See Thomas N. Brown, *Irish-American Nationalism, 1870-1890* (Philadelphia: Lippincott, 1966), 39.

50. Ellen Skerrett, "The Development of Catholic Identity among Irish Americans in Chicago, 1880-1920," in Meagher, *From Paddy to Studs,* 126-27; David Montgomery, *Beyond Equality: Labor and the Radical Republicans, 1862-1872* (New York: Knopf, 1967), 127.

51. See John Patrick, "The Cleveland Fenians: A Study in Ethnic Leadership," *Old Northwest* 9 (Winter 1983-1984): 311-13, 316, 321, 323; Mushkat, *Fernando Wood,* 159-60; Roland Tappan Berthoff, *British Immigrants in Industrial America, 1790-1850* (Cambridge: Harvard University Press, 1953), 194; Montgomery, *Beyond Equality,* 132; Baum, *Civil War Party System,* 109; Brown, *Irish-American Nationalism,* 41.

52. See *New York Times,* July 13, 1870, and July 8, 1871; Handlin, *Boston's Immigrants,* 220.

53. Altina L. Waller, "Community, Class, and Race in the Memphis Riot of 1866," *Journal of Social History* 18 (Winter 1984): 233-34, 240-41.

54. Archdeacon, *Becoming American,* 100.

55. Brown, *Irish-American Nationalism,* 180; Raymond A. Mohl, *The New City: Urban America in the Industrial Age, 1860-1920* (Arlington Heights, Ill.: Harlan Davidson, 1985), 93-95; Bridges, *City in the Republic,* 151; Jay P. Dolan, *The Immigrant Church: New York's Irish and German Catholics, 1815-1865* (Baltimore: Johns Hopkins University Press, 1975), 168; Maxwell Whiteman, *Gentlemen in Crisis: The First Century of the Union League Club of Philadelphia, 1862-1962* (Philadelphia: Union League Club, 1975), 105; Mushkat, *Fernando Wood,* 176.

56. Dolan, *Immigrant Church,* 163-64; Lannie, *Catholics, Protestants, and Public Education,* 55.

57. Montgomery, *Beyond Equality,* 51. Note that this was the era of Bismarck's Kulturkampf in Germany and, in 1870, of newly unified Italy's suspension of Vatican territorial sovereignty. See also Les Wallace, *The Rhetoric of Anti-Catholicism: The American Protective Association, 1887-1911* (New York: Garland, 1990), 33; Diane Ravitch, *The Great School Wars: New York City, 1805-1973: A History of the Public Schools as Battlefield of Social Change* (New York: Basic Books, 1974), 93-94.

324   *Notes and References*

58. Paul Kleppner, *The Cross of Culture: A Social Analysis of Mid-western Politics, 1850-1900* (New York: Free Press, 1970), 116; Sker-rett, "Development of Catholic Identity," 130.

59. Dolan, *Immigrant Church,* 159.

60. William S. McFeely, *Grant: A Biography* (New York: Norton, 1981), 393; Gerald N. Grob, *Workers and Utopia: A Study of Ideological Conflict in the American Labor Movement, 1865-1900* (Chicago: Quadrangle, 1969), 26; Robert D. Parmet, *Labor and Immigration in Industrial America* (Boston: Twayne, 1981), 50.

61. McFeely, *Grant,* 394; Brown, *Irish-American Nationalism,* 47.

62. *Chicago Tribune,* February 23 and 24, 1875; Richard Schneirov, "Class Conflict, Municipal Politics, and Governmental Reform in Gilded Age Chicago, 1871-1875," in *German Workers in Industrial Chicago: A Comparative Perspective,* ed. Hartmut Keil and John B. Jentz (Dekalb: Northern Illinois University Press, 1983), 198, 211-20.

63. Mohl, *New City,* 111-12; Montgomery, *Beyond Equality,* 377-78; Bridges, *City in the Republic,* 152.

64. Norman H. Clark, *Deliver Us from Evil: An Interpretation of American Prohibition* (New York: Norton, 1976), 50; Ruth Bordin, *Woman and Temperance: The Quest for Power and Liberty, 1873-1900* (Philadelphia: Temple University Press, 1981), 57.

65. Donald L. Kinzer, *An Episode in Anti-Catholicism: The American Protective Association* (Seattle: University of Washington Press, 1964), 8-10.

66. Kleppner, *Cross of Culture,* 114-15; Brown, *Irish-American Nationalism,* 139; Handlin, *Boston's Immigrants,* 215-16.

67. Hayes, *Diary and Letters,* 3: 273-74, June 3, 1875, entry.

68. See Stevens, *Cyclopedia of Fraternities,* 303; William L. Ellsworth, Commander of the Keystone Council of the American Alliance and Corresponding Secretary of the Grand Council of the United States of the American Alliance, to Kenneth Rayner, August 21, 1878, Kenneth Rayner Papers, Southern Historical Collection, University of North Carolina, Chapel Hill; *American Protestant,* July 18, 1874; Berthoff, *British Immigrants,* 191; Sydney Ahlstrom, *A Religious History of the American People* (New Haven: Yale University Press, 1972), 853; Stevens, *Cyclopedia of Fraternities,* 301, 310-11, 317.

69. See Edwin Seligman and Alvin Johnson, *Encyclopedia of the Social Sciences,* 15 vols. (New York: Macmillan, 1931), 6:424.

70. John Brinkerhof Jackson, *American Space: The Centennial Years, 1865-1876* (New York: Norton, 1972), 192-93.

71. For thumbnail sketches, see Stevens, *Cyclopedia of Fraternities,* 317, 301.

72. Shaw, "Making of an Immigrant City," 266-67, 102, 128, 116-18.

73. Douglas V. Shaw, "Political Leadership in the Industrial City: Irish Development and Nativist Response in Jersey City," in *Immigrants in Industrial America,* ed. Richard L. Ehrlich (Charlottesville: University Press of Virginia, 1977), 93-94; Shaw, "Making of an Immigrant City," 200-3, 215-16, 225-27.

74. Shaw, "Making of an Immigrant City," 202, 225, 190.

75. James H. Campbell, "New Parochialism: Change and Conflict in the Archdiocese of Cincinnati, 1878-1925," in *Ethnic Diversity and Civic Identity: Patterns of Conflict and Cohesion in Cincinnati since 1820,* ed. Henry D. Shapiro and Jonathon D. Sarna (Urbana: University of Illinois Press, 1992), 96; Christopher J. Kauffman, *Faith and Fraternalism: The History of the Knights of Columbus, 1882-1982* (New York: Harper & Row, 1982), 83.

76. Kinzer, *Episode in Anti-Catholicism,* 74-75.

77. Kinzer, *Episode in Anti-Catholicism,* 75-76; Wallace, *Rhetoric of Anti-Catholicism,* 36.

78. See Dumenil, *Freemasonry,* 237 n. 12; Stevens, *Cyclopedia of Fraternities,* 218-21; Loyal Orange Institution of the United States of America, *Constitution and By-Laws* (Philadelphia: Loyal Orange Institution, 1884), 3; Ladies' Loyal Orange Association of the United States and Canada, *Fourteenth Annual Report of the Supreme Grand Lodge* (Boston: Loyal Orange Institution, 1896); Kinzer, *Episode in Anti-Catholicism,* 23; Stevens, *Cyclopedia of Fraternities,* 238; Thomas K. Donnalley, *Reminiscences of Forty-Seven Great Suns* (Philadelphia, 1908), 230.

79. Dumenil, *Freemasonry,* xi, 88, 63-64, 109; Mark C. Carnes, *Secret Ritual and Manhood in Victorian America* (New Haven: Yale University Press, 1989), 3; Max Weber quoted in Schmidt, *Fraternal Organizations,* 45.

80. Carnes, *Secret Ritual and Manhood,* 1-5.

81. Brotherhood of the Union, *Supreme Laws, Order of Business, and Rules of the Order of the Supreme Circle* (Philadelphia: Brotherhood of the Union, 1888), 18; American Protestant Association, *Proceedings . . . at Its 39th Annual Session,* 15, 5; *Office of the Right Worthy*

Grand Secretary, American Protestant Association (Philadelphia, 1888), 4.

82. Patriotic Order, Sons of America, *Something about the Order,* 2, 6, 9-11; Patriotic Order, Sons of America, *Official Pocket Directory* (Philadelphia, 1889), 6-7, 59-60.

83. OUAM, *How to Become a Member of the Order . . . Together with the Laws of the Life Insurance Department, Principles of the Order, Etc.* (New York: G. H. Burton, 1882), 3-5; National Council of the Daughters of Liberty, *Constitution . . . and Laws for the Government of the Life Insurance Department* (New York, 1887), 35; Roy Rosenzweig, *Eight Hours for What We Will: Workers and Leisure in an Industrial City* (Cambridge, England: Cambridge University Press, 1982), 88; Stevens, *Cyclopedia of Fraternities,* 302-3.

84. Stevens, *Cyclopedia of Fraternities,* 310, 105; *Minutes of the Proceedings of the Grand Lodge of the Junior American Protestant Association of the United States* (Scranton, Penn., 1890), 201-2.

85. Stevens, *Cyclopedia of Fraternities,* 309, 317; *Constitution of the Loyal Men of American Liberty of Massachusetts* (Boston, 1890), 4, 5.

86. *Constitution and By-Laws of the Get-There Benefit Association* (Newburyport, Mass., 1890), 3-5; Stevens, *Cyclopedia of Fraternities,* 327.

87. *By-Laws of the United Order of Native Americans* (San Jose, 1888), 18.

88. Higham, *Strangers in the Land,* 61; Stevens, *Cyclopedia of Fraternities,* 292, 310.

89. Wilson L. Gill, manuscript draft of the organizational proposal for the Young People's Society to Promote Practical Patriots, dated July 1891, collection of the New York Public Library. Gill called for the affiliation of the group with such organizations as the Sons and Daughters of the American Revolution and the Patriotic Sons of America as well as with such mainstream educational institutions as the Chautauqua Lyceum and the American Association for the Advancement of Science; *Report of the Patria Club Committee on Ways and Means for Developing a Deeper Interest among Young People in Affairs of Government and Citizenship* (New York, c. 1894), 1, 3; in the collection of the New York Public Library.

90. Stevens, *Cyclopedia of Fraternities,* 322.

Chapter 6

1. [Obituary of Charles E. Gildersleeve], *New York Times,* November 5, 1911; "Washington's Birth-Day," *Republic* 1 (April 1851): 188.

2. David P. Page, "Bishop Michael J. Curley and Anti-Catholic Nativism in Florida," *Florida Historical Quarterly* 45 (October 1966): 103; Robert B. Rackleff, "Anti-Catholicism and the Florida Legislature, 1911-1919," *Florida Historical Quarterly* 50 (April 1971): 354-55.

3. Kauffman, *Faith and Fraternalism*, 168-69; Buenker, *Urban Liberalism*, 173.

4. Frederick Jackson Turner, "Social Forces in American History," *American Historical Review* 16 (January 1911), reprinted in *Frontier and Section: Selected Essays of Frederick Jackson Turner*, ed. Ray Allen Billington (Englewood Cliffs, N.J.: Prentice-Hall, 1961), 158.

5. See Higham, *Strangers in the Land*, 189; and Barbara Miller Solomon, *Ancestors and Immigrants: A Changing New England Tradition* (Chicago: University Chicago Press, 1971), 198.

6. See Higham, *Strangers in the Land*, 110.

7. Archdeacon, *Becoming American*, 144-45; Parmet, *Labor and Immigration*, 53; Higham, *Strangers in the Land*, 42-44.

8. Archdeacon, *Becoming American*, 145; Higham, *Strangers in the Land*, 99.

9. See Higham, *Strangers in the Land*, 101, 58, 69.

10. Timothy J. Meagher, "Introduction," in Meagher, *From Paddy to Studs*, 9; Alexander DeConde, *Ethnicity, Race, and American Foreign Policy* (Boston: Northeastern University Press, 1992), 56.

11. For discussions of Strong, see Dorothy Ross, "The Liberal Tradition Revisited and the Republican Tradition Addressed," in *New Directions in American Intellectual History*, ed. John Higham and Paul Conkin (Baltimore: Johns Hopkins University Press, 1979), 122; Wallace, *Rhetoric of Anti-Catholicism*, 31-32; and Richard Hofstadter, *Social Darwinism in American Thought* (Boston: Beacon, 1955), 178.

12. Wallace, *Rhetoric of Anti-Catholicism*, 29-30; Kinzer, *Episode in Anti-Catholicism*, 22.

13. *Minutes of the Wisconsin Baptist Assembly, 1880* (Madison, 1880), 23; *Watchman*, October 27, 1881; Charles P. T. Chiniquy, *Fifty Years in the Church of Rome* (New York: Fleming H. Revell, 1886).

14. For a discussion of all these issues, see Ahlstrom, *Religious History*, 722-24, 815-20.

15. Gary Ross Mormino, *Immigrants on the Hill: Italian-Americans in St. Louis, 1882-1982* (Urbana: University of Illinois Press, 1886), 149; Jay Dolan, "Catholic Attitudes toward Protestants," in *Uncivil Religion: Interreligious Hostility in America*, ed. Robert N. Bel-

lah and Frederick E. Greenspahn (New York: Crossroad, 1987), 75; Kinzer, *Episode in Anti-Catholicism,* 89-90.

16. Kauffman, *Faith and Fraternalism,* 1, 71.

17. See John Gilmary Shea, "Protestant Churches and Churchgoers," *American Catholic Quarterly Review* 7 (July 1882): 427-86; Bernard McQuaid, "The Decay of Protestantism," *North American Review* 136 (February 1883): 135-36; John Ireland, *The Church and Modern Society,* 2 vols. (New York, 1903), 1:81.

18. Archdeacon, *Becoming American,* 106-7; Skerrett, "Development of Catholic Identity," 121.

19. Anton H. Walburg, *The Question of Nationality in Its Relation to the Catholic Church in the United States* (Cincinnati: Herder, 1889), excerpted in *The Church and the City, 1865-1910,* ed. Robert D. Cross (Indianapolis: Bobbs-Merrill, 1967), 117-20, 122.

20. Archdeacon, *Becoming American,* 107-8.

21. See Wallace, *Rhetoric of Anti-Catholicism,* 47-48; and Kinzer, *Episode in Anti-Catholicism,* 88.

22. Martin E. Marty, *Pilgrims in Their Own Land: 500 Years of Religion in America* (Boston: Little, Brown, 1984), 283-84; Dolan, "Catholic Attitudes," 80; Kauffman, *Faith and Fraternalism,* 38-39, 101; Kinzer, *Episode in Anti-Catholicism,* 170, 96; Bennett, *Party of Fear,* 174.

23. See Humphrey J. Desmond, *The APA Movement: A Sketch* (Washington, D.C.: New Century Press, 1912), 157; James J. Kennearlly, "Catholicism and Woman Suffrage," in *Catholicism in America,* ed. Philip Gleason (New York: Harper & Row, 1970), 85; Kinzer, *Episode in Anti-Catholicism,* 26.

24. Kinzer, *Episode in Anti-Catholicism,* 26; Kennearlly, "Catholicism and Woman Suffrage," 86-87.

25. Archdeacon, *Becoming American,* 109; Kleppner, *Cross of Culture,* 158; Kinzer, *Episode in Anti-Catholicism,* 64.

26. Samuel T. McSeveney, *The Politics of Depression: Political Behavior in the Northeast, 1893-1896* (New York: Oxford University Press, 1972), 102, 106; Ravitch, *Great School Wars,* 141.

27. See Kinzer, *Episode in Anti-Catholicism,* 20, 142; Brown, *Irish-American Nationalism,* 140-41.

28. *Ritual and Full Information Concerning the American Patriotic League* (New York, 1891), 1, 4-6.

29. See *National League for the Protection of American Interests* (New York, 1896), 4, 6, 10; *To the U.S. Senate, A Protest and Petition*

by the National League for the Protection of American Institutions (New York, 1890), 2; Kinzer, *Episode in Anti-Catholicism,* 55-56.

30. "The 'American Party,' " *San Antonio Express,* August 24, 1887.

31. *Address of S. E. Church at the National Convention of the American Party Held at Washington, August 14, 1888* (Washington, D.C., 1888), 1-4, 9-10; Kinzer, *Episode in Anti-Catholicism,* 21.

32. See APA, *Thirty-ninth Annual Session,* 17. The organization's officers reported corresponding with Henry Baldwin for two years preceding a unifying conference of "patriotic" orders held in New York City on May 7, 1889. See also Kinzer, *Episode in Anti-Catholicism,* 80, 123, 213.

33. Archdeacon, *Becoming American,* 113, 96; Higham, *Strangers in the Land,* 15.

34. Melvyn Dubovsky, *Industrialization and the American Worker,* 2d ed. (Arlington Heights, Ill.: Harlan Davidson, 1985), 10; Arthur Mann, *One and the Many: Reflections on the American Identity* (Chicago: University of Chicago Press, 1979), 77.

35. Mann, *One and the Many,* 129.

36. Meagher, Introduction to *From Paddy to Studs,* 7-8.

37. See Yaroslav J. Chyz, "Fraternal Organizations of Nationality Groups," in *One America: The History, Contributions, and Present Problems of Our Racial and National Minorities,* ed. Francis J. Brown and Joseph Slabey Rovcek (New York: Prentice-Hall), 392; Kathleen Neils Conzen, David A. Gerber, et al., "The Invention of Ethnicity: A Perspective From the U.S.A.," *Journal of American Ethnic History* 12 (Fall 1992): 28.

38. Timothy J. Meagher, "Irish, American, Catholic: Irish-American Identity in Worcester, Massachusetts, 1880 to 1920," in Meagher, *From Paddy to Studs,* 86; Rosenzweig, *Eight Hours for What We Will,* 27.

39. Conzen et al., "Invention of Ethnicity," 21; Kauffman, *Faith and Fraternalism,* 83.

40. Solomon, *Ancestors and Immigrants,* 47-48; Brown, *Irish-American Nationalism,* 134; Kleppner, *Cross of Culture,* 117.

41. U.S. Bureau of Labor, *First Annual Report of the Commissioner of Labor, March 1886* (Washington, D.C., 1887), 245.

42. See Humbert S. Nelli, *Italians in Chicago, 1880-1930: A Study in Ethnic Mobility* (New York: Oxford University Press, 1970), 126-27; John V. Baiamonte Jr., *Spirit of Vengeance: Nativism and*

Louisiana Justice, 1921-1924 (Baton Rouge: Louisiana State University Press, 1986), 65-66.

43. Parmet, *Labor and Immigration,* 52; Higham, *Strangers in the Land,* 46; Grob, *Workers and Utopia,* 84-85.

44. Parmet, *Labor and Immigration,* 57.

45. Ibid., 57, 146, 137; Grob, *Workers and Utopia,* 185; Higham, *Strangers in the Land,* 175.

46. Bordin, *Woman and Temperance,* 87.

47. For more on the Anti-Saloon League, see Clark, *Deliver Us from Evil,* 94; for more on the saloon and working-class culture, see Rosenzweig, *Eight Hours for What We Will,* 101, 89, 77, 223.

48. Klaus Ensslen and Heinz Ickstadt, "German Working-Class Culture in Chicago: Continuity and Change in the Decade from 1900 to 1910," in Keil and Jentz, *German Workers,* 238; Mohl, *New City,* 130, 102.

49. Bordin, *Woman and Temperance,* 112-13; Kennearlly, "Catholicism and Woman Suffrage," 85-86; David H. Bennett, "Women and the Nativist Movement," in *'Remember the Ladies': New Perspectives on Women in American History: Essays in Honor of Manfred Blake,* ed. Carol V. R. George (Syracuse: Syracuse University Press, 1975), 84.

50. See Mohl, *New City,* 116.

51. For background on Bowers and the beginnings of APA, see Kinzer, *Episode in Anti-Catholicism,* 36; John Higham, "The Mind of a Nativist: Henry F. Bowers and the APA," in John Higham, *Send These to Me: Jews and Other Immigrants in Urban America* (New York: Atheneum, 1975), 69; Desmond, *The APA Movement,* 7; Matthias, "Know Nothing Movement in Iowa," 182-83; and Wallace, *Rhetoric of Anti-Catholicism,* 59.

52. Kinzer, *Episode in Anti-Catholicism,* 92; Desmond, *APA Movement,* 49; Wallace, *Rhetoric of Anti-Catholicism,* 64.

53. Kinzer, *Episode in Anti-Catholicism,* 45-46; Wallace, *Rhetoric of Anti-Catholicism,* 72-73.

54. Desmond, *APA Movement,* 36-37; Kinzer, *Episode in Anti-Catholicism,* 99; Wallace, *Rhetoric of Anti-Catholicism,* 65.

55. Kinzer, *Episode of Anti-Catholicism,* 50-54.

56. Ibid., 42; Wallace, *Rhetoric of Anti-Catholicism,* 98-99, 71.

57. Kinzer, *Episode in Anti-Catholicism,* 128, 78; McSeveney, *Politics of Depression,* 94.

58. McSeveney, *Politics of Depression,* 121; Desmond, *APA Movement,* 72.

59. Lowell J. Soike, *Norwegian Americans and the Politics of Dissent, 1880-1924* (Northfield, Minn.: Norwegian-American Historical Association, 1991), 59; Kinzer, *Episode in Anti-Catholicism,* 84.

60. Desmond, *APA Movement,* 88; Kinzer, *Episode in Anti-Catholicism,* 221-22.

61. Desmond, *APA Movement,* 92-93; Kinzer, *Episode in Anti-Catholicism,* 237.

62. See McSeveney, *Politics of Depression,* 137, 185-86; Kleppner, *Cross of Culture,* 349.

63. Kinzer, *Episode in Anti-Catholicism,* 150, 100, 138; McSeveney, *Politics of Depression,* 67, 140.

64. Kinzer, *Episode in Anti-Catholicism,* 176, 201; Higham, *Strangers in the Land,* 72; McSeveney, *Politics of Depression,* 107.

65. McSeveney, *Politics of Depression,* 141; Lloyd P. Jorgenson, "The Oregon School Law of 1922: Passage and Sequel," *American Catholic Historical Review* 54 (October 1968): 455.

66. Humphrey Desmond's early-twentieth-century account of the American Protective Association made much of Sims's exposé; see *APA Movement,* 70.

67. Kinzer, *Episode in Anti-Catholicism,* 177; McSeveney, *Politics of Depression,* 99.

68. For a variety of views on internativist connections, see Wallace, *Rhetoric of Anti-Catholicism,* 62-66, 84-87; Kinzer, *Episode in Anti-Catholicism,* 59, 68-69, 101-2; Stevens, *Cyclopedia of Fraternities,* 303.

69. Kinzer, *Episode in Anti-Catholicism,* 68-69, 101.

70. McSeveney, *Politics of Depression,* 95, 138-39.

71. "The Know Nothings," *Providence Journal,* reprinted in *Houston Post,* November 27, 1893.

72. DeConde, *Ethnicity, Race, and American Foreign Policy,* 57-62; Berthoff, *British Immigrants,* 202; David Noble, *The Progressive Mind: 1890-1917,* rev. ed. (Minneapolis: Burgess, 1981), 15.

73. Solomon, *Ancestors and Immigrants,* 84.

74. See, for example, E. A. Freeman's *Comparative Politics* (New York, 1874), which was among the first academic treatises to link American constitutionalism to putative northern European cultural traditions. For discussion of other examples, see Solomon, *Ancestors and Immigrants,* 63.

75. Solomon, *Ancestors and Immigrants,* 70-71.

76. Frederick Jackson Turner, "The Significance of the Frontier in American History," in Billington, *Frontier and Section,* 51. Turner's paper was first published in the American Historical Association annual report for 1893 (Washington, D.C., 1894).

77. Richard Hofstadter, *Social Darwinism in American Thought* (Boston: Beacon, 1955), 182.

78. The most thorough treatment of the founding and development of the IRL is found in Solomon, *Ancestors and Immigrants,* esp. 99, 104-6, for the early history.

79. John Higham, "The Politics of Immigration Restriction," in Higham, *Send These to Me,* 40; Archdeacon, *Becoming American,* 146; Solomon, *Ancestors and Immigrants,* 108-9.

80. Kinzer, *Episode in Anti-Catholicism,* 204; Higham, *Strangers in the Land,* 103; Solomon, *Ancestors and Immigrants,* 119, 124.

81. Solomon, *Ancestors and Immigrants,* 124-25; Archdeacon, *Becoming American,* 162.

82. Parmet, *Labor and Immigration,* 64; Whiteman, *Gentlemen in Crisis,* 180-81.

83. Solomon, *Ancestors and Immigrants,* 79, 154.

84. Mormino, *Immigrants on the Hill,* 176; Higham, *Strangers in the Land,* 118.

85. Arthur A. Goren, *The American Jews* (Cambridge: Harvard University Press, 198), 37, 43.

86. For Higham on anti-Semitism, see "Anti-Semitism and American Culture," "Another Look at Nativism," "Ideological Anti-Semitism in the Gilded Age," and "Social Discrimination against Jews, 1830-1930," in *Send These to Me,* 176, 110, 128, 148.

87. Edward S. Shapiro, "John Higham and Anti-Semitism," *American Jewish History* 76 (December 1986), 204, 202, 210; David A. Gerber, "Introduction: Anti-Semitism and Jewish-Gentile Relations in American Historiography and the American Past," in *Anti-Semitism in American History,* ed. David A. Gerber (Urbana: University of Illinois Press, 1986), 4.

88. See Goren, *American Jews,* 13, 21; Jonathon D. Sarna, "Jewish-Christian Hostility in the United States: Perceptions from a Jewish Point of View," in Bellah and Greenspahn, *Uncivil Religion,* 6-7, 10, 14, 17; Marty, *Pilgrims in Their Own Land,* 289; Jonathon D. Sarna, "A Sort of Paradise for Hebrews: The Lofty Vision of Cincinnati Jews," in Shapiro and Sarna, *Ethnic Diversity and Civic Identity,* 134.

89. Sarna, "Paradise for Hebrews," 134; Higham, "Another Look," 122.

90. Eli N. Evans, *Judah P. Benjamin: The Jewish Confederate* (New York: Free Press, 1988), 18, 110, 138, 208, 167.

91. Moses Rischin, *The Promised City: New York's Jews, 1870-1914* (New York: Harper & Row, 1970), 261; Solomon, *Ancestors and Immigrants,* 8, 38; Whiteman, *Gentlemen in Crisis,* 162; DeConde, *Ethnicity, Race, and American Foreign Policy,* 53.

92. Evans, *Judah Benjamin,* 83; Goren, *American Jews,* 19-20.

93. Richard Hofstadter, *The Age of Reform: From Bryan to FDR* (New York: Vintage, 1960), 78-80; McSeveney, *Politics of Depression,* 186-88, 103-4; Rischin, *Promised City,* 259; Higham, *Strangers in the Land,* 92; Higham, *Send These to Me,* 126.

94. Sarna, "Jewish-Christian Hostility," 8-10; Solomon, *Ancestors and Immigrants,* 171.

95. C. Vann Woodward, *Tom Watson: Agrarian Rebel* (New York: Rinehart, 1955), 442-43. Frank, an Atlanta factory manager from a New York Jewish family, had been convicted with slim evidence of the murder of a young woman employee. National outcry about the trial caused Georgia's governor to commute execution to life imprisonment. Frank was subsequently taken from jail by a mob and killed.

96. Stuart Creighton Miller, *The Unwelcome Immigrant: The American Image of the Chinese, 1785-1885* (Berkeley: University of California Press, 1969), 151; DeConde, *Ethnicity, Race, and American Foreign Policy,* 50.

97. Parmet, *Labor and Immigration,* 25; Alexander Saxton, *The Indispensable Enemy: Labor and the Anti-Chinese Movement in California* (Berkeley: University of California Press, 1971), 3, 71, 118.

98. Saxton, *Indispensable Enemy,* 172; Miller, *Unwelcome Immigrant,* 189; DeConde, *Ethnicity, Race, and American Foreign Policy,* 73; S. W. Kung, *Chinese in American Life: Some Aspects of Their History, Status, Problems, and Contributions* (Seattle: University of Washington Press, 1962), 85.

99. Saxton, *Indispensable Enemy,* 88; Higham, "Politics of Immigration Restriction," 35; Miller, *Unwelcome Immigrant,* 163, 185.

100. Miller, *Unwelcome Immigrant,* 199; Higham, *Send These to Me,* 185.

101. Hofstadter, *Social Darwinism,* 189-91; Higham, *Strangers in the Land,* 166; DeConde, *Ethnicity, Race, and American Foreign Policy,* 75-76.

102. For summaries of some key racial nativist literature, see Higham, "Politics of Immigration Restriction," in *Send These to Me,* 47; R. Fred Wacker, *Ethnicity, Pluralism, and Race: Race Relations Theory in America before Myrdal* (Westport, Conn.: Greenwood, 1983), 16; and Solomon, *Ancestors and Immigrants,* 140.
103. Marty, *Pilgrims in Their Own Land,* 285.
104. Kauffman, *Faith and Fraternalism,* 107, 159, 139, 52.
105. Meagher, "Irish, American, Catholic," 86-87; Higham, *Strangers in the Land,* 174.
106. Higham, *Strangers in the Land,* 70, 116, 123-24; Whiteman, *Gentlemen in Crisis,* 199-200.
107. Parmet, *Labor and Immigration,* 153-54; Lawrence H. Fuchs, "Immigration Reform in 1911 and 1981: The Role of Select Commissions," *Journal of American Ethnic History* 3 (Fall 1983): 59; Solomon, *Ancestors and Immigrants,* 196.

Chapter 7

1. For a description of the Klan parade, see David M. Chalmers, *Hooded Americanism: The History of the Ku Klux Klan* (New York: New Viewpoints, 1976), 186-87. David Bennett (*Party of Fear,* 229) offers some of the colorful names that Klan chapters adopted.
2. See Kinzer, *Episode in Anti-Catholicism,* 242.
3. Wiebe, *Search for Order,* 295.
4. See Buenker, *Urban Liberalism,* 218, 205.
5. Wiebe, *Search for Order,* 210.
6. For diverse treatments of the demise of Victorianism (although the term itself is specifically Rose's), see Rose, *Victorian America,* 255; Wiebe, *Search for Order,* 130; and Lynn Dumenil, "The Insatiable Maw of Bureaucracy: Antistatism and Education Reform in the 1920s," *Journal of American History* 77 (September 1990): 523.
7. Higham, *Strangers in the Land,* 200.
8. Woodward, *Tom Watson,* 419-24; Higham, *Strangers in the Land,* 184.
9. Buenker, *Urban Liberalism,* 175, 177, 180; Skerrett, "Development of Catholic Identity," 132.
10. See Rackleff, "Anti-Catholicism and the Florida Legislature," 356-61; and Page, "Anti-Catholic Nativism in Florida," 11.
11. See *Tallahassee Daily Sun,* April 30, 1915.
12. Page, "Anti-Catholic Nativism in Florida," 113.

13. Rackleff, "Anti-Catholicism and the Florida Legislature," 352, 363-65.

14. Kauffman, *Faith and Fraternalism,* 162-63.

15. Dennis Clark, *Erin's Heirs: Irish Bonds of Community* (Lexington: University of Kentucky Press, 1991), 151-52; Buenker, *Urban Liberalism,* 185-88.

16. Clark, *Deliver Us from Evil,* 125-26.

17. Noel P. Gist, "Secret Societies: A Cultural Study of Fraternalism in the United States," *Journal of Missouri Studies* 15 (October 1940): 42, 48; Gist numbers the Junior Order, United American Mechanics, at about 131,000 in 1905, 202,000 in 1910, 185,500 in 1915, and 275,000 in 1920. Kauffman, *Faith and Fraternalism,* 154, 188. The commission was authorized in August 1914 but did not really go into business until early 1915. It was suspended after the United States entered World War I in 1917 and the Knights of Columbus took up other causes.

18. Solomon, *Ancestors and Immigrants,* 150.

19. Hofstadter, *Social Darwinism,* 179-90; Wacker, *Ethnicity, Pluralism, and Race,* 13, 15.

20. Steven J. Ross, "Struggles of the Screen: Workers, Radicals, and the Political Uses of Silent Film," *American Historical Review* 96 (April 1991): 339-40, 351.

21. For discussions of the fate of the literacy test bills, see Parmet, *Labor and Immigration,* 155; and Higham, *Strangers in the Land,* 193, 203.

22. See DeConde, *Ethnicity, Race, and American Foreign Policy,* 83.

23. Gerd Korman, *Industrialization, Immigrants, and Americanizers: The View from Milwaukee, 1866-1921* (Madison: State Historical Society of Wisconsin, 1967), 149; Rosenzweig, *Eight Hours for What We Will,* 160.

24. Korman, *Industrialization, Immigrants, and Americanizers,* 158.

25. Frances Kellor, in *Immigrants in America Review* 1 (September 1915): 3-5.

26. For a good description of these organizations and their role in the Americanization movement, see Frederick C. Luebke, *Bonds of Loyalty: German-Americans and World War I* (DeKalb: Northern Illinois University Press, 1974), 205-20.

27. Leo P. Ribuffo, *The Old Christian Right: The Protestant Far Right from the Depression to the Cold War* (Philadelphia: Temple University Press, 1983), 5-6.

28. See Higham, *Strangers in the Land,* 199, 215.

29. John F. McClymer, "Gender and the 'American Way of Life': Women in the Americanization Movement," *Journal of American Ethnic History* 10 (Spring 1991): 11.

30. Parmet, *Labor and Immigration,* 179; Bennett, *Party of Fear,* 186; McClymer, "Women in the Americanization Movement," 8.

31. Dennis J. Clark, "Intrepid Men: Three Philadelphia Irish Leaders, 1860 to 1920," in Meagher, *From Paddy to Studs,* 105; J. Joseph Huthmacher, *Massachusetts People and Politics, 1919-1933* (New York: Atheneum, 1969), 26; Edward Cuddy, "The Irish Question and the Revival of Anti-Catholicism in the 1920s," *American Catholic Historical Review* 67 (April 1981): 237.

32. William D. Jenkins, *Steel Valley Klan: The Ku Klux Klan in Ohio's Mahoning Valley* (Kent, Ohio: Kent State University Press, 1990), 20.

33. Lynn Dumenil, "The Tribal Twenties: 'Assimilated' Catholics' Response to Anti-Catholicism in the 1920s," *Journal of American Ethnic History* 11 (Fall 1991): 23-24; Ahlstrom, *Religious History,* 890-91; Towey, "Kerry Patch Revisited," 154.

34. Cuddy, "Irish Question," 237.

35. Dumenil, "Assimilated Catholics," 42; Dumenil, "Insatiable Maw of Bureaucracy," 507.

36. See Patrick Renshaw, *The Wobblies: The Story of Syndicalism in the United States* (New York: Doubleday, 1967), 2; Goren, *American Jews,* 57.

37. Robert K. Murray, *Red Scare: A Study in National Hysteria, 1919-1920* (New York: McGraw-Hill, 1964), 46, 37; Bennett, *Party of Fear,* 189.

38. Clark, *Deliver Us from Evil,* 128-30, 9; Buenker, *Urban Liberalism,* 189-95.

39. Paul Davis Chapman, *Schools as Sorters: Lewis M. Terman, Applied Psychology, and the Intelligence Testing Movement, 1890-1930* (New York: New York University Press, 1988), 41-42.

40. See Wacker, *Ethnicity, Pluralism, and Race,* 29; Chapman, *Schools as Sorters,* 108, 110, 129; Thomas F. Gossett, *Race: The History of an Idea in America* (New York: Schocken, 1965), 374; Alan M. Kraut, "Silent Strangers: Germs, Genes, and Nativism in John Higham's *Strangers in the Land,*" *American Jewish History* 76 (December 1986): 150.

41. Dumenil, "Insatiable Maw of Bureaucracy," 499, 506-11.

42. Huthmacher, *Massachusetts People and Politics,* 68-69.

43. Dumenil, "Assimilated Catholics," 38; M. Paul Holsinger, "The Oregon School Bill Controversy, 1922-1925," *Pacific Historical Review* 37 (August 1968): 330.

44. Gary Gerstle, *Working-Class Americanism: The Politics of Labor in a Textile City, 1914-1960* (Cambridge, England: Cambridge University Press, 1989), 47.

45. Chalmers, *Hooded Americanism,* 85; Holsinger, "Oregon School Bill Controversy," 327, 335; Jorgenson, "Oregon School Law of 1922," 459, 457.

46. DeConde, *Ethnicity, Race, and American Foreign Policy,* 87; Cuddy, "Irish Question," 238-42; Huthmacher, *Massachusetts People and Politics,* 27.

47. *Masonic Observer,* June 25, 1921.

48. Dumenil, *Freemasonry,* 124, 134.

49. Cuddy, "Irish Question," 251; Dumenil, "Assimilated Catholics," 34; Kauffman, *Faith and Fraternalism,* 263.

50. Huthmacher, *Massachusetts People and Politics,* 21, 27; DeConde, *Ethnicity, Race, and American Foreign Policy,* 94.

51. For discussions of ethnic politics in the postwar period, see Cuddy, "Irish Question," 252, 243; DeConde, *Ethnicity, Race, and American Foreign Policy,* 97; and Huthmacher, *Massachusetts People and Politics,* 29, 36, 42.

52. Parmet, *Labor and Immigration,* 68; Murray, *Red Scare,* 124, 140; Rudolph J. Vecoli, "Anthony Caparo and the Lawrence Strike of 1919," in *Labor Divided: Race and Ethnicity in United States Labor Struggles, 1835-1960,* ed. Robert Asher and Charles Stephenson (Albany: State University of New York Press, 1990), 281-82.

53. See Murray, *Red Scare,* 61, 94, 193-96, 14.

54. Ibid., 84, 98; Ross, "Struggles of the Screen," 348.

55. See Bennett, *Party of Fear,* 193.

56. See Gossett, *Race,* 37; Higham, *Strangers in the Land,* 271; and Parmet, *Labor and Immigration,* 176.

57. Higham, *Strangers in the Land,* 305, 307, 215; Parmet, *Labor and Immigration,* 173-75, 178-80.

58. Parmet, *Labor and Immigration,* 183, 188; Higham, "Politics of Immigration Restriction," 55; Higham, *Strangers in the Land,* 318; DeConde, *Ethnicity, Race, and American Foreign Policy,* 102.

59. William Pencak, *For God and Country: The American Legion, 1919-1941* (Boston: Northeastern University Press, 1989), 46, 30, 9; *Catholic Standard and Times,* November 3, 1923.

60. Dumenil, *Freemasonry,* 146.

61. See ibid., 116, 145, 184, 124-26.

62. Chalmers, *Hooded Americanism,* 29.

63. Chalmers, *Hooded Americanism,* 30; Woodward, *Tom Watson,* 449-50.

64. Jenkins, *Steel Valley Klan,* 2.

65. Richard K. Tucker, *The Dragon and the Cross: The Rise and Fall of the Ku Klux Klan in Middle America* (Hamden, Conn.: Archon, 1991), 23; Chalmers, *Hooded Americanism,* 21.

66. Tucker, *Dragon and the Cross,* 25-26, 35-36.

67. Huthmacher, *Massachusetts People and Politics,* 87.

68. Ibid., 88; Holsinger, "Oregon School Bill Controversy," 329.

69. Kathleen M. Blee, *Women of the Klan: Racism and Gender in the 1920s* (Berkeley: University of California Press, 1991), 64, 121.

70. Jenkins, *Steel Valley Klan,* 5; Chalmers, *Hooded Americanism,* 35, 115.

71. Chalmers, *Hooded Americanism,* 34; Leonard J. Moore, *Citizen Klansmen: The Ku Klux Klan in Indiana, 1921-1928* (Chapel Hill: University of North Carolina Press, 1991), 94; Jenkins, *Steel Valley Klan,* 9. Blee, *Women of the Klan,* 140.

72. *Smart Set* (March 1923).

73. Huthmacher, *Massachusetts People and Politics,* 90, 98.

74. Leonard J. Moore, "Historical Interpretations of the 1920s Klan: The Traditional View and the Populist Revision," *Journal of Social History* 24 (Fall 1990): 342.

75. Moore, "Interpretations of the 1920s Klan," 342; Moore, *Citizen Klansmen,* 11-12; Nancy MacLean, *Behind the Mask of Chivalry: The Making of the Second Ku Klux Klan* (New York: Oxford University Press, 1994), 71, 87, 100.

76. Chalmers, *Hooded Americanism,* 113; Moore, "Interpretations of the 1920s Klan," 346.

77. Moore, *Citizen Klansmen,* 52, 26; Jenkins, *Steel Valley Klan,* 110; Dumenil, *Freemasonry,* 143; Moore, "Interpretations of the 1920s Klan," 352.

78. Moore, *Citizen Klansmen,* 191, 57, 90; Moore, "Interpretations of the 1920s Klan," 353, 351, 348.

79. Clark, *Deliver Us from Evil,* 134; Jenkins, *Steel Valley Klan,* 91.

80. See Charles C. Alexander, *Crusade for Conformity: The Ku Klux Klan in Texas, 1920-1930* (Houston: Texas Gulf Coast Historical Association, 1962), v.

81. Hiram Wesley Evans, "The Klan's Fight for Americanism," *North American Review* 213 (March, April, and May 1926).

82. See Jenkins, *Steel Valley Klan,* 23.

83. Robert Alan Goldberg, *Hooded Empire: The Ku Klux Klan in Colorado* (Urbana: University of Illinois Press, 1981), 147; Jenkins, *Steel Valley Klan,* 88; Moore, "Interpretations of the 1920s Klan," 352.

84. Goldberg, *Hooded Empire,* 168; Jenkins, *Steel Valley Klan,* 88; Moore, "Interpretations of the 1920s Klan," 351; Blee, *Women of the Klan,* 2, 33, 7; MacLean, *Behind the Mask of Chivalry,* 116-17.

85. See Goldberg, *Hooded Empire,* 169; Jenkins, *Steel Valley Klan,* 97, 58.

86. Goldberg, *Hooded Empire,* 178-79; Jenkins, *Steel Valley Klan,* 162.

87. Chalmers, *Hooded Americanism,* 296; Charles C. Alexander, *The Ku Klux Klan in the Southwest* (Lexington: University of Kentucky Press, 1965), 242.

88. Alexander, *Crusade for Conformity,* 77; Moore, *Citizen Klansmen,* 182; Alexander, *Klan in the Southwest,* 237.

89. Alexander, *Klan in the Southwest,* 233-34.

90. Chalmers, *Hooded Americanism,* 290; Jenkins, *Steel Valley Klan,* 114, 109.

91. David Chalmers recognizes the offhandedness of early Klan anti-Semitism in *Hooded Americanism,* 110. Leo P. Ribuffo discusses the anti-Semitic campaign of the *Dearborn Independent* in *The Old Christian Right: The Protestant Far Right from the Great Depression to the Cold War,* (Philadelphia: Temple University Press, 1983), 10, 12. Seymour Martin Lipset and Earl Raab capture the internationalist bent of anti-Semitism in *The Politics of Unreason: Right-Wing Extremism in the United States* (New York: Harper & Row, 1970), 136.

92. Higham, "Social Discrimination against Jews, 1830-1930," in Higham, *Send These to Me,* 160, 163; Mann, *One and the Many,* 124-25; Solomon, *Ancestors and Immigrants,* 204-5.

93. Gist, "Secret Societies," 42.

94. See Carnes, *Secret Ritual and Manhood,* 151-55.

95. Higham, "The Transformation of the Statue of Liberty," in Higham, *Send These to Me,* 83-84.

96. Robert H. Wiebe, *The Segmented Society: An Introduction to*

the Meaning of America (New York: Oxford University Press, 1975), 69; Clark, *Erin's Heirs,* 190.

97. Archdeacon, *Becoming American,*171.

98. See the *Junior American* 8 (1933): 5; Charles H. Litchman, *Improved Order of Red Men,* ed. Carl R. Lemke (Waco, 1964), 522-23, 564; Pencak, *For God and Country,* 259.

99. Archdeacon, *Becoming American,* 128; Higham, "Politics of Immigration Restriction," 57; Mormino, *Immigrants on the Hill,* 218; Baylor, "Klans, Coughlinites, and Aryan Nations: Patterns of American Anti-Semitism in the Twentieth Century, *American Jewish History* 76 (December 1986): 183–85.

Index

to, xxi–xxii, 26–30, 34–37, 50, 54; in
west, 86–87; women in, 132–33; *see
also* autonomy
naturalization, xix, xxii, 55, 116, 223; and
military service, 246; and voting
rights, 216; waiting periods for, 18,
53, 74, 84, 106–7, 138–39, 213
Naturalization Act (1906), 223
New York City, 55, 106, 146, 208; Central
Park, 133–34; education in, 56,
57–58, 121; 1835 election, 52; and
municipal reform, 73–83, 89, 90, 92,
175–76, 202; population growth in,
41–42, 46; as port of disembarkation,
46–47, 54, 194, 221; riots, 53, 78; St.
Patrick's Cathedral, 174; Socialist
party in, 249
New York Native American Democratic
Association (NADA), 40, 53
Noah, Mordecai, 135, 226

O'Connell Guards, 52
Odd Fellows, International Order of, 36,
64, 71, 184, 253, 265
Order of the American Star, 97
Order of the American Union, 178, 180
Order of the Star-Spangled Banner
(OSSB), 88, 92–94, 96, 97, 105, 113
Order of United American Mechanics
(OUAM), 1, 68–69, 86, 87, 133, 185,
247; in Baltimore strike, 95; and contract labor, 221–22; and immigration,
233; Junior Order, 193, 218, 222, 232,
242, 274, 276; organizing principles
of, 131–32; women in 132
Order of United Americans (OUA), xxi,
xxii, 1, 36, 79–82, 88–92, 97, 133, 145;
ceremonies, 190, 235, 265; after Civil
War, 165; financial benefits, 103;
growth of, 89, 90, 104; in Jersey City,
179; members' occupations, 129–30,
131; on voting rights, 106, 138;
women in, 132

Palmer, A. Mitchell, 256, 257
Paludan, Phillip Shaw, 152, 158, 164, 167
paramilitary organizations, 134, 136, 175

Patriotic Daughters of America, 69, 85,
185
Peace Democrats, 161, 167
Pearson, Charles: *National Life and Character,* 221
Pelley, William Dudley, 277
Phelps, Wilbur, 191
Philadelphia, 42, 58–64, 68–69, 85–86, 90,
134, 164; American party in, 94, 97,
147; reform in, 175; riots in, 61–62,
76–77; schools controversy in, 59–60
Pierce, Franklin, 92, 107, 108
political parties, 107, 111–15; anti-Catholic
sentiment in, 176; and immigrant
vote, 52, 107, 108, 172; and
"machines," 172, 175–76; mass, 44,
109; nomination procedures, 109–10;
see also individual parties
Polk, James K., 84
Populist movement, 215, 227
Powderly, Terrence, 209
Probasco, Harriet, 69
Progressive movement, 211–12, 236, 244,
245
Prohibition, 238, 250, 251, 268, 270
prohibitionism, 127–28, 242; *see also* temperance societies
Prohibitionist party, 240
Protestantism, American, 9, 10, 13, 23, 24,
31, 119–20, 189; and anti-Catholicism, 34, 52, 181–82, 196–202, 227,
239, 241, 262; and fundamentalism,
197; and Indian missions, 181; and
Ku Klux Klan, 264, 265, 268, 269–70,
272; schisms in, 34, 43, 197; and
women, 201, 211, 217
"pursuit of happiness," 11–12, 22

racism, xix–xx, 277; and citizenship, 15;
and immigration restriction, 228–31,
278; internationalist, 224, 231, 277
Rayner, Kenneth, 105, 108, 128, 177
"red scare," 255–57; *see also* antiradicalism, bolshevism
Reed, David A., 260
reform movements, xix, 32, 74, 211–12,
244

The Author

Dale T. Knobel is Provost and Dean of the Faculty at Southwestern University in Georgetown, Texas, where he also holds an appointment as Professor of History. He joined the Department of History at Texas A&M University in 1977, after earning a B.A. at Yale and a Ph.D. at Northwestern, and served in faculty and administrative roles through the academic year 1995-1996. A specialist in American ethnic and race relations, he is the author of *Paddy and the Republic: Ethnicity and Nationality in Antebellum America,* the coauthor of *Prejudice,* and a contributor to *Immigrant America: European Ethnicity in the United States.* His articles on ethnic stereotypes, nativist ideology, and nineteenth-century fraternalism have appeared in such journals as *New York History, Journal of American Studies, Civil War History, Journal of American Ethnic History,* and *Western Historical Quarterly.*